Food Across Borders

Published in cooperation with the William P. Clements Center for Southwest Studies, Southern Methodist University.

Food Across Borders

EDITED BY MATT GARCIA,
E. MELANIE DUPUIS, AND
DON MITCHELL

RUTGERS UNIVERSITY PRESS
NEW BRUNSWICK, CAMDEN, AND NEWARK,
NEW JERSEY, AND LONDON

Library of Congress Cataloging-in-Publication Data

Names: García, Matt, editor. | DuPuis, E. Melanie (Erna Melanie), 1957– editor. | Mitchell, Don, 1961– editor.
Title: Food across borders / edited by Matt Garcia, E. Melanie Dupuis, and Don Mitchell.
Description: New Brunswick : Rutgers University Press, [2017] | Includes bibliographical references and index.
Identifiers: LCCN 2016053283| ISBN 9780813591971 (hardcover : alk. paper) | ISBN 9780813591964 (pbk. : alk. paper) | ISBN 9780813591988 (e-book (epub)) | ISBN 9780813591995 (e-book (mobi)) | ISBN 9780813592008 (e-book (web pdf))
Subjects: LCSH: Food habits—North America. | Cooking, American—Social aspects. | United States—Emigration and immigration—Social aspects.
Classification: LCC GT2853.N7 F66 2017 | DDC 394.1/2097—dc23
LC record available at https://lccn.loc.gov/2016053283

A British Cataloging-in-Publication record for this book is available from the British Library.

Published in cooperation with the William P. Clements Center for Southwest Studies, Southern Methodist University.

∞ The paper used in this publication meets the requirements of the American National Standard for Information Sciences—Permanence of Paper for Printed Library Materials, ANSI Z39.48–1992.

www.rutgersuniversitypress.org

Manufactured in the United States of America

For Cheva Garcia and the many food chain workers
who make meals possible throughout North America

Contents

Maps

Food Across Borders

CHAPTER 1

Food Across Borders

AN INTRODUCTION

E. Melanie DuPuis, Matt Garcia, and Don Mitchell

Eating is a border crossing. The act of choosing what to put into our mouths is a kind of "boundary-work" in which we sort out the line between what is us and what is other.[1] Similarly, eating is a transgression in which we violate the wholeness that is our bodily selves and bring the outside in. It is not surprising, then, that as territories became nations, the act of eating became a metaphor for solidarity, belonging, and exclusion: the line we draw and defend against the outside. Boundaries can also be that place where new ways of being get worked out and incorporated into a new whole.[2] This book is about all three kinds of boundary-work: the exclusions, the solidarities, and the transformations that occur when we negotiate boundaries in the process of producing, procuring, preparing, and consuming food.

Food is a great way to understand what borders do: the bodily, societal, cultural, and territorial transformations that occur as physical sustenance flows across, or stops at, a boundary. In other words, borders are dynamic entities that give us a reason to pause and think about the constitution of food systems, nations and places, and ourselves, as they change over time and through space. The stories in this book focus on transformative moments and dynamic forces in our food practices that invite such contemplation. From the rise of Thai American cuisine, to the celebration of the ancient grain quinoa, to the hyperexploitative conditions that many immigrant farmworkers face, the way we produce food, the way we eat, and what we eat have frequently hinged on the flow of people, foods, memories, and worldviews across borders. Focusing on North America, this volume explores, at every scale, *how* borders define our food systems and our food identities. For example, some of the chapters in this book explore what constitutes "American" in our cuisine—old, invented, and new—which has always depended on a liberal crossing of borders by people, commodities, and capital, from "the line in the sand" that separates Mexico and the United States, to the grassland "OTM" (Other than Mexico) boundary with Canada, as well as the internal borders of sovereign indigenous nations.

The stories told in this volume highlight the contiguity between the intimate decisions we make as individuals concerning what we eat and the social and geopolitical boundary-work we carry out (or that is carried out in our name) to secure nourishment, territory, and belonging. They examine how borders have mattered historically and how, in an age of "globalization," borders continue to play a major role in how people and nations define and redefine themselves—and their foodways.[3] Such redefinitions involve new cuisines and new immigrants who introduce new ways of cooking that force the nation to question the boundaries between "us" and "them." At the U.S.-Mexico border, Yankee settlers rejected chile-based foods during the U.S. conquest of the Southwest in the nineteenth century. Today, their great-grandchildren embrace the "*sazón*"[4] of "Mexican food" whether they turn to white "Mexican" cuisine gurus like Diana Kennedy or Rick Bayless, grab burritos at the fast-food drive-thru, or visit the *fútbol*-drenched local mom-and-pop restaurants that cater to a primarily immigrant clientele. Even a cultivar with a name like New Mexico #9 Chile is the product of both a border-crossing germplasm and an immigrant agronomist: Fabián García.

Meanwhile, in the labor camps on dairy farms or in the small kitchens of those same local restaurants, Mexican immigrants cultivate gardens or improvise with non-Mexican ingredients to re-create a version of native dishes that have been forever changed by their displacement from their origins. Yet the goal is often to re-create a "taste of home" in much the same way that World War II American army canteens mobilized and procured "the familiar" in daily meals to give soldiers familiar flavors in their rations. Such is also true of nations within nations, like the Blackfeet Reservation in Montana where tribal ranchers adapted traditional cooperative livestock raising practices to fend off redistribution of land and the destruction of their homelands. In multiple ways and in many places and times, the stories told in this volume demonstrate that American food choices have both reified *and* compromised sovereign borders, both breached static "ethnic notions" of taste *and* produced contradictions in our food preferences, both solidified prejudices *and* made us rethink who we are. The result is a rich (sometimes distressing, sometimes exhilarating) social history and geography of food, food systems, and foodways that allow us to see anew the multifarious struggles and adaptations, oppressions and innovations, customs and cultures, that make up something as mundane, essential, and vital as the food we eat.

We offer this volume, in part, as an important corrective to the current (often liberal) duality of global and local, built on the assumption that we, as a society, will create a better world by becoming conscientious locavores who will save the planet by eating ingredients cultivated close to home. "Home" is itself a concept defined by boundary work, such as when farmers' markets define "local" by the farm's distance from the point of sale (that is, how far is too far to be considered "local" or "homegrown"?). Our contributors confirm that crossing borders has been a feature of our North American food system for a long time, a condition that will not likely change soon. Equally important, we aim to disrupt the comforting notion that recipes and foodways—how we prepare, procure, provision, and produce food—have traveled with us, unchanged, over many miles and generations. This is not to say that our pasts are unimportant; they are just not absolute and pure. Finally, many of the contributors to this volume remind us that cuisine and food provisions have sometimes been a product of struggles over borders. Such transgressions of borders and the creation of new ones through conflict and conquest have made us eat differently and, therefore, think differently about ourselves.

Our attention to borders—and our occasional use of the term "transborder"—comes out of a deep appreciation for the literature of border studies that spans several decades. Gloria Anzaldúa's canonical book *La Frontera/Borderlands* in 1987 established the notion that to live in the borderlands may start with the geopolitical reality of the U.S.-Mexico border, but it also involves a psychological, sexual, and spiritual state of existence for the many people who find themselves crisscrossing North American borders. Anzaldúa's articulation of "a *new mestiza* consciousness" and a "consciousness of the Borderlands" has served as a guiding theory for scholars conducting more empirical studies of migration. Lynn Stephen suggests that Zapotec Indians who migrate between their native Oaxaca in southern Mexico and California and Oregon to do farm labor are not just "transnational" but "transborder" migrants. Her interpretation is derived from an appreciation of Anzaldúa but also from her observation that these workers "move across many borders and live multisited lives." Migrants' high degree of connectivity and their negotiation of racial and ethnic boundaries within and beyond Mexico permeate their experience regardless of where they might find themselves at any moment. Several scholars in this volume describe similar negotiations of boundaries and a border consciousness among immigrant workers and farmers in the Northeast borderlands and along the eastern seaboard, as well as in the familiar borderlands of the Southwest. We, too, are inspired by Anzaldúa's theory and agree with Stephen that the lives of many migrants must be classified as "transborder rather than just simply transnational."[5]

To explore these ideas, we focus on three different border spaces and crossings: (1) The body itself as a metaphor for the Nation and the definition of "good food" as a metaphor for both the creation and defense of national identity. As this bodily border space is at once reinforced and renegotiated, an irony arises because (2) the food that creates an American "us" requires people crossing territorial borders in order to provide labor to produce that food. From soil to restaurant table, immigrant food workers are vital to the maintenance of the American food system. At the same time, our reliance on food grown outside the United

States means that (3) food, itself, increasingly crosses U.S. borders to provide the key ingredients of an ever-evolving American cuisine. The scholars in this book grapple with all three of these border crossings, looking at the struggles, the ironies, and the new collectivities formed by our hidden and evolving transborder food system. We will see that the history of American food is one in which borders create both belonging and displacement, often leading to transformations of cuisine in processes more interesting and rich than captured by the simple word "assimilation." These transformations are both embodied and territorial, with body and territory entwined in the creation of new ways of eating and living.

To understand these three kinds of boundary, we will start with some background. First we look into the history of the body as a long-standing metaphor for the nation as a social order bounded in territory. We then look at how American cuisine has in fact depended on bodies crossing borders. Finally, we examine how in a growing but not new phenomenon, American cuisine is increasingly dependent on the global flow of foods across its borders. In these three processes, identity, power, belonging, memory, and conflict play major roles in the continual transgressive transformation that is American eating.

BODY AND NATION

At the end of the nineteenth century, Emile Durkheim sought to explain the nature of society as more than just a collection of individuals. Durkheim was a supporter of the French republicans who fought against the monarchistic idea of a nation united by obedience to hierarchical authority. In a nation that had alternated for over a century between a republic and a monarchy, understanding exactly what brought a nation together was still under debate. Interestingly, these arguments about nation revolved around a particular metaphor: the body, an idea that came to the fore during the Enlightenment and manifested itself during the French Revolution as the *corps-etat*, or "body politic." The English Enlightenment philosopher Thomas Hobbes had earlier argued that the king did not rule on the basis of divine right but from an agreed-upon social contract in which individuals consent to join together under a sovereign. Hobbes expounded these ideas in *Leviathan*, a treatise with a frontispiece illustrating the king's body as made up of numerous tiny individuals. Hobbes's idea of the nation as a body formed by the consent of the governed drew upon and yet contrasted with earlier monarchical ideas of the king as the bodily manifestation of God, a "divine right" passed down through ancestral lineage. These concepts of monarchy were rooted in even earlier ideas, particularly Plato's metaphor of the state as a body in *The Republic*, and the Christian idea of the Eucharist as the body of Christ eaten by the shared community.

Durkheim adapted this metaphor of the social body to describe a unified modern state order. But unlike Hobbes, he explained society not as a predetermined social contract between individuals but as a product of the interdependence of individuals due to the division of labor. He described society as a body with specialized organs—representing the different roles in modern society—all of which were necessary for a functioning whole. In support of his republican beliefs, Durkheim envisioned the French republican nation as a group of individuals in solidarity with each other through their mutual dependence. This understanding of society became the foundation for modern concepts of the nation and nationalism.

The body therefore became a metaphor used to describe both solidarity and perceived national threats. In this way, national borders become the line between us and other, and the idea of the nation as a body surrounded by a protected skin a way to explain both borders and belonging. In his famous Iron Curtain speech, Winston Churchill described the British-American alliance as joined by "sinews" against the threat of Communism. The Iron Curtain defined the borders of the democratic body, delineating "the free" from people trapped under Communism, but it also demarcated the democratic body that had to be kept safe from Communism, often represented as "germs" in anti-Communist propaganda.[6] At the same time, American nativist groups, from the late nineteenth century to today, used bodily metaphors to argue against the acceptance of various kinds of immigrant populations—and their foods—as contaminating the national body.[7]

It's not surprising, then, that Cold War anthropologists defined cultures through their foods, studying what food was civilized or "cooked" and what was "raw" or "rotten" and dangerous. Anthropologists Claude Levi-Strauss and Mary Douglas both used food choice as a metaphor for society itself and noted the danger of the mouth as a place that represented both the solidarity of belonging and the danger of transgression. "Digestion," as Ambrose Bierce once observed, "is the conversion of victuals into virtues." That which is necessary is turned into that which is good, the good being the civilized and safe "us."[8]

Today's increased food consciousness has produced a healthy reminder of the stakes involved in eating, but it has also heightened anxiety about which borders are crossed and how we manage them. In an immigrant society such as the United States, this anxiety is particularly apparent. Frederick Kaufman calls this country "one of the most gut-centric and gut-phobic societies in the history of human civilization," and Julia Child described the American public as "deathly afraid" of its food: "I am sure that an unhappy or suspicious stomach, constricted and uneasy with worry, cannot digest properly." She saw this threat extending to all of society, adding, "if digestion is poor, the whole body politic suffers." We have certainly witnessed such pathology in our own time. For some individuals, the fear of food has produced eating disorders or pursuits for perfection that consume their daily lives. The concern over where our food comes from has generated distrust in neighboring countries (that is, Mexico) that have always been critical to provisioning the United States. Worse—as the 2016 presidential candidacy of Donald Trump showed us—displaced anger about foreign workers crossing U.S. borders to harvest crops has produced a new nativism that fails to appreciate the labor of those who toil in the fields.[9]

For most of its history, the American body has been a battleground for any number of forces seeking hegemony. Dieticians and food conglomerates, "food gurus" and political activists, adventurous friends and travel writers, all try to influence Americans' choices of what to eat. In doing so, these foodies want to become an adviser to, if not the arbiters of, what passes through the border and into the body.[10] If borders define what we eat, then border skirmishes (as well as the effort to "win hearts and minds") matter.

Yet daily food practices continually challenge today's dietary arbiters. What if, as Meredith Abarca describes in her chapter, you eat sweet potatoes with your tortillas? What if you are an Anglo who eats chiles (like the women Katherine Massoth profiles)? Or, like the Blackfeet Mike Wise examines, you are a Native American who ranches cattle rather than hunts buffalo? Where do you belong if your eating takes you across cultural borders, if your eating practices are not pure, if you are, in Mary Douglas's terms, in dangerous territory? These examples show that the common phrase "you are what you eat" or even "you are where you eat" is much too static, hewing too closely to the notion that people eat primarily according to a timeless place that, in fact, does not exist. We are culinary subjects, as Meredith Abarca calls us, our cuisine reflecting not just where we come from but where we are going.

But eating can also be a kind of invasion, a colonization through the colon. As Rachel Laudan has described, those victorious in war have often also conquered the bodies of their subjects by imposing an imperial cuisine.[11] In peacetime, food has been used to discipline the unruly, the marginal, and the foreign to eat a proper "national" diet[12]—a process that also helps determine who belongs to the nation and who does not.[13] Cuisine, then, arises both through border crossing and border policing.

Despite this policing, people do make choices. Those who are compelled to redefine themselves are also pulled into new types of eating, such as the new middle classes around the world who have adopted the Standard American Diet as a way to mark their new social status. In fact, the Standard American Diet is invading stomachs at the global level, leading to the globalization of American dietary diseases.[14] Yet even those who cross dietary borders with aspirations to raise their social status take their mouths, their tastes, and their memories with them. People who evoke the concept of "good food" often associate it with the place they call "home." Yet tastes rooted in place, rooted in a sense of belonging, get rerouted to new homes, new lands, as "belonging" becomes "longing." Memories of food and place shape new landscapes—for example, the gardens immigrant workers have cultivated behind barns on dairy farms in Vermont described by Teresa Mares, Naomi Wolcott-MacCausland, and Jessie Mazar, or the small commercial farms of settled-out immigrants in Virginia that Laura-Anne Minkoff-Zern alerts us to. Their adaptation to new lands and new ingredients gives birth to new tastes, even as they try, not always successfully, to maintain certain roots, spices, and combinations. In their struggles we see that their—our—culinary subjectivities are possessive and dynamic: possessive, in that we have an ideal in our minds, tastes, and imagination of dishes; dynamic, in that we have to adapt to changes in access as a result of our mobility.

In memory food tends to come from a timeless place, or an ancient place, often occupied by a grandma. "Just eat what your great-grandma ate" advises Michael Pollan as part of his "Food Rules."[15] Pollan's idea of goodness as existing in the past echoes so many others who speak the language of nostalgia when representing "the good." Placing goodness in a nostalgic past, however, suggests that there are morally correct choices over ones that deviate from a more perfect way of eating. This search for a past "good" fixes our notion of what is correct in a time and place, placing a boundary around it and turning it into an ideal that redeems what is lost. Such a view makes present lives morally suspect. Nostalgic indulgences of this sort enable those on the move to regain wholeness but also creates the power to exclude. In the extreme, these practices can set one group apart from the rest, creating a sense of superiority.

Yet those who lose access to their home foods can also lose the intactness of self.[16] To lose one's food sovereignty is to lose contact with one's territorial belonging as well as one's own body. The laborers who make bodily sacrifices every day in unjust working conditions far from home are sacrificing both on the factory floor—the dairy barn, the fields of Mexico, or the restaurant kitchens that José Antonio Vázquez-Medina examines in his contribution—and in their lack of access to foods that make them who they are. Repossession of longed-for foods, which may entail a whole history of chain migration and the development of intricate networks of provisioning—as Tanachai Mark Padoongpatt explores in his chapter on the rise of Thai cuisine in the United States—enables a repossession of one's culinary subjectivity (and perhaps its sharing with others) as well as one's bodily intactness.

So, then, what do we do with memory, particularly what Meredith Abarca calls "palate memory"? How do we deal with its various manifestations, as described in the chapters of this book, like "*sazón*" and "yum"? How does recapturing taste become, as Padoongpatt tells us about Thai cuisine, a way of regaining "wholeness"? What is it that the cooks in José Vasquez-Medina's chapter seek when they strive to re-create foods from home? What is this part of the brain that Abarca tells us is embedded—perhaps encrusted—with past tastes and previous generations? Authenticity may be a dream, but dreams are sticky, particularly ones associated with home, wholeness, belonging, and the hippocampus (the portion of the brain responsible for emotion and memory). Dreams tend to be timeless and placeless. And, like dreams, memories tend to be inconsistent and open to multiple interpretations. When is the idea of authentic food, such as the chiles that are "*los correctos*" for immigrants in Vermont, the pull of wholeness and when is it a way to privilege some cultures and classes over others? Kellen Backer's story of World War II military cuisine shows how the idea of a national, nutritionally perfect, and affordable cuisine marginalized other cuisines as imperfect. Katherine Massoth shows that white settlers in nineteenth-century New Mexico denigrated local cuisine as unsanitary and uncivilized. When do definitions of home foods create belonging, and when do they marginalize and denigrate?

These chapters explore these questions, looking in particular at marginal cuisine dreams and homeless tastes. As it turns out, academics began to question authenticity around the same time that Thai and Mexican cooks began to create restaurants that sought to capture the tastes of home. Simultaneously, corporations began to willfully (and profitably) create restaurants that indulged in the lie that they were delivering an authentic culinary experience (for example, Olive Garden's "Tour of Italy" dishes).

Food memories, in other words, play multiple roles. For those marginalized and misrepresented, food memory has been a way to represent wholeness and belonging. The desire to be whole, to belong and be "authentic," can be a resistance to the marginalization from a central cuisine whose authenticity and perfection go unquestioned because it is ubiquitous. It can also be a response to the cultural appropriation of certain cuisines. Palate memory, therefore, can be a resistance to the kinds of cultural dismemberment immigrants experience when they leave home and cross borders. In their displacement they seek home through the palate. As a result, food also moves, as packages with the right chiles arrive in upstate Vermont or new supermarkets selling kaffir lime leaves appear in Los Angeles. Or, as in Michael Wise's chapter, people leave home to visit Congress and defend their right to their own land and livelihood. Yet the defense of home is not necessarily the defense of a timeless past. The Blackfeet visit Congress not to reclaim their past as buffalo hunters but to defend their collective organization based on a re-created wholeness. The Blackfeet re-created their idea of home by building upon traditional notions of selfhood and a relationship to nature based on cattle ranching and self-sufficiency in reservation food production. Similarly, Fabián García did not attempt to recapture the chile pepper of his Chihuahua childhood home, as William Carleton shows in his chapter, but to remake that pepper into something that could be modernized, canned, and eaten by those whose "palate memories" did not include hot food. The Mexican restaurant cook in José Vásquez-Medina's story who seeks to re-create her home mole succeeds not by recovering the lost seasoning, but by replacing it with Coca-Cola (unless, as is possible, that was the seasoning even at home). And Vásquez-Medina's Mexican restaurant cooks, who are trying to re-create tastes of home, are in restaurants with other cooks from other small towns with other tastes—so that sometimes the soup has cumin in it and sometimes it does not. The menu is an amalgam of each of these cooks—recipes imparted by grandmothers, dishes prepared and eaten in different small towns across Mexico, and recommendations for substitute ingredients shared by way of phone calls back home. As recipes become successful on the "front stage" of restaurant menus, they are passed on from cook to cook, and from restaurant to restaurant, to become a part of American cuisine regardless of origins.

Marygold Walsh-Dilly's chapter shows how these moral categories can change as home foods cross over territories and borders. The word "Indio" is a derogatory slur in Bolivia, where producers refer to themselves as "campesinos." Yet as the word travels to packages on American supermarket shelves, it becomes part of the sales pitch. "Good" food in this case draws upon ancient Inca grandmas, yet where that past Inca civilization resides, such nostalgia does not exist. In Western sales romanticism, "Indio" stands for a preindustrial nostalgia, one that has been appropriated to sell everything from cigars to vacations. In the case of quinoa, this ethnic marker is used to sell a product of peasants struggling to reclaim a moral dignity, in a place that uses that same word to represent them as a degraded group. The irony in this case is that those peddling quinoa as an indigenous product are often fair trade solidarity groups, the ones who have brought this economic boon to Bolivian peasants, representing them in the romantic terms that have no romance in their own country.

Mary Murphy's chapter shows a different role for borders and belonging. World War I made "the previously imperceptible line" between Canada and the United States "a line of judgment." Citizens began to police one another, and morals hardened as borders did. As "wartime regulations inscribed more clearly what had been a fairly invisible national border," they created moral differences "in the intimate daily acts of eating." As a result, "innocuous items like sugar and flour became instruments of policing and judgment." Borders require surveillance if they are to maintain their integrity. The hardening of borders, therefore, lessens the possibilities of hybridity, or mixing, and raises the wall between good and bad, so that transgression—in Murphy's case the transgression of eating too much flour or sugar—pits one neighbor against another. Consequently, a monitoring of neighbors once considered similar became subject to differences in loyalties and lifestyles, producing distrust where previously there had been familiarity and solidarity, conflict where there had been peace if not harmony.

BODIES CROSSING BORDERS

In the wake of the September 11, 2001, terrorist attacks, Congress reorganized border policing, abolishing the Immigration and Naturalization Service and reorganizing its Border Patrol into the Customs and Border Protection (CPB) agency. At the same time, it extended CPB's jurisdiction to 100 miles from the north and south borders and all coasts. Two-thirds of all residents in the United States now live within CPB jurisdiction (Map 1).

While Mexico has traditionally been the focus, border surveillance along the Canada-U.S. border has taken on added urgency in recent years. Maine and Florida are now entirely legal border zones. Very little of New York or Vermont are outside the zone. Within the 100-mile zone, CPB agents can establish checkpoints along the roads and ask for IDs and documentation, stop cars without probable cause or indications of an infraction, and fly drones for high-resolution surveillance (even over private property) and use them to track individuals. They can detain "suspected" illegal immigrants—including, not infrequently, immigrants who are here legally but do not have their papers on them (which is not required for travel within the States). Within 25 miles—a space that contains all of San Francisco and Oakland, much of greater New York City, a good deal of Chicago, and whole bands of productive farmland along the Mexican and Canadian borders—agents can enter private property without a warrant. As one reporter says: "On any given day, it [the 'Homeland Security State'] can stand between you and the grocery store."[17] For Mexican and Central American immigrant workers on the dairy farms of northern New York and Vermont, as Kathleen Sexsmith and Teresa Mares and her colleagues discuss in their chapters, living in the border zone means workers rarely leave their farms for fear of detention and deportation. It is not uncommon for their employers to do all the grocery shopping for them so they can remain hidden in the milking sheds or their apartments and bunkhouses far back from the road.

"Immigrant" is a word that comes from the Latin "to move." Immigrants leave home and enter the homes of others, sometimes even living on their farms. As with the immigrants in Teresa Mares's and Katherine Sexsmith's chapters, New York and Vermont dairy workers have frequently made long, perilous journeys, often from Central America, risking life and paying significant sums to smugglers as they cross into and through Mexico. By the time they work their way to the northernmost reaches of the continental United States to secure work, as Sexsmith shows, they may have to pay an additional fee to a previous job holder in order to take his or her place on the milking machines.[18] The monetary and bodily cost of crossing borders is exceptionally high, and thus many dairy workers along the Canadian border (like their compadres working in meatpacking plants in Nebraska and South Dakota, fruit orchards in the Northwest, restaurants in Chicago and Atlanta, tobacco and vegetable farms in North Carolina and Virginia, chicken processing plants in Arkansas and Delaware, and any number of other links in the food commodity chain) are reluctant to contact authorities to report workplace abuses such as below-minimum wages, wage theft, or unsafe working and housing conditions. Nor are many willing to risk exposure should they become sick or injured. Consequently, many immigrant workers avoid

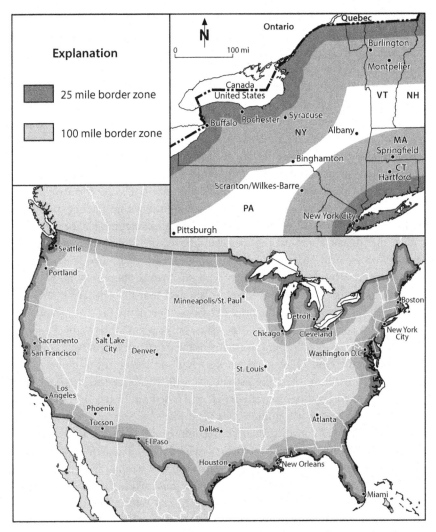

Map 1. The U.S. border is a zone, not only a line. Within 25 miles of any U.S. border, Customs and Border Protection agents can enter private property without a warrant if they suspect undocumented people might be present. Within 100 miles, they may establish checkpoints along roads to check IDs, stop cars without probable cause or indications of an infraction, and fly drones (even over private property) for high-resolution surveillance of individuals. Cartography by Syracuse University Cartographic Laboratory & Map Shop.

treatment, compounding public health problems and raising obvious concerns about food safety.[19]

The border regulates the nature of labor relations in most food industries, establishing how and at what cost food is produced. Farm owners have long understood this. As California developed into one of the most productive and profitable farming regions in the world, for example, the primary question confronting growers has always been, and remains, how shall they secure a labor force appropriate to the demands of an industry—with its high-seasonality and discontinuous production—that requires massive inputs of labor for brief moments over the course of the year (for a week or two, perhaps), but then for much of the year, hardly any labor at all. With high, and largely fixed, input costs (for land, fertilizer, pesticides, seeds, packing and shipping, and credit), growers have demanded—or, as they see it, their viability as food producers has required—constant access to cheap, flexible labor, the one cost over which they feel they might have some control. Their solution from the beginning has been to look beyond California and the United States, recruiting labor first from China, then Japan, southern Europe, Scandinavia, the Philippines, Mexico, the Dust Bowl states, then Mexico again, and now increasingly Central America. The struggle to grow food is a struggle over who can cross the border—and how.[20]

The economist Lloyd Fisher long ago showed that the primary interest of commercial growers was less the price of labor—their desire for "cheap labor"—and more its controllability.[21] Over the years, farmers have thus lobbied aggressively for "guest worker" programs (many of the dairy workers in New York and Vermont are there on H-2A guest worker visas and are meant to be here only temporarily), winning their biggest success with the "bracero program" that began as a war emergency program in 1942 and lasted until 1964. Over the course of the program, some 4.6 million jobs were filled by braceros, who typically worked on six-week contracts, had no freedom of job mobility, and were relatively easily returned to Mexico if farm owners did not like them. Their conditions of labor were close to indenture, a situation that has hardly changed as the bracero program has been replaced with other guest worker programs. Indeed, a recent investigation by the Southern Poverty Law Center found many H-2A farmworkers to be toiling in conditions "close to slavery."[22]

Geared primarily toward the needs of agribusiness (though in its early years it also provided temporary workers to the railroads), the bracero program reinforced the domination of heavily capitalized farms over smaller farmers, helping to cement into place the industrial system of food production that is now the focus of so much concern by food activists. The dynamics were complex. On the one hand, access to what seemed like an unlimited supply of temporary, largely powerless, labor allowed highly capitalized growers to experiment with new, expensive technology. For example, the development of vacuum cooling during World War II (part of the significant reorientation of American food technologies during the war that Kellen Backer traces in his chapter) allowed for field-packing of iceberg lettuce beginning around 1950. But this required investment in both vacuum-packing facilities and new, mobile field-packing machines, a significant capital outlay. At the same time, the new lettuce picking and packing process required an *increase* in the number of field workers. Mechanization did not replace human labor in this instance, it demanded more of it. And the bracero program, which brought workers over the border under controlled circumstances, provided the predictable, inexpensive labor that made the gamble worth it for those farmers who could afford the new technology. This in turn led to a consolidation of lettuce growing into fewer, increasingly corporate, hands.[23]

On the other hand, by 1960 the technology and new plant varieties were in place to allow for mechanized canning-tomato harvesting. But adoption of the technology was halting, at best, until it became clear, in 1963, that the bracero program was going to end and growers would lose access to that source of cheap, controlled labor. Indeed, when braceros were plentiful, growers actively resisted research into mechanization. But now, fearful that the border might be shut altogether, growers quickly adopted the new technology, especially as banks, concerned that the crops would not be harvested, stopped making loans to tomato growers. In 1963, less than one-half of 1 percent of the harvest was machine-picked. By 1966, almost all of it was. Simultaneously, tomato growing was consolidated. The new machines demanded larger fields (in excess of 100 acres) to be viable. Between 1964 and 1975, total tomato acreage increased 109 percent and average farm size increased by 168 percent, but the number of tomato farmers decreased by 18 percent. Meanwhile, despite fears of a labor shortage, wages dropped for laborers working as sorters on the machines compared to the tomato harvesting workers they replaced.[24]

If guest worker programs (or other border-management programs) transform how food is produced, they also change the nature of the border itself. As the historian David Gutiérrez has shown, the government managed the flow of agricultural labor and betrayed the temporary nature of the migration not only by creating a guest worker program but also by simultaneously encouraging braceros to skip their contracts or forego the program altogether to become undocumented immigrants, even as it made a show of cracking down on undocumented workers in the fields, as with "Operation Wetback" in 1954.[25] The border itself, as a frontier that had to be crossed, together with laws governing immigration and citizenship, remade the border zone into a sieve, a destination, and a waiting room. The border functioned as a sieve when the bracero program drained Mexico of potential contributors to the Mexican economy during the prime years of braceros' lives, reworking Mexican agricultural landscapes and extending an economic and political imbalance between the two countries that already existed.[26] The United States' economic dominance was strengthened, encouraging continued migration of former braceros and their families as the program ended, now as undocumented immigrants.

During the bracero program, American growers and officials fought to get recruitment centers in Mexico located as near to the border as possible, not only to reduce transportation costs but also because they knew that many of those waiting to be selected—or who failed to be selected—would seek to enter the United States anyway. The border became a destination and a waiting room. American studies scholar Alicia Schmidt Camacho reveals, the lure of U.S. agriculture—and the Border Industrial Program (the maquiladora program) that began in 1965 as a partial replacement for the bracero program—contributed to a massive shift of the Mexican population northward and the urbanization of the border on the Mexican side.[27] Perhaps not coincidentally, this northward shift of population also created a large pool of available labor as food production itself moved south across the border in the wake of the bracero programs' demise and, especially, the significant opening of the border for the movement of goods with the North American Free Trade Agreement (NAFTA) in 1994.

Of course, movement by workers or others across America's borders has not always been so fraught, as William Carleton makes clear in his examination of the life of Dr. Fabián García. Born in Mexico, raised in northern New Mexico, and working at what became New Mexico State University in Las Cruces, Garcia traveled back and forth across the border during the first decades of the twentieth century, securing plant varietals for his chile breeding program and consulting with Mexican farmers and government officials. Garcia's work as an agriculture extension officer extended across the border as a matter of course. His frequent travels into Mexico were essential to the nature of the work he did, and thus the new commercial chiles he bred. Similarly, the Hispano cooks that white women travelers drew on in their search for and transformation of New Mexican cuisine—as a detailed by Katherine Massoth—were typically part of extended families that lived on both sides of the border. Indeed, before 1848 there was no border (Map 2). Even after it was imposed as a result of the Treaty of Guadalupe Hidalgo and the Gadsden Purchase (1853), movement across the line was rarely impeded. Only much later did a line in the sand (or, more accurately, on a map) become hardened into a more-or-less effective barrier to the movement of people and things that give food its taste—that make a cuisine.

And sometimes the movement of people across a border that is truly consequential for national cuisines has nothing to do with food production and preparation, at least at first, as Padoongpatt explains. The earliest Thai immigrants came to the United States as students, responding to shifting geopolitical realities in Southeast Asia as well as the rapid expansion of the American higher education system in the postwar era. Once here, though, they longed for the food of home, and thus had to invent ways to procure the ingredients. In the process

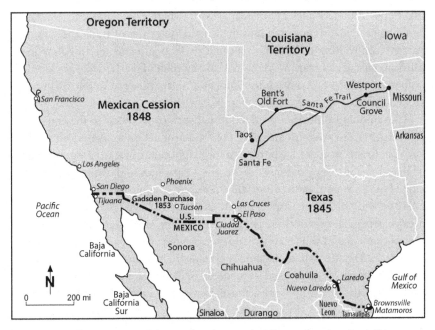

Map 2. Northern Mexico and the southwestern United States, showing the shifting border between the two, the Santa Fe Trail, and key border region cities. Cartography by Syracuse University Cartographic Laboratory & Map Shop.

they helped invent Thai (American) cuisine and launch a whole segment of the restaurant business.

FOOD CROSSING BORDERS

The story Padoongpatt tells is important. Thai restaurateurs and grocers had to create whole new networks of provision. Sometimes they would smuggle seeds and plants from Southeast Asia into the United States and provide them to willing farmers in hopes of developing a local source for key ingredients (which was not easy given U.S. Customs agents' heightened scrutiny of travelers from Southeast Asia as they sought to interrupt drug shipments). Sometimes they would experiment with local foodstuffs they hoped would mimic ingredients they could not get. Ultimately, some of the more enterprising ones created import-export businesses to bring in packaged goods from Thailand and fresh produce from Mexico. In the case of Mexican imports, Thai entrepreneurs had to overcome U.S. Department of Agriculture (USDA) restrictions on "foreign foods" thought to harbor diseases that they believed threatened U.S. agriculture. Pramorte Tilakamonkul, a proprietor of the pioneering Bangkok Market in Los Angeles, persevered more than others. By the mid-1980s, he had help create two Foreign Trade Zones in Sinaloa, Mexico, where Thai fruits and vegetables could be grown and imported into the United States free of trade and Customs barriers confronting other food imports (see Map 3 in chapter 5). Before long, Mexican farmers and farmworkers in Tilakamonkul's Free Trade Zones supplied 90 percent of the fall and winter Southeast Asian produce imported into the United States.

Tilakamonkul's Mexican production network contributed to the emergence of a post-bracero program movement of food production for American markets and restaurants south of the border. At the height of the bracero program, nearly all the white asparagus and most of the green asparagus sold commercially in the United States were produced in California's San Joaquin Delta region. By 1970, all white and much green asparagus production had been relocated to northern Mexico, where labor costs were cheaper. At the time, white asparagus was almost always canned, and thus traveled and stored easily. Green asparagus is likewise durable, and relatively hard to damage in transit. These characteristics—together with their heavy labor demands—made them likely candidates to quickly move south when the bracero program ended, becoming early "transnational" vegetables. But global markets in agricultural commodities are hardly new. Wheat, rice, and other grains, sugar, spices, oils, liquors, and meats have long been globalized.

The history of the banana provides the best evidence of our dependence on transnational networks for our food. By the end of the nineteenth century the banana was America's most popular fruit, even though it—the very quintessence of the American cereal-based breakfast—could not even be grown within the country. Sicilian immigrants began large-scale commercial production of bananas in Central America in the 1880s, and within only twenty years bananas had surpassed apples as the leading fruit consumed in the United States. America's preference for this new fruit had a profound influence not only at home but across the borders in the places where it was grown. If the railroad was the "octopus" of nineteenth-century America—a term used to describe monopolies that control a significant part of the U.S. economy—then cultivation of bananas gave rise to the Latin American equivalent "El Pulpo" of the twentieth century: the United Fruit Company.[28] Under the leadership of Sam Zemurray, United Fruit drove U.S. foreign policy in Central America, facilitated a coup d'etat in Guatemala, and built one of the most influential businesses in the hemisphere.[29] During the 1960s and 1970s, a Polish immigrant, Eli Black, leveraged United Fruit to control agriculture within and outside the United States under the banner of United Brands. Until his suicide in 1975 (Black leaped to his death from the forty-fourth floor of the Pan American building in midtown Manhattan, about to be exposed for bribing the president of Honduras to lower tariffs—that is, to lower borders for his company's goods) United Brands managed an agricultural empire that stretched from the fields of California, across the border into Mexico, and on south through Central and South America. As a transnational corporation growing and selling vegetables and fruits inside and outside of the United States, United Brands also facilitated the movement of large number of workers throughout the Americas to participate in its harvests.[30]

The misdeeds of Black occurred even as the United States enacted policies that increased the interdependence of food production throughout the hemisphere and beyond. Beginning in 1973, the United States started reversing the practice of paying farmers *not* to produce surplus food, a policy established by the Agricultural Adjustment Act of 1933, which sought to stabilize prices by managing farmers' productivity and avoiding overproduction. Instead, the Nixon administration, under advisement from Secretary of Agriculture Earl Butz, encouraged farmers to produce with reckless abandon and sell at any price since the federal government would now make up the difference between the real cost and the sale price.[31]

Nixon simultaneously pursued the expansion of farm exports by eliminating barriers to selling U.S. agricultural products abroad. He followed the advice of another adviser, the investment banker and presidential assistant Peter Flanigan, who recommended "the fullest possible liberalization of policies with regard to agricultural trade"—at least for U.S.-produced goods seeking global markets, if not vice versa.[32] The policy achieved the desired results: the trade surplus on agricultural goods went from $1.56 billion in 1972 to $10.53 billion in 1974. The twin policies of removing New Deal policies that minimized surpluses and removing trade barriers in order to sell the new surpluses on the world market fundamentally reshaped the methods and purpose of food production in the United States. Under these conditions, U.S. agriculture served not only to feed America but also to increase revenues through exports.

A massive restructuring of the food system and the North American agricultural economy in the 1970s hastened a new world order that currently shapes what we eat and who makes that food possible. In the 1990s, trade agreements were negotiated (NAFTA in 1994), trade organizations were created (as the General Agreement on Tariffs and Trade became the World Trade Organization in 1995), and congressional acts were passed (the "Freedom to Farm Act"—the Federal Agricultural Improvement and Reform [FAIR] Act of 1996), all of which extended and deepened trade liberalization and food exports and imports.[33] These agreements and governing bodies have lowered tariffs among nations (if not all Customs barriers, as Padoongpatt shows) and facilitated investment in Mexican agriculture by U.S. growers at the expense of workers on both sides of the border.

For example, Jack Pandol, a grower who fought unionization of his grape fields in Delano, California, during the heyday of the United Farm Workers in the 1960s and 1970s, planted several thousand acres of grape vines on the Mexican side of the Sonoran desert after the passage of NAFTA, tapping into a large pool of labor the bracero and maquiladora programs had helped create.

He quickly produced so many grapes, at such low labor cost, that he drove U.S. competitors from the market. The resulting closure of several farms in nearby Riverside County on the U.S. side resulted in hundreds of farmworkers losing their jobs. When the workers applied for unemployment benefits and worker retraining, or "Trade Adjustment Assistance" under the original NAFTA agreement, the California Employment Development Department ruled that only forty-three "permanent" employees qualified. The rest of the employees, the department determined, had not yet begun to pick for the season, and therefore were ineligible.[34] Under NAFTA, capital and production—and the foods central to American diets—move more easily across borders than do workers' rights. Indeed, a recent *Los Angeles Times* exposé detailed how Mexican agricultural production, like its U.S. counterpart, is frequently characterized by withheld wages, child laborers, and abysmal working conditions. On some Mexican megafarms employees were held against their will. Entitled "They Treated Us Like Slaves," the December 10, 2014, story was part of a series, "Product of Mexico," which captured how borders make such abuses possible by exporting exploitative labor practices southward while increasing the bounty of affordable produce moving northward.

The cross-border influence of financial power increasingly stretches in both directions. In addition to Jim Pandol & Company (begun by Jack Pandol) and other U.S. agribusinesses, Mexican agricultural conglomerates have invested deeply in farms that fuel U.S. consumers' appetites for fresh fruits and vegetables. Over the last decade, Mexican agricultural exports to the United States have increased threefold and now exceed $7.5 billion in business per year. As one measure of this increase, Mexican tomatoes now account for approximately 50 percent of all tomatoes consumed in the United States. Several of these Mexican producers—among them Rene Produce and Agricola San Emilio—sell almost all their produce to U.S. supermarkets and restaurants, including Walmart, Whole Foods, Safeway, Olive Garden, and Subway. Until the recent revelations of horrid working conditions, the Mexican government celebrated these farms as model producers. Rene alone made $55 million in 2014 selling its tomatoes to Whole Foods. Whole Foods, meanwhile, made claims of "social responsibility" in its labor practices.[35]

The embarrassment of being associated with inhumane treatment of workers has led industry leaders to embrace reform, but on their terms. While Walmart has called for more accountability from Mexican producers, it has also chosen to work with the Mexican Ministry of Agriculture to establish labor standards.[36] Such an approach is a form of "corporate social responsibility" that deviates dramatically from the "worker-driven social responsibility" demanded by the Coalition of Immokalee Workers (CIW) in Florida, for example.[37] Under the Fair Food Program created by CIW pressure, growers participate in a "penny per pound" program that funds a grievance system for workers on Florida's tomato farms, and involves workers themselves in the audit of grower practices (activists in upstate New York and Vermont have organized for a system like this to govern dairy workers like those Sexsmith describes, even as their efforts are strongly opposed by farmers' organizations).[38] The existence of unequal monitoring and grievance procedures on either side of the border threatens the progress made by the CIW, since the tomatoes produced in Mexico and the United States compete for the same supermarket shelf space.

The illegibility of origin for so many of the foods we consume—and thus of the relations of their production—has generated opposition to highly industrialized production (and processing) and advocacy for the restoration of accountability. Advocates for locally grown produce on small, often community-supported farms have come to define a politics of localism that raises the esteem of farm work and has returned some of us to seasonal diets. The rapid growth of local farmers' markets (like the ones that Laura-Anne Minkoff-Zern's Virginia farmers find themselves frequently excluded from) has been one important consequence of this movement. A second response has been the push for country of origin labeling (COOL) legislation, which has been fiercely resisted by large transnational growers and food processors, meat packers, and the like. A third response has been to support "fair trade," a system of marketing that, as Marygold Walsh-Dilley makes clear, is often happy to trade on the presumed "authenticity" of indigenous peoples and ethical treatment, so that consumers can seek to resolve the contradictions of globalized food production not through a retreat into localism, but to become more global than ever.

All three responses depend on a sense of autonomy and authenticity of place that is somewhat illusory given the challenge of differential access to healthy food and our societal dependence on a transnational food system. As the long history of the global exchange of foods indicates—from the spread of taro throughout the Pacific, to the transfer of potatoes from the Americas to become the primary starch in Europe, to United Fruit's conquest of Central America to sell bananas for North Americans' breakfast cereal, to the yams that came to the Americas with some of Meredith Abarca's forebearers, to the lemongrass and kaffir limes smuggled into California by Thai immigrants, to the contemporary spread of pseudo-grains like the quinoa Marygold Walsh-Dilley examines in her chapter—"local food" is an oxymoron, even if localized production and distribution systems and regionalized cuisines may not be. More positively, then, the new politics of food, from localism, to COOL, to fair trade (to say nothing of activism against the use of genetically modified organisms [GMOs]), represents an effort to gain more control over the forces of globalization that define when, how, and why food crosses borders.

Food Across Borders: Bodies, Nations, and Border Crossings

Shifts like these in transborder relations of food production, procurement, and preparation—as well as eating—require a reorientation of how food scholars understand borders and borderlands. Beginning with Américo Paredes's ground-breaking work in the 1950s, border studies scholars have reversed the popular notion that borders and borderlands are "culturally diluted and marginal to the interests of the state," a claim that was always debatable because what happens at borders—how and if they are policed, what is and is not let through—is itself significantly defined by what happens in the core.[39] By now, it is obvious that what happens at the borders defines the nation. This volume shows this to be especially true of food.[40] Borders are, in this sense, internalized in the foods we eat, part and parcel of their very conditions of possibility.

The chapters in this volume revise our understandings of borders, border-lands, and border crossings (and thus of nation and home) by focusing on the intimate borders of the body and community as well as the territorial borders of states. Collectively, the chapters show that neither the intimate nor the geo-political can be understood in isolation from the other. Individually, each chapter presents a case study in how borders and border crossings are internalized in food. Food moving across borders remakes home, creating the potential to satisfy yearnings for remembered dishes through imported ingredients. It makes possible the achievement of culturally specific (if changing) practices of *sazón* and sensations of "yum." Bodies moving across borders additionally make food production itself possible, from the cooks in Chicago and Houston's small Mexican restaurants to the large dairy farms on the Canadian border that produce the milk that goes into a quintessentially American invention, "Greek" yogurt (developed in its commercial form by a Turkish immigrant). The erecting of boundaries, as well as the dismantling and transgression of them, constitutes an important element in defining what we eat, how we eat, and what it means when we consume food.

What these boundaries mean is not static even though they appear fixed. Borders are frequently demarcated by walls, hard to breach and difficult to climb over (and when they operate like this, the consequences for immigrant workers can be devastating). Just as often, however, they function like membranes: allowing some things to pass, transforming others, and keeping yet others out altogether. The borderlands that result—bodily, cultural, or territorial—can be spaces of creative intermixing or create zones of intensive policing and constriction. The chapters that follow show that food and the act of eating offer perhaps the best place to observe both of these dynamics as they exist in North America's past, present, and likely future.

NOTES

1. Thomas. F. Gieryn, "Boundary-Work and the Demarcation of Science from Non-Science: Strains and Interests in Professional Ideologies of Scientists," *American Sociological Review* 48 (1983): 781–795.

2. Geoffrey Bowker and Susan Leigh Star, *Sorting Things Out: Classification and Its Consequences* (Cambridge, MA: MIT Press, 1999).

3. Though the global "food sovereignty" movement is not directly addressed in this volume, the stories told in *Food Across Borders* nonetheless ought to have great relevance for social movements currently struggling for it in their locales, regions, and nations—and for immigrants seeking work in far-flung corners of America as Teresa Mares, Naomi Wolcott-MacCausland, and Jessie Mazar make clear in chapter 10. Food sovereignty entails the right to define food as belonging to the territory, as the right to a "culturally appropriate" cuisine, and, perhaps especially, as the right to have local and national food security not be at the mercy of outside corporate or geopolitical forces. Sovereignty, therefore, involves borders on the ground and people drawing those borders. People imagine community through the bounded places where they live and eat. Yet when people cross those boundaries, they become involved in new conversations about who and where they are. All this matters for any decent notion of food sovereignty based on a progressive, interconnected sense of place rather than a reactionary or nationalist one. On the "progressive sense of place," see Doreen Massey, *Space, Place and Gender* (Minneapolis: University of Minnesota Press, 1994).

4. Loosely translated, "*sazón*" encompasses an act of seasoning that includes not only spices but also the skill and experience a cook brings to a dish. See José Vásquez-Medina's chapter in this volume, and Meredith Abarca, *Voices in the Kitchen: Views of Food and Women from Working Class Mexican and Mexican-American Women* (College Station: Texas A&M Press, 2006).

5. Gloria Anzaldúa, *Borderlands/La Frontera: The New Mestiza* (1987; repr., San Francisco: Aunt Lute Books, 1999), 99–101; Lynn Stephen, *Transborder Lives: Indigenous Oaxacans in Mexico, California, and Oregon* (Durham, NC: Duke University Press, 2007), 6, 19–23.

6. Philip White, *Our Supreme Task: How Winston Churchill's Iron Curtain Speech Defined the Cold War Alliance* (New York: Public Affairs, 2012), 187, 192.

7. E. Melanie DuPuis, *Dangerous Digestion: Politics and Dietary Reform in America* (Berkeley: University of California Press, 2015); J. David Cisneros, "Contaminated Communities: The Metaphor of 'Immigrant as Pollutant' in Media Representations of Immigration," *Rhetoric & Public Affairs* 11.4 (2008): 569–601; Natalia Molina, *Fit to Be Citizens?: Public Health and Race in Los Angeles, 1879–1939.* (Berkeley: University of California Press, 2006).

8. Claude Levi-Strauss, *The Raw and the Cooked* (New York: Harper, 1968); Mary Douglas, "Deciphering a Meal," *Daedalus* (Winter 1972): 61–81; see also Deborah Lupton, *Food, the Body and the Self* (London: Sage, 1996); Elspeth Probyn, *Carnal Appetites: Foodsexidentities* (New York: Psychology Press, 2000).

9. Frederick Kaufman, *A Short History of the American Stomach* (Orlando, FL: Houghton Mifflin Harcourt, 2008); Julia Child *The Way to Cook* (New York: Knopf, 1989), xi.

10. DuPuis, *Dangerous Digestion.*

11. Rachel Laudan, *Cuisine and Empire: Cooking in World History* (Berkeley: University of California Press, 2013).

12. Though as Kellen Backer shows in this volume, "national cuisine" itself has to be invented. Not only that, inventing it is a logistical problem.

13. Richard Pillsbury, *No Foreign Food: The American Diet in Time and Place* (Boulder, CO: Westview Press, 1998); Rachel Slocum and Arun Saldhana, eds., *Geographies of Race and Food: Fields, Bodies, Markets* (Farnham, UK: Ashgate, 2013); Helen Zoe Viet, *Modern Food, Moral Food: Self-Control, Science, and the Rise of Modern American Eating in the Early Twentieth Century* (Chapel Hill: University of North Carolina Press, 2013).

14. DuPuis, *Dangerous Digestion*, 106.

15. Michael Pollan, *Food Rules: An Eater's Manual* (New York: Penguin, 2009).

16. Psyche Williams-Forson has shown how African American women created not just a cuisine in the face of racism, but through that cuisine a home and a source of power, showing just how important a produced, reproduced, rooted, and shared culture of food can be for the formation of subjectivity and for the exercise of power. Psyche Williams-Forson, *Building Houses Out of Chicken Legs: Women, Food, and Power* (Chapel Hill: University of North Carolina Press, 2006).

17. Todd Miller, "66 Percent of Americans Now Live in a Constitution-Free Zone," *Nation*, July 15, 2014, http://www.thenation.com/article/66-percent-americans-now-live -constitution-free-zone/.

18. On the perilous journey, see Joe Nevins, *Operation Gatekeeper: The Rise of the "Illegal Alien" and the Making of the U.S.-Mexico Boundary* (New York: Routledge, 2002); Ken Ellingwood, *Hard Line: Life and Death on the U.S.-Mexico Border* (New York: Pantheon, 2004); Don Mitchell, "Work, Struggle, Death, and Geographies of Justice: The Transformation of Landscape in and beyond California's Imperial Valley," *Landscape Research* 32 (2007): 559–577.

19. A. Bugarin and E. Lopez, *Farmworkers in California* (Monograph CRB-98–007), (Sacramento: California Research Bureau, California State Library, 1998); S. Arcury and T. Quandt, eds., Special Section: Health Risks in Agricultural Work—Occupational and Environmental Health Risks in Farm Labor, *Human Organization* 57(3): 331ff.

20. The literature is vast, but some starting points are Cletus Daniel, *Bitter Harvest: A History of California Farmworkers, 1870–1941* (Ithaca, NY: Cornell University Press, 1981); Don Mitchell, *The Lie of the Land: Migrant Workers and the California Landscape* (Minneapolis: University of Minnesota Press, 1996); Richard Steven Street, *Beasts of the Field: A Narrative History of California Farm Workers, 1769–1913* (Stanford, CA: Stanford University Press, 2004). For an analysis of the California agricultural political economy more generally, see Richard Walker, *The Conquest of Bread: 150 Years of Agribusiness in California* (New York: New Press, 2004).

21. Lloyd Fisher, *The Harvest Labor Market in California* (Cambridge, MA: Harvard University Press, 1953).

22. Don Mitchell, *They Saved the Crops: Labor, Landscape, and the Struggle Over Industrial Farming in Bracero-Era California* (Athens: University of Georgia Press, 2012); Matt Garcia, *A World of Its Own: Race, Labor, and Citrus in the Making of Greater Los Angeles, 1900–1970* (Chapel Hill: University of North Carolina Press, 2002); Mae Ngai, *Impossible Subjects: Illegal Aliens and the Making of Modern America* (Princeton, NJ: Princeton University Press, 2004); Manuel García y Griego, "The Importation of Mexican Contract Laborers to the United States, 1942–1964," in *Between Two Worlds: Mexican Immigrants in the United States*, ed. David Gutierrez (Wilmington, NC: Jaguar/SR Books, 1996), 45–85; Kelly Lytle Hernandez, *Migra! A History of the U.S. Border Patrol* (Berkeley: University of California Press, 2010); Southern Poverty Law Center, *Close to Slavery: Guest Worker Programs in the United States* (Montgomery, AL: SPLC, 2007), 5, 19.

23. Mitchell, *They Saved the Crops*, 204–106.

24. Ibid., 411–415.

25. David Gutiérrez, *Walls and Mirrors: Mexican Americans, Mexican Immigrants, and the Politics of Ethnicity* (Berkeley: University of California Press, 1995); Mitchell, *They Saved the Crops*, 229–256; Juan Ramon García, *Operation Wetback: The Mass Deportation of Undocumented Mexican Workers in 1954* (New York: Praeger, 1980); Kitty Calavita, *Inside the State: The Bracero Program, Immigration, and the I.N.S.* (New York: Routledge, 1992), 53–61.

26. Gilbert G. Gonzalez, *Guest Workers or Colonized Labor: Mexican Labor Migration to the United States* (Boulder, CO: Paradigm, 2006).

27. Alicia Schmidt Camacho, *Migrant Imaginaries: Latino Cultural Politics in the U.S.-Mexico Borderlands* (New York: New York University Press, 2008).

28. Dan Koeppel, *Banana: The Fate of a Fruit That Changed the World* (New York: Hudson Street Press, 2007), xiii.

29. Rich Cohen, *The Fish That Ate the Whale: The Life and Times of America's Banana King* (New York: Farrar, Straus, and Giroux, 2012), 12.

30. Thomas McCann, *An American Company: The Tragedy of United Fruit* (New York: Random House, 1988).

31. Michael Pollan, *The Omnivore's Dilemma: A Natural History of Four Meals* (New York: Penguin Books, 2006), 52.

32. Matt Garcia, *From the Jaws of Victory: The Triumph and Tragedy of Cesar Chavez and the Farm Worker Movement* (Berkeley: University of California Press, 2014), 132.

33. Raj Patel, *Stuffed and Starved: The Hidden Battle for the World Food System* (New York: Melville House Publishing, 2007).

34. David Bacon, *The Children of NAFTA: Labor Wars on the U.S.-Mexico Border* (Berkeley: University of California Press, 2004), 20–21, 36.

35. *Los Angeles Times*, December 7, 2014.

36. *Los Angeles Times*, February 12, 2015.

37. http://ciw-online.org/.

38. http://www.fairfoodprogram.org/.

39. Américo Paredes *"With His Pistol in His Hand": A Border Ballad and Its Hero* (Austin: University of Texas Press, 1958); Claire F. Fox, *The Fence and the River: Culture and Politics at the U.S.-Mexico Border* (Minneapolis: University of Minnesota Press, 1999), 2. Other border theorists such as José David Saldívar have worked to reconstitute a holistic "Greater Mexico" culture in the borderlands that must have existed prior to the Treaty of Guadalupe Hidalgo, and persisted in the borderlands culture of the late twentieth century. See José David Saldívar, *Border Matters: Remapping American Cultural Studies* (Berkeley: University of California Press, 1997), 12. And Mexican cultural theorist Néstor García Canclini regards *la frontera* (the border) as a "laboratory for postmodernism" where the aspirations of progress, as conceived by states, conflicts with the reality of human and environmental degradation to produce a new "hybridity" that is indicative of what both nations, the United States and Mexico, have become. Néstor García Canclini, *Culturas Híbrisas: Estrategias para Entrar y Salir do la Modernidad* (Mexico City: Grijalbo, 1990), 23.

40. See, for example, Robert R. Alvarez Jr., *Mangos, Chiles, and Truckers: The Business of Transnationalism* (Minneapolis: University of Minnesota Press, 2005); Hernández, *Migra!*; Camacho, *Migrant Imaginaries*; Rachel S. John, *A Line in the Sand: A History of the Western U.S.-Mexico Border* (Princeton, NJ: Princeton University Press, 2012); Geraldo L. Cadava, *Standing on Common Ground: The Making of a Sunbelt Borderland* (Cambridge, MA: Harvard University Press, 2013); Peter Andreas, *Border Games: Policing the U.S.-Mexico Divide* (Ithaca, NY: Cornell University Press, 2000); Joseph Nevins, *Operation Gatekeeper*.

CHAPTER 2

Afro-Latina/os' Culinary Subjectivities

ROOTING ETHNICITIES THROUGH ROOT VEGETABLES

Meredith E. Abarca

VIANDA: *The sustenance and food of rational men:*
So it has been said, from the Latin meaning of Vivanda,
because it helps [men] to live and strengthens life.
—*Diccionario de autoridades,* 1737

El abuelo Larios, my great-grandfather, was a blonde, blue-eyed, fair-skinned man born in Cordillera, Michoacán, México (Figure 2.1). He had a peculiar eating habit, which has become my most vivid memory of him. *Camotes* (sweet potatoes) and bananas, more so than *tortillas,* were never absent from his meals. It did not matter if he was eating a hot *caldo de res, sopa de fideo,* a bowl of beans, rice, *chiles rellenos,* or *tamales*—to all of his food he would add slices of either banana or cooked camotes, along with a few drops of lemon. Growing up, literally, in two restaurants owned by my grandmother, Aurora Larios Cárdenas, in Nuevo Laredo, Tamaulipas, México, I saw other people eating corn or flour tortillas with their food. Not my great-grandfather. Nor my mother, Liduvina Vélez Larios, who inherited her grandfather's palate for camotes (not so much for bananas). As a matter of fact, she self-identifies as a *camotera,* one who eats camotes. It is not uncommon for my mother to make her *merienda,* or last meal of the day, a piece of baked camote and a glass of milk. Over the years, I have noticed that I, too, share a palate for camotes with my mother and my great-grandfather. While I do not go out of my way to eat or cook with camotes, the aroma of baked yams or sweet potato soup wafting through my house during late fall and most of winter is a common occurrence (Figure 2.2).

Figure 2.1. The author's great-grandfather, whose love of *camotes* (sweet potatoes) has been passed down through the family. Photo from the author.

Figure 2.2. A bowl of sweet potatoes and yams in the author's kitchen. Photo by the author.

Our food choices communicate something of who we are.[1] They reflect how we respond to our physical, socioeconomic, and cultural milieu. With our current global food industry, our food choices are determined by geography (what is available where we live?) and by economics (what can we actually afford to buy?). The culturally symbolic meaning that food choices carry, however, extends beyond the boundaries of our location of residency and socioeconomic status. The stories that enter our bodies with the foods we consume reflect complex and complicated intimate social acts of how we present and represent ourselves. The narratives and scenarios[2] by which such forms of representation are expressed tell stories of our personal and collective subjectivities.[3]

The idea that we are what we eat is certainly not new. However, I hope to expand this notion by addressing the embodied performance, sensory articulation, and collective palate memories shared within groups whose histories have intertwined their lives. Throughout Latin America and the Caribbean, the lives of people with ancestral origins in Africa have mixed with the lives of Amerindians (as well as other ethnic/European groups) for hundreds of years. As early as the 1500s, Africans crossed the Atlantic as soldiers, merchants, servants, nuns, and slaves. In the context of this chapter, culinary subjectivities underscore how and what *systems* of knowledge(s) people of African background have added to the Latina/os' food practices. More particularly, my interest is in examining how food's historical significance has been shared and transmitted across time and space via collective sensory memories. In order to tease out the process by which Afro-Latina/os share and transmit collective sensory memories, I link French sociologist Claudie Fischler's concept of the "principles of taste" (gustatory) and Puerto Rican historian Cruz Miguel Ortíz Cuadra's notion of "palate memory." Both of these notions are vessels that archive people's cultural knowledge(s). These systems of knowledge are stored in the body and its senses, making them of particular importance in the process of gathering (hi)stories[4] of those who have left little to no written historical records, as is the case with people of African ancestry throughout the Americas. The principles of taste and the palate memory are vital sources that express lived (hi)stories that informed the culinary subjectivities of Afro-Latina/os. Here I explore how this form of embodiment assists in the process by which a collective system of knowledge(s) is performed to "generate, record, and transmit"[5] across time and space cultural values, beliefs, and customs that are expressed through people's food practices, in particular those that share a common African culinary influence.

AFRO-LATINA/OS

How does the opening anecdote of my family's multigeneration of *camoteros* relate to a chapter on Afro-Latina/os' culinary subjectivity? What does my family's palate for camotes have to do with the food practices of Afro-Latinos? Who are Afro-Latinos? My family comes from an area in Mexico with a significant African history, a site where people with African background reside. While my family has never acknowledged an African ancestral heritage, the range of phenotypes and hairstyles within my family gene pool indicates that possibility. If my family does have African heritage and does not acknowledge it, we are not unique in this cognitive lapse. Yet as the overall gist of this chapter suggests, in some of our foodways such African inheritance is performed.

The term "Afro-Latina/o" serves three functions. First, the notion Afro-Latina/o[6] as an identity label addresses what historically, politically, and ideologically two other interethnic labels, *mestizo* and *mulato*, have had a tendency to leave out. Mestizo usually refers to the mixture of Europeans and Amerindians—and tends to leave out people of African ancestry.[7] Mulato is used to identify people of African and European background—leaving Amerindians out. Yet the Spanish Casta System/Las Castas created during the colonial period in what is now known as the Global South clearly indicates the range of inter-connection between these groups: Europeans, Amerindians, and Africans. In the shift from colonies to independent nations, however, many countries projected an idea of the national citizen that underplayed the presence and influence of Africans in the social and cultural fabric of the new countries.[8] In leaving the eth-nic category of "Black" out of the census, as many Latin American and Caribbean countries did, not only were Africans not formally acknowledged but, subse-quently, their culinary influences have historically not been recognized as being part of national cuisines.

Without reducing Chicana cultural critic Gloria Anzaldúa's body of work to one single poem, it is worth mentioning one here to show the difference between conceptual and embodied performative knowledge. In her poem "To Live in the Borderland Means You . . . ," Anzaldúa acknowledges the historical presence of people of African ancestry in the Americas as she writes that *mestiza* conscious-ness "means / . . . that denying the Anglo inside you / is as bad as having denied the Indian or Black."[9] As the poem goes on to describe how such consciousness is lived, food enters Anzaldúa's poetic performance: "To live in the Borderlands means to / put *chile* in the borscht, [and] eat whole wheat *tortillas*."[10] In this moment of an embodied culinary subjectivity, Anzaldúa leaves out the Afri-can influence and foregrounds the Anglo (or European) with the mentioning of borscht and wheat and highlights Amerindians by speaking of *chile* and the technique of making tortillas.[11] The specific influence of what blacks have added to the culinary subjectivity of those living in the borderlands of multiple cultural intersections—for example, *barbacoa de res, caldo de olla, moros y cristianos*, and *arroz con leche*[12]—remains absent in Anzaldúa's poem.

Second, the use of "Afro-Latina/os" as a collective term for those with an ances-tral African background born and living in Latin America, the Caribbean, or the United States allows me not to confine the exploration of culinary subjectivities to one single geographical area. This is particularly important as food knowl-edge travels with people's migrations that expand beyond national and cultural boundaries; it is then adopted and modified due to the availability of ingredients in new geographical contents, but its historical linage remains. For example, *fufu* (also spelled *foofoo, foufou*, and *fufoto*) is a ubiquitous porridge in West and Cen-tral Africa often made of yams.[13] It is abundant in Yoruban cooking, where it is kneaded into a consistency of stiff dough until it resembles a loaf of bread.[14] The knowledge of fufu was brought to the Caribbean islands by African slaves, where it became a staple food made of flour derived from the cassava plant—which is native to the Americas, not Africa. If cassava is not available, maize flour is used. Other substitutes include plantains, which are cooked and made into a doughlike consistency. Throughout the Caribbean, fufu is also found as a porridge made of mashed sweet potatoes, also native of the Americas. In contemporary Puerto

Rico, fufu gave creation to the *mofongo* made mainly with plantains and yucca. While on his journey searching for "blackness" through six Latin American and Caribbean countries, Henry Louise Gates Jr. is offered fufu in Veracruz, México. Gates, however, ends his journey in Mexico stating that people do not recognize their African heritage. What this lack of recognition actually expresses is a "failure" of both Gates and many Mexican people to be fully aware how much history and culture foods and food practices convey.

The third purpose the term "Afro-Latina/o" serves is to "remap our existing concepts of the Americas." By exploring the performative acts of Afro-Latina/os' culinary subjectivities, we can "use embodied performance to trace trajectories and forms of interconnectedness"[15] between multiethnic people. In the realm of food and in the context of this chapter, this embodied performance shows how people of African ancestry and Latina/o heritage have accepted each other's staple foods. Describing the significance of cassava, for example, Ortíz Cuadra states how it was "the principle food in the diet of the [original] native population" of the Americas, and, "in the aftermath of the conquest, [it] became part of the diet of the emergent interethnic society."[16] Fischler elaborates on this acceptance by differentiating between complementary and supplementary foods. Complementary foods are those that are "newly" introduced alongside foods that already play a significant role as a staple for a particular group. In the case of people with an African ancestry, this might mean plantains or yams next to cassava or sweet potatoes; rice next to corn; black-eyed peas next to pinto beans. Complementary foods, according to Fischler, become a valuable dietary food but do not replace the original staple. The similarity between foods—cassavas and yams, for example—allows for their "complementary" relationship. Supplementary foods refer to those that, once introduced to an area, become part of people's core diet. Fischler explains that it is only through an "intense interethnic contact" that newly introduced foods are accepted as a supplement to a people's diet.[17]

(Re)mapping African culinary influence in the Americas adds to our understanding of the success story of the ethnic restaurants Frederick Douglass Opie traces in "Eating, Dancing, and Courting in New York Black and Latino Relations, 1930–1970." He claims that restaurants introduced African Americans to some Latin American foods while also introducing Latinos to soul (African American) food. He describes food sold in certain restaurants that included things like: "traditional Cuban food [such as] roasted pork cooked on a spit over charcoals or *mafungo*, a ball of crisp pork mixed with a variety of batters [and] *mofongo con chicharrones*, mashed green plantains mixed with mashed fried pig skin and covered with garlic, onion, and hot peppers sauce. . . . [A] 'so-called Panamanian restaurant' sold soul food [along with] 'food that you would think is completely South American' with a cornmeal base."[18] The main reason Opie offers as to why African Americans and Latina/os were willing to eat in these places is that they could get "good inexpensive food."[19] However, pork, plantains, corn, and

peppers have historically been part of the diet of Africans, in Africa and the diaspora, and of Latina/os (that is, people with Amerindian heritage) for hundreds of
years either as supplementary or complementary foods. The (hi)stories embedded in these foods, therefore, have been embodied as part of a culinary knowledge by people with these ethnic and racial backgrounds for thousands of years.

When an African influence is recognized within the eating habits of the
Americas, the (hi)stories conveyed through culinary performances help us
explore how people carved social and cultural interethnic relationships. In tracing
these interethnic connections, we can examine "the mechanisms that allow a culture to transmit, to reproduce, and to evaluate the food choices and values linked
to such food"; we can analyze the ways "individuals internalize the general culinary rules, taxonomies, changes in taste caused by time, geography, and socioeconomic factors affecting their cultural group"; and we can avoid romanticizing
the idea of tradition by taking note of the "degree of liberty [that] individuals
have to make changes to culinary notions of a collective group."[20] Therefore, the
term "Afro-Latina/o," for the three reasons mentioned here, serves to (re)map
the intertwining of the African Diaspora with other cultures of the Americas,
particularly Amerindians. By exploring ways in which a group of people's food
knowledge has been shared to form new food practices, we can begin to speak
of an Afro-Latina/o culinary subjectivity that reflects *transculinary* affirmations,
resilience, and adaptations informed by the gustatory principles of taste and palate memory.[21]

PRINCIPLES OF TASTE AND PALATE MEMORIES IN VIANDAS

Using culinary subjectivity to (re)map an Afro-Latina/o identity instead of solely
relying on race or ethnicity allows for an affirmation of an African heritage while
by-passing racial prejudice embedded in a country's national discourse, as is
clearly the case in Reyita's story. In her ethno-memoir, *Reyita: The Life of a Black
Cuban Woman in the Twentieth Century*, while admitting her active process of
erasing "blackness" from her gene pool, through her food Reyita acknowledges
a sensory affirmation of her Afro-Latina cultural identity. Reyita speaks of how
as the darkest child in a large family she grew up feeling rejected by her own
mother. This rejection led her to continually pray for a marriage to a good white
man so that her children would be lighter skinned. Perhaps due to a national
sentiment of racism in Cuba, Reyíta refers to her cooking simply as "traditional
Cuban food."[22] This includes her signature dishes of *malanga*, a *vianda*/root
vegetable, pudding, and *ajiaco* stew, which includes viandas/root vegetables as
its base. Scholars have found that both malangas and ajiaco carry connections
between black Cubans and people of Africa.[23] The malanga pudding presented
as traditional Cuban cooking connects Reyíta to an Africa sensory heritage;
through it, Reyíta keeps this link alive.

In the section "Loves comes in through the kitchen door," Reyíta asks her daughter, who is the ethnographer of Reyíta's story, if she remembers how to cook her malanga pudding. Although we do not hear the response, Reyíta's reaction suggests that her daughter does not remember. She states, "Women aren't too keen on cooking these days."[24] In an effort not to have her daughter's sensory knowledge and memory forget her mother's culinary creation, Reyíta shares the process of cooking the pudding by recalling an embodied practice: "You boil the malangas with a little salt, and then purée them, add milk boiled with cinnamon, anise, nutmeg, clove, vanilla, white sugar, to taste, and butter. After you've got it all blended, you pour it into a pan greased with butter. You put it on the fire over a slow flame and cover it with a lid filled with hot coals so it gets golden brown on the top and the bottom; if you've got an oven you can bake it. Take it off the heat after thirty or forty minutes. Let it cool and turn it out onto a serving plate. It's delicious!"[25] In providing the recipe to her daughter, and by extension to us, and because malangas are both Cuban and African in their origins and are similar to yams, Reyíta's concerns might not only be about the loss of her invention but also about her daughter's disconnect from her African ancestry. Furthermore, by including the detail of placing the malanga pudding on a serving plate, a gesture is symbolically made to the act of sharing the flavors of this dish; thus a moment of a collective shared palate memory with others can be established. Through her action of marrying a white Cuban, she hopes to protect her children from a nationalist racism. Through the descriptive performance of her malanga pudding, Reyíta reaffirms an African ancestral heritage.

Viandas, of which malanga is part, perform a significant role in Afro-Latina/os' shared collective sensory memory. Viandas in the Caribbean and Mexico are staple foods such as "cassava, tannier, and their likeness," such as yam, sweet potato, taro, breadfruit, and "including plantains and unripened bananas."[26] What makes these particular foods fitting to the Latin etymology of vivanda, as the "things necessary for living" and that "help . . . strengthen life," is their "characteristics that made them universally valuable."[27]

Viandas carry significant agricultural, nutritional, cultural, and psychological values. Agriculturally, they can be "reproduced and grown in different types of soil, [and] withstand radical shifts in weather conditions."[28] Nutritionally, depending on the vianda, they provide a number of dietary and medicinal benefits. Culturally, a number of such viandas are associated with religious/spiritual beliefs. Psychologically, they affirm the ability of survival, as they have become "the food[s] that enable people to live when other food stuffs [are] scare; . . . tubers and their cousins invariably became the fail-safe of [a] most secure option."[29]

One of the (hi)stories evoked with viandas is the drive for basic survival; they are foods that sustain in time of need. Returning to the shared palate for camotes within my family, it is quite possible that in the case of my great-grandfather they did function as the safety net against hunger. However, this has not been the case for my mother's palate for camotes, and certainly it is not the case for me. Yet camotes do represent a core aspect of our diets; they are integral to our cuisine and thus our culinary subjectivities. So what other (hi)stories are conjured by camotes as a vianda, or malangas for Reyita and her family within a Cuban context?

Before a food becomes a shared cultural tradition identifiable by a group's palate memory, such an item has to have already been established as a group's principles of taste. Fischler defines the principles of taste in gustatory terms as the interconnection of two distinct aspects. First, it is through taste that we make judgments (at time moral ones) regarding what is or is not safe to eat in terms of a food's toxicity, and methods to best cultivate, gather, and prepare a food; this form of taste also reflects already established social and cultural norms of a given society. The second aspect involved in the principles of taste is that they are "strongly marked by affectivity [and] colored by emotion."[30] These two functions of taste establish certain foods as simultaneously normative, universal, and objective as well as private, emotional, and subjective.[31] The yam, for example, meets both of Fischler's criteria. The nutritional value of a yam—high protein content, rich in phenylalanine and threonine, and moderate in potassium, vitamin B6, and vitamin C—can be seen as an example of the first function. Regardless of where yams are cultivated and consumed, these qualities remain. An example of the second is the emotions connected to the belief that some people have that suggests the only way to ensure a bountiful harvest of yams is to offer "three portions of cooked yams, part of which have been mixed with palm oil to Mawu (God)."[32] Only within certain cultural belief systems this is an undeniable truth. The principles of taste aid people in having an "opinion about food, around which and through which [they] communicate daily to each other who they are."[33]

The way Fischler defines the principles of taste as being simultaneously objective and subjective brings to mind cookbook writer Elizabeth Rozin and psychologist Paul Rozin's theory of "culinary themes." For the Rozins, "most of the world's people seem to belong to well-marked cuisine groups that create culinary products with distinctive and describable gustatory themes."[34] Another way to think of gustatory themes is the notion of a sensory biography that José Antonio Vázquez-Medina explores in his chapter "'Cooking Mexican': Negotiating Nostalgia in Family-Owned and Small-Scale Mexican Restaurants in the United States," included in this collection. These gustatory themes or sensory biographies are created by the use of specific spices, ingredients, and culinary techniques that carry the meaning of traditional culinary flavors across time and space in a group's shared collective memory. This kind of memory becomes a depository of culinary knowledge(s) that is stored and reenacted through our senses. People's culinary collective memory manifests traditions' significances of either everyday or ceremonial events because traditions "can act upon people only because they . . . carry history as a living thing in themselves."[35]

In *Biography of a Runaway Slave*, Miguel Barnet presents an ethnographical-historical account of Esteban Montejo's life. In recalling his years as a slave, as a Cimarron (runway), and as free black man in Cuba, many of Montejo's references to food illustrate how the principles of taste as gustatory themes reflect a collective sensory memory by which culinary knowledge(s) is established and transmitted across time. Montejo's life-narrative is of particular interest in the context of this chapter in terms of the sensory and embodied process of recognizing an African-ness within culinary traditions despite the fact that, as he states, "Today, there are no Africans in Cuba."[36] Even with Montejo's own admission of there being "no Africans in Cuba," a substantial part of his (hi)story revolves around food, including rituals with a direct link to African food knowledge, culture, and values. A few examples of how Montejo remembers the consumption of some viandas (and other foods) show how culinary subjectivities reflect acts of agency that endure over time. According to food historian Candice Goucher, this is the case because food practices are embodied "in aspects . . . such as ritual, belief and gendered relations."[37]

The first food reference comes when Montejo learns to eat "'taters." These are often translated as potatoes, but in the context in which he mentions them, he means root vegetables and, in particular, the taro plant. "I learned from the old timers [Africans on plantations] to eat 'taters, which are very nutritious. . . . If you eat them everyday, especially taro, you wont have bone trouble. In the woods there are lots of those wild 'taters. The taro has a big leaf that shines at night. You recognize it right away."[38] This knowledge from the "old timers" proved vital once he became a Cimarron, for while on the run he was able to identify what to eat. Taro literally became a food necessary for life, as are all viandas.

After slavery was abolished in Cuba and Montejo, like many others, became free but remained poor, food memories continued to mark his life's narrative. In recalling poor people's breakfast he states, "Poor people had coffee and sweet potato. The tastiest kind of sweet potato cooked over the ashes, the African way. . . . If you didn't have a grinder, you had a mortar and pestle. Hand-ground coffee is the kind I like the best because it keeps its aroma. That's probably just an idea of mine, but an idea is an idea."[39] As it turns out, Montejo's "idea" is actually supported by Western/scientific theories of memory.

Recent studies in neurogastronomy reveal why and how the senses and emotions, both connected to the principles of taste, are linked to memories.[40] Neuorogastronomical studies show not only how food triggers memories but also how it helps in creating, remembering, and forgetting certain food-centered cultural and social dynamics. Sensory stimuli caused from eating or drinking affects the function of the hippocampus. This brain structure is not only "critical for the formation of declarative or explicit memories," but it is also part of the limbic system responsible for the regulation of drives and emotions.[41] In this Western paradigm, food affects a brain structure that links both memory and emotions. Montejo's idea links a sensory/bodily memory—the actual use of the hand, the smell, and the taste of coffee—to emotions of, perhaps, a nostalgic past. After stating that hand-ground coffee is best, he says, "Before coffee plantations got bigger, coffee was sold in the pharmacy. After that by peddlers in the street."[42] By nostalgic past, I refer to the fact that the flavor, quality, and taste of coffee are likely not ones that have remained constant through these three procurement processes. Yet, in Montejo's memory, its emotional value continues unchanged.

In another food scenario, Montejo connects memories and emotions marked by the passing of time when he speaks of his love for fritters, or fried root vegetables. "Anytime an African did something, he did it well. He brought the recipe from his land, from Africa. Of the things I liked . . . the best were the fritters [of yuca, black-eyed peas, taro] that you don't see around anymore because . . . these days, people don't have the gusto to make those things. They make food without salt or lard, and it isn't worth a mustard seed."[43] In these few comments, Montejo's recollection links New World foods as integral to diets associated with a collective past of older folks. While Africans brought embodied recipes from their land to make fritters, the actual production of such dishes reflects a *transculinary* performance. Both *yuca* and taro are native to the Americas, yet they have become supplements as foodstuffs that enter into the category of remembering "African fritters."

For younger generations, however, cooking without "gusto" suggests a path of how modernity forgets.[44] Salt has not always been an easily accessible commodity to flavor food. Once pork was introduced to the Americas, poor people used lard as a condiment to flavor food. Forgetting the process by which people learned to flavor their food expresses an individual's disconnect with the nuances of embodied culinary system(s) of knowledge. Such disengagement does not necessarily suggest that all of a group's sensory collective memories are completely erased; rather, such knowledge(s) is simply dormant and stored in our sensorial repertoire. Gusto, while often translated as enthusiasm, refers to taste and appetite. Adding gusto to the performance of cooking is a sensual remembrance that food both nourishes the body and emotionally feeds the self. If gusto is not added, then one runs the risk of cooking something not "worth a mustard seed." Montejo's culinary subjectivity reveals recollections full of *gusto* for even as he claims that there are "no Africans in Cuba," African culinary knowledge(s) remains a vital (hi)story expressed through his palate memory.

What makes a person's palate memory so central to a group's collective sensory memory is that palate memory is created by "a kind of intimate bond with food and diet molded by material circumstances."[45] In her essay "Kitchens," Puerto Rican historian, poet, and essayist Aurora Levins Morales describes this collective sensory memory. It is the smell, texture, and ritual of peeling a green banana—a plantain, which in Puerto Rico is categorized as a vianda—that links her kitchen in California with the kitchens and women of her childhood in Puerto Rico:

> It's a magic, a power, a ritual of love and work that rises up in my kitchen, thousands of miles from those women . . . who twenty years ago taught the rules of its observance to me, the apprentice, the novice, the girl cook: . . . "Always peel the green banana under cold water, *mijita,* or you'll cut your fingers and get *mancha* on yourself and the stain never comes out: that black sap stain of *guineo verde* and *plátano,* that stain that marks you forever."
>
> So I peel my bananas under running water from the faucet, but the stain won't come out, and the subtle earthy green smell of that sap follows me, down from the mountains, into the cities, to places where banana groves are like green dreams, unimaginable by daylight: Chicago, New Hampshire, Oakland. [In] the immigrant markets of other people, . . . now and then . . . I find a small curved green bunch to rush home, quick, before it ripens, to peel and boil, bathing in the scent of its cooking, bringing the river to flow through my own kitchen now, the river of my place on earth, the green and musty river of my grandmothers, dripping, trickling, tumbling down from the mountain kitchens of my people.[46]

In the act of peeling a green banana (a plantain), Levins Morales's palate memory connects her physical act of cooking in California with a community thousands of miles away. The "stain that marks" her "forever" with its "subtle earthly green smell" shows how this performative act of her culinary subjectivity links her cooking in California with a community thousands of miles away. Her culinary subjectivity is one that crosses borders, incorporating interethnic food practices, as Levins Morales comes from a Jewish and black Puerto Rican family.

Ortíz Cuadra offers other examples of the kind of bonds a palate memory creates, which lead to colletive sensory memoires: "a mother's cooking, the frequent repeating of various diets and meals, and the 'principle[s] of taste.'" Furthermore, he suggests that palate memory evokes "fixation[s] on flavors and taste, and—at times—sensations of estrangement."[47] It also connects "food and dishes with vital experiences and remembrance."[48]

The effectiveness of a palate memory to become part of a group's collective sensory memory is due to multiple forms of embodied and sensory recognition. Collective sensory memory is "always operating in conjunction with other memories."[49] The names of dishes signal historical and social memories: cognitive memory. Through foods related to rituals and ceremonies, cultural and spiritual values and beliefs are manifested: episodic memory. It is through the senses—smell, taste, touch, sight, and hearing—that the reproduction of (unwritten) recipes takes place: sensorial memory.[50] It is through habitual bodily movements in the act of watching, dicing, kneading, baking, serving, offering, and sharing food, that culinary subjectivities are performed and displayed: embodied memory. In these sensorial embodied moments, our body expresses a totality that words cannot do alone. Our bodies play an imperative role in archiving cultural memories as they take place on "the body's surface[,] its tissues,"[51] and its organs. In the context of Afro-Latinos, perhaps Afro-Mexicanos, the centrality of the body and memory is further underscored through the Mexica's ontology that the organ that houses memory is the heart. Sensory collective memory "links the deeply personal with the social, [and] like the heart, [it] beats beyond our [cognitive] capacity to control it"; it is "a lifeline between the past and the future."[52]

In his description of Puerto Rican *pasteles*, a tamal-like food for which no formal written recipe existed prior to 1930, Ortíz Cuadra illustrates how the individual's palate memory informs a group's collective sensory memories. The main ingredient in pasteles is plantain, a vianda introduced to Puerto Rico via Africa. Without a written recipe, the preparation of this dish was done (and continues to be done) with the guidance of a bodily sensory memory. The task of performing the preparation of pasteles—mashing the plantains into a dough consistency, wrapping them in banana leaves, and cooking them by boiling—is always associated with a religious event, as throughout Puerto Rico they are mostly prepared only during Christmas and the Epiphany. Ortíz Cuadra further explains, "Whoever has made pastel, in one form or another, is well aware that the task is complicated and requires considerable focus, organization, and judgment, along with something that cannot be planned—an intuitive sense of how the dish will best come together."[53] Here we are reminded of the objective and subjective aspects of the principles of taste by which foods' (hi)stories are negotiated, as pasteles are not made by an authentic and unchanging single recipe. "For example, the first step in the process—softening the banana leaves prior to enfolding the dough in them (or, *amortiguarlas*)—has always been the subject of differing interpretations. . . . The same lack of uniformity characterizes the preparation of the dough. . . . The filling, too, varies from kitchen to kitchen, its content often determined by what food happens to be on hand at the appointed time, as well as by the likes and dislikes of household members."[54] Despite so many changes, pasteles remain central to traditional Puerto Rican holiday food.

A tradition filled with multiple possible modifications reflects what philosopher Pierre Nora sees as the "permanent evolution" of a group's collective memory. For him, a group's collective memory (as well as an individual's palate memory) is always "open to the dialectic of remembering and forgetting, . . . vulnerable to manipulation and appropriation, susceptible to being long dormant and periodically revived. . . . [It] nourishes recollections that may be out of focus or telescopic, global or detached, particular or symbolic. . . . [It] installs remembrance within the sacred. . . . [It] is by nature multiple and yet specific; collective, plural, and yet individual. . . . [It] takes root in the concrete, in spaces, gestures, images, and objects."⁵⁵ To Nora's list we must add that collective memory is also formed and kept alive through food practices. What remains constant in a seemly never-ending change within culinary traditions are the normative/objective aspects by which a group defines a food as their own while simultaneously bathing such selections with affective reasons: the principles of taste. The palate's memory—guided by the principles of taste, the senses, and the body—enables us to recognize the symbolic characteristics associated with significant social and cultural episodic aspects of our culinary subjectivities.⁵⁶ Through embodied performance, we open the possibility to be able to taste that who we are today is seasoned with the culinary (ever-changing) inheritance we have received throughout history from those who make up our ancestral gene-*cultural* pool.

A Camotera "I Yam"

It is time to return to the personal antidote about my family's palate for camotes. My mother self-identifies as a camotera. I do not know if my great-grandfather made the same claim, and I know I never have. But considering how often he ate camotes and how often I eat them, I would venture to say that we, too, are camoteros. Now, what does our self-identification have to do with the food practices and (hi)stories of Afro-Latina/os, with the recognition of an African-ness in the performative act (eating camotes) of our culinary subjectivities? The answer to this question probably begins with the historical interconnection and confusion between camotes and yams and the fact that my family comes from Michoacán and Guerrero, two states with a substantial Afro-Mexican population. Teasing out the differences and similarities of these two viandas, camotes and yams, might show how these root vegetables and their symbolic (ritual) significance have facilitated their status as a supplement staple for both people of African ancestry and Latinos, (re)mapping the (hi)stories of African disporic people in the Americas. How does this relate to my family? Neither the Larios side of my family, mostly fair-skinned, blue- or green-eyed people, nor the Cárdenas side, mostly dark *moreno* people, has ever claimed an African cultural mixture to be part of our genealogy. However, as more social efforts are made to unearth and address the third racial root of *mestizaje*, my family is learning about our African gene inheritance. As more information comes to light about the presence of people of African ancestry in Mexico and what social, cultural, and political contributions they have made to the nation, information has been published in different social media that the forty-fourth president of Mexico, Lázaro Cárdenas, my grandmother's uncle, was a *mulato*. Even without this familial knowledge, to what degree do we acknowledge this interethnic ancestry through our culinary subjectivities based on the foods we consume?

The Spanish word *"camote"* comes from the Nahualt *"camotli,"* which means *raíz convestible*, suggesting that any edible root goes under the category of *camotli*: sweet potatoes, yams, cassava, malanga, potatoes, taro, carrots, and/or beets. Over the years, camotes have come to refer only to sweet potatoes. When the Europeans first encountered them in Hispaniola, they were described by the Taíno name *batata*.[57] Eventually *"batata"* was transformed into "potato," but the sweet potato in its botanical genus and family name kept its Taíno linguistic heritage: *Ipomoea batata*. Camotes are believed to be one of the first domesticated plants in the world. While camotes have not received as much scholarly attention as forming a central part of the diet and culture of people of the Americas as corn has, for example, their nutrient content makes them quite valuable, especially for the poorest sectors of the population. Camotes, as with most *viandas*, are easy to cultivate, are cooked in various ways, and can be stored for a long time, and most of all they are rich in complex carbohydrates, dietary fiber, and beta-carotene. Since food expresses something of who we are, camotes then connect my family historically, culturally, and linguistically to diverse Amerindian groups.

But what about an African link? At a linguistic level, this link is perhaps one often based on confusion. In the United States, the words "sweet potato" and "yam" are often used interchangeably despite that fact that these two root vegetables do not belong to the same botanical family and are quite different in a number of ways. Yams (*Dioscorea Dioscoreceae*) are considered to be one of the most important indigenous crops in West Africa. They are a central staple for protein and calorie consumption for over 40 percent of the population. Due to their high protein content (something the sweet potatoes do not have), they are used as a food to feed infants. The importance of yams within a cosmological world vision is reflected both in its etymology and harvest rituals. "Yam" comes from the West Africa word "nyam," which is possibly from the Fula (Fulani) language. As a verb it means to eat, and as a noun it stands for food. The combination of this verb-noun stresses the idea that yams are a food that sustains people and life—it incorporates the Spanish concepts of *nutrir* (to nourish) and *alimentar* (to feed).

Yams sustain life through ritual/spiritual contexts. Nigerian novelist Chinua Achebe, in *Things Fall Apart*, addresses this idea in his description of the Feast of the New Yam, which sets the stage for the novel: "It was an occasion for giving thanks to Ani, the earth goddess and the source of all fertility. Ani played a greater part in the life of the people than any other deity. She was the ultimate judge of morality and conduct. And what was more, she was in close communication with the departed fathers of the clan whose bodies had been committed to earth."[58] The (hi)stories associated with yams involve a social and cosmic worldview: community, moral conduct, kinship among the living and the dead, and connection between the spirits of deities, humans, and earth. All of these (hi)stories were brought to the Americas during the transatlantic slave trade. Once in the Americas, people of African background transferred their cultural knowledge and association of yams to sweet potatoes due to their similarity in appearance. Sweet potatoes became a supplementary staple for Africans and their descendants. Haitian novelist Edwidge Danticat shows this to be the case with the first food reference in her novel *Breath, Eyes, Memory*: sweet potato pudding.[59] The pudding is for a communal potluck that had started "a long time ago"[60] to commemorate a collectivity of labor in the fields that no longer exist as most people do not have fields to clear and plant. Yet the value of conviviality remains, and the scent, flavor, and texture of sweet potatoes mark their presence as people "get together, eat, and celebrate life."[61] Sweet potatoes become, in this novel, the depository of traditions and values associated with yams in places like West Africa. While "true" yams are not easily accessible in the Americas, their significance remains alive in the consumption of sweet potatoes.

Ralph Ellison shows this transfer of cultural significance between yams and sweet potatoes when the narrator of *Invisible Man* proclaims, "I yam what I am!" as he bites into the sweetness of a steamed yam he bought from a street vendor. Just a few minutes before this declaration, the narrator had asked of himself: "Who was I, how I have come to be?"[62] His answer comes in the form of a yam: "I took a bite, finding it sweet and hot as any I'd ever had. . . . I walked along, munching the yam, just as suddenly overcome by an intense feeling of freedom."[63] Due to such emotion, he buys two more. When the vender tells him, "I can see you [are] one of those old fashioned yam eaters," he replies, "They're my birthmark."[64] Considering that true yams are not often found in the United States, a strong possibility exists that what the narrator ate was a sweet potato. The (hi)stories evoked by these two root vegetables have been so interconnected that it is hard to know where one begins and one ends. In Spanish, at least in Mexico, "*camotes*" means both sweet potatoes and yams. Symbolically, then, either of these two *viandas* embodies the narrator's culinary subjectivity.

Addressing *Invisible Man* points out the culinary (hi)stories that link people of African background with Latinos (here I stress the Amerindian ethnicity of a Latina/o identity). People of African background and Amerindians (pure blood and mestizos) have long shared similar spaces of labor and residency, thereby creating interethnic social and cultural networks. Due to such proximity, their traditions, values, stories, and practices are shared and exchanged. Such exchanges, however, are not always at a conscious level, but at a sensory and embodied level that takes place through the consumption of each other's foods. I see a strong connection between the narrator of *Invisible Man* and my family's act of claiming a culinary subjectivity via two root vegetables that symbolically and imaginatively link the (hi)stories of people of African ancestry with those of Amerindian heritage. In the context of Latin America and the Caribbean, this mixing of culinary (hi)stories reflects Afro-Latina/os' culinary subjectivities.

CULINARY SUBJECTIVITIES

Recently I asked my mother why she likes camotes, to which she replied: "Because they are sweet; they are nutritious; they are roots and we have to eat our roots."[65] Her statement of eating "our" roots could simply mean the importance of eating viandas (that which keeps and strengthens life), but this reference to roots grounds my mother in the history and culture of camotes, both sweet potatoes and yams. They also represent roots within our family. After all, my own palate's memory for camotes comes from the intimate bond by which I connect the principles of taste: the universal nutritional value of this vianda with the subjective/affective meaning I give to my mother's cooking. I cannot recall eating camotes as a child, but wouldn't it be safe to say that a self-identified camotera would nourish and feed her children with a little something of who she is?

But there is more to my mother's reasons for eating our roots. Her statement explains much of what I think a culinary subjectivity expresses as a marker of identity: an embodied/sensory performative act that nourishes and feeds our sense of who we are culturally and historically. Our culinary subjectivities emerge from two distinct functions food performs that are succinctly expressed in the Spanish words of "*nutrir*" (to nourish) and "*alimentar*" (to feed). *Nutrir* is the process of biologically sustaining the body with proteins, nutrients, and calories. Food nourishes the physical body. *Alimentar*, as the act of feeding and eating, encompasses the symbiotic process of sustaining the social, cultural, imaginative, spiritual, and affective self. Our culinary subjectivity, therefore, weaves "evocations, connotations, [and] significations that extend from the dietary to the poetic" and from the material to the symbolic.[66] Eating our cultural and historical roots, our viandas, sustains our life and gives meaning to it.

Our culinary subjectivities are defined, as I have shown here, by the principles of taste that links us to the migratory histories of people who have been responsible for establishing certain foodstuffs as supplementary to our diets. What makes this link possible is that our gustatory performative acts defined by our palate memory reflect a poly-temporality: past, present, and future. In the case of eating viandas—Esteban Montejo's tora, Reyita's malanga pudding, Levins Morales's green plantains, the "invisible" man's yams, my family's camotes—this poly-temporality (re)maps an African culinary influence in our eating habits. As we eat a variety of viandas (and other foods) in the Americas, recollections of the past are enacted; the embodied, sensory, and textual narratives and expressions used to bring to life such past memories ensure their continuation in the future. This continuation, however, displays a range of complimenting and conflicting processes of exchanges. Methods of growing, gathering, sharing, and preparing food maintain a historical continuity that expands to incorporate new palates, flavors, and textures born out of socioeconomic and geographical realities that reflect people's migratory patterns. The performative acts of our culinary subjectivities, therefore, are not stifling authentic replicas of such a past; while informed by the past, they are embodied expressions of burgeoning sociocultural identity constructions. Culinary subjectivities are lived, archived, recognized, and performed viscerally.

This visceral way of knowing, expressing, and sharing with others' complex (hi)stories of people's "values, choices, and cultures[s]"[67] deserves critical examination to explore the nuances by which food does in fact say something about who we have been, who we are, and who we might become. Clearly, culinary subjectivities informed through the principles of taste and the palate memory, which together create collective sensory memories for particular groups of people, are not limited to the study of African influences in Latina/os food practices. My particular interest emerges from a desire to acknowledge that the "third root" (*la tercera raiz*) of mestizaje throughout the Americas, the African root, has always been central to many Latina/os' cultural and historical identity. A challenge black Latina/os, particularly those living in the United States, are often made to feel is the need to assert cultural affiliation with either African Americans, where they do not fit comfortably, or with Latin Americans, where part of who they are is not recognized. In Latin America, as in the case with my own family, an African cultural heritage often does not enter the radar as forming part of people's cultural identities. Yet the visceral root-ness of a cultural identity based on our food practices can enable in many (of us) the ability to savor the flavors of an Afro-Latina/o culinary subjectivity.

NOTES

1. See, for example, Roland Barthes, "Towards a Psychosociology of Contemporary Food Consumption," in *Food and Culture: A Reader*, ed. Carole Counihan and Penny Van Esterik (New York: Routledge, 2013), 23–30.

2. Diana Taylor, in *The Archive and the Repertoire: Performing Cultural Memory in the Americas* (Durham, NC: Duke University Press, 2003), makes a compelling case for framing embodied and performative acts of knowledge in terms of scenarios, as these acts "do not reduce gestures and embodied practices to narrative description" (16). Scenarios, she explains, are "durable, transposable dispositions. That is, they are passed on and remain remarkably coherent paradigms of seemingly unchanging attitudes and values. Yet they adapt constantly to reigning conditions. . . . Scenarios refer to more specific [embodied performance/knowledge] of cultural imaginings" (31). The value in analyzing food moments in narratives through the idea of scenarios is that it reminds us of how culinary knowledge is in fact transmitted beyond the written word.

3. Subjectivity, as a philosophical concept, presupposes that all people are inherently subjects rather than objects. Subjects have the quality of possessing perspectives, experiences, feelings, beliefs, and desires that shape and are shaped by the culture and society in which they live. Subjectivity, however, does not mean free will; it is a process that defines both our indiviudal self as well as the process of socialization. Since no individual lives in complete social, cultural, and environmental isolation, our actions (physical, emotional, intellectual, and spiritual) of self-definition are in constant negotiation (often resulting in contradictory attitudes) with those of others who might hold more economic, political, or religious social power. What one must remember is that our subjectivity (which informs how we

define ourselves) is never static but is constantly undergoing change as we navigate our relations within our society, which in turn change in response to economic and environmental global changes.

4. The spelling of (hi)story is to express a weaving of genres as history and narrative. I also use this to evoke two different words in Spanish, *historia* and *cuento*, thereby addressing two ideological, social, and cultural understandings of a given material circumstance. My use of (hi)story resonates with Miguel Barnet's views on the value of inserting "history into . . . narrative, [which] working like a compass and a walking stick, has meant as much for subjectivism as for testimonial realism, the two tendencies that go linked together in a single strategy that incites and provokes new ideological trails." Miguel Barnet, *Biography of a Runaway Slave*, trans. W. Nick Hill (Willimantic, CT: Curbstone Press, 1994), 203–204.

5. Taylor, *Archive and the Repertoire*, 21.

6. The use of Latina/o throughout this chapter is to be understood as reflecting an ethnic group whose ancestry includes both Amerindians and Europeans. It is also to be understood as referring to people in Latin America, the Caribbean, and the United States.

7. The rhetoric of *mestizaje*, not only within Mexican and Mexican American contexts but also throughout most of Latin America and parts of the Caribbean, has historically rendered black communities invisible. Therefore, a national ideology of mestizaje fails to recognize black communities' contributions to the cultural, social, economic, and political fabric of a nation. See Laura A. Lewis, *Chocolate and Corn Flour: History, Race, and Place in the Making of "Black" Mexico* (Durham, NC: Duke University, 2012); and Bobby Vaughn, "México Negro: From the Shadows of Nationalist Mestizaje to New Possibilities in Afro-Mexican Identity," *Journal of Pan African Studies* 6.1 (2013): 227–240.

8. See the foreword, preface, and introduction to Anita González, *Afro-Mexico: Dancing Between Myth and Reality* (Austin: University of Texas Press, 2010).

9. Gloria Anzaldúa, *Borderlands/La Frontera: The New Mestiza*. (San Francisco: Spinsters/ aunt lute), 194. The historical significance of this reference to "black" is the political, social, and cultural invisibility that this ethnic group has had within the Mexican national consciousness of mestizaje.

10. Ibid.

11. See Jeffery M. Pilcher, *Planet Taco: A Global History of Mexican Food* (New York: Oxford University Press, 2012).

12. See Raquel Torres Cerdán, *La cosine afromestiza en Veracruz* (Veracruz, MX: Instituto Veracruzano de Cultura, 1995).

13. See Candice Goucher, *Congotay! Congotay!: A Global Hisotry of Caribbean Food* (New York: M. E. Sharpe, 2014); see also Igor Cusack, "African Cuisine: Recipes for Nation-Building," *Journal of African Cultural Studies* 13.2 (December 2000): 207–225

14. William Bascom, "Yoruba Cooking," *Africa* 21.2 (April 1951): 124.

15. Taylor, *Archive and the Repertoire*, 51.

16. Ortíz Cuadra, *Eating Puerto Rico*, 125.

17. Claude Fischler, *El (h)omnívoro: El gusto, la cocina, y el cuerpo* (Barcelona: Editorial Anagrama, 1995), 156; see also Ortíz Cuarda's work and his inclusion of these concepts in his study of Puerto Rico's food history, culture, and identity.

18. Frederick Douglass Opie, "Eating, Dancing, and Courting in New York Black and Latino Relations, 1930–1970," *Journal of Social History* (2008): 86, 94.

19. Ibid., 86.

20. Fischler, *El (h)omnívoro*, 34.

21. Sociologist Fernando Ortiz developed the concept of transculturation to address the process of how blacks had the ability to coexist within and inform national cultures. Transculturation is closely link to W. E. B. Du Bois's theory of double consciousness. Transculturation especially addresses the ability to maneuver multiple cultural dispositions. Ortiz's theory, while it sees identity formation as fluid, tends to essentialize such fluidity through a directional process that moves from the traditional African customs, beliefs, and so forth, to

a more "progressive" modern, national identity. My own use of transculinary is to address the fluidity of culinary knowledge and values but not to essentialize one (the African) over another (Amerindian/European). Instead, my effort is to show how blending of equally valuable food knowledge(s) creates new forms of Afro-Latina/o culinary subjectivities that are neither African nor Latino but both.

22. María de los Reyes Castillo Bueno, *Reyita: The Life of a Black Cuban Woman in the Twentieth Century* (Durham, NC: Duke University Press, 2000), 114.

23. See Cusack, "African Cuisines," 2000.

24. Castillo Bueno, *Reyita*, 114.

25. Ibid.

26. Ortíz Cuadra, *Eating Puerto Rico*, 123–124.

27. Joseph B. Solodow, *Latin Alive: The Survival of Latin in English and Romance Languages* (Cambridge: Cambridge University Press, 2010), 134.

28. Ibid., 122.

29. Ibid., 123. For an excellent example of how a vianda provides all four of these aspects to a community, see Ryan N. Schacht, "Cassava and the Makushi: A Shared History of Resiliency and Transformation" in *Food and Identity in the Caribbean*, ed. Hanna Garth (New York: Bloombury, 2013).

30. Fischler, *El (h)omnívoro*, 89.

31. Ibid.

32. Robert Hall, "Food Crops, Medicinal Plants, and the Atlantic Slave Trade," in *African American Foodways: Explorations of History and Culture*, ed. Anne L. Bower (Urbana: University of Illinois Press, 2007), 19.

33. Sidney Mintz, *Tasting Food, Tasting Freedom: Excursions into Eating, Culture, and the Past* (Boston: Beacon Press, 1996), 97–98.

34. Elizabeth Rozin and Paul Rozin, "Culinary Themes and Variations," in *The Taste Culture Reader: Exploring Food and Drink*, ed. Carolyn Korsmeyer (New York: Berg, 2005), 35.

35. Paul Connerton, *The Spirit of Morning: History, Memory, and the Body* (New York: Cambridge University Press, 2011), E-book, Loc. 3365–3371.

36. Barnet, *Biography of a Runaway Slave*, 129.

37. Goucher, *Congotay! Congotay!*, xix.

38. Barnet, *Biography of a Runaway Slave*, 50.

39. Ibid., 141.

40. See Gordon M. Shepherd, *Neurogastronomy: How the Brain Creates Flavor and Why It Matters* (New York: Columbia University Press, 2012).

41. John S. Allen, *The Omnivorous Mind: Our Evolving Relationship with Food* (Cambridge, MA: Harvard University Press, 2012), 152.

42. Barnet, *Biography of a Runaway Slave*, 141.

43. Ibid.

44. Paul Connerton, in *How Modernity Forgets* (New York: Cambridge University Press, 1989), states: "What is being forgotten in modernity is profound, the human-scale-ness of life, the experience of living and working in a world of social relationships that are known. There is some kind of deep transformation in what might be described as the meaning of life based on shared memories, and that meaning is eroded by the structural transformation in the life-spaces of modernity" (5). The shared memories that gusto, as it relates to taste and appetite, provides in the contexts of food preparation run the risk of being forgotten.

45. Ortíz Cuadra, *Eating Puerto Rico*, 2.

46. Aurora Levins Morales, "Kitchens," in *Currents from the Dancing River: Contemporary Latino Fiction, Nonfiction, and Poetry*, ed. Ray Gonzalez (New York: Harcourt Brace, 1994), 30.

47. Ortíz Cuadra, *Eating Puerto Rico*, 2.

48. Ibid.

49. Taylor, *Archive and the Repertoire*, 82.

50. See David Howe, ed., *Empire of the Senses: The Sensual Cultural Reader* (New York: Berg, 2005); and Carolyn Kormeyer, ed., *The Taste Culture Reader: Experiencing Food and Drink* (New York: Berg, 2005).

51. Connerton, *Spirit*, Loc. 60–64. Connerton argues, "Cultural memory occurs as much, if not more, by bodily practices . . . as by documents and texts. This memory takes place on the body's surface and in its tissues and in accordance with levels of meaning that reflect human sensory capacities more then cognitive categories." These bodily recollections have their "own articulateness, history and purposes" (Loc. 5–55).

52. Taylor, *Archive and the Repertoire*, 80–82.

53. Ortíz Cuadra, *Eating Puerto Rico*, 150.

54. Ibid., 150–151.

55. Pierrie Nora, "Between Memory and History: Les Lieux de Mémoire," in *Theories of Memory: A Reader*, ed. Michael Rossington and Anne Whitehead (Edinburgh: Edinburgh University Press, 2007), 146.

56. David E. Sutton. *Remembrance of Repasts: An Anthropology of Food and Memory* (New York: Berg, 2001), 101–102.

57. The Taíno are related to the Arawakans, a group of Amerindians in northeastern South America who lived in the Greater Antilles, which included Cuba, Jamaica, Hispaniola (Haiti and the Dominican Republic), and Puerto Rico at the time when Christopher Columbus arrived to the New World.

58. Chinua Achebe, *Things Fall Apart* (New York: Anchor Books, 1994), 33.

59. Edwidge Danticat, *Breath, Eyes, Memory: A Novel* (New York: Vintage Books, 1994), 9.

60. Ibid., 11.

61. Ibid., 12.

62. Ralph Ellison, *Invisible Man*, 2nd ed. (New York: Vintage, 2010), 259.

63. Ibid., 264.

64. Ibid., 266.

65. Phone conversation on January 22, 2015.

66. Fischler, *El (h)omnívoro*, 16–17.

67. Massimo Montanari, "Historia, alimentación, historia de la alimentación," In *Problemas actuals de la historia*, ed. José María Sánchez et al. (Salamanca: Universidad de Salamanca, 1993), 24–25.

CHAPTER 3

"Mexican Cookery That Belongs to the United States"

EVOLVING BOUNDARIES OF WHITENESS IN NEW MEXICAN KITCHENS

Katherine Massoth

In the opening to *Mexican Cookbook* (1934), Erna Fergusson writes, "Mexican food has, ever since the 'American Occupation,' been a part of the Southwestern diet. . . . Mexican food has become part of the national cuisine."[1] If we were to trust her, it would appear Anglos have always savored aspects of New Mexican and Mexican foodways. However, Fergusson's cookbook is a product of the dynamic culinary borderlands between Anglos and Hispanas/os that evolved after the United States annexed New Mexico in 1848.[2] Fergusson's *Mexican Cookbook* illuminates the changing Anglo relationship to New Mexican food from annexation to the time of publishing. By selectively appropriating recipes and ingredients, Fergusson drew a boundary between American, New Mexican, and Mexican foods that mimicked the politics of inclusion and exclusion along the U.S.-Mexico border. Using Fergusson's cookbook as an endpoint, this chapter discusses how middle-class Anglos strategically narrated racial and ethnic differences in New Mexico through their taste buds. Rather than viewing the rise of New Mexican food as simply an innocuous desire to taste the food of another, I consider food as an additional site of cultural contention in establishing the boundaries of whiteness. By providing snapshots of Anglos' reactions to New Mexican food depending on the larger political and social processes, this chapter highlights the subtle, but significant, ways Anglos repeatedly shifted culinary boundaries to separate "us" from "them" in the U.S.-Mexican borderlands.

In New Mexico, kitchens and dining spaces have been dynamic sites for both border making and boundary crossing and have contributed to the social construction of the border between "New" and "Old" Mexico in the Southwest.

Immediately after the U.S.-Mexico War and throughout the territorial period (1850–1912), New Mexico was not fully part of the United States, and Anglo settlers needed to maintain a distinction between themselves and Hispanas/os. During this period, Anglos established culinary borderlands to place themselves above Hispanas/os and American Indians and claim their whiteness.[3] These culinary borderlands marked New Mexican food as indigestible due to middle-to-upper-class Anglo standards of spice and cleanliness. Eventually Anglos reshaped this culinary borderland. After the arrival of the railroad in 1878 and growing cries for statehood, Anglos began embracing aspects of New Mexican culture in hopes the larger United States would do the same. Finally, during the first three decades of the twentieth century, when Mexican immigration rapidly increased, Anglos again needed to define their place in the Southwest to separate themselves from Hispanas/os and Mexicans. After statehood, Anglo women selectively appropriated New Mexican foodways without regard for the lived reality of Hispanas/os or acknowledging a history of discrimination toward Hispanas/os. In the process, Anglo women, like Erna Fergusson, strategically constructed New Mexican food as part of a Spanish regional culture separate from Mexico but still not fully American.

These domestic negotiations over the place of New Mexican food on the Anglo table signal the subtle ways concerns over whiteness appear as simply differences of communities along the U.S.-Mexican border. Whiteness is a malleable set of social and cultural boundaries that reify the social category of white, not just the racial category, and attempts to define the boundaries of acceptable differences. In the United States, Anglos have been the definers of who belongs to "us" and to "them."[4] Cultural customs are central to how the United States determined which groups were permitted entry, deserved full citizenship, or accessed the benefits of whiteness.[5] If we consider the nation as home and homemaking as a performance of identity, then it is clear how cooking could function in creating boundaries and performing nationhood.[6] In the process of homemaking, people establish their difference and compete for power by deciding who and what belongs, and what is excluded in the home.[7] Moreover, through conscious acts of choosing what food is safe or indigestible, people create culinary boundaries. Along culinary borderlands, people work to guard their foodways, blend ingredients, and/or appropriate recipes. The acts of policing the boundary between the mouth and stomach assist in producing power and justifying constructions of racial difference and political inequality.[8] In New Mexico, the initial act of disgust and the eventual appropriation of food culture served to support middle-class Anglo power in the region by denigrating Hispanas/os and Mexicans. Anglos defined the differences of the local food to maintain and evolve their perceptions of Hispanas/os as the racial and ethnic other.

Between the 1910s and 1940s, wealthy Anglo women such as Erna Fergusson used cookbooks and cookery writing to define New Mexican foodways for a U.S.

audience.[9] Erna Fergusson was born into a prominent Albuquerque family in 1888. Her mother, Clara Huning Fergusson, was the daughter of wealthy German immigrants, and her father, Harvey Fergusson, migrated from Alabama in 1882, was a territorial political representative, and served in Congress after statehood.[10] With these pioneer and political roots, Fergusson fashioned herself into a travel writer and historian by glorifying New Mexico's Spanish past as ancient and disappearing. While Fergusson mostly wrote fiction and travel articles, her *Mexican Cookbook*, published in 1934 and republished in 1940 and 1945, is regarded as a classic of southwestern literature and a ripe source for understanding the appropriation of Hispana/o foodways.[11] Fergusson's *Mexican Cookbook* is one piece in a larger collection of cookbooks and cookery articles by Anglo women that reflect the greater trend in New Mexico (and the Southwest) to appropriate and possess Hispana/o food at the cost of the Hispana women who cooked and carried this heritage. Fergusson's recipes allowed Anglo women to control, within their kitchen, the cleanliness, the flavor of dishes, and the heat of chile. Through the recipes she included and excluded, Fergusson defined the appropriate New Mexican food for a middle-class white palate. Moreover, the culinary boundaries early Anglo settlers established in the mid-nineteenth century influenced how Fergusson imported New Mexican food into the Anglo kitchen.

INITIAL DISTASTE

Contrary to Erna Fergusson's assertion that New Mexican food was smoothly annexed into the U.S. national cuisine in 1848, archival fragments reveal many Anglos did not initially find the food enjoyable or even palatable immediately after annexation. In correspondence, journals, and newspapers from the second half of the nineteenth century, middle-class Anglos documented the different foods they encountered. After annexation, newly arrived Anglos grappled with how to establish their power in the region, even in their daily activities. Anglos were a minority of the population in New Mexico, with only about 8,690 settling by 1870.[12] Due to the higher population of Hispanas/os and tension between the legal and social definitions of whiteness, Anglos needed to construct daily boundaries between the United States and Mexico, "Americans" and "non-Americans," white and non-white, to secure control of the region and support the national cause of manifest destiny. Cultural customs, especially foodways, became a readily available tool for Anglos in mapping these distinctions and establishing Anglo superiority.[13] Anglos made sense of the larger politics of annexation by distinguishing what was American or non-American food. While some Anglos eventually appreciated New Mexican foodways, the negative stereotypes predominate in the historical records, even among those who saw themselves as proponents of southwestern culture.

The majority of Hispanas/os in New Mexico were adversely affected by racial politics and land grant disputes following annexation even though they were demographically dominant. The Treaty of Guadalupe Hidalgo ended the U.S.-Mexico War and established the present-day border in 1848 by annexing Texas, Colorado, Arizona, California, Nevada, Utah, and New Mexico. At the time, approximately 75,000 Spanish-speaking people lived in these portions of northern Mexico.[14] New Mexico was the most populated, with 61,525 Hispanas/os.[15] The treaty established a central paradox by legally constructing Mexicans as white and citizens, while in legal application and social practice Anglos treated Mexicans as racially inferior and non-white. Under the 1790 Naturalization Act, only "whites" could be naturalized as U.S. citizens, and since the treaty guaranteed them citizenship, Mexicans were now legally white. However, the treaty stipulated full citizenship would come after Hispanas/os proved their worthiness of membership through proper demeanor, deference, gender comportment, and whiteness. Moreover, Anglos socially constructed Hispanas/os as non-white due to their physiognomy, leisure habits, Spanish language, food and material cultures, and Catholicism.[16] Hispanas/os were borderline white citizens.[17]

In their initial reactions, Anglos focused on the ubiquitous chile. They complained about its overuse and powerful piquancy, identifying chile as nearly indigestible. For example, while traveling the Santa Fe Trail in August 1846, Susan Shelby Magoffin, a trader's wife, could not finish a meal of blue corn tortillas and chile verde a Hispano family in Las Vegas served her because of the dish's piquancy. She explained in her diary, "I could not eat a dish so strong, and unaccustomed to my palate."[18] Similarly, in September 1870 Sarah Louise Wetter, the wife of the secretary of the New Mexico Territory, wrote her brother, "cant eat Chili a favorite dish of the Mex, well in fact all they eat [sic]."[19] In another encounter with chile, in December 1884 journalist Charles Fletcher Lummis ate his first chile in Carnuel, New Mexico. In an article written for an Ohio newspaper, Lummis reported, "This was my first venture on chili colorado [sic], and will be my last. One not used to eating fire might just exactly as well chew up a ripe red pepper raw and swallow it."[20] Throughout the annexed region, Anglos made similar comments about the ingredients used by people of Mexican descent. According to anthropologist Mario Montaño, Anglos in Texas noted the "strong spices" and "poor quality ingredient," which meant Mexican food was "unhealthy and unfit for human consumption."[21] The distaste for chile was more than a preference. During the mid-nineteenth century, U.S. expansionism and domesticity bound the nation and home. Bodies were central to maintaining the boundaries of both.[22] Anglos worried that what they put into their bodies would affect their morals and the health of the nation. Moreover, beginning in the 1830s, many middle-to-upper-class Anglos understood that minimizing spice was a method of maintaining their class and social distinction.[23] In these subtle but repeated remarks about chile and digestion, Anglos encoded chile with their ideas of difference.

Besides noting the predominance of chile in New Mexico, the notions of piquancy or spiciness served to mark the differences between those who could and could not eat it. Anglos used the tolerance for chile's heat and the prominent use of the chile in the regional foodways as a symbol of the physical and moral differences between themselves and Hispanas/os. Rancher Elizabeth Smith Collins reminisced of the chile in 1894, "A fair idea of the amount of red peppers used by the Mexicans may be arrived at by considering the fact that their bodies are so impregnated by the vegetable that after death they dry rather than decay, and a wild animal, which would devour with avidity the body of other than they, will pass them without molestation."[24] Collins's image of a desiccated, unburied Mexican body—one even animals would not eat—contrasts greatly with Anglo ideas of the body after death. During the second half of the nineteenth century, Anglos romanticized death and emphasized properly beautifying the corpse and respecting the dead. Through embalming, elaborate burials, and postmortem portraits, disintegration and corruptibility of the body were halted and the body remained unchanged and reunited with the living in heaven.[25] Collins's comment on chile reflects another way Anglos used the human body to consolidate power after the U.S.-Mexico War. By remarking that over-consumption of chile changed the body, Anglos suggested not only cultural but also physical differences of Hispanas/os and Mexicans.[26]

The chile could also reveal how Hispanas/os were deviants and untrustworthy. Charles Fletcher Lummis provided insight into how Anglos attached the bodily response to the chile's spice to the supposed characteristics of Hispanas/os. Reflecting on the chile in 1892, Lummis wrote, "I sprang up with a howl of pain and terror, fully convinced that these 'treacherous Mexicans' had assassinated me by quick poison. . . . My mouth and throat were consumed with living fire, and my stomach was a pit of boiling torture. . . . That was only *chile colorado* [*sic*] . . . which liked to the Mexicans *mucho*."[27] Lummis's initial response to the heat was attached to the prevalent stereotype of Hispanas/os as tricksters or deviants, and they must have poisoned him. Along with many other cultural differences, such as Catholicism, skin tone, and the Spanish language, foodstuffs and consumption practices were integral in how Anglos determined racial and social differences.[28]

By documenting their disgust and inability to eat spicy food, many Anglos drew a boundary between white and non-white bodies. The chile posed a risk to Anglos in the borderlands because of the centrality of chile in Hispano foodways and their need to establish themselves as superior in the region. This is not to say Anglos did not consume spicy food. Instead, to maintain their whiteness and social power in the region, Anglos had to self-police the amount of spice that entered their mouths in comparison to Hispanas/os and Mexicans.

While traveling through the territory, some middle-class Anglo women also used their notions of cleanliness in kitchens and dining spaces to mark the differences between "us" and "them." In 1846, Susan Shelby Magoffin initially anticipated a nice meal in Las Vegas because the table was covered in a "clean white cloth." Her opinion changed when a Hispano placed a "cloth so black with dirt and greese [sic]" on the table; she added, "how my heart sickened." There were "neither knives, forks or spoons," which meant Magoffin had to eat in the tradition of the region—with her hands or tortillas—out of the same clay pot as her Hispano hosts. These different food customs could have potentially contributed to the contamination of her body.[29] Not only had the heat of chile stopped Magoffin from eating in Las Vegas but also so had the apparent dirtiness of the dining space and unfamiliar custom of eating. Lydia Spencer Lane, the wife of Lieutenant William Bartlett Lane, complained about the cleanliness at a dining establishment while traveling to Santa Fe from Fort Union in 1867. After asking the Hispana proprietress for a cup, Lane was shocked when the woman "took up a glass the men had used, seized one of their soiled towels, and began to polish the tumbler. . . . I found my appetite had gone, and I ate no more that morning."[30] The lack of the appropriate markers of middle-class white American society indicated for Magoffin and Lane their meals would be unappetizing and unclean. By refusing to drink from a tumbler not cleaned to her standards and even refusing to continue eating, Lane protected her white body from contamination. Magoffin's and Lane's central criticisms were the filthiness of the people and their foodstuffs, pointing to the importance of cleanliness and purity in their own bodies. Similar to Lummis in Carnuel, who feared chile as potential poison, Magoffin's and Lane's reactions hint to a fear about what New Mexican kitchen practices could potentially do to their bodies.

Women like Magoffin and Lane were actively policing and protecting not only their bodies but the national body as well by holding to their ideas of cleanliness after moving to New Mexico. Cleanliness was a central trope during U.S. nineteenth-century expansion because bodily deportment was enmeshed in the construction of race and class differences. Since the early Republic, Anglos used cleanliness and homemaking practices as indicators of the health, future, and superiority of the home and nation. As the United States expanded, Anglo politicians and reformers grew concerned about the domestic ramifications of a growing population that included foreign and non-white bodies. Through their standards of cleanliness, Anglos needed to mitigate the threat of foreigners being absorbed into the nation, home, and body.[31] Middle-class and elite Anglos feared unclean food, cooks, or utensils might contaminate their pure bodies. Contamination of the body through eating dirty or spicy food would not only cause disorder in the white body but could potentially cause dysfunction in the national project of expansion.

Differences in cleanliness mattered during the territorial period because Anglos needed to maintain their social and political dominance due to their low population and recently established political power. In their research on the construction of racial difference in Arizona and New Mexico, historians Linda Gordon and Pablo Mitchell, respectively, found that place complicates simply looking at cleanliness as a health or class issue.[32] Since the West had different ethnic and racial structures, Anglos used their constructions of cleanliness to modify the boundaries of whiteness to exclude Mexicans and Hispanas/os. Anglos used cleanliness to determine "us" and "them." For example, the Anglo epithet for people of Mexican descent—"greaser"—arose from the Anglo perception of Mexican food as greasy after their arrival to the Texas borderlands in the mid-nineteenth century.[33] In New Mexico, clean dishes, white walls, white table linens, and white clothing denoted safe spaces for consumption and were linked to ideas of higher civilization.[34] Expressions of poisoning and contamination helped Anglos construct an image of Hispanas/os lacking the social distinction of true, white U.S. citizens. Anglos depicted those who did not keep homes up to their standards as non-white, inferior, and unfit for citizenship.[35]

Repeated descriptions of dishes and kitchens of New Mexico in the archival records reveal the subtle ways Anglos expressed ideas of race and class differences along the U.S.-Mexican border after 1848. While they often ate "foreign" ingredients and increasingly came to enjoy them, Anglos originally constructed a culinary borderland and distanced the United States from Mexico by generalizing New Mexican foodways as spicy, dirty, and suspect. Through culinary borderlands, racial and ethnic tensions manifest themselves as threats of outsiders and a fear of food poisoning.[36] Anglos used their eastern and middle-class constructions of cleanliness and spice to police the boundaries between New Mexican bodies and their own "pure," white bodies. Anglo concerns for white linens, clean hands, and bland food were rituals of the nation to protect the boundaries of whiteness.

As the railroad rapidly brought more Anglos to the region after 1878 and the luster of being new settlers wore off, Anglos gradually adapted New Mexican foodstuffs into their homes, even when they expressed distaste. While Anglos did not leave written records describing their decision to incorporate local foods, it is likely they felt safe crossing the culinary borderlands they had earlier established due to their growing population, their increased exposure to the dishes, and the increasing availability and sanitation of canned goods. However, this was a slow process. From extant records, it is evident that by the 1880s Anglo women had privately reinterpreted New Mexican dishes or ingredients in their kitchens. For example, Alice Kirk Grierson and Martha Summerhayes, both army wives, included recipes such as green chile stuffed with macaroni, *albóndigas*, and "Spanish soups" in their manuscript cookbooks.[37] Anglo women did not leave written explanations about their decisions to incorporate Hispano foodstuffs.

Given their relationships with local workers, it is likely Anglo women learned the recipes by observing their domestic laborers or by asking Hispanas to teach them.[38] While living in the Arizona Territory in the 1870s, Martha Summerhayes noted in her memoir that she observed Spanish-Mexican women prepare *carne seca* and tortillas.[39] As Anglos increasingly learned New Mexican recipes, grew regional ingredients, and adapted the foodstuffs into their kitchens, Hispana/o cooks, servers, and farmers became increasingly irrelevant in their ability to eat New Mexican style.

Moreover, the availability of chiles and chile powder safely grown, produced, and canned by Anglos probably increased Anglos' willingness to eat chile. U.S. producers started marketing canned chile, chile sauce, and chile powder in the 1870s.[40] In Texas, William Gebhardt, a German immigrant, began manufacturing prepackaged Mexican dinners of chili con carne and selling Gebhardt's Eagle Chili Powder [*sic*].[41] The ability to purchase chile produced and sold by Anglos allowed other Anglos to taste the other without actually having to encounter Hispanas/os. For example, in 1889 Mary Douglass purchased "a second can of Colorado chili" at Fort Marcy's commissary in Santa Fe.[42] However, while having a piqued interest in New Mexican food, as the nineteenth century closed, many Anglos were still adamant in narrating that the traditional preparation of chile was too spicy and the dining spaces were dirty. Anthropologist John Bourke ended his 1895 catalog of New Mexican foodstuffs by reminding the reader, "Neither shall I rush impetuously to the defence of Mexican cookery . . . as a general rule, there is an appalling liberality in the matter of garlic, a recklessness in the use of chile colorado or chile verde, and an indifference to the existence of dirt and grease."[43] As the nineteenth century ended, Anglo inhabitants of New Mexico demonstrated an increased desire to eat chile but not in the same manner as New Mexicans.

It is difficult to document why Anglos changed their eating preferences given the extant records, but a growing population and pressing concerns over statehood clearly played a role. By 1880, the territory's population had jumped to 120,000 people, from 61,547 in 1850.[44] Even though Hispanas/os faced social and legal discrimination, they still had economic and political power, with many elite Hispanos holding positions of power during the late territorial period and even after statehood.[45] Within the territory, Anglos clamored for statehood because they had nonvoting representation in Congress and wanted national policies to reflect their interests.[46] However, citizens of the greater United States repeatedly denied New Mexico statehood due to the concerns regarding the mixed Hispana/o and American Indian population of the territory. Whiteness was the central theme in statehood debates. In New Mexico, both Hispanas/os and Anglos were legally white, but outside the territory Anglos constructed whiteness differently. The Anglo fear surrounding statehood throughout the rest of the United States was about potentially giving full citizenship, equal representation, and legal equality to Hispanas/os and American Indians, and thus upsetting the racial hierarchy.[47] Given this continued tension over maintaining power over Hispanas/os, even as the nineteenth century ended, Anglos still held anxiety over their own degree of whiteness.

After statehood, Anglos and Hispanas/os continued to vie for claims to whiteness to separate themselves from Mexican immigrants. This was particularly evident in New Mexico because in Arizona, California, and Texas, Anglos quickly became the majority population and claimed political control by the turn of the twentieth century. However, in New Mexico, Hispanas/os made up 60 percent of the population in 1912, the only annexed state to retain a Hispana/o advantage.[48] As they lost land and political influence, elite Hispanas/os redefined their whiteness by emphasizing themselves as being Spanish in ethnicity and American in nationality, which allowed them to claim whiteness and place themselves above working-class Mexican immigrants.[49] Simultaneously, Anglos sought additional ways to circumscribe their own whiteness and maintain the racial hierarchy because Hispana/o claims to whiteness appeared more fluid and many Hispanas/os still maintained some local autonomy. As historian John Nieto-Phillips explains, during the first half of the twentieth century, Anglos' "phobias turned to fascination."[50]

APPROPRIATING NEW MEXICAN COOKERY

During the first three decades of the twentieth century, Anglos reshaped their relationship to New Mexico's history and food as the boundaries of whiteness continued shifting after statehood. A rise in immigration throughout the United States inflamed nativist sentiments, and Anglos became more intolerant of racial, ethnic, religious, and class differences.[51] Economic and political unrest in Porfirian Mexico led many Mexican nationals to move north for labor opportunities. Between 1910 and 1930, the number of immigrants from Mexico to the United States increased by 300 percent and the number of Mexican-born residents in New Mexico increased by 140 percent.[52] In 1917, and again in 1924, Congress passed immigration acts that established new requirements for entry, expanded border patrol, and instituted a quota system to maintain the supposed homogenous nature of the nation.[53] The quota did not apply to immigrants from the Western Hemisphere but contributed to overall anti-immigrant sentiment and to a pull for Mexican immigrants to replace other "cheap labor."[54] As demand for Mexican immigrant labor increased, being "Mexican" came with increasing stigma. There was a rise in de facto segregation and Americanization programs that further marginalized people of Mexican, Chinese, Japanese, and southern and eastern European descent.[55] Tensions over who belonged and who did not shaped national policy and daily life because labor became more competitive and war strained the economy and morale. In turn, the racial hierarchy of whiteness dispossessed many Mexican-descent people of full citizenship, even though statehood in 1912 granted all non-indigenous residents the privileges of citizenship.

By the 1910s, Anglos in New Mexico began publicly appropriating the Spanish past into their own national narrative and tourist industry. Anglo boosters, journalists, and merchants sold a Spanish heritage to maintain their power over Hispanas/os and increase tourism and economic interest in the Southwest as a distinct region within the United States. Anglos found the "Spanish myth" alluring because of the nostalgia and escape from industry and urban settings.[56] In their use of the Spanish myth, Anglos constructed Hispanas/os as primitive vestiges of the Spanish past, distancing them from Mexican immigrants but still lower than Anglos.[57] Through selective appropriation, Anglos were able to "disdain yet desire" and "reject yet posses," as historian Phoebe Kropp explains, many aspects of Hispano culture, especially their material culture, architecture, and foodways across the Southwest.[58] For example, Anglos sexualized Mexican American women's relationship to chile cooking at the Alamo and romanticized the Dons and Doñas of the California missions.[59] Charles Fletcher Lummis, who feared "treacherous Mexicans" poisoned him with chile, became a proponent of the Spanish past by promoting tourism in Southern California.[60] Nevertheless, the celebration of the Spanish past did not stop Anglos from acquiring Spanish-land grants from Hispanas/os, practicing wage discrimination and segregation, or denying Hispanas/os their civil rights.[61] As the Spanish myth grew in New Mexico, Hispanas/os increasingly lost political power and control over their land, and were often forced to Americanize and speak English. Moreover, the appropriation increased Hispanas/os' inability to control their culture.[62] Besides economic benefits, the sociopolitical benefits of the Spanish myth allowed Anglos to maintain power and redraw the boundaries of whiteness at the cost of Hispanas/os and Mexican immigrants.

Using the myth of the Spanish past, New Mexican kitchens served as a vantage point from which Anglo women during the first three decades of the twentieth century helped redraw the boundaries of whiteness. Prior to World War II, restaurants were not the center of foodways and dining in the United States.[63] Instead, cookbooks, like Erna Fergusson's, served as an entry point for New Mexican food's entrance into many middle-class Anglo kitchens. Published in 1934, Fergusson's cookbook was a product of the Anglo fantasy of Spanish life in the Southwest. Her foreword to *Mexican Cookbook* especially reveals how Anglos felt they had the right to possess Hispano food, like their desire to possess the land. Fergusson told her readers, "Mexican food has, ever since the 'American Occupation,' been a part of the Southwestern diet. . . . Mexican food has become part of the national cuisine." This language of the boundaries of possession also ends her introduction: "The recipes in this book are limited to those which were in common use when the province of New Mexico was a part of the Republic of Mexico. They represent Mexican cookery that belongs to the United States."[64]

She separated New Mexico from its Mexican heritage and transferred New Mexican food to be now part of "American food," paralleling the annexation of New Mexico. By claiming ownership of New Mexican foodways for the United States, Fergusson attempted to deny Hispanas/os the ability to control the traditions central to their identities.

Fergusson celebrated the Spanish past of New Mexico in the cookbook but used a benevolent tone when describing Hispanas/os. In 1928, she wrote about Hispanas/os, calling them Mexicans, in *Century Magazine*. With a telling choice of words, she asked the white reader to care about the process of Americanization in New Mexico because "thousands of boys and girls in their teens are mingling with our boys and girls in the schools." She noted, "The Mexican people of New Mexico are foreign to the American amalgamated citizen." While this article is separate from the cookbook, we can clearly see her intentions to introduce Anglos to New Mexicans and their foodways because they were exotic and could not be simply incorporated into the body politic. Furthermore, Fergusson added, "New Mexico as a part of the United States, must, of course live an American life." Fergusson was clear that Hispanas/os needed to Americanize—particularly in their labor, language, and education.[65] In her acts of simultaneously rejecting and possessing the Spanish-Mexican past, Fergusson used domesticity and Americanization programs to entrench Anglo whiteness while selectively appropriating Hispana/o southwestern foodways in the process.

The conflict between claims of appreciation of New Mexican foods but disgust for people of Mexican heritage is evident in the concurrent rise in Americanization programs during the 1930s and 1940s. In the first half of the twentieth century, the U.S. concern for changing the diets of Hispanas/os, Mexican Americans, and Mexican nationals continued, especially by focusing on recently arrived Mexican immigrants. In the Southwest, U.S. reformers developed campaigns to combat the "Mexican problem"—a supposed propensity for delinquency, poor housing, illiteracy, and disease among Mexicans in the United States.[66] Reformers also focused on the diets of immigrants from southern and eastern Europe to discourage them from eating spicy food and nonmeat dishes.[67] Americanization programs sought to force people of Mexican descent to reject their traditional foodways in the hopes of creating good citizens in the kitchen.[68] Their concern over diet and citizenship is evident in their teachings that the typical noon lunch of ethnic-Mexican children consisted of a "folded tortilla with no filling," which "became the first step in a life of crime." Instead, reformers taught, "The modern Mexican woman should replace tortillas with bread, serve lettuce instead of beans, and broil instead of fry."[69]

By writing the cookbook and documenting Hispanas' recipes, Fergusson crossed the culinary borderland in 1934 and imported recipes so other Anglo women would not have to leave their safe kitchens to taste the exotic and foreign. Fergusson provided recipes for atole (corn gruel), frijoles (beans), enchiladas, and chile con carne, all of which are now considered staple dishes in New Mexico. She included a three-page section on "Chile" and a chile sauce recipe, demonstrating how Anglos' palates adapted. However, the traditional distrust of chile is not far off. Fergusson suggested, "Commercial canned chile may be substituted in equal proportions."[70] In the early twentieth century, most white-authored cookbooks suggested buying canned chile, such as the Anglo-produced Golden State Brand or Gebhardt's, instead of making red or green chile at home.[71] At the same time, Anglo reinterpretations of New Mexican dishes are sprinkled throughout the cookbook. She included a recipe for "Green Chile and Sandwiches" (bread covered in mayo and canned green chiles), "Spanish Meat Loaf" (a traditional American meatloaf with canned green chiles), and even a southern dish of "Crackling Corn Bread."[72] Through these recipes, Fergusson removed the threat of contamination and overly spiced food by placing the control of the ingredients, recipes, and cooking into Anglo women's hands and kitchens.

While Fergusson appeared to have a deep reverence for New Mexican foodways, she discussed Hispanas and their kitchens as museum exhibits of a dying way of life. To separate Anglo kitchens from Hispana kitchens, Fergusson employed comparisons of modern white kitchens and ancient New Mexican kitchens. While describing the "great kitchens" of New Mexico in a section named "Then," she wrote the "food was cooked over open fires in iron and copper pots . . . these methods were the result of conditions so primitive that we can scarcely believe them now." This type of description even entered her tortilla recipe. She explained that traditional corn tortillas could only be made by someone who had "a line of Indian ancestry running back about five hundred years."[73] These descriptions, while appearing nostalgic and appreciative, essentialized Hispanas' culture as static, and highlighted the mixed blood of New Mexicans. The myth that North Americans brought modernity and civilization to non-Western and indigenous societies assumes their ethnic heritage and traditions remained unchanged without white guidance.[74]

Fergusson characterized Hispanas' labor in the kitchen as ancient and unchanged. She wrote, "All old and excellent cooks maintain that the full flavor of Mexican cookery depends upon doing everything as in the old days, when women worked slowly with their hands and only the simplest equipment."[75] Her comments signaled a belief that Hispanas/os practiced an outdated way of life different from U.S. industrial practices and Anglo women's kitchens. She neglected to recognize other Hispana cooking practices, which included canning, pre-ground masa, mass-produced tortillas, and even their own cookbook authors.[76] The use of U.S. industry and modernization was applied elsewhere in the adaptation to New Mexican chile. As William Carleton demonstrates, in the public realm Dr. Fabián García worked with the Extension Service at New Mexico State University to make the New Mexican chile palatable at the national level during the early twentieth century. To avoid appropriating primitive, and thus non-middle-class and non-white, kitchen practices, Fergusson consulted a domestic science teacher, Estelle Weisenbach. Weisenbach tested all of Fergusson's recipes and found them "practicable for a modern cook in a modern kitchen." Fergusson explained, "Mechanical devices can lessen the strain on the human back. Commercial products may often be substituted for ingredients that call for laborious preparation. And all the ingredients may now be bought ready and correctly prepared."[77] After removing the Hispanas' procedures from the recipes, Fergusson permitted some New Mexican foods to enter safely Anglo stomachs and kitchens.

Fergusson claimed the authority to alter the Hispanas' procedures in the kitchen and determined certain procedures were no longer necessary, as there were "modern" ways to prepare the dishes. While Weisenbach's modern recommendations to Fergusson attempted to save women's time and labor in the kitchen, Anglos entangled ideas of modernization in homes with ideas of class, citizenship, white superiority, and gender roles. So-called modern housekeeping and cooking techniques were not aimed at actually eliminating women's domestic labor but instead at preserving white middle-class homogeneity and gender roles. The ability to purchase kitchen appliances was a symbol of Anglo class status and modernity.[78] Anglo women could not claim their whiteness if they cooked like Hispanas. If Anglo women followed the traditional procedures of Hispanas, they would have performed the practices that justified the lower racial status of Hispanas and Mexicans, providing a recipe for upsetting the established racial hierarchy and denaturalizing whiteness. In this process of removing the traditional women's labor of grinding corn and making tortillas, Fergusson provided models on how other Anglo women could import New Mexican foodstuffs and dishes into their kitchens that fit the normative models of modern, middle-class white domesticity.

Even though Fergusson wrote of a dying tradition, the actual content of the cookbook betrays the crucial role of Hispanas in educating Anglos about their foodways. Fergusson explained in the "Mexican Cookery" chapter, "Most of these recipes were given [to] me by Dona Lola Chaves de Armijo."[79] The Armijo family was an elite Albuquerque-based Hispano family of the Spanish colonial era. Lola Chávez de Armijo, former New Mexico territorial and state librarian, was an active feminist until her passing in 1929.[80] Additionally, Fergusson noted that Mela Sedillo, Señora Máxima Tafoya de Salazar, and Señora Florinda Barela contributed advice and recipes.[81] These women's recipes were the ones Weisenbach Americanized. By telling the reader she relied on Hispanas for advice, Fergusson established the authenticity of the cookbook and her ability to transmit the recipes. Fergusson worked as a border agent between Hispanas' kitchens and Anglo women's kitchens. She relied on Hispanas to acquire insider knowledge—she risked crossing the culinary border—so other white women would not have to do so. Estelle Weisenbach served as an inspector to transform the ingredients and procedures that were neither modern nor American enough. Despite this exploitation, it is crucial to recognize the agency of Hispanas who contributed greatly to the ability for Anglo women to produce cookbooks on Mexican, New Mexican, and southwestern foodways.

There is no reason to doubt Erna Fergusson's, and others', sincere interest in New Mexican cookery. Obviously, Anglos relished certain dishes and New Mexican ingredients. However, to look uncritically at Anglo-authored cookbooks as a form of appreciation ignores the reality of life in the borderlands. In the process of writing, Fergusson asserted her authority to selectively appropriate New Mexican dishes and ingredients without negating her racial status. Moreover, while cultural appropriation implies intercultural exchange occurred, in these exchanges racial and class hierarchies still existed in which Anglos maintain power. As Marygold Walsh-Dilley demonstrates in her study on quinoa, the appropriation of foodstuffs and foodways often comes at the cost of the heritage and livelihood of native or non-white peoples. Appropriating New Mexican food was a method of eating and exploring the racial other while subordinating them. Fergusson was not alone in this action. For example, in an 1933 article on New Mexican food and recipes, Elizabeth Willis DeHuff explained it was worth trying New Mexican foods because "in trying them out one has a delightful feeling of daring and exhilaration—that feeling that always comes when exploring new fields."[82] The cookbook, and similar cookery texts from the first half of the twentieth century, provided Anglos a gateway to taste the romanticized and exoticized New Mexican food without having to interact directly with Hispanas/os.[83] Moreover, the recipes provided a taste of New Mexican food in a sanitized fashion so as not to disrupt the boundaries of whiteness while eating.

RED OR GREEN?

By examining acts of eating and cooking with a keen eye on the larger political and social motives driving such actions, I argue the politics of performing whiteness and racial differences were intertwined with daily life in New Mexico. Long after the present-day U.S.-Mexico border was drawn in the sand, Anglos used their kitchens and food choices to reshape racial boundaries and to claim their place in the region. By the 1930s, distaste changed to desire. However, the disgust for people of Mexican descent remained even as Anglos' cravings for New Mexican food increased. Anglos not only wanted to assimilate Mexicans and Hispanas/os but also make New Mexican food digestible and safe for the nation—to whiten it. Twentieth-century cravings for southwestern cuisine represent what food scholar Amy Bentley calls the "cultural domination of borderlands foodways."[84] By appearing to absorb New Mexican food through their cravings, the Anglo appropriation, marketing, and mass consumption of New Mexican foods erase the history of anti-Mexican discrimination in the borderlands. The evolving process of Anglo distaste in the second half of the nineteenth century to Anglo appropriation in the early twentieth century centered on removing people's agency—Mexican, Mexican American, and American Indian—and their lived history, culture, and status in the region.

The culinary tourism Fergusson encouraged is still found throughout the United States in the form of fast food and chain restaurants that celebrate their ability to make some version of Mexican or southwestern food and to do so cheaply.[85] Since the mid-twentieth century, the New Mexican specialties of red or green chile have predominated in the state's tourist industry. Travelers to New Mexico, regardless of their ethnicity, race, or class, view tasting New Mexico via its chile as an essential part of their southwestern visit.[86] In 1996, New Mexico passed a state question—"Red or Green?"—due to the importance of chile production in the state agriculture and tourist industries. Nevertheless, the chile is still a popular racist symbol for Latinas/os among Anglos. The heat of a chile is now a mark of pride as menus note "Gringos should order with caution" at Carlos Murphy's chain restaurant in San Diego, California.[87] Moreover, for its "special report on America's Latinos," the *Economist* featured an American flag made of denim material, jeweled stars, and chiles replacing the red stripes on the cover of the March 14, 2015, issue. In the accompanying article, titled "How to Fire Up America," the conclusion is subtitled "Chilies in the mix," with no discussion of foodways.[88] This chile cover and spicy rhetoric create a mental image of Latinas/os as chiles themselves, evoking Collins's nineteenth-century description of spicy decaying bodies.

Similar to the Anglo women who wrote cookbooks and profited through appropriation, Anglo-owned companies and restaurants are selling Americanized and commercialized New Mexican and Mexican food often off the backs of underpaid Mexicans and Mexican Americans. Since the early 1990s, salsa has outsold ketchup, and Doritos and Tostitos are the second and third, respectively, best-selling snack chips in the country.[89] Old El Paso Products, owned by Pillsbury and situated over 1,000 miles from the U.S.-Mexican border, is the top producer of Mexican commercial food in the United States.[90] In its commercials, Taco Bell claims that entering its restaurant is an act of border crossing. The late-1960s Frito Bandito commercials even suggested simply opening a bag of chips allowed one to cross into Mexico.[91] The availability of southwestern and New Mexican cookbooks, foodstuffs in the market, and fast food restaurants allows Anglos to experience the culture without interacting with the people.[92]

While it might be tempting to ask whether Erna Fergusson's recipes were authentic New Mexican food, the more important point is she expressed the lived reality of the U.S.-Mexico borderlands, a place where the history of U.S. annexation remains part of daily life and conversations, maybe even over plates of chile verde. Fergusson inherited a practice of using foodways to construct her racial and class status in New Mexico vis-à-vis other Anglo women. Anglos engaged in debates over the boundary between "us" and "them" from within the kitchen. Besides the rich food history, Fergusson's cookbook demonstrates that within the kitchen the tensions of who was "American," "Mexican," and "white" played out daily through questions of what ingredients and procedures could be included or excluded and under what conditions. These decisions are a continuation of the politics of manifest destiny and whiteness Anglos brought to the borderlands in the 1840s. As Erna Fergusson decided what dishes and methods the "American way" would improve, her choices were reminiscent of Susan Shelby Magoffin's distaste for chile verde and Lydia Spencer Lane's refusal to drink from a glass tumbler cleaned by a Hispana.

NOTES

1. Erna Fergusson, *Mexican Cookbook* (Albuquerque: University of New Mexico Press, 1934), n.p.

2. Due to the fluidity of ethnic and racial identities, I use widely accepted terms when discussing heterogeneous groups of people for cohesion. Anglos are whites of non-Spanish descent. American refers to their cultural customs. Hispanas/os are New Mexicans who claimed a white Spanish identity, and New Mexican refers to their foodways, even when others refer to it as Mexican food. Mexican American refers to U.S. citizens of Mexican descent outside of New Mexico. Mexicans refers to Mexican citizens and/or recently arrived immigrants.

3. Pablo Mitchell, *Coyote Nation: Sexuality, Race, and Conquest in Modernizing New Mexico, 1880–1920* (Chicago: University of Chicago Press, 2005), 23.

4. Ruth Frankenberg, *White Women, Race Matters: The Social Construction of Whiteness* (Minneapolis: University of Minnesota Press, 1993), 197; Matt Wray, *White Trash and the Boundaries of Whiteness* (Durham, NC: Duke University Press, 2006), 5–6, 139.

5. Matthew Frye Jacobson, *Whiteness of a Different Color: European Immigrants and the Alchemy of Race* (Cambridge, MA: Harvard University Press, 1998), 1–12.

6. Amy Kaplan, *The Anarchy of Empire in the Making of U.S. Culture* (Cambridge, MA: Harvard University Press, 2002), 23–26.

7. Yen Le Espiritu, *Home Bound: Filipino American Lives Across Cultures, Communities, and Countries* (Berkeley: University of California Press, 2003), 2.

8. Jeffrey Pilcher, "Was the Taco Invented in Southern California?," *Gastronomica* 8.1 (February 2008): 30–32; Kyla Wazana Tompkins, *Racial Indigestion: Eating Bodies in the 19th Century* (New York: New York University Press, 2012), 1; E. Melanie DuPuis, *Nature's Perfect Food: How Milk Became America's Drink* (New York: New York University Press, 2002), 8–11.

9. In 1916, Alice Stevens Tipton wrote the first official cookbook on New Mexican food, *New Mexico Cookery*, for the State Land Office, to promote the state's agriculture among Anglo residents. However, this cookbook was not popular or widely circulated. Alice Stevens Tipton, *New Mexico Cookery* (Santa Fe: Bureau of Publicity of the New Mexico State Land Office, 1916).

10. David Remley, *Erna Fergusson, Southwest Writers Series*, no. 24 (Austin, TX: Steck-Vaughn, 1969), 5.

11. Robert Franklin Gish, *Beyond Bounds: Cross-Cultural Essays on Anglo, American Indian & Chicano Literature* (Albuquerque: University of New Mexico Press, 1996), 16.

12. Carey McWilliams, *North from Mexico: The Spanish-Speaking People of the United States* (New York: Praeger, 1990), 113.

13. Charles Montgomery, *The Spanish Redemption: Heritage, Power, and Loss on New Mexico's Upper Rio Grande* (Berkeley: University of California Press, 2002), 9.

14. David Weber, *The Mexican Frontier, 1821–1846: The American Southwest under Mexico* (Albuquerque: University of New Mexico Press, 1982), 217.

15. McWilliams, *North from Mexico*, 113.

16. David Weber, *Myth and the History of the Hispanic Southwest* (Albuquerque: University of New Mexico Press, 1987), 153; Tomás Almaguer, *Racial Fault Lines: The Historical Origins of White Supremacy in California* (Berkeley: University of California Press, 1994), 8.

17. Laura Gómez, *Manifest Destinies: The Making of the Mexican American Race* (New York: New York University Press, 2007), 4–5; Jacobson, *Whiteness of a Different Color*, 230; Pablo Mitchell, *West of Sex: Making Mexican America, 1900–1930* (Chicago: University of Chicago Press, 2012), 4; Richard Griswold del Castillo, *The Treaty of Guadalupe Hidalgo: A Legacy of Conflict* (Norman: University of Oklahoma Press, 1990), 190; Katherine Benton-Cohen, *Borderline Americans: Racial Division and Labor War in the Arizona Borderlands* (Cambridge, MA: Harvard University Press, 2009), 6–7.

18. Susan Shelby Magoffin, *Down the Santa Fé Trail and into Mexico: The Diary of Susan Shelby Magoffin, 1846–1847*, ed. Stella M. Drumm (New Haven, CT: Yale University Press, 1926), 93–94.

19. Letter from Sarah Louise Wetter, Santa Fe, New Mexico, to Sam, September 4, 1870, Henry Wetter Papers, Fray Angélico Chávez History Library, Santa Fe, New Mexico.

20. Charles Fletcher Lummis, *Letters from the Southwest, September 20, 1884 to March 14, 1885*, ed. James Byrkit (Tucson: University of Arizona Press, 1989), 179–180.

21. Mario Montaño, "Appropriation and Counterhegemony in South Texas: Food Slurs, Offal Meats, and Blood," in *Usable Pasts: Traditions and Group Expression in North America*, ed. Tad Tuleja (Logan: Utah State University Press, 1997), 51.

22. Amy Greenberg, *Manifest Manhood and the Antebellum American Empire* (New York: Cambridge University Press, 2005); Kaplan, *Anarchy of Empire*.

23. Tompkins, *Racial Indigestion*, 62–68, 81–86; Jeffrey Pilcher, *¡Que Vivan los Tamales! Food and the Making of Mexican Identity* (Albuquerque: University of New Mexico Press, 1998), 65.

24. Elizabeth Smith Collins, *The Cattle Queen of Montana: A Story of Personal Experience during a Residence of Forty Years in the Far West*, comp. Charles Wallace (St. James, MN: C. W. Foote, 1894), 36.

25. Martina Will de Chaparro, *Death and Dying in New Mexico* (Albuquerque: University of New Mexico Press, 2007), 175–178; James Farrell, *Inventing the American Way of Death, 1830–1920* (Philadelphia: Temple University Press, 1980), 10; Gary Laderman, *The Sacred Remains: American Attitudes toward Death, 1799–1883* (New Haven, CT: Yale University Press, 1996), 54.

26. Sidney Mintz reminds us that "people who eat strikingly different foods or similar foods in different ways are thought to be strikingly different, sometimes even less human." Sidney Mintz, *Sweetness and Power: The Place of Sugar in Modern History* (New York: Penguin, 1985), 3.

27. Charles Fletcher Lummis, *A Tramp Across the Continent* (New York: Charles Scribner's Sons, 1892), 137.

28. For an analysis on the centrality of the body in territorial and statehood politics, see Mitchell, *Coyote Nation*.

29. Magoffin, *Down the Santa Fé Trail*, 94.

30. Lydia Spencer Lane, *I Married a Soldier* (Albuquerque: University of New Mexico Press, 1987), 149.

31. Kathleen Brown, *Foul Bodies: Cleanliness in Early America* (New Haven, CT: Yale University Press, 2009), 150, 185, 191; Kaplan, *Anarchy of Empire*, 12, 18–19; Amy Greenberg, "Domesticating the Border: Manifest Destiny and the 'Comforts of Life' in the U.S.-Mexico Boundary Commission and Gadsden Purchase, 1848–1854," in *Land of Necessity: Consumer Culture in the United States–Mexico Borderlands*, ed. Alexis McCrossen (Durham, NC: Duke University Press, 2009), 98–101.

32. Linda Gordon, *The Great Arizona Orphan Abduction* (Cambridge, MA: Harvard University Press, 1999); Mitchell, *Coyote Nation*.

33. Américo Paredes, "The Problem of Identity in a Changing Culture: Popular Expressions of Culture Conflict Along the Lower Rio Grande Border," in *Views Across the Border: The United States and Mexico*, ed. Stanley Ross (Albuquerque: University of New Mexico Press, 1978), 69.

34. See, for example, John Bourke, *On the Border with Crook* (New York: Charles Scribner's Sons, 1891), 57–59; George Rutledge Gibson, *Journal of a Soldier Under Kearny and Doniphan*, ed. Ralph Bieber (Philadelphia: Porcupine Press, 1974), 359; Magoffin, *Down the Santa Fé Trail*, 56.

35. Mitchell, *Coyote Nation*, 35–37, 131–132, 155.

36. Pilcher, "Was the Taco Invented in Southern California?," 30–32.

37. Alice Kirk Grierson, *An Army Wife's Cookbook*, ed. Mary Williams (Tucson, AZ: Southwest Park and Monuments Association, 1972), 24–25; Martha Summerhayes, "Cookbook of Martha Summerhayes No. 1," Arizona Historical Society, Tucson.

38. Cheryl Foote, "Chiles, Frijoles and Bizcochitos: Recording, Preserving and Promoting New Mexico's Culinary Heritage," *Tradición Revista* 18.3 (September 2013): 99.

39. Martha Summerhayes, *Vanished Arizona: Recollections of the Army Life of a New England Woman* (Salem, MA: Salem Press, 1911), 156–159.

40. Gustavo Arellano, *Taco USA: How Mexican Food Conquered America* (New York: Scribner, 2012), 220; Jeffrey Pilcher, *Planet Taco: A Global History of Mexican Food* (New York: Oxford University Press, 2012), 118.

41. Arellano, *Taco USA*, 177–178.

42. Mary C. Douglass Papers, 1888–1889, Fray Angélico Chávez History Library, Santa Fe, NM.

43. John Bourke, "The Folk Foods of the Rio Grande Valley and of Northern Mexico," *Journal of American Folklore* 8.28 (January–March 1895): 53–54.

44. Mitchell, *Coyote Nation*, 2, 17.

45. Ibid., 17–18; David Maciel and Erlinda Gonzales-Berry, eds., *The Contested Homeland: A Chicano History of New Mexico* (Albuquerque: University of New Mexico Press, 2000), 84.

46. Amy Bridges, "Managing the Periphery in the Gilded Age: Writing Constitutions for the Western States," *Studies in American Political Development* 22 (Spring 2008): 39.

47. John Nieto-Phillips, "Spanish-American Ethnic Identity and New Mexico's Statehood Struggle," in Maciel and Gonzales-Berry, *Contested Homeland*, 97–98, 116–134.

48. Evelyn Nakano Glen, *Unequal Freedom: How Race and Gender Shaped American Citizenship and Labor* (Cambridge, MA: Harvard University Press, 2002), 145.

49. John Nieto-Phillips, *The Language of Blood: The Making of Spanish-American Identity in New Mexico, 1880s-1930s* (Albuquerque: University of New Mexico Press, 2004), 73–92.

50. Ibid., 49.

51. Arnoldo de León and Richard Griswold del Castillo, *North to Aztlán: A History of Mexican Americans in the United States*, 2nd ed. (Wheeling, IL: Harlan Davidson, 2006), 85.

52. George Sanchez, "'Go After the Women': Americanization and the Mexican Immigrant Woman 1915–1929," Working Paper Series No. 6 (Stanford, CA: Stanford Center Chicano Research, 1984), 3; María Rosa García-Acevedo, "The Forgotten Diaspora: Mexican Immigration to New Mexico," in Maciel and Gonzales-Berry, *Contested Homeland*, 218–220.

53. George Sánchez, *Becoming Mexican American: Ethnicity, Culture, and Identity in Chicano Los Angeles, 1900–1945* (New York: Oxford University Press, 1993), 17–55; Jacobson, *Whiteness of a Different Color*, 83–90.

54. McWilliams, *North from Mexico*, 173–174, 195–197.

55. Nakano Glen, *Unequal Freedom*, 163.

56. Nieto-Phillips, *Language of Blood*, 147.

57. Montgomery, *Spanish Redemption*, 11, 16–17; McWilliams, *North from Mexico*, 43–66.

58. Phoebe Kropp, *California Vieja: Culture and Memory in a Modern American Place* (Berkeley: University of California Press, 2006), 7.

59. Suzanne Bost, "Women and Chile at the Alamo: Feeding U.S. Colonial Mythology," *Nepantla* 4.3 (2003): 493–522; Lawrence Culver, *The Frontier of Leisure: Southern California and the Shaping of Modern America* (New York: Oxford University Press, 2010).

60. Nieto-Phillips, *Language of Blood*, 152–159.

61. Montgomery, *Spanish Redemption*, 128–131, 157.

62. Nieto-Phillips, *Language of Blood*, 147–148, 170.

63. Barbara Shortridge and James Shortridge, eds., *The Taste of American Place: A Reader on Regional and Ethnic Foods* (Lanham, MD: Rowman and Littlefield, 1998), 185.

64. Fergusson, *Mexican Cookbook*, n.p.

65. Erna Fergusson, "New Mexico's Mexicans: The Picturesque Process of Americanization," *Century Magazine* 116 (August 1928): 437–438, 441.

66. McWilliams, *North from Mexico*, 188–191.

67. DuPuis, *Nature's Perfect Food*, 118.

68. Charlotte Biltekoff, *Eating Right in America: The Cultural Politics of Food and Health* (Durham, NC: Duke University Press, 2013), 27.

69. Sánchez, *Becoming Mexican American*, 102.

70. Fergusson, *Mexican Cookbook*, 11.

71. See, for example, Charles Parnell Leahy, *Spanish-Mexican Cookbook* (Culver City, CA: Murray & Gee, 1949); and Tipton, *New Mexico Cookery*.

72. Fergusson, *Mexican Cookbook*, 37, 88.

73. Ibid., 4–5, 88.

74. Pilcher, "Was the Taco Invented in Southern California?," 26.

75. Fergusson, *Mexican Cookbook*, 3.

76. Arellano, *Taco USA*, 112–114, 199–204; Pilcher, *Planet Taco*, 130–157; Joan Jensen, "Canning Comes to New Mexico: Women and the Agricultural Extension Service, 1914–1919," *New Mexico Historical Review* 57.4 (October 1982): 361–386. Hispanas such as Fabiola Cabeza de Baca, Cleofas Jaramillo, and Margarita Cabeza de Baca wrote cookbooks about their Spanish heritage and are the subjects of separate research.

77. Fergusson, *Mexican Cookbook*, 3.

78. Sherrie Inness, *Dinner Roles: American Women and Culinary Culture* (Iowa City: University of Iowa Press, 2001), 71–73, 86–87; Ruth Schwartz Cowan, *More Work for Mother* (New York: Basic Books, 1983), 100–110.

79. Fergusson, *Mexican Cookbook*, 3.

80. Tey Diana Rebolledo, *Nuestras Mujeres: Hispanas of New Mexico: Their Images and Their Lives, 1582–1992* (Albuquerque, NM: El Norte Publications, 1992), 30–32.

81. Fergusson, *Mexican Cookbook*, 2.

82. Elizabeth Willis DeHuff, "Cookery as of Old," *New Mexico Magazine* 11 (February 1933): 46.

83. Pilcher, "Was the Taco Invented in Southern California?," 30.

84. Amy Bentley, "From Culinary Other to Mainstream America: Meanings and Uses of Southwestern Cuisine," *Southern Folklore* 55.3 (1998): 239.

85. Culinary tourism is a form of racial and ethnic othering, as it paints the tourist as daring and open while reifying white food as normative. Jennie Germann Molz, "Eating Difference: The Cosmopolitan Mobilities of Culinary Tourism," *Space and Culture* 10.1 (February 2007): 77–93; Lisa Heldke, *Exotic Appetites: Ruminations of a Food Adventurer* (New York: Routledge, 2003), xv–xviii.

86. Foote, "Chiles, Frijoles and Bizcochitos," 98.

87. Laresh Jayasanker, "Tortilla Politics: Mexican Food, Globalization, and the Sunbelt," in *Sunbelt Rising: The Politics of Place, Space, and Region*, ed. Michelle Nickerson and Darren Dochuk (Philadelphia: University of Pennsylvania Press, 2011), 316.

88. "How to Fire Up America," *Economist* 414.8929 (March 14, 2015): 15.

89. Bentley, "From Culinary Other to Mainstream America," 238. Number one is Lay's Potato Chips.

90. Glenn Collins, "The Americanization of Salsa," *New York Times*, January 9, 1997.

91. Bentley, "From Culinary Other to Mainstream America," 242–245.

92. Inness, *Dinner Roles*, 88–108; Pilcher, "Was the Taco Invented in Southern California?," 30.

CHAPTER 4

"Cooking Mexican"

NEGOTIATING NOSTALGIA IN
FAMILY-OWNED AND SMALL-SCALE
MEXICAN RESTAURANTS IN THE UNITED STATES

José Antonio Vázquez-Medina

From the first moment I started working in a small-scale kitchen in Houston, I noticed a hostile atmosphere between the two cooks who were rushing to fill the breakfast orders that were piling up.[1] The tension became even more obvious a few hours later, when a client sent back a dish that had been prepared wrong, due to a lack of communication between the cooks. This culminated in an argument about who had made the mistake. This incident, however, had a deeper source: the rivalry due to different ways of cooking that existed between the two workers who were in charge of preparing breakfast, a rivalry based in competing nostalgias—the taste of their respective Mexican homes.

Once the peak hour had passed, one of the cooks told me I should eat, because it was getting late. She immediately served me a bowl of chicken soup that she had been preparing with my help. While making it a few hours earlier, she had mentioned to me that she was from a rural community in San Luis Potosí, where ground cumin is always added to the soup during the final stages, and that was what made the difference. As she served me the dish, carefully adding the vegetables and meat, she said that her soup had earned high praise: "Taste it! You'll see, it tastes like the soup from over there" (referring to the flavor of chicken soup prepared in Mexico). "Various Mexican chefs with restaurants here in Houston have come just to try the soup, and they have all congratulated me," she said, waiting for my reaction to the soup. When she turned to finish preparing another dish that was waiting, the other cook approached me, and lowering her voice, said, "She thinks she's the only one who knows how to make this soup, but the truth is mine turns out better. Mine has better seasoning. Later on, I'll make it for you so you can taste it. The steps aren't the same. She complicates things when she cooks. Just because she's the one in charge, she thinks she does everything well."

This chapter explores the development and negotiation of what I will call "culinary nostalgia" among the social actors who play a role in these restaurants. The specificities of preparing Mexican cuisine in U.S. restaurant establishments cross three borders: the border-crossed embodied individual as containing the authentication of flavors—what Meredith Abarca refers to as *"sazón"*[2]—(re)-created in the American restaurant kitchen; the transfer of nostalgic culinary knowledge from the private sphere of families—particularly mothers—to the public in these restaurants; and the border itself, which prompts the struggle over the definition of an *original* cuisine from a sending-nation with many communities of origin. These struggles create a new *culinary order*, with its own canons and emotionally charged contests, responsible for re-creating the Mexican homeland—from which bodies, *sazón*, and the Mexican nation come.[3]

As I learned in that kitchen in Houston, the tension is more than a day-to-day tale of workplace tensions that can happen in any restaurant. The cooks' desire to demonstrate their expertise in preparing chicken soup also shows how, in the quest to replicate the flavors associated with Mexico, a nostalgic ideational process involving tastes from the past take the cook back to his or her most personal memories of home, family, and community of origin. When one tries to replicate these flavors outside of Mexico, they acquire a *national* character. That is, the regional, personal, and private tastes of home become the flavors of the Mexican nation upon crossing the geopolitical border. On the other hand, the quest to replicate such flavors leads to a nostalgic search for *sazón* memory that in fact is re-created anew, creating a sui generis Mexican cuisine that is produced in these restaurants in the United States.[4]

RESTAURANTS AND THE MEXICAN-AMERICAN MIGRATORY PROCESS

As many studies have shown, kitchens offer an ideal stage for analyzing the interactions among the social actors who work in them.[5] Jean Pierre Hassoun maintains that restaurants should be considered total social spaces that facilitate the observation not only of interactions between the actors who work there but also of the acquisition of status, belonging, and political affiliation that are manifested in these spaces. At the same time, the restaurants act as living registries of the historical and urban transformations of the places where they are found.[6] In adding to these conversations, my observations in Mexican restaurant kitchens show that the questions of belonging and affiliation are even more complex, as they intersect with a memory of flavors on the other side of a national border, one that is dangerous to cross. Ethnicity and kinship also impact the way that social dynamics in the restaurant develop. In the case of family and small-scale establishments in the United States, analyzing their kitchens serves to define and redefine what it means to be Mexican and to "cook Mexican" in the United States.[7]

Restaurants are also border spaces for another reason: they facilitate migratory flows and are often a "first stop" on some of the more recurrent labor supply chains for Mexicans in the United States.[8] Therefore, Mexican restaurants can be examined as initial nodes or links in the migratory chains for border-crossing bodies, one of the first points of arrival for migrants in the United States.[9] Mexican restaurants are places where the new migrants often establish initial contacts with their fellow émigrés and receive job training, or, in the best-case scenario, establish their own businesses. Therefore, within the kitchen, one notes the flow of culinary information and its resulting appropriation by the cooks. These assertions are corroborated by Jacobo,[10] who manages the kitchen in a small restaurant in Houston:

> When I arrived, I settled in with a friend of my godfather, who had another friend who worked here in the restaurant, and he told me that the owner was from San Luis, and there was the possibility [of work] here. I stayed for a year, almost two. I never had worked in the kitchen, but I learned quickly. A taquero [taco maker] who worked here taught me all the tricks, I think because he was also from San Luis and he wanted to give us a hand. Later on, I brought my wife and my small daughter. My second child was born here. When my wife arrived, I was able to get her a job here also, and that's why we both work here. It lets us to have schedules that work with the children.

Jacobo's statements indicate how family and small-scale establishments owe their success to the fact that the industry allows flexibility in hiring and in legal questions: migratory status alone does not determine whether one can work. Knowing someone or having been recommended, as well as sharing cultural traits such as a common language and community of origin, all serve to create a comfortable work environment.[11] Hiring fellow nationals fosters a discourse of *helping* or giving back to the sending community, which puts the owner's image and status in a favorable light in that community. The total community of the restaurant, therefore, creates a nostalgia for the community of origin that binds the workers and the owners together.

Yet the discourse of helping—and the nostalgia it is based upon—hides the control of costs for the growing establishment through negotiable working hours and salary rates. Since kitchen work generally does not require technical, specialized, or professional skills, its activities can be carried out by anyone. These conditions also foster a kind of continuous, legitimized exploitation by one's own community, which is disguised by shared national, regional, and/or kinship ties. Indeed, among owners of these restaurants, I was able to observe a general tendency toward exploitative working conditions that was hidden under a discourse of solidarity with their community of origin. Along these lines, Elisa, a cook and owner of a family restaurant in California, told me:

> The majority of people from my town come and devote themselves to opening a restaurant. When they go [to Mexico], they say to our compatriots: "Come on over, I'll give you a job," but for many who accept [their offer], the goal is not to stay with them. It's more like a springboard. Many people said that they didn't pay well, so they really only arrive in San Diego because they know someone there, some relatives or people from home, and that gives them a place to start. From there they go wherever they want.

The status of restaurant work as an initial form of entry into the United States, in addition to showing how family and community networks merge, also facilitates the flow of culinary information that circulates in these establishments. Essentially, people's mobility inherently enables the sharing of operational knowledge, which can then be replicated and appropriated by the cooks in these restaurants. In that setting, there are two key players who foster the exchange of culinary information: the owners, or those in charge of managerial, functional, and operating practices; and the cooks, who become part of the staff and replicate the information gained by experience during their personal migratory journeys.

FROM INFORMATION FLOW TO NEGOTIATING NOSTALGIA: THE ROLE OF PERMANENT OR LONG-TERM MIGRANTS IN THE KITCHENS

In order to explain how the question of nostalgia is negotiated in these restaurants, it is necessary to identify the structure that facilitates the restaurants' operational processes. First, the permanent or long-term migrants are part of an organization in which culinary knowledge has already been systematized, and their power base depends on the demonstration of such knowledge. Their importance lies in the transmission of knowledge and the ways in which they use it for management, training, and delegating tasks to their fellow countrymen, who work as food preparers, helpers, dishwashers, busboys, and servers in the same establishment.

When Victor, the manager of a small restaurant in Chicago, was showing me how they make large quantities of rice and explaining the difficulty of getting it to turn out right, he asked Salvador, the dishwasher, if he was busy. When Salvador replied that he was available, Victor called him over to help cook the rice. When Salvador went back to his workstation, Victor told me: "This young guy is being taken advantage of. I'm teaching him so that he'll be able to work in the kitchen soon, or, if he wants to leave here, at least he'll know how to do a few things."

With respect to the relationship between permanent and temporary migrants who join a business, preferential treatment can sometimes result from being related by blood, or from having common cultural characteristics, food customs, or a shared place of origin with the other workers. These connections afford more autonomy to the migrant who has been recently assigned to culinary tasks. This in turn promotes the exchange of culinary information. Linda, the owner of a restaurant in Chicago, made this comment about the cook who had leaned out the pass-through window from the kitchen: "This cook hasn't been with us long, but even though he's quiet he's a good guy. He's from Guerrero, and he already showed us how to make a mole sauce [a traditional sauce made with ground chiles, seeds, and spices] and a fish dish the way they're made in his village, and we've added them to the menu." In this case, the cook represented an embodiment of a particular culinary practice affiliated with a particular Mexican community. The addition of another regional cuisine in this case was considered an asset, as opposed to the situation where the definition of true Mexican chicken soup was in contest.

The cook's contribution to menu development through his particular *sazón* memory gave him agency, empowered him as an agent of culinary information, and created a comfortable atmosphere that reinforced the dynamic of closeness between the actors who work together in the restaurant. Tere, who was able to start her own business in Houston when she got divorced, explains: "The goal was to form a good team. What I wanted was to make a really big family. I try to make sure that the new arrivals feel good—the cooks, the young women who work as waitresses, everyone. Even those who leave almost always come back. If they happen to get pregnant or get married, they come back later. I haven't fired anyone." Although Tere's statements make it clear that she wishes to treat the workers as part of an extended family to guarantee a harmonious atmosphere in the restaurant, it's hard not to overlook the paternalistic character of her words. Among the proprietors of family-owned and small restaurants, I found that there exists a generalized discourse around the notion of treating workers like members of the family in order to justify the unstable working conditions that are found in most of these establishments. Nevertheless, the recent arrivals accept such conditions because these restaurants represent their first foray into the U.S. job market. For this reason, staff turnover is a recurrent phenomenon in Mexican restaurants in the United States, a fact that—like the exploitation of the newly arrived workers—belies the idea of solidarity through shared nostalgia.

The circulation of *sazón* memory through the body of restaurant workers means that restaurants become sites of cultural diffusion that set up channels for the circulation and appropriation of culinary information. In such settings, information is constantly refreshed due to the arrival of new individuals with new *sazón* memories who facilitate the exchange of information in the kitchens. However, these processes are not carried out in a systematic way, since often these establishments are the migrants' first experience in a kitchen outside of the domestic environment.

From Nostalgia to Agency: The Development
of *Sazón* by Cooks at the Individual Level

What happens when new migrants enter the world of food preparation for the first time? How is this immersion experience handled when it occurs in a migratory context where personal and work lives intersect?

In order to address these questions, I analyze how the process of developing *sazón* associated with a particular form of nostalgia represents the epitome of the culinary knowledge that is put into practice in these restaurants. I take into consideration the intriguing proposal by Meredith Abarca in this volume about *culinary subjectivity*, as well as the principle of *culinary competence* that Fabio Parasecoli suggests, in which he explains how cooks draw from their memories as well as their sensory and life experiences to develop the technical skills needed for culinary work.[12]

As Abarca explains, culinary subjectivity, to a certain degree, requires the individual to carry out a thoughtful and reflective exercise about *what one was* in order to understand *what one is*, by activating both memory and sensory experience. Taking a more pragmatic approach, Parasecoli maintains that culinary competencies are a set of tools for developing skills over time, and that they acquire new meaning within the context of the migratory experience. *Sazón* memory is a kind of "sensory biography" as proposed by Phillip Vannini and his colleagues to understand how cooks manage their internal sensory registries to be able to reproduce the flavors they associate with their nostalgic memories of their home cuisine.[13] Such nostalgia is embodied in and draws on "body memory" to analyze the practices that enable cooks to develop culinary skills. Embodied nostalgia becomes culinary knowledge.[14] Thus, the references to, and constant memories of, the knowledge, flavors, practices, and culinary techniques that cooks associate with Mexico and consciously try to re-create in the United States become a way of acquiring labor skills in Mexican restaurants in the United States. The kitchens of family-owned and small-scale Mexican restaurants in the United States are stages where this nostalgia is constantly activated, due to the diffuse sensory stimuli that are released when food is being prepared. These memories, besides demonstrating a longing for home, to an extent also guide the culinary praxis of Mexican cuisine in the United States: they contribute to the development and negotiation of *sazón*.

Culinary nostalgia is relational, in that it brings the private sphere of the family into the public sphere. Josué gives an example of this when relating how a menu was created in the restaurant where he worked. The transfer of knowledge from the domestic to the public sphere was apparent from the use of key reference figures for the cooks engaged in culinary work:

> I continue to make flan (or try to) like my mom; I even make *pastel de elote* [a dish made with sweet corn, similar to cornbread] like she taught me. I still

make rice the way she taught me. . . . It's not her same seasoning but at least I use the processes that she used, to try to at least get the same results that she did . . . her advice is always foremost in my mind. . . . The other cook, a guy from Silao, added a dish [to the menu] that his mother had taught him to make. . . . Another cook, from Salvatierra, Guanajuato, remembered the dishes that his mother used to make for him, and he added those too.

Josué's narrative shows how the collectivization of individual memories facilitates the flow of culinary information in the kitchen. Thus, culinary information that crosses the border from the domestic setting to the public sphere of the restaurant promotes the systematization of nostalgia. The memories contribute an added emotional value to the sensory registry of flavors.

Additionally, the transmission of domestic knowledge to the public arena is expressed in terms of authenticity, which is a marketable value for such Mexican restaurants in the United States.[15] In the words of Elisa from California, the restaurants' success is due to the fact that they are able to reproduce the flavor of *home*: "It's the same seasoning as home, we don't know any other way to cook. If you eat a taco here, it's the same as eating one in my house. I almost always try to make food that I like, because if I like it, others will like it too. I think that's why people come back, because they see that it tastes like home. That's what people here [in the United States] look for the most." Elisa's statements return us to the initial proposal of this chapter: how crossing the geopolitical border also requires the readjustment of connections or personal associations at the national level. Thus, the flavors of home not only represent an added incentive to the cuisine, they also become a means of national identification. This phenomenon has a direct impact on how culinary work is performed in family and small-scale restaurants.

In trying to replicate the flavors of a place not physically accessible in the day-to-day experience of food preparation in Mexican restaurants in the United States, the cooks implement emotional mechanisms that govern culinary practices. These become a ritualized enactment of nostalgia in the kitchen as those moments of introspection in which nostalgia fuses with the work experience: cooks verbally express their longing for certain people, places, or situations, and the work itself becomes an act of remembrance and nostalgia. Such ritualization is made possible by the constant stimuli in the workplace; they evoke the people, places, and situations that are emotional reference points for the kitchen worker, even though they are not physically present.

Once we had finished with all the food production and no more clients were in the restaurant, I asked Elisa what else I could help her with. She began to make corn tortillas using a process that I had never seen before: the only partially cooked tortilla on the griddle was cut horizontally and spread out with a spatula to make it thinner, to be fried later. While continuing to focus on the task at hand, she said:

It's great that you're here for these few days so that you can learn how to make "*tostadas raspadas*" [fried tortillas topped with chicken, carrots, and potatoes]. Whenever I make them, you can't imagine how much they remind me of my village! I can't make too many because they get stale, that's why they aren't on the menu. But the people from Michoacán already know that I make them and they ask for them. The bad part is that they take a lot of work, and you have to get the hang of when to scrape them because you can easily burn yourself, and then they don't turn out well. Whenever I make them, I remember helping my aunt with them; she had a stand right outside her house. Even though there were a lot of eateries around there, hers always had the most customers.

Elisa's comments make clear how the techniques involved in the preparation process make up part of a sensory experience that, combined with memory, take her back to the past when she used to carry out the same operations in her village in Mexico. In producing the *tostadas raspadas*, Elisa sets in motion a combination of affective examples and sensory experiences that is triggered whenever cuisine from home is prepared. In this way, memories and sensations associated with food preparation in Mexico tend to be continually expressed when certain dishes are re-created in the United States. Accordingly, for cooks like Elisa, the success of kitchen labor is determined by the faithful replication of the flavors associated with those dishes in the communities where they originated.

Attaining the flavors that are etched in the cook's sensory biography denotes him or her as an agent of creative process, and this has the power to transport both the cook and the potential client back to their community of origin. The food preparer who successfully manages to transfer his or her own *sazón* from the domestic to the public sphere is empowered and given agency. Such a cook can bring the memories of a community to life, and that translates into social recognition. A unique feature of the immigrant kitchen is that it is also a lab for sensory experimentation. This allows the cooks to be on a continuous quest to reproduce flavors from home, in spite of the fact that the process of food preparation in the restaurant setting is not the same as a home kitchen. As a result of the accessibility of ingredients and their organoleptic properties, the cook starts up a sensory machine. It runs on memory and helps the cook develop a personal creative process—based on his or her own memory bank.

As Abarca states in her paradigm of the epistemology of the senses, sensory approximations are the first step in determining how a cook will alter the flavor.[16] By means of this memory bank, the cook can judge the degree to which the original recipe should be followed, and can also predict the possible favorable or unfavorable effects of changing the dish. Then, using the memories in his or her sensory biography as a reference, the cook adapts the ingredients at hand to re-create the flavors of each dish, as can be seen in the following testimony: "I began to make mole here, but not only did it not turn out the same (I don't know if it

was the chiles or what), I also couldn't find everything it needed. One day I realized that it lacked a bit of sweetness, and it occurred to me that I could add just a
tiny bit of Coca-Cola. Since that day, I make it like that. I just have to let it cook a
bit longer on a low heat, without letting it boil. Many people come back for [my]
enchiladas de mole because they say it tastes like the mole from over there." Crossing the border—and thus confronting challenges of procurement[17]—encourages
creativity in culinary practices. The desire to re-create certain flavors associated
with Mexico gives the cook the freedom to experiment and be creative, and this
shows the ways in which memory becomes flexible, along with the flexible work
processes of Mexican restaurants. Essentially, the attempt to re-create dishes in
itself creates a new culinary order: new ways of preparing food are adopted, and
new ingredients are added to the internal registries of *Mexican flavors*, which are
then traced back to the flavors of home.

The discussion so far has focused on the cooks who already had some degree
of experience in the kitchen before immigrating. However, what happens to
migrants who have their first contact with culinary processes after they arrive?
In this case, they employ mnemonic techniques, rooted in body memory, to try
to reproduce the flavors. From this perspective, it is clear that the use of *body
memory*, based on mnemonics, is used to evoke physical similarities in taste.
These help the cook who has little or no experience to replicate operational processes, to be creative, and to approximate the *sazón* they seek. This strategy for
reproducing the necessary steps becomes legitimized within the memory bank of
the cook's sensory biography. In this sense, Luz, the cook from Houston, narrates
how her brother with little experience in the kitchen was able to re-create a salsa,
and how this accomplishment improved his social situation:

> My brother works in a kitchen, and it's going well for him. He started in a
> Mexican [restaurant], and began to make a few things, you should have seen
> him. Back in Mexico he would not have stepped into the kitchen, but he called
> all my aunts from here so that they could explain everything to him. He made
> a really good salsa that's only made in the tiny village we come from between
> Morelos and Guerrero. They gave him the recipe, and he started making it in
> the restaurant, using what my aunts had told him and from what he remem-
> bered seeing our mother do at home. He kept trying it until he got it right.
> Some Arab clients tasted it and they liked it so much that they invited him
> to go work in their restaurant. He says it was because of the salsa; they even
> offered to take care of his immigration papers so that he could stay on as
> their chef.

As noticed in Luz's account, culinary knowledge and its material expression in
reproducing recipes become a market commodity and a form of mobility for
those cooks who are able to re-create the food and flavors of Mexico.

Those who manage to develop their own style of cooking and are capable of replicating certain flavors acquire a work skill that can be thought of in terms of agency. The cooks must master and systematize the process of experimentation by faithfully reproducing the flavors recorded in their individual memory banks, and by taking maximum advantage of the equipment and ingredients that are at their disposal. Their *sazón* becomes the skill of transforming nostalgia into knowledge. This information becomes part of a corpus of culinary knowledge and technical skills that are highly valued in the transmigration context, where faithfully re-creating the flavors of the homeland can yield, in practical terms, recognition.

Inside the kitchen, being perceived as someone who works efficiently and has developed a recognizable personal style conveys more status to the cook. The conscious use of culinary skills adds value to the cook's work. In the case of cooks who are employees, it helps them move up the kitchen hierarchy and earn a higher income. For the restaurant owner, having an expert cook who can successfully reproduce the flavors of Mexico guarantees a constant flow of clients, which strengthens the business.

However, this explicit recognition can produce tensions in the workplace. The fact that one cook is given enhanced status can foment hostility and envy among others who work in the same restaurant. This can result in mistreatment, as shown in the following situation that took place in Houston. In a family restaurant there, I witnessed how the cook, Sara, made rice. I asked her how she could cook more than 2 kilos at once and still manage to produce rice with such good texture:

You should have seen how hard it was! I came here and nobody knew how to do it. In Mexico I was a secretary and I didn't know how to cook—I always bought [prepared] food because I didn't have time. When I came here [to work in the taco restaurant] there was a woman who was a real know-it-all, and she made fun of me because I didn't know how to make rice. She said that she was the *queen* of rice, that everyone loved hers. One would think that by virtue of being Mexican, a fellow Mexican would lend you a hand, and even more so because most of the people here are from a small town. You know what we say there, that small-town folk are very nice, but this lady wasn't like that. On her day off it was my job to make the rice and I didn't know how. So I asked her how to do it. Can you believe that she gave me the wrong recipe? The next day she said to me, your rice turned out really bad. That was when I realized she had given me the wrong recipe. Without her realizing it, I began to notice that she put in a little more of this or a little more of that. I saw, for example, that she put in a lot more oil than she had told me, and that's why the rice turned out so well for her. Little by little I learned how to do it and I got over my fear, until it started to turn out well for me.

As shown by Sara's statement, one's culinary competence through *sazón* memory becomes a means of gaining recognition, allowing cooks to gain status in the workplace. But when these cooks realize how easily the final product can be reproduced by their peers, tensions are created.

Such tensions can trigger a new social dynamic that determines how workers interact in the culinary setting. Although the transmission of knowledge opens a channel for the flow of culinary information, it also allows recipes to be treated as goods that are susceptible to plagiarism. Saul, a circular migrant, narrates the following account about his aunt's business in northern Texas:

> My aunt was the first to start making *gorditas de revoltillo* [a dish of scrambled eggs and spicy salsa] when she opened her business there. She showed a few cooks how to make gorditas with the same seasoning that the people here [in Mexico] use. Now in all the Mexican restaurants in her town you can find *gorditas de revoltillo*. The cooks learned how to make them, and after quitting, they left to go make them somewhere where they are paid a little more. They're practically selling her recipe for less than a dollar and that's not right.

Demonstrating one's expertise takes on a material form when explored in terms of *sazón*, and also in terms of agency. However, the agency built up in the kitchen becomes vulnerable in the work context, because embodied culinary competence is mobile. José, the owner of a restaurant in Chicago, expressed his discontent with employee turnover and how it impedes culinary efficiency: "The bad thing is that [the cooks] don't stay long, and then new ones come that don't know how to do anything; they only know how to serve food, or open cans. Then they take what they've learned here and try to open their own businesses." Migrants who are new additions to the labor force are active players that perform culinary functions. This kind of migrant is a key individual in re-creating flavors, due to the knowledge they acquired either in Mexico or in other Mexican restaurants in the United States.

In the same way, they are agents for the circulation and transmission of knowledge about how other restaurants are run, as Tere states when speaking about the concept of her *taquería*:

> He [her ex-husband] was a taco-maker at another Mexican restaurant, he was really good. He had been operating the griddle for about seven years. The restaurant he worked in was always full, and he worked the griddle. But when he came here [to the United States] he didn't know anything, everything he knows he learned here. He learned to be a taco-maker here in Houston, back there he didn't know anything. After three months of marriage, we decided to take a chance and open a *taquería*. He went for it and I supported him, because he knew all the tricks, and knew the menu backwards and forwards. As a matter of fact, the menu we have comes from "Jalisco," one of the first [Mexican]

restaurants in Houston. It's the most traditional, it's like the *taquerías* down there in Jalisco. I had worked as a waitress in other restaurants here. I also knew the business of running a dining room.

The circulation of information for the systematization of culinary knowledge is neither fluid nor completely explicit. On the contrary, many times the turnover of personnel brings tensions between workers and bosses, producing questions of who should possess and use culinary knowledge. Jorge, owner of a Mexican restaurant, expressed the following with obvious anger: "There's nothing that disturbs an owner more than when an employee who worked in the kitchen—above all a cook—leaves and opens his own place, and copies the recipes. As a regular customer, you know when the chef changes." Beyond the negotiations and tensions inside the kitchen, the exchange of culinary information allows for the creation of an original cuisine that is constantly adapting. The fluidity of this cuisine, thanks to the negotiating of the *sazón*, points to the creation of an original cuisine classified as "Mexican" in restaurants the United States.

The Flow of Information within the Restaurant Kitchens: The Creation of an Original Mexican Cuisine in the United States

Due to the flow of culinary information, as well as the adaptations undergone by a migrating Mexican cuisine, the United States has seen the evolution of an original Mexican cuisine, one that is recognized and accepted by food preparers and Mexican consumers as a cuisine in its own right. During its formation, negotiating the *sazón* is the creative process carried out by cooks to replicate various flavors. Although these flavors adapt to the context in which they are being prepared, they still follow the original cuisine's principles of seasoning as practiced in Mexico. In this sense, Arjun Appadurai points out that in the current global environment, the shaping of national cuisines needs to be viewed within the framework of the contemporary order: they do not remain static in a single territory.[18] As Parasecoli explains, migrating cuisines "undergo various degrees of transformation due to the availability of ingredients, the exposure to different flavors and techniques and the need to adapt to a dissimilar rhythm of life."[19] Abarca analyzes this phenomenon in the transborder domestic spheres where an original cuisine is developing that could be accepted as a typical Mexican cuisine that reflects the cultural fluctuations faced by migrants.[20] Such a cuisine consists of examples of the original cuisine prepared in Mexico, but incorporates new ingredients and culinary equipment in its preparation. Furthermore, it is forming under U.S. standardization processes, and this requires a rethinking of the culinary grammar.

In the public domain of restaurants, in addition to strengthening migratory networks, this phenomenon brings other processes into the kitchen: the exchange of culinary information and the creation of new dishes that are developed as a result of the synthesis of culinary knowledge. As Rosy from Chicago explains: "Here some of us cook one way and some another. Gradually our methods combine all together. People come with different seasonings, different ways. But it's OK, we learn from everyone. We have a lady here from Veracruz and another from Puebla. They taught us how to make *mole* as it's made where they come from. We showed them how to make *asado* [barbecued beef or pork]. In the end, I think they made *asado* better than we did." Recipes can thus be considered decipherable codes for the purposes of replicating them, but they are also permeated by the environments in which they're being prepared.[21]

Something like a culinary grammar—an accepted order that regulates how a specific group cooks and eats—arises. In the context of the United States, established standards, from the preparation and serving of food, to portion size and courtesies extended to clients, shape this grammar. These aspects account for a restructuring that makes use of the standards on time, timing, portions, and types of service seen in the United States. This is explicitly noted by José, owner of the Chicago establishment:

> You'll notice that everything here comes with rice and beans, even the *antojitos* [a generic name for corn-base dishes, central to the Mexican national diet]. You can't serve small portions here, they give you a lot of food everywhere. I think that's why in all the Mexican restaurants you have to serve rice and beans. You always have to add a lot of sauce. In addition, you can't leave out the pico de gallo, guacamole and sour cream to accompany everything. Wherever you go, you'll find it—all the Mexican restaurants do it. We have some Mexicans here who do not eat chile, so you have to make the dishes so they taste just like in Mexico, but also be sure not to make them too spicy or they won't come back.

José's comments exemplify how culinary orders are being restructured. This restructuring shows the negotiating that cooks must do in order to get started in the U.S. food industry.

Along with the legitimizing process for Mexican cuisine in the United States comes the creation of dishes that follow the principles of seasoning and the preparation techniques commonly used in Mexico, while acquiring variations that allow them to be considered original dishes. Such dishes are the result of the continuous cross-border flow and exchange of culinary information by migrants with diverse backgrounds and different ways of cooking in Mexico. They carry this information along, and help create a unique cuisine formed by the synthesis of regional cuisines that come together in the restaurant kitchens.

BEYOND THE LINE: RETHINKING THE BORDER IN CULINARY PRACTICES

The cooking "line" is the last frontier that separates the kitchen from the dining room or from the service area. The cooks are on the line to transform ingredients into dishes. In one kitchen, not all the workers are allowed to go beyond the preparation line. The line is also the border that divides two countries. In both worlds, it is the last point from which a different reality can be seen.

In sum, the negotiations of geopolitical, symbolic, and temporary borders demonstrate the complexity of preparing food in a context of transnational migration. The manifestation of social dynamics in the kitchen encourages a rethinking of territories and territorialities with regard to culinary practices. Food preparation as a social fact becomes more complex when placed in the migratory context, where cuisine can impact, and be impacted by, the personal and collective influences of the migrant subjects. In small-scale and family-owned restaurants in the United States, an original cuisine is evolving that expresses the culinary nostalgia felt by its preparers. They are developing a Mexican cuisine with its own unique traits, one that is being created beyond the territorial limits of the Mexican nation-state.

NOTES

1. In this chapter, family restaurants are fixed establishments controlled by a nuclear family, with or without the involvement of members of the extended family. The culinary work and service are established, although they may be flexible. Each social actor has an assigned function, although he or she can get involved in other functions. Food preparation and service are not standardized, although the tasks that each person has are well established. There is no strategic planning for the menu planning or for cost control. The menu can change depending on the accessibility of the products used. Small-scale restaurants might have begun as family restaurants that, due to expansion as a result of success and affluence, require a greater number of staff who are not necessarily family members. Duties are distributed inside and outside of the kitchen, and even though it is less flexible, the culinary tasks are redistributed when someone leaves the job. There is a common hierarchy, with a cook in charge (but not a chef) and a couple of multifunctional helpers. The processes of preparation, presentation, and service tend to lack rigorous standardization.

2. As Meredith Abarca notes, translating the word "*sazón*" into English is difficult. "*Sazón*" has connotations beyond the simple act of seasoning a dish, since it reflects the expertise, personal journey, and skill of the subjects who prepare food. Meredith Abarca, *Voices in the Kitchen: Views of Food and the World from Working-Class Mexican and Mexican-American Women* (Austin: University of Texas Press, 2006).

3. Jesús Contreras and Mabel Gracia, *Alimentación y Cultura: Perspectivas Antropológicas* (Barcelona: Ariel, 2005), 39–40.

4. In order to explain these processes, I undertook a culinary ethnography by working as a cook and participating observer in four family or small-scale restaurants in three different regions of the United States: the San Joaquin Valley in California, metropolitan Chicago, and Houston, Texas. I also completed semistructured interviews in Mexico and the United States as complements to my observations. In Mexico, I interviewed returning migrants who had worked as cooks in small Mexican restaurants in the United States. In the United States, I interviewed other social agents who were key to the restaurants' operation: owners of the

establishments, service personnel, and a few regular clients. The fieldwork was carried out during 2012 and 2013.

5. Gary Alan Fine, *Kitchens: The Culture of Restaurant Work* (Berkeley: University of California Press, 2009).

6. Jean Pierre Hassoun, "Restaurant dans la Ville? Monde Doceurs et Amertumes," *Ethnologie Francaise* 44.1 (2014): 5–10.

7. Sylvia Ferrero, "Comida sin Par: Consumption of Mexican Food in Los Angeles: 'Foodscapes' in a Transnational Consumer Society," in *Food Nations: Selling Taste in Consumer Societies*, ed. Warren Belasco and Philip Scranton (New York: Routledge, 2009), 202.

8. Ruth Gomberg-Muñoz, *Labor and Legality: An Ethnography of a Mexican Immigrant Network* (New York: Oxford University Press, 2011).

9. Liliana Rivera defines nodes or nodal points as physical or symbolic spaces that assemble and distribute the flow of people, money, capital, and symbolic goods, and that further allow interconnections between migratory and work trajectories in the context of transnational migration between Mexico and the United States. Liliana Rivera, "La Geografía de los Flujos y los Sitios Articuladores en un Circuito Migratorio Complejo: Avances de Investigación," in *Migración, Procesos Productivos, Identidad y Estigmas Sociales: Lecturas desde la Antropología*, coord. Juan Cajas (Ciudad de México: Universidad Autónoma del Estado de Morelos, 2010), 37.

10. Some of the names that appear in this text were changed to protect the confidentiality of my subjects.

11. Anuradha Basu, "Immigrant Entrepreneurs in the Food Sector: Breaking the Mould," in *Food and the Migrant Experience*, ed. Anne J. Kershe (Aldershot: Ashgate, 2002), 149–167.

12. Fabio Parasecoli, *Bite Me: Food in Popular Culture* (New York: Berg, 2008).

13. A sensory biography is the series of sensorial memories with specific meanings in the life trajectory of the subject who has experienced them. In this way, the perception of meaning attached to sensorial stimuli is part of the individuality of the subject, due to the affective associations involved. Phillip Vannini, Deniss Waskul, and Simon Gottschalk, *The Senses in Self, Society and Culture: A Sociology of the Senses* (New York: Routledge, 2014).

14. Paul Connerton states that the body is a receptacle for memory that allows the execution of certain actions and practices learned or perceived in the past that can be used as a skill for dealing with some situations in the present. Paul Connerton, *How Societies Remember* (Cambridge: Cambridge University Press, 1989), 72.

15. Jeffrey Pilcher, *Planet Taco: A Global History of Mexican Food* (Oxford: Oxford University Press, 2012).

16. Abarca, *Voices in the Kitchen*.

17. See the chapter in this volume by Tanachai Mark Padoongpatt.

18. Arjun Appadurai, "How to Make a National Cuisine: Cookbooks in Contemporary India," *Comparative Studies in Society and History* 30 (2008): 3–24.

19. Fabio Parasecoli, "Food, Identity and Cultural Reproduction in Immigrant Communities," *Social Research* 81 (2014): 420

20. Meredith Abarca, "Authentic or Not, It's Original," *Food and Foodways Explorations in the History and Culture* 12.1 (2004): 1–25.

21. Priscilla Ferguson, "Culinary Nationalism," *Gastronomica: The Journal of Food and Culture* 10 (2010): 102–109.

CHAPTER 5

"Chasing the Yum"

FOOD PROCUREMENT AND THAI
AMERICAN COMMUNITY FORMATION
IN AN ERA BEFORE FREE TRADE

Tanachai Mark Padoongpatt

The grand opening of the Bangkok Market in Hollywood, California, in 1971 marked a watershed moment in the history of Thai food culture and Thai American community formation in the United States. Pramorte "Pat" Tilakamonkul, a Thai immigrant who arrived in Los Angeles at the age of twenty-six, opened the grocery store on the northwest corner of Melrose Ave. and N. Harvard Blvd. Inside, small checkout counters with conveyor belts partitioned the cozy store into two sections. Five aisles lined the west end, with a produce aisle stocked with Thai basil, kaffir limes, golf-ball-size greenish-white Thai eggplant, lemongrass, jackfruit, and green papaya, to name a few. In the other aisles sat sixteen types of canned curry paste; different varieties of smoked, pickled, or dried fish in bags, cans, or freezer packs; and high-quality long-grain white and flavored rice in 25-, 50-, and 100-pound bags. On the east end of the store, customers could find Thai butchers behind the meat counter preparing cuts of beef, pork, chicken, and assorted organ meats next to a wide array of seafood imported from Asia and a variety of fresh fish not available elsewhere in Los Angeles.[1] It was the first of its kind.

This article explores the acquisition of Thai foodstuffs, or food procurement, as a Thai American community building practice in Los Angeles. Focusing on U.S. trade policy and barriers from the 1960s to the 1980s, the era before free trade under the North American Free Trade Agreement (NAFTA), it analyzes shifting trade conditions that shaped the pursuit of Thai food. Before the Bangkok Market opened its doors in the early 1970s, most Thai and Southeast Asian produce and ingredients were not widely available in Los Angeles. As a result, early Thai home cooks, chefs, and restaurateurs turned to local ingredients to simulate Thai flavors in dishes. However, as they tried to reproduce the complex

and balanced Thai flavor profile of salty, sour, sweet, creamy, and of course hot/
spicy—or "yum"—the lack of Thai and Southeast Asian ingredients exacerbated
the crisis of identity among a geographically dispersed Thai immigrant population. To illustrate how and why Thais worked to resolve this crisis through food
procurement, I chart the first wave of Thai migration and settlement patterns
in Los Angeles spurred by U.S. Cold War intervention in Thailand, detail Thai
migrants' attempts to re-create Thai dishes in Los Angeles, and then examine
Thai entrepreneurs who worked to establish a local supply of Thai and Southeast
Asian ingredients by opening grocery stores and creating import/export companies that connected Thailand, Los Angeles, Fresno, and Mexico.[2]

A number of scholars have examined the way racial and ethnic populations
employed food to shape communities and identities throughout U.S. history.[3]
Whereas most tend to treat cooking and gustatory consumption as the most
important aspects of community building and identity formation, I argue that
there is much to be gained by focusing on procurement.[4] In this chapter, food
procurement expands and nuances our understanding of the way borders shape
social relations and impact people's lives. To get at how central procurement was,
historically, to community formation I ask: what did securing "proper" ingredients mean for early Thai immigrants in Los Angeles? In what ways did procuring Thai foodstuffs contribute to Thai American community building and
formation? For Thai immigrants, tracking down and securing a supply of
"authentic" ingredients were integral to the reconstruction of "wholeness" at a
moment of physical and social dislocation in a new environment.[5] Taste and flavor were therefore essential to processes of Thai American community and identity formation, both real and imagined. In addition, food procurement was a
collective effort that brought people together and cultivated social and economic
networks, and was crucial to the development of early Thai America because
Thais had very few formal organizations (labor unions, political groups, social
clubs), cultural activities, or community spaces that could otherwise bring
them together.

But this story is not about food and community formation alone. The Bangkok Market helped create the conditions of possibility for Thai food culture in
the United States and thus the formation of a Thai American community centered on foodways. It is because Tilakamonkul and his business partners negotiated the web of U.S. trade policies and barriers that the Bangkok Market came
into existence, Thai restaurants opened, and Thai dishes prepared without using
too many substitute ingredients—all of which allowed community to form.
Most important, an emphasis on procurement highlights the significance and
saliency of U.S. borders in the making and defining of Thai food culture in Los
Angeles. On the one hand, Thai migration was a product of the United States
expanding its influence beyond its borders into Thailand. U.S. intervention in
Thailand during the Cold War, coupled with U.S. immigration policies, directly

shaped a Thai migration pattern characterized by large numbers of Thais who gained entry with legal student and tourist visas. On the other hand, borders also determined Thai immigrants' access to foodstuffs from Thailand and Southeast Asia. The U.S. nation-state, through a tangled network of import trade regulations, government agencies, and free trade zones, regulated when, where, and how "foreign" foodstuffs entered the country. Yet policymakers, scientists, and inspectors working for these entities did more than just patrol U.S. border spaces for prohibited food. They also influenced, both discursively and in their maintenance of the border, notions of nation, citizenship, and belonging by linking these concepts to food safety and public health.

THAI STUDENTS TASTE LOS ANGELES

Thais began arriving to the United States in large numbers during the late 1950s. The first wave occurred between 1945 and 1965 and was made up primarily of male government officials, political elites, and formally educated middle-class Thais from urban Bangkok. The second wave happened after the passage of the Hart-Cellar Act, or the Immigration and Nationality Act of 1965. This second wave altered gender and class dynamics among Thai Americans because it included a significantly higher number of women, younger migrants, tourists, and students, and a lower number of professionals. Between 1965 and 1975, Thais arrived at a rate higher than any other immigrant group, as the United States admitted a total of 25,705 Thai immigrants, 95,183 Thai non-immigrants, and 396 Thai Americans.[6] By the late 1970s, there were an estimated 100,000 Thai immigrants and Thai Amerians in the United States.[7]

Unlike other Southeast Asians who entered the United States during this period, Thais were not refugees fleeing war or political strife. However, U.S. foreign policy and militarization in Southeast Asia did, in fact, facilitate Thai migration to the United States. From the 1950s to the 1970s, the United States established a U.S. embassy and the Southeast Asian Treaty Organization headquarters in Bangkok as well as military bases (especially air bases) throughout the country. At the same time, the U.S. State Department also engaged in "cultural diplomacy" by developing educational and cultural exchange programs through organizations such as the Peace Corps and Fulbright Foundation. This intervention opened the way for the arrival of thousands of U.S. state and military officials, businessmen, educators, students, volunteers, and tourists to Thailand.

The U.S. presence in Thai society played a profound part in the demographic composition of Thai America. For example, the restructuring of Thailand's education system along American lines allowed young Thais to learn about U.S. culture and society through interactions with U.S. citizens and firsthand experience in exchange programs. These encounters encouraged middle-class Thais to pursue student visas to study in the United States. By the 1970s, roughly 30,000

Thai students were enrolled in colleges and universities across the United States.[8] While certainly a "middle-class" migration, many Thais would eventually use these "nonimmigrant" student visas as a way to bypass stricter immigration requirements and settle in the country.[9] About 42 percent of Thai immigrant women who arrived between 1965 and 1975 entered as wives of U.S. citizens, typically American GIs.[10]

Initially, Thais settled in different parts of the United States and therefore did not establish a distinct or sizable "ethnic enclave." The top destination for Thais was California, followed by Massachusetts, Connecticut, New York, Michigan, Illinois, Ohio, Texas, and Florida.[11] The early settlement pattern reflected the impact of U.S. intervention on Thai migration. Thais typically lived where they studied—near college or university campuses that granted them student visas. In addition, the Thai women married to American GIs and other U.S. citizens found themselves in large cities as well as small towns far away from other Thais.[12]

But by the early 1970s, Los Angeles became home to the largest Thai population in the United States and outside of Thailand. The number of Thais in Los Angeles (including those without legal status) grew from 300 to 400 in 1965 to an estimated 40,000 by the late 1970s.[13] Although early studies reasoned that Thais settled in Los Angeles because of warm climate "comfortable for Asian people" and the city's reputation for racial/ethnic diversity, given Thai migration patterns across the United States more broadly it is more likely that Los Angeles's large number of colleges, universities, and trade and adult schools served as the primary "pull" factor.[14] Indeed, the top destinations after California were New York, Illinois, Ohio, Michigan, Connecticut, and Massachusetts—which were not necessarily places where Thais found a warm climate or racial and ethnic anonymity. What these places had were colleges and universities. So as with national patterns, early Thai settlement in Los Angeles also did not resemble an ethnic enclave. Rather, it was scattered—at times 30 miles apart—as Thai students lived mostly near their respective campuses and schools.

Even though American intervention in Thailand familiarized Thais with U.S. culture and society, the migration and scattered settlement pattern led to a jarring sense of disjunction and fragmentation. As a result, life for Thai students consisted of going to school, working low-wage part-time jobs, and social isolation. According to geographer Jacqueline Desbarats, who examined Thai migration patterns closely during this period, Thai students often found college to be more academically demanding and financially burdensome than they anticipated. Since many had to pay for their education with family or personal funds, a number were forced to either drop out of school or violate the terms of their I-20 student visas to find unskilled and underpaid employment.[15] Urai Ruenprom, who arrived in Los Angeles in 1964 at the age of thirty-six, recalled having to attend 8 a.m. classes at Los Angeles City College then work full time as a hotel janitor until 11 p.m., four days a week, to pay for and complete his studies.[16] To

help alleviate loneliness, students like Ruenprom established informal social networks as well as formal organizations such as the Thai Association of Southern
California, which was established in 1961 (as Thai Student Association of Southern California) to help increase sociability and promote unity among Thais.[17]

Yet perhaps the most disappointing part of life in the United States for Thai
students was the absence of Thai food. As a result, they were forced to try a variety
of other cuisines. Thai students found "American" fare—typically steaks, ham-
burgers, and sandwiches—to be good, but too bland. And even though many
in Thailand associated the consumption of steak in America with wealth and
high social status, the flavor profile of a grilled or pan-fried cut of red meat was
relatively basic (seasoned mainly with salt, pepper, and butter) in comparison
to Thai-style beef dishes, such as *sueh long hai* (crying tiger) and *nue nam tok*
(waterfall beef). Malulee Pinsuvana, an "expert in Thai cooking" from Thailand
who traveled often to the U.S. West Coast, including to Los Angeles, witnessed
firsthand during this period the unsatisfied craving among her compatriots. In
her cookbook, *Cooking Thai Food in American Kitchens*, Pinsuvana asserted: "I
understand the longing of so many Thais living there [Phoenix and Los Angeles]
for their native food. It is not that American food is not good, or that other types
of food, Mexican, French, Italian and Chinese to name a few are not delicious,
but their taste is not quite satisfying enough. In other words, Thais must have
Thai food."[18] The closest the students could get to Thai food was Chinese food.
But the flavor profile of most Chinese dishes at the time, which were Cantonese,
was salty, sweet, sour, pungent, and sometimes bitter.[19] So while similar, Chinese
food was distinctly different from the more expansive "yum" that typified Thai
cooking: salty, sweet, sour, creamy, and hot/spicy.[20]

The yearning for "yum" reflected not simply a craving for better-tasting and
therefore more-satisfying food. It was also informed by a desire to reconnect
with Thailand, which was critical as a way to alleviate feelings of isolation, loneliness, and disruption caused by migration. Thai food represented a tangible way
for Thais in Los Angeles to re-create and relive a familiar, comforting Thailand
displaced in time and space. Most important, it had the power to aid this nostalgia neurologically through taste and smell. Meredith Abarca and others have
demonstrated that while there is indeed a strong relationship between food and
emotional memory, it is the combination and interplay between gustatory (taste,
texture) and olfactory senses (smell), what David Sutton calls "synesthesia,"
that serve as a conduit to emotions and memories in the brain.[21] Drawing on
recent studies in neurogastronomy, Abarca explains in her essay that the "sensory
stimuli caused from eating or drinking affects the function of the hippocampus,"
a region of the brain that is critical to the formation of memories as well as "part
of the limbic system responsible for the regulation of drives and emotions."[22]

The power of food to trigger emotional memories in the brain, according
to Abarca, also cultivates the formation of individual "palate memories" and

subjectivities that become central to a group's shared sensory collective memory and speak to "lived (hi)stories" and a "kind of intimate bond with food and diet molded by material circumstances."[23] Ultimately, the craving for authentic Thai flavors captures the power and significance of the sensory experience of eating. Along with social and symbolic meaning, eating evokes, neurologically, food memories from the homeland. Having the right ingredients and foodstuffs to re-create "yum," then, became extremely critical as the craving could only be effectively satiated through gustatory and olfactory consumption.

Thus, even without Thai restaurants or grocery stores in Los Angeles where they could get the key ingredients to make Thai cuisine, Thai students began re-creating their own versions of Thai dishes at home. One of the more popular dishes was *moo tod gratiem prik Thai* (garlic and white pepper pork) over white rice. Another dish was boiled eggs with chili paste over rice. Soon, a number of Thai students started hosting Thai potluck dinner parties that allowed them to connect and socialize with fellow classmates and, occasionally, non-Thai English-language teachers whom they often invited to the gatherings. A few capitalized on their culinary skills and the demand for Thai food. In fact, Thai college students appear to have been the first to open and operate Thai restaurants in the United States. While no definitive record exists on when and where the first Thai restaurant opened (though it was in Southern California), we do know that early restaurants were temporary, mostly small makeshift shops intended to serve a Thai student clientele that planned to return to Thailand once they completed their studies.[24] One example is Surapol Mekpongsatorn, who opened a noodle stand near the University of California–Los Angeles (UCLA) sometime in the early 1960s. His noodle soups sold well enough that he once boasted to friends that he made "so much cash he had to sleep on it under his bed."[25] Some Thais even remember placing lunch orders with a Thai couple, Arunee and Udom, who took phone orders during the evening, prepared the lunches, and then delivered them to worksites the next day. The question is: where did they get the ingredients to prepare these dishes?

CHASING THE "YUM"

Anyone who created, or attempted to create, Thai dishes in 1960s Los Angeles procured ingredients in three main ways. First, they substituted ingredients available in local supermarkets for Thai ones. Marie Wilson's *Siamese Cookery* (1965), the very first Thai cookbook printed in the United States, reflects this approach while underscoring the scarcity of Thai ingredients. Wilson, a homemaker from West Los Angeles, became smitten with Thai food after she traveled to Thailand in the 1950s to marry her fiancé, who was teaching English in Bangkok as a Fulbright scholar. Consider her recipe for "Khrung Kaeng," or Shrimp Curry:

1 tbsp. ground coriander

1 tbsp. ground caraway seed

1 tsp. turmeric; 1 tsp. pepper

¼ tsp. cayenne pepper

½ tsp. freshly grated nutmeg

2 tbsp. anchovy paste

2 tsp. vinegar

Combine coriander, caraway, turmeric, pepper, cayenne, nutmeg and blend. Add anchovy paste and vinegar and mix well. Store in a small airtight jar in refrigerator.[26]

Here, Wilson's recipe suggests using anchovy paste to capture the saltiness of fish sauce and cayenne pepper for the spiciness of Thai chili peppers.[27] In addition, when she told her Thai friends in the United States about using sour cream in place of coconut cream for Thai curry dishes, she said they "approved enthusiastically as soon as they tasted a curry made with it."[28] Wilson's Thai friends, however, had already been experimenting with cow's milk, sweet cream, and buttermilk to replace coconut cream/milk. Thais especially relied on Chinese ingredients to simulate Thai flavors. They shopped at Chinese groceries in Chinatown, such as the well-known and well-stocked Yee Sing Chong supermarket, to buy produce, sauces, rice, and other foodstuffs along with utensils and dishware. But while they could easily find soy sauce in stores, staples like Thai fish sauce and curry paste, which served as the base for all Thai curries, were not available.[29]

Another common practice was to pack dried and canned goods as well as fruits and vegetables and bring them into the United States—legally and illegally. Although U.S. Customs did allow Thais to enter the country with certain foodstuffs, typically canned and processed foods, only a small amount intended for personal use was admissible. Almost all plants and produce were prohibited or required an import permit. Faced with these restrictions, small cohorts of Thai entrepreneurs began smuggling banned ingredients by traveling back to Thailand to collect plants, fruits, and vegetables native to Southeast Asia such as lemongrass, galanga, and Thai basil (as well as seeds) and sneaking them into the United States inside suitcases.[30] Therefore, producing the complex and balanced Thai flavor profile in dishes required more than just creativity, ingenuity, and a skilled palate—but participation in unlawful activities. Yet attempting to smuggle Thai foodstuffs was difficult, in large part because the U.S. Customs Service had become increasingly concerned with the trafficking of narcotics and illicit drugs from Southeast Asia's "Golden Triangle."[31]

Lastly, the chase for "yum" ultimately led to the discovery of a small grove of "kaffir" lime (citrus hystrix) trees in the citrus town of Riverside, California, roughly 60 miles away from Hollywood. The kaffir lime, or *makrut*, is native to Southeast Asia and is an indispensable ingredient in Thai cuisine.[32] It is used not for the juice of the citrus fruit, which is very bitter to the taste, but instead for the pungent flavor of the zest and aromatic leaves. Some *makrut* had made its way into the United States and was donated to Riverside's Citrus Variety Collection in 1930.[33] In the 1960s, the collection, now part of the University of California–Riverside, was the only place in the country where one could find kaffir limes, as it was illegal to import Asian-grown citrus due to fears of the spread of canker disease. So when Thais in Los Angeles first learned about these *makrut* trees, they began organizing carpools to travel roughly 120 miles roundtrip—about two hours—in order to procure the prized ingredient. Once there, the group picked bunches of *bai makrut* as well as lemongrass shoots.[34] Upon returning home, they froze the leaves in plastic bags and preserved them for later use in making *nam prik pao* (chili paste) and *nam prik kaeng* (curry paste), the base components for spicy Thai stir-fry dishes, curries, and soups—namely *tom yum*.

There clearly was a shortage of Thai foodstuffs in 1960s Los Angeles. But why? One could argue that the shortage simply reflected a lack of demand given that Thais had yet to arrive in large numbers. Yet the range of procurement strategies Thais performed—substitutions, smuggling, and willingness to trek long distances—strongly suggests there was a passionate desire and that a consumer base existed, one that included non-Thais. Thus, the answer has more to do with U.S. trade policy, specifically import regulations, than with the relatively small Thai population. To be clear, U.S. trade policy on imports during this period was not heavily restrictive. On the contrary, it was as liberal or "free" as it had ever been.

In the post–World War II period, the United States joined other capitalist nations to reduce tariffs and non-tariff barriers to trade. They helped to establish and participated in the General Agreement on Tariffs and Trade (GATT), a multilateral agreement that functioned as the main entity for the regulation of world trade.[35] By the 1960s, over eighty nations participated in GATT (Thailand was not a member but adhered to its principles) as it governed an estimated 80 percent of world trade.[36] However, Congress still placed barriers and restrictions on fruits, vegetables, and plants, banning some from entry altogether, as it did with Asian-grown kaffir limes and leaves. And regardless of how liberal the trade policy, it was still necessary to have the wherewithal and knowledge to navigate the dizzying system of policies and procedures in order to make large and steady supplies of Thai and Southeast Asian foods available to consumers.

No one responded to the Thai American demand for a steady supply of Thai ingredients more than Pramorte Tilakamonkul. When Tilakamonkul opened the Bangkok Market grocery store and import company in 1971, he had been living in Los Angeles for several years and knew firsthand the dire Thai food situation.

There was only one Thai restaurant in the entire city and no grocery stores that sold Thai or Southeast Asian foodstuffs.[37] He also recognized that the Thai population in Los Angeles was growing and that it would continue to grow. Tilakamonkul's son, Jet, who grew up working in the grocery store, recalled nearly forty years later that his father "had the vision to say 'hey, there's a ton of Southeast Asian people here and we need to eat things like green papaya and long beans and jackfruit, [be]cause we don't have any.'"[38] So from the beginning Tilakamonkul very much understood food procurement as a form of community sustenance.

At the same time, of course, Tilakamonkul wanted to capitalize on a potentially lucrative economic opportunity and business niche in an industry he knew well, and one that did not require formal education or English-language skills. He certainly had the pedigree to be a food-based entrepreneur. Tilakamonkul was born in southern China's Hainan Province. He spent most of his youth, however, in urban Bangkok after his parents moved his six brothers and him from China to Thailand in the 1950s to escape Communism.[39] While in Bangkok, he grew up learning the food and restaurant business from his parents, who became restaurateurs after opening a family-operated Thai-Chinese shophouse in a predominantly Hainanese section of the city, selling food and coffee to residents in the neighborhood.[40] He would model the Bangkok Market after this shop.

By the mid-1960s Tilakamonkul decided to leave Thailand for the United States with help from his brother and Mexican sister-in-law who were already living there.[41] He arrived in Los Angeles in 1966 and settled in East Hollywood, a neighborhood with a few other Thais as well as immigrants from Latin America and Eastern Europe.[42] For Thai immigrants, the local economy at the time offered mostly low-wage, part-time, unskilled jobs with no benefits in either the growing service sector or garment work for the apparel industry. Furthermore, East Hollywood was in shambles. Global economic restructuring, deindustrialization, and the continuation of policies that funneled resources away from urban cores and to the suburbs in Los Angeles helped to produce this cheap exploitable immigrant labor pool as well as ghettoes. These conditions were, however, ripe for establishing a small retail store. Small retail operations required minimal start-up capital, paid cheap rent, and faced less competition with larger chain supermarkets typically found in white neighborhoods.

Confronting U.S. Trade Barriers

The significance of Tilakamonkul's accomplishments and why and how the Bangkok Market even came to be cannot be fully grasped without a knowledge of trade policies and conditions in the 1970s and 1980s. Tilakamonkul and other Thai food industry entrepreneurs confronted a number of problems as they tried to procure ingredients for Thai cooking in order to nurture Thai community formation in Los Angeles. Importing goods from Thailand into the United States was a process that involved an intricate global distribution network and multiple players with different, often competing, interests. First, import companies such as Bangkok Market Inc. had to purchase foodstuffs directly from overseas companies or from agents of those companies with offices in the United States. Next, importers often hired a customs broker—an independent operator to handle the logistics of planning and orchestrating the entry of goods.[43] Once the goods crossed formal U.S. boundaries, the import company could either have the customs broker arrange transportation for delivery or hire a trucking firm to drive the goods to local warehouses, from where they would ultimately be distributed to retail stores or sold to other importers. Then there was the ship itself, which functioned as a "multimillion dollar floating business" that freighted goods stored in large containers across the Pacific Ocean.[44] From 1968 to 1977, the volume of Thai foreign trade grew from roughly $1.9 million to $8 million, with agricultural products accounting for 60 percent of total export value.[45] On average, Thailand shipped 11.5 percent of exports to the United States over this period.[46] The top export items included rice, tapioca, rubber, maize, sorghum, beans (mung), tobacco leaves, and shrimp and seafood.

To import foods for his market, Tilakamonkul and his partners had to deal with the intricate labyrinth of nation-state import-export policies in both Thailand and the United States. In Thailand, the National Economic and Social Development Plans (NESDP) set the guidelines for all of Thailand's foreign trade. In the 1970s, NESDP's primary objectives were to increase export volume, seek new markets, and diversify production to create new export commodities.[47] In addition, the Ministry of Commerce was in charge of import-export control and trade promotion, while the Department of Foreign Trade dealt with export promotion, import-export licensing, and establishing standards for export products.[48] With few exceptions, Thailand's authorization system allowed companies to export commodities "freely" without undue restrictions.

The U.S. nation-state depended on an equally complex web of federal departments and agencies to make sure importers complied with existing trade laws and regulations. Whereas Congress was largely responsible for setting trade and import policies, the Food and Drug Administration (FDA), the U.S. Department of Agriculture (USDA), and the U.S. Customs Service were the key entities that administered and enforced the policies and therefore policed U.S. borders. The FDA monitored shipments of all drugs, cosmetics, and foods other than meat and poultry.[49] The USDA, on the other hand, oversaw only meat and poultry imports and in 1972, with the creation of the Animal and Plant Health Inspection Service (APHIS), also assumed the responsibility of "protecting and promoting" U.S. animal and plant health in order to safeguard U.S. agriculture from invasive foreign pests and diseases.[50] Lastly, the U.S. Customs Service, under the U.S Treasury Department, was in charge of classifying and valuing imports, determining rates and duties on imports, and collecting them. Customs also supervised the entry and unloading of vessels, vehicles, and aircraft as well as enforced laws prohibiting the importation of restricted goods, drugs, and other contraband.[51] While these entities attempted to work in concert, each operated with different resources: Customs and the USDA had computerized management systems to expedite their efforts—the FDA did not; and the USDA had goods delivered to it whereas Customs and the FDA had to travel to inspection sites.[52]

Just as Bangkok Market Inc. was trying to get established, U.S. foreign trade policy swung to a protectionist stance amid rising anti-import sentiment in the United States. The post–World War II "golden age" of American capitalism came to an abrupt halt as the country entered an economic recession. U.S. corporations saw their profits fall. Working-class living standards stagnated. At the same time, the rapid growth of capitalist systems of production around the world, particularly in Asia and the Pacific, exposed U.S. corporations to serious international competition.[53] In 1971, for the first time in the twentieth century, the United States imported more goods than it exported.

In response, support for "trade liberalization" waned among the business, labor, and agricultural communities. These groups blamed imports for the recession, sparking an economic nationalism historian Dana Frank has referred to as "one of the longest, deepest waves of Buy American campaigns in U.S. history," which encouraged U.S. consumers to buy products made only in the United States to help save jobs by fighting the encroachment of foreign-made goods at the border.[54] The debate over imported goods was also highly racialized. Asian imports, such as Japanese cars, came to represent the growing threat of Asian capital and Asian workers on the U.S. economy and the "native" (white) worker.

The protectionist sentiment sparked attempts to restrict, or at least slow down, the flow of foreign imports. But the United States could not impose higher tariffs to meet the demands for protection. Higher tariffs would have violated GATT regulations. Instead, Congress turned to non-tariff barriers as the trade restriction mechanism of choice: measures, policies, and practices other than a tax or duty designed to restrict imports and therefore protect U.S. companies and the domestic market from foreign competition. U.S. non-tariff barriers included complex regulatory systems, quotas, bans, safety standards, burdensome Customs inspections, and lengthy entry procedures. By the 1980s, the United States witnessed a sharp rise in non-tariff barriers that captured the total reappraisal of trade liberalization under GATT.

Unfortunately for Tilakamonkul and the Bangkok Market, the United States used non-tariff barriers on food imports, especially fruits, vegetables, and plants. The amount of food imported into the United States rose incredibly in the 1980s, pushing the United States to rely more heavily on non-tariff barriers to protect its borders. In 1983, approximately 32 billion pounds of foreign food entered the United States. By 1988, 40 billion pounds of food were imported.[55] The non-tariff barriers on foreign foods stemmed from concerns over the potentially destructive impact of imported goods on public and environmental health, specifically "native" species of plants, fruits, and vegetables vital to the U.S. agricultural industry.[56] It was at this time that the USDA, on top of banning Asian-grown *makrut* from entry into the United States, placed *makrut* under federal quarantine for canker because it did not trust the standards used by Asian nations to test for the disease.[57] Unlike cars, clothing, electronics, and other manufactured products, when it came to Asian food imports there did not appear to be the same level of anxiety about foreign companies taking jobs or competing directly with U.S. agriculture and food companies. One would have been hard-pressed, for instance, to find a grower in the United States who raised kaffir limes, lemongrass, or Thai eggplant to sell in the commercial market—or a U.S. curry paste manufacturer. In other words, there was not a major agribusiness lobby working to keep out Asian foodstuffs because of economic competition. Instead of economic infiltration, foreign food imports represented disease and pest infiltration.

Along with quotas, bans, and quality standards, the U.S. Customs Service emerged as an effective and omnipresent non-tariff barrier. As a federal enforcement agency, Customs was not a formal trade barrier, but its bureaucratic procedures and activities slowed the import process down. In essence, Customs acted as a non-tariff barrier in practice. Customs enlarged its operations dramatically during this period to try and keep pace with the rapid growth of food imports. It bolstered its personnel, invested in larger processing facilities, and implemented a nationwide computer network to expedite entry procedures and inspections. The agency spent roughly $900 million a year to accomplish this but generated a revenue of over $15 billion annually in duties, tariffs, fines, forfeitures, and seizures for the U.S. government.[58] As the bureaucratic and physical infrastructure of the U.S. Customs Service expanded, so did the responsibilities of Customs officers and inspectors. Typically, agents measured arriving shipments against quotas, subjected them to tariffs, and checked for narcotics, bacteria, and insects—or "drugs and bugs."[59] These actions were carried out in any place in the United States, within Customs waters, or within an authorized Customs enforcement area. By the 1980s, Customs agents also had to enforce over 2,000 regulations of more than forty agencies, including the FDA and USDA-APHIS. For instance, even though 95 percent of the tonnage of imported food in 1988 fell under FDA jurisdiction, it all had to first pass through Customs.[60] Furthermore, Congress weaponized Customs agents by granting them the right to carry firearms, make an arrest without a warrant, and "perform any other law enforcement duty that the Secretary of the Treasury may designate."[61]

In a way, the U.S. Customs Service did more than just police the border by keeping out food at physical border spaces. It also participated in social and cultural border making: drawing stark lines between nonthreatening "native" foods and invasive "alien" ones to determine which foods belonged and which ones did not, at times using scientific research to justify the exclusion.[62] Customs gave the impression that "foreign" foods were more dangerous than domestic foods. In doing so, it played a role in constructing and defining the U.S. nation-state as modern, safe, and pest- and disease-free while constantly under threat from the "torrent" of contaminated imported foods.[63] Bonnie Aikman, spokesperson for the USDA, revealed to the *Los Angeles Times* in 1987, "We [USDA] worry a lot about this . . . for example, just one orange carried by an incoming passenger may have introduced the Mediterranean fruit fly to California in 1980. More than $100 million was spent by the USDA and the state of California before the fly was eradicated."[64] Aikman highlighted both the environmental and economic dangers of poorly or uninspected imported meats and produce at a moment in which federal, state, and local governments became increasingly strapped for funds. A 1989 *Washington Post* article reported that the "rising tide of foreign foods," coupled with budget cuts on government agencies, put pressure on inspectors patrolling the nation's borders and "raised concerns about whether troublesome foods are reaching American tables and if public health is being adequately protected."[65] The article also stated that about 40 percent of sampled imported goods (2 percent of all imports) did not meet FDA standards. In addition, Customs, USDA-APHIS, and the FDA helped to disseminate these ideas by informing both importers and overseas travelers about the risks of foreign foods through pamphlets, booklets with lists of restricted items, and posters.[66]

The notion that foreign food imports were uniquely hazardous to U.S. safety gained enough traction to compel some members of the import community, and even officials who worked for enforcement agencies, to respond. They believed that Customs, FDA, and USDA-APHIS import procedures resulted in the depiction of all imported food as bad or worse than domestic food. Richard Sullivan, president of the Association of Food Industries, Inc., a trade group for importers, claimed that inspection methods produced misleading statistics that "create the impression that imported foods are dangerous."[67] Sullivan pointed specifically to the FDA's system of checking 9 percent of all shipments and testing only 2 percent of them in a lab. He argued that because the FDA only sampled imported goods deemed suspicious, it usually found problems since it looked in "problem areas." Others tried to invalidate the idea that imported foods were more dangerous simply because they were foreign by turning attention to domestic food safety. Robert Gaylord, international field supervisor for the USDA's Baltimore division, told the *Washington Post* that he had seen "a lot more wholesome beef from overseas" than what was produced in the United States.[68]

For importers, the expansion of Customs operations and responsibilities meant cumbersome entry, inspection, and processing procedures for foodstuffs in transit. The Ports of Los Angeles and Long Beach were particularly bad. With booming trade across the Pacific Rim, Los Angeles became a main hub for imports and Customs activity in the nation. It was the primary port complex for

Bangkok Market Inc. The value of imports that came through the ports grew at a faster rate than any other major U.S. port, reaching $48.7 billion in 1988. But the increased volume and value of imports at both ports burdened West Coast Customs inspectors with a workload 50 percent higher than others around the country.[69] As a result, Customs simply could not check and clear all arriving imports. Instead, it inspected only 10 percent of all shipments (releasing 90 percent at the dock), relying on on-site import specialists and computers to determine which cargoes to examine.[70]

Not surprisingly, delays in processing and routine inspections also caused headaches for import companies. A 1986 study commissioned by both West Coast port authorities and shipping interests found that the Los Angeles and Long Beach ports had the worst processing delays on the entire West Coast: Customs only cleared 9 percent of imports selected for examination in less than eight hours—whereas other ports on the West Coast had a clearance rate of 42 percent under eight hours. What's more, Customs was in no way a uniform operation. It was decentralized, and agents often had to make decisions on-site, which made the process opaque and at times inconsistent. The authors of the 1986 study took notice that importers were "increasingly selecting ports and carriers which offer the most trouble-free customs clearance."[71]

Sidestepping Trade Barriers and Foreign Trade Zones

Faced with these trade conditions and the discursive landscape around foreign foods, Tilakamonkul decided to sidestep the heightened barriers. He vertically integrated Bangkok Market Inc. and created new source regions to grow Thai and Southeast Asian produce (Map 3). While Bangkok Market Inc. managed to import canned and packaged items like fish sauce, curry paste, and dried fish, it of course struggled to import fruits, vegetables, and plants. USDA-APHIS banned Asian-grown kaffir limes and placed them under federal quarantine. It also started quarantining shipments of Asian-grown lemongrass because of rust disease.[72] In response, Tilakamonkul and his partners (some of whom participated in smuggling Thai foodstuffs) attempted to cultivate these and other crops in different parts of Southern California. It was perfectly legal to grow and sell kaffir-limes as well as lemongrass domestically in California, so long as one could provide documentation to prove that they were, in fact, grown in the United States.[73] After failed attempts in Chino and San Diego, California, due to inappropriate climate conditions, the group partnered with a wholesale company in Fresno, California, S.S.K. Produce Inc.[74] Tilakamonkul discovered that California's Central Valley's climate was ideal for growing Thai plants and produce.

As much as he cared about bringing food to his people, Tilakamonkul was just as driven to increase profits. He restructured Bangkok Market Inc. so that

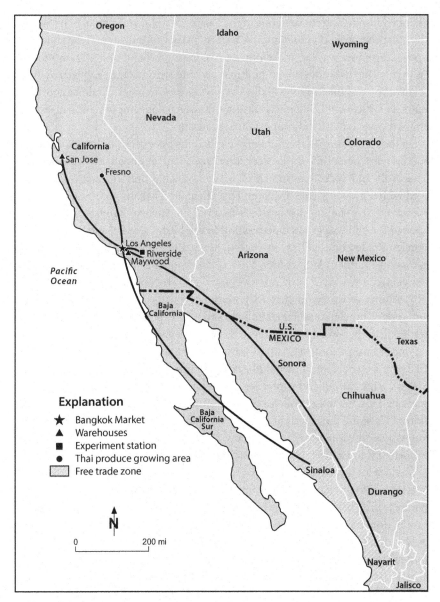

Map 3. Bangkok Market, Inc.'s North American "empire" established by Pramorte "Pat" Tilakamonkul and his son Jet to overcome restrictions on the importation of Asian produce and the expense of importing processed Thai ingredients while profiting from the growing demand for Thai cuisine. Cartography by Syracuse University Cartographic Laboratory & Map Shop.

the company controlled the entire supply chain: production, wholesale, distribution, and retail. In addition to the retail store, Tilakamonkul opened two family-operated import warehouses, one in the Northern California city of San Jose and the other in Maywood in Southern California's City of Industry. The warehouses opened up more ways to make money. According to his son, Jet, Pramorte was "a trendsetter" who developed multiple revenue streams and "monetized every segment of this business. Basically, our produce companies would support our markets, which would support our restaurants. And our import company would support our markets and support our restaurants."[75]

In the mid-1980s, Tilakamonkul expanded the operations of Bangkok Market Inc. even further. While the grocery store brought an abundance of locally grown Thai fruit and vegetables, much of it was available only on a seasonal basis. And with a growing Thai and non-Thai clientele, Tilakamonkul sought a year-round supply—he and his partners found it in Mexico. Bangkok Market Inc. applied for and was granted permission to establish, operate, and maintain two Foreign Trade Zones (FTZs) in Sinaloa, Mexico, creating a global trade network across the southern U.S. border.[76] FTZs, also known as "Free Trade Zones," are designated areas in or near ports of entry that, by law, are treated as outside of Customs territory, in that they eliminate tariffs and other trade barriers and reduce bureaucratic regulations in order to expedite and encourage global trade.[77] In other words, FTZs allowed companies to effectively circumvent the regime of import control Customs was trying to maintain. Bangkok Market Inc.'s FTZs grew 90 percent of the Southeast Asian produce that came into the United States during the fall and winter seasons. Jet, who spent a number of his teenage years helping his father oversee the operations in Mexico, describes the conditions: "These are thousands of Mexicans that are growing our food. [They] don't know how to eat it, [they] don't know what the hell to do with it, and they're exporting it to us. It's really amazing to see."[78]

Besides a year-round supply of Thai and Southeast Asian produce, Bangkok Market Inc. found FTZs to be advantageous for other equally, if not more, important reasons. For one, they represented a "frictionless"—near magical—space of production, handling, and importing/exporting full of exemptions and special powers for U.S. businesses. Dara Orenstein contends that FTZs "deterritorialized rather than delineated the nation, creating archipelagos of murky sovereignty and unsettling what it meant to be or buy 'American.'"[79] This meant that U.S. import restrictions no longer applied to foreign, specifically Asian-grown, produce—because such produce was no longer "foreign," but American. Customs agents assigned to the zones also reduced the dutiable value of goods produced there, which helped to lower or eliminate tariffs. In addition, FTZs allowed businesses to avoid not only U.S. Customs oversight and regulations but U.S. labor and environmental laws as well.[80] As a physical site, FTZs were "isolated, enclosed, and policed" spaces with facilities for loading, unloading, handling, storing, producing, and shipping items by land, water, or air.[81] FTZs throughout the twentieth century were generally regarded as foreign land although "foreign in a domestic sense," which had "all the familiar trappings of a militarized national border: guards, customs agents, barbed wire."[82]

Moreover, a major reason why it was appealing to establish FTZs in Mexico was because of changes happening in the country's agricultural sector at the time. The Mexican government enacted policies in the 1980s that altered the Mexican agricultural industry to be more privatized, market-oriented, and foreign-capital friendly, essentially prepping the country for NAFTA. The support for increased commercial-based production of crops spawned an entrepreneurial class of Mexican growers looking for ways to tap into the capitalist marketplace, especially in the United States. From the perspective of the Mexican growers, investing in "exotic" crops opened a smaller yet more stable market that lessened the possibility of the glut that occurs in bigger markets. Such investment provided surer access to U.S. consumers, as Southeast Asian crops did not compete in the marketplace with crops produced by U.S. Big Agriculture.[83]

Creating a Thai American Community

Between the mid-1960s and the late 1980s, U.S. border practices through food trade policy had a profound impact on the Thai immigrants' ability to procure and cook what they considered to be authentic Thai dishes. A complex regulatory system of government agencies acted as barriers to the importation of Thai foodstuffs as the U.S. nation-state tried to selectively benefit from and manage the increased flow of foreign foods. Tilakamonkul and fellow Thai entrepreneurs negotiated the hardening of U.S. borders in a range of ways, but perhaps most effectively by turning to FTZs, where U.S. regulations and enforcement were not nearly as pronounced.

In short, the opening of the Bangkok Market grocery store was a formative event. It established a central place to procure foodstuffs necessary to make Thai food. It also led to the creation of other businesses like import/export companies and encouraged food growing in California's Central Valley and, later, FTZs in Mexico. But above all, Tilakamonkul and his partners' negotiation of complex non-tariff barriers, from restrictions to enforcement agencies, made it easier for Thai entrepreneurs to open restaurants and "authentic" Thai dishes to be cooked at home. The Bangkok Market created the conditions of possibility for a Thai American community to take shape around foodways.

As the first Thai grocery store in the United States, the Bangkok Market grocery store appeared to serve as a magnet for Thai migration to and within Los Angeles. Within a few years of its opening, a majority of the city's Thai population moved to the Mid-Wilshire and East Hollywood area, near the intersections of Wilshire and Olympic Boulevards and Hollywood and Western Boulevards

Figure 5.1. The front entrance to Bangkok Market in 2016. However unprepossessing its facade, the Bangkok Market serves as a central node of Thai American cuisine and culture. Photo by the author.

Figure 5.2. The rear entrance to Bangkok Market with a glimpse of the abundance of foods available inside. Photo by the author.

(Figures 5.1 and 5.2).[84] East Hollywood, a predominantly white neighborhood just a decade earlier, was transitioning into a multiracial and multiethnic space. Thais settled there along with other immigrant groups from Latin America as well as Armenia.[85] Although the area was in "decline" with "pimps, hookers, and drug dealers" mingling in and around blighted or empty buildings, the neighborhood around the store had grown into a small Thai enclave lined with Thai travel agencies, newspaper presses, auto shops, beauty parlors, and other businesses established to attract and serve Thai newcomers.[86] At least one-third of these businesses, though, were food and restaurant related. As geographer Jacqueline Desbarats observed in 1979, two interrelated processes were at work in East Hollywood: Thai businesses located to serve their clientele, and in turn the residential choice of Thai newcomers was influenced by these businesses as well as the location of earlier immigrants and employment opportunities.[87]

Thai food-related businesses in Los Angeles also cultivated social networks and economic gains that turned them into incubators for Thai American community development. They often provided financial backing to launch Thai-language newspapers and community organizations, and supported the growth of early Thai American community leaders. The success of the Bangkok Market, for example, propelled Tilakamonkul to a leadership role in other Thai community building efforts. He played a key part in the founding of Wat Thai of Los Angeles in 1979—the first and largest Thai Buddhist temple in the nation—and eventually served as its executive vice president.[88]

At another level, the Bangkok Market served as an important "location" where Thais constructed racial and ethnic identity and formed a "cultural community" out of a population that was largely geographically dispersed across Southern California.[89] Tilakamonkul tightened the link between food and identity for Thais in Los Angeles by providing them with tangible, edible symbols of ethnic identity they used to mark themselves as distinctly "Thai." Scholars like Linda Espana-Maram and Sudarat Disayawattana have illustrated the way ethnic newspapers reflect common group experience and how they express a groups's values, heritage, and changing sense of identity, especially for group members spatially apart.[90] Newspapers like the monthly *Thai Citizen News* certainly fostered an "imagined" sense of community among Thais through news about Thailand and local events. But, simply put, not all Thais in Los Angeles read Thai-language newspapers—yet every Thai immigrant and Thai American shopped for, cooked, or ate Thai food. So in many ways, the Bangkok Market operated as a community institution, serving as a location where Thais went for face-to-face socialization that fostered a sense of real community in Los Angeles.

The history of food procurement in the making of the early Thai American community in Los Angeles helps clarify the messy, complicated, yet meaningful relationship between food and borders taken up in this anthology. It historicizes both the academic and popular view that increased globalization in the

1990s made foodways an important part of community formation, especially for a growing number of immigrant and diasporic populations in the United States. As a story that played out at least a decade before NAFTA and the formation of the World Trade Organization (successor to GATT), the myriad ways that Thais acquired ingredients to reproduce Thai flavors and literally nourish a sense of community show what "globalization" looked like from the mid-1960s to the late 1980s.

And borders mattered. The U.S. nation-state shaped Thai food culture by not only expanding its influence into Thailand to generate and facilitate Thai migration patterns to the United States but also by enacting mechanisms—quotas, quality standards, and inspections—that determined whether Thai immigrants would have access to the foods they wanted and needed once they arrived. Any conversation about how and why immigrant communities fight to maintain cultural continuity or forge transnational identities by cooking and eating must at least consider the way nation-state policies mediate these very processes. Immigrants do not just bring their foods with them. They bring only what the United States allows them to, or what they get away with smuggling in. Also, the fact that Thais got nearly all "native" produce from Riverside, Fresno, and later Mexico demonstrates how borders can also short-circuit and redirect procurement routes, or open up new ones altogether. This pushes us to think about where "foreign" food actually comes from and disrupts the notion of "authentic ingredients" as defined by country of origin. Which is more "authentic": California-grown kaffir lime or Thailand-grown kaffir lime? Who decides?

While borders shape food, this exploration of Thai food procurement also serves as a vivid example of how food shapes borders, both discursively and materially. More specifically, food imports informed U.S. border making and border maintenance in the late twentieth century. The proliferation of the flow of foreign imports across borders and into the United States did not mean that nation-state boundaries softened or became more porous. On the contrary, this growth was matched by the expansion of trade barriers and federal agencies as well as the rapid increase of border policing and enforcement by the U.S. Customs Service. These borders, reinforced by food science research and officials who patrolled the physical borders, were charged with confronting and protecting against bacteria, pests, diseases, and other agricultural threats in food imports.

Shifting the spotlight to food procurement helps us better understand that the historical interplay between food and community building in the United States is intertwined with nation-state policies and practices. Investigating everyday practices of cooking and eating certainly offers insight into the way immigrants and other marginalized groups rely on food to create and strengthen social bonds, form identities and subjectivities, and reproduce the homeland as they grapple with life in U.S. society outside the purview of the state, or from the "bottom up." But centering our analysis on procurement illuminates how U.S. food policies, food systems, global trade, border making, and border maintenance defined the look, feel, and very livelihood of ethnic communities.

NOTES

1. Colman Andrews, "Fare of the Country: With Satay and Tiger Prawns, Fiery Thai Food Is a Hit in L.A.," *New York Times*, July 6, 1990.

2. Here, I use "ingredients" and "foodstuffs" interchangeably to refer to the food or substances used in cooking. This includes packaged and canned goods like coconut milk and curry paste, as well as fresh fruit and vegetables such as kaffir lime and lemongrass.

3. Hasia Diner, Donna Gabaccia, Psyche Williams-Forson, Dawn Mabalon, and Rachel Slocum, to name a few, have all illustrated that marginalized groups throughout the twentieth century, especially immigrants, re-created familiar foods and cooperated with each other to prepare them and make them available on a community basis. See Hasia Diner, *Hungering for America: Italian, Irish, and Jewish Foodways in the Age of Migration* (Cambridge, MA: Harvard University Press, 2001); Donna R. Gabaccia, *We Are What We Eat: Ethnic Food and the Making of Americans* (Cambridge, MA: Harvard University Press, 1998); Psyche Williams-Forson, *Building Houses Out of Chicken Legs: Black Women, Food, and Power* (Chapel Hill: University of North Carolina Press, 2006); Dawn Bohulano Mabalon, "As American as JackRabbit Adobo: Cooking, Eating, and Becoming Filipina/o American before World War II," in *Eating Asian America: A Food Studies Reader*, ed. Robert Ku, Martin F. Manalansan, and Anita Mannur (New York: New York University Press, 2013); Rachel Slocum, "Thinking Race through Corporeal Feminist Theory: Divisions and Intimacies at the Minneapolis Farmers' Market," *Social & Cultural Geography* 9 (December 2008): 849–869. See also Anita Mannur and Valerie Matsumoto, eds., *Amerasia Journal: Meat versus Rice: New Research on Asian American Foodways* 32 (Los Angeles: University of California–Los Angeles, 2006); Frederick Douglass Opie, *Hog and Hominy: Soul Food from Africa to America* (New York: Columbia University Press, 2008); Haiming Liu and LianLian Lin, "Food, Culinary Identity, and Transnational Culture: Chinese Restaurant Businesses in Southern California," *Journal of Asian American Studies* 12 (June 2009): 135–162. These scholars also used food as an analytical category to enhance theories of community formation by demonstrating, for instance, that transnationalism and globalization are more than abstract ideas but are tangible realities, and that newcomers negotiate U.S. racial, class, and gender structures in the textures of everyday life. In essence, they treat food as a site that functions as a point of identification and community, particularly for peoples displaced by migration. Or, as David Sutton has written, food is "especially useful in understanding experiences of displacement, fragmentation, diaspora, and the reconstruction of 'wholeness'" for those who are seeking "firm ground under their feet." See David E. Sutton, "Synesthesia, Memory, and the Taste of Home," in *The Taste Culture Reader: Experiencing Food and Drink*, ed. Carolyn Korsmeyer (New York: Berg, 2005), 305. The goal is to reveal the power that seemingly insignificant daily practices have on the way people interact with and change their social, cultural, and natural environments.

4. For instance, Diner asserted in *Hungering for America* that "we might define a community as a group of people who eat with each other" because preparing and consuming food at a common table "solidifies social bonds within families, between households, and among individuals who consider themselves friends." See Diner, *Hungering for America*, 4. At least one exception is Robert Alvarez's work on Mexican *troqueros* (truckers) who transported food across the U.S.-Mexico border since the passage of the North American Free Trade Agreement (NAFTA), which offers a glimpse into how food procurement shapes community. While Alvarez's study of "transnationalism from below" does not focus specifically on community formation, as an anthropologist he was able to uncover the way Mexican

long-haul *troqueros* formed and tightened bonds between family members and fictive kin networks as they brought produce from the interior of Mexico across the border into the United States. See Robert R. Alvarez Jr., *Mangos, Chiles, and Truckers: The Business of Transnationalism* (Minneapolis: University of Minnesota Press, 2005).

5. By using the term "authentic" to describe the sought-after Thai ingredients, I do not wish to suggest that these ingredients are objectively authentic, given that there are different and competing measurements for what is or isn't "authentic." Rather, I use it to refer to what Thais considered or believed to be authentic Thai ingredients—and they defined these largely by taste and flavor profile as well as by country of origin and/or region (Southeast Asia). David Sutton's use of the concept of "wholeness" builds on James Fernandez's work on "returning to the whole," which Fernandez developed by studying the way groups in West Africa used religious revitalization to try to combat alienation and become whole under conditions of colonialism. See Sutton, "Synesthesia, Memory, and the Taste of Home," 305; and James Fernandez, *Bwiti: An Ethnography of Religious Imagination in Africa* (Princeton, NJ: Princeton University Press, 1982).

6. Jacqueline Desbarats, "Thai Migration to Los Angeles," *Geographical Review* 69 (July 1979): 302. The total numbers are from Nutta Vinijnaiyapak, "Institutions and Civic Engagement: A Case Study of Thai Community in Los Angeles" (Ph.D. diss., University of Southern California, 2004), 15. Vinijnaiyapak cites Narong Kaeonil, "The Thai Community in Los Angeles: An Attitudinal Study of Its Socio-Economic Structure" (Ph.D. diss., United States International University, 1977).

7. Desbarats, "Thai Migration to Los Angeles," 305.

8. Kaeonil, "Thai Community in Los Angeles," 33–34.

9. Jiemin Bao has described Thai immigration to the United States as a "middle-class" migration and claims that this is due to the fact that Thais arrived as students. However, Bao did not account for poor and working-class Thais who used student visas simply to gain entry into the United States. Jiemin Bao, "Thai Middle-Classness: Forging Alliances with Whites and Cultivating Patronage from Thailand's Elite," *Journal of Asian American Studies* 12.2 (June 2009): 163–190.

10. Desbarats, "Migration to Los Angeles," 306.

11. Ibid., 312–313.

12. For a fascinating look into the lived experiences of Thai war brides in the United States, see Orapan Footrakoon, "Lived Experiences of Thai War Brides in Mixed Thai-American Families in the United States" (Ph.D. diss., University of Minnesota, 1999).

13. Sudarat Disayawattana, "The Craft of Ethnic Newspaper-Making: A Study of the Negotiation of Culture in the Thai-Language Newspapers of Los Angeles" (Ph.D. diss., University of Iowa, 1993), 54.

14. Ibid., 59.

15. Desbarats, "Thai Migration to Los Angeles," 307.

16. Urai Ruenprom, interview by author, North Hollywood, CA, December 18, 2008.

17. Disayawattana, "Craft of Ethnic Newspaper-Making," 54.

18. Malulee Pinsuvana, *Cooking Thai Food in American Kitchens* (Bangkok: Thai Watana Panich Press, 1976), preface ("From the Author").

19. Andrew Coe, *Chop Suey: A Cultural History of Chinese Food in the United States* (New York: Oxford University Press, 2009), 85–87.

20. Of course not all Thai people enjoy the same types of dishes, as people in most communities do not all eat the same foods in the same ways. The distribution and consumption of food have been historically determined by age, gender, class, and region, to name a few factors, which highlights internal group differences and complexities. That said, Thai cuisine is often characterized by this flavor combination, or "yum." Chef Jet Tilakamonkul once said at one of his many cooking demonstrations that "yum is the perfect balance between hot, sour, salty and sweet" and that in cooking Thai food, one must "chase the yum and use the country-specific ingredients, and you will make authentic food." Canda Fuqua,

Corvallis-Gazette Times, February 8, 2013. See also Penny Van Esterik, *Food Culture in Southeast Asia* (Westport, CO: Greenwood Press, 2006), 39.

21. Meredith E. Abarca, this volume; Sutton, "Synesthesia, Memory, and the Taste of Home," 305. See also C. Nadia Seremetakis, "The Breast of Aphrodite" and Deborah Lupton, "Food and Emotion" both in Korsmeyer, *Taste Culture Reader*.

22. Abarca, this volume.

23. Ibid.

24. Lois Dwan, "Roundabout," *Los Angeles Times*, February 27, 1972; Jean Barry, *Thai Students in the United States: A Study in Attitude Change* (Ithaca, NY: Southeast Asia Program, Department of Asian Studies, Cornell University, 1967), 30.

25. Prakas Yenbamroong, interview by author, Hollywood, CA, January 13, 2010.

26. Cecil Fleming, "A Happy Task—Getting to Know Thai Cuisine," *Los Angeles Times*, January 6, 1966.

27. Marie Wilson, *Siamese Cookery* (Rutland, VT: Tuttle Press, 1965), 35.

28. Wilson, *Siamese Cookery*, 36.

29. Jet Tilakamonkul, interview by author, Hollywood, CA, October 16, 2007.

30. Ibid.

31. The "Golden Triangle" refers to the geographic area where the borders of Thailand, Burma, and Laos meet, which during the 1960s and 1970s emerged as the world's major cultivator of opium and heroin. U.S. intervention in Southeast Asia during the Cold War sparked the explosion of an illegal flow of heroin into the United States that drew the attention of U.S. drug enforcement agencies and U.S. Customs. See Ron Chepesiuk, *Bangkok Connection: Trafficking Heroin from Asia to the USA* (Dublin: Maverick House, 2014); and Ko-lin Chin, *Golden Triangle: Inside Southeast Asia's Drug Trade* (Ithaca, NY: Cornell University Press, 2009).

32. I understand that the term "kaffir" is a racial slur commonly used outside of the United States. White colonialists, for instance, used it as derogatory term to insult black Africans, and its power to offend grew more intense in apartheid-era South Africa. Even though there is still debate about the etymology of the word and its meaning in relation to limes, I still want to recognize its history as a derogatory term. However, I use "kaffir" in the article because I want to place in front of readers the exact terminology used.

33. USDA, ARS, National Genetic Resources Program, *Germplasm Resources Information Network—(GRIN)* [Online Database] National Germplasm Resources Laboratory, Beltsville, MD, http://www.ars-grin.gov.4/cgi-bin/npgs/acc/display.pl?1434184; Tilakamonkul interview. The availability of "exotic" citrus in the region appears to be true: http://www.citrusvariety.ucr.edu/history/index.html.

34. Tilakamonkul interview.

35. John H. Jackson, "The General Agreement of Tariffs and Trade in the United States Domestic Law," *Michigan Law Review* 66. 2 (December 1967): 250; Charles S. Pearson, *United States Trade Policy: A Work in Progress* (Hoboken, NJ: Wiley Press, 2004), 7.

36. Jackson, "General Agreement of Tariffs and Trade," 250.

37. Tilakamonkul interview; Andrews, "Fare of the Country."

38. Tilakamonkul interview.

39. Kathleen Squires, "The Next Generation: Jet Tila, The Charleston LA," *Zagat*, September 27, 2013, https://www.zagat.com/b/the-next-generation-jet-tila-the-charleston-la.

40. Kelly DiNardo, "Travel Q&A: Chef Jet Tila Talks About Travel's Influence on His Cooking and the Importance of Getting Lost," *MapQuest Discover*, December 2, 2014, http://www.mapquest.com/travel/articles/chef-jet-tila-food-network-los-angeles-21001185; Squires, "Next Generation."

41. Jet has mentioned on multiple occasions that his family was able to come to Los Angeles because of his Mexican aunt who sponsored them to come to the United States. "Q&A: Chef Jet Does Bistronomics," http://www.marpop.com/whats-new/qa-chef-jet-tila/. In a recent interview with Travels in Taste website, he mentions: "I have a natural affinity toward

Mexican food and culture, but mine goes deeper than my native city to my family tree. When my uncle moved to the U.S. from Thailand, he fell in love with a woman named Dora Lucero and married her almost instantly. Soon there were Thai/Chinese/Mexican cousins running around." http://www.travelsintaste.com/jet_tila__favorite_local_spots__antojos _df-listing2616.aspx.

42. Squires, "Next Generation."

43. Eugene T. Rossides, U.S. Import Trade Regulation (Edison, NJ: BNA Books, 1986), 56–57.

44. Carole Sugarman, "A Matter of Imports: The Challenge of Tracking the Rising Tide of Foreign Foods," Washington Post, December 6, 1989.

45. General Agreement on Tariffs and Trade (GATT), Provisional Accession of Thailand, Memorandum on Foreign Trade Regime, April 24, 1979, 3.

46. Japan was the top buyer of Thai exports, bringing in about 25 percent of Thailand's total exports each year between 1968 and 1977. Ibid., 4.

47. Ibid., 2; Yanee Srimanee and Jayant Kumar Routray, "The Fruit and Vegetable Marketing Chains in Thailand: Policy Impacts and Implications," International Journal of Retail & Distribution Management 40.9 (2012): 658, 666–667.

48. GATT, Provisional Accession of Thailand, Memorandum on Foreign Trade Regime, 8.

49. Sugarman, "Matter of Imports." For a useful overview on the origins of federal oversight and the responsibilities of the USDA and the FDA when it comes to domestic food supply and imports, see Marion Nestle, Safe Food: Bacteria, Biotechnology, and Bioterrorism (Berkeley: University of California Press, 2003), 50–61 and chapter 3.

50. Sugarman, "Matter of Imports"; United States Department of Agriculture—Animal and Plant Health Inspection Service, "A 40-year Retrospective of APHIS, 1972–2012" (Washington, D.C.), 4.

51. Rossides, U.S. Trade Import Regulation, 489.

52. Sugarman, "Matter of Imports."

53. In Buy American, historian Dana Frank explains that this increased global competition was a matter of "chickens coming home to roost." She writes that at the same time the American Century seemed limitless in the early 1960s, the billions of dollars the United States spent to bring Japan and Germany into the capitalist orbit resulted in competition and the rise of industrial powerhouses—steel, auto, machine tools, electrical manufacturing—which ultimately led to the crisis of the 1970s and 1980s. Moreover, the Allied powers agreed not to allow these countries to spend money on military endeavors. Dana Frank, Buy American: The Untold Story of Economic Nationalism (Boston: Beacon Press, 1999), 126.

54. Ibid., 132.

55. Sugarman, "Matter of Imports."

56. George Stein, "Keeper of the Ports: Customs Service Directs Record Traffic Flow," Los Angeles Times, March 20, 1988; APHIS, "A 40-year Retrospective of APHIS, 1972–2012," 5.

57. Barbara Hansen, "Thai Markets Short on Kaffir Lime Leaves," Los Angeles Times, June 30, 1999.

58. Stein, "Keeper of the Ports."

59. Ibid.

60. Sugarman, "Matter of Imports."

61. The Comprehensive Crime Control Act of 1984 and the Trade and the Tariff Act of 1984 authorized Customs officers to carry firearms and make arrests. Prior to 1984, the authority of Customs agents to make arrests was limited, as they could only do so for breach of navigation laws or for violations of the narcotic drug and marijuana laws. See Rossides, U.S. Import Trade Regulation, 512–513.

62. Peter Coates's American Perceptions of Immigrant and Invasive Species: Strangers on the Land (Berkeley: University of California Press, 2006) offers an insightful analysis of how this type of border-making process played out in U.S. history but within the context of flora and fauna instead of food. Coates argues that U.S. fears over its "ecological identity," and how

that anxiety helped construct American national identity, is not a new phenomenon. In fact, the relationship between naturalism, nativism, and nationalism in America dates back to the mid-1800s, when ideas and discourses about "invasive" species intersected with national identity and cultural nationalism.

63. Sugarman, "Matter of Imports."

64. Stein, "Keeper of the Ports."

65. Peter S. Greenberg, "Customs Is Cracking Down on Forbidden Fruits," *Los Angeles Times*, March 22, 1987.

66. For example, Customs published a pamphlet called *Know Before You Go* to inform overseas travelers about what foods they were not allowed to bring back. In addition, the USDA also published a seventeen-page booklet called *Traveler's Tips* that listed food items that were acceptable to bring back into the United States. Greenberg, "Customs Is Cracking Down."

67. Sugarman, "Matter of Imports."

68. Ibid.

69. Stein, "Keeper of the Ports."

70. This was pretty consistent with other agencies as well. For example, in 1970 the FDA was able to inspect about 20 percent of the 500,000 imported entries. But by 1987, the FDA-regulated imports reached 1.5 million, and the agency was able to check the documents of only 9 percent of the goods and physically sample 2 percent in their labs—40 percent of which did not meet FDA standards. Sugarman, "Matter of Imports."

71. Stein, "Keeper of the Ports."

72. Charlyne Varkonyi, "Major Ingredients in Thai Food Harder to Find," *Los Angeles Times*, July 12, 1990.

73. Hansen, "Thai Markets Short on Kaffir Lime Leaves."

74. Tilakamonkul interview.

75. Squires, "Next Generation."

76. A public or private corporation had to submit an application to the Foreign-Trade Zones Board and have it approved in order to establish, operate, and maintain a zone. Rossides, *U.S. Import Regulation*, 73.

77. Ibid., 70.

78. Tilakamonkul interview.

79. Dara Orenstein, "Foreign-Trade Zones and the Cultural Logic of Frictionless Production," *Radical History Review* 109 (Winter 2011): 48.

80. Ibid., 54. There is not enough evidence to suggest that Bangkok Market exploited Mexican workers, although labor exploitation and low wages are characteristic of FTZs.

81. Rossides, *U.S. Import Regulation*, 70.

82. Orenstein, "Foreign-Trade Zones and the Cultural Logic of Frictionless Production," 47.

83. Joel Millman, "Stir Fry: Mexican Vegetables in U.S. Woks—Fewer Import Controls, Lower Costs Increase Demand for Bok Choy," *Wall Street Journal*, March 5, 1998.

84. Chanchanit "Chancee" Martorell, interview by author, Hollywood, CA, December 18, 2009; James Paul Allen and Eugene Turner, *The Ethnic Quilt: Population Diversity in Southern California* (Northridge: Center for Geographical Studies, California State University, Northridge, 1997), 159–160.

85. Allen and Turner, *Ethnic Quilt*, 101, 102, 104, 105; 1960 United States Census Tract Record 90029, Los Angeles County; 1970 United States Census Tract Record 90029, Los Angeles County; 1980 United States Census Tract Record 90029, Los Angeles County.

86. Jet Tila quoted in David Pierson and Anna Gorman, "A New Take on Thai Town," *Los Angeles Times*, August 2, 2007.

87. Desbarats, "Thai Migration to Los Angeles," 316.

88. Wat Thai of Los Angeles, *Phra Tamrachanuwat* (North Hollywood: Wat Thai of Los Angeles), 151.

89. Rick Bonus, *Locating Filipino Americans: Ethnicity and the Cultural Politics of Space* (Philadelphia: Temple University Press, 2000), chapter 3. In her work on Chinese in St. Louis and in Huping Ling, ed., *Asian America: Forming New Communities, Expanding Boundaries* (Piscataway, NJ: Rutgers University Press, 2009), Ling defines "cultural community" as a community without physical boundaries that creates a sense of identity through cultural activities and organizations.

90. Linda Espana-Maram, *Creating Masculinity in Los Angeles' Little Manila: Working-Class Filipinos and Popular Culture, 1920s–1950s* (New York: Columbia University Press, 2006), 37; Disayawattana, *Craft of Ethnic Newspaper-Making.*

CHAPTER 6

Crossing Chiles, Crossing Borders

DR. FABIÁN GARCÍA, THE NEW MEXICAN
CHILE PEPPER, AND MODERNITY IN THE EARLY
TWENTIETH-CENTURY U.S.-MEXICO BORDERLANDS

William Carleton

New Mexico's official state question—"Red or Green?"—inquires tongue-in-cheek about chile preference to celebrate one of the state's leading crops and economic engines. Implicitly, the question also signals pride for New Mexico's Hispanic and Native cultural heritage. This official display of pride came roughly a century after New Mexican politicians and other territorial elites debated, in explicitly racist terms, whether New Mexico was modern and white enough to become fully incorporated into the Union.[1] As these elites sought to distance New Mexico's population from its indigenous heritage and its neighbors to the south, a Mexican-born horticulturalist at New Mexico's land-grant college, Dr. Fabián García, bred a new chile variety that embodied an alternative vision of modernity for New Mexico. The new chile pepper encouraged a more industrialized, more culturally inclusive borderlands and set the course for an industry that would eventually define the state's cultural identity.

García held an important position on the U.S.-Mexico border as a cultural and agricultural intermediary that shaped his work with the iconic chile. As horticulturalist at New Mexico College of Agriculture and Mechanical Arts (NMAM), later New Mexico State University (NMSU), in Las Cruces, New Mexico—positioned more squarely in the borderlands than any other land-grant college in the United States—García helped disseminate cultural and agricultural change in all directions in early twentieth-century New Mexico. The number 9 chile, as García called the new variety, was more than simply the first scientific and industrial chile pepper; it embodied a pan-Hispanic and nationally inclusive vision for New Mexico that encouraged cultural transformations both within and beyond the borderlands. García's efforts transformed more than the chile's genetics; his efforts represented the first major step in producing a modern crop that the nation as a whole could more readily consume. Perhaps better than any other single crop variety, the number 9 chile reveals the intersections among modernity, race, and nation within the wider economic and cultural network of the early twentieth-century U.S.-Mexico borderlands.

CHILE CULTURE

Fabián García was "born of humble parents" in 1871 in Chihuahua, Chihuahua Mexico. His grandmother, after his parents died, brought him to the mountains of southern New Mexico two years later, where as a boy he recalled being terrified by encounters with Apaches. His grandmother eventually landed a job in Las Cruces with the prominent Casad family, who treated him "as a member of the family, in all respects," and sent him to grade school and then NMAM, which they had helped found. García became a naturalized U.S. citizen in 1889, graduated from NMAM's inaugural class of 1894, and shortly thereafter joined the faculty as a horticultural assistant. He worked on a wide range of projects at the college (particularly with fruit trees), spent a year of graduate work at Cornell University in 1899–1900, and in 1907 married Julieta Amador, whose family had deep-rooted business and social connections with Mexico. His disparate experiences and connections from an early age cut across cultural, class, and geopolitical lines.[2]

When he began his seed trials in 1907 as the college's newly appointed horticulturalist, García sought to transform the chile pepper from a regionally significant crop into a national one (Figure 6.1). Already the most culturally and commercially significant crop for many Hispanic farmers throughout the state, the chile pepper, García believed, could be improved. He bred for a more consistent, narrower, fleshier, and more peelable chile for canning purposes. He also sought a milder pepper to appeal to people elsewhere in the country unaccustomed to pungent flavors.[3] Such transformations in the chile would require hard work on his part, but would also require a transformation on the part of the farmers who grew the crop and the consumers who bought it. Farmers needed to be more diligent seed savers and embrace a scientific approach to agriculture, he argued. He believed people outside the Southwest had to "educate" themselves about traditionally Hispanic foods of Mexico and the U.S. Southwest in order to embrace the chile. Cultural changes, within and outside the Southwest, came part and parcel with agricultural ones.

Hispanic farmers throughout New Mexico grew the chile pepper more than any other non-grain crop, and regarded it as a symbol of their heritage. In 1848, topographical engineer William Emory described the chile pepper as "the glory of New Mexico," and a food that "the Mexicans considered the chef-d'ouvre of the cuisine, and seem really to revel in it."[4] Forty years later, an 1884 *Rio Grande Republican* article reaffirmed *chile colorado* as the "national dish" of the "native"

Figure 6.1. Dr. Fabián García in 1907, the year he was appointed chief horticulturalist at his alma mater, the New Mexico College of Agriculture and Mechanical Arts (renamed New Mexico State University in 1960). Photo by Fred Feldman, El Paso, Texas. Courtesy New Mexico State University Library, Archives and Special Collections.

population in Las Cruces, and several generations later, farther north, Fabiola Cabeza de Baca reflected, "When we think of New Mexican foods, naturally the chile dishes come first." The chile pepper—growing in the field, drying by the house, and simmering in the pot—provided a defining mark on the cultural landscape of New Mexico and a source of collective pride. "Unless one has watched the farm families as they weave and string the chile pods," Cabeza de Baca explained, "one has missed a delightful work of art and skill."[5]

Throughout much of New Mexico during the late nineteenth and early twentieth centuries, chile peppers were just as important commercially as they were culturally. The *Rio Abajo (Albuquerque) Press* reported on February 2, 1863, that Congress took "fifty thousand dollars out of the pockets of the people of the United States to make us good roads for intercommunication and the transportation of chile colorado to market." Several decades later, the rail connection between Santa Fe and Colorado had gained the nickname "Chili Line," by many accounts because of the loads of chile peppers it carried out of the state. While chile production had peaked in some northern New Mexico counties by the turn of the century, chile production in other northern areas was still increasing as late as 1924. In that same year, Fabián García estimated that growers exported 75 percent of the crop grown in Santa Fe County out of state.[6]

In the southern part of the state at the turn of the century, commercial production was more limited. Fabián García neither mentions chiles in his lengthy 1903 summation of horticulture in the state nor in an updated report to the National Irrigation Congress in 1908. Only in 1910 did his revised report include the chile, describing it as principally a crop grown by "Mexican farmers."[7]

Nonetheless, García explains in his 1908 *Chile Culture* that "the use of chile in the United States is increasing every year; the American people are beginning to cultivate a taste for it, and thus a greater demand is being created for this vegetable."[8] The increasing popularity of canned green chile provided the most promising development for the chile industry. Canneries in both Los Angeles and Las Cruces had begun canning green chile, mainly for local and regional consumption. Theodore Rouault started a canning business in Las Cruces in 1896, and grew the majority of the vegetables for it. Business thrived. In 1903, he saw no need to ship any canned goods east because he had "a ready market in New Mexico, Texas, and Arizona for the product of my cannery and, indeed, I can not meet the demand, especially for the canned green chili. The greater portion of my goods find a market right here in New Mexico."[9]

García saw great potential in this emergent canning industry and sought to develop a chile specifically suited for it. He later recalled that the success of the canning industry, along with the difficulty of peeling and processing native chile, led to the initial experiments. García explained in 1934: "The old native pods formerly used in the green chile industry were usually quite wrinkled, with a sunken shoulder and a thin flesh. In peeling the pod, if it had a sunken shoulder, the women who used to do the peeling had first to get the skin from inside the stem and as it went over the ridge from the stem end it would break off. Since millions of pods had to be handled in this way, we felt that a variety easier to peel would be an economical development for the industry."[10] By principally breeding for traits that would transform the chile into an efficient, cannable export crop that could be grown and processed on larger scales, García bred the first chile variety to be eaten primarily green and year-round for markets near and far. A chile bred to be canned green not only helped make the future state question possible in any season of the year, it also suggests that the question of Red or Green is also a question of traditional versus modern.[11]

García bred the chile by methodically crossing and selecting for desirable traits among fourteen strains over several successive seasons (Figure 6.2). He planted each strain in small test plots, recorded their performance under a variety of controlled conditions, and within a few years began discarding ones that performed poorly. After several seasons of initial selecting, he sent the seeds of the most promising strains to "collaborators"—farmers throughout New Mexico—who grew them and reported how they performed under a variety of conditions. After roughly a decade of such careful and methodical experiments, strain number 9

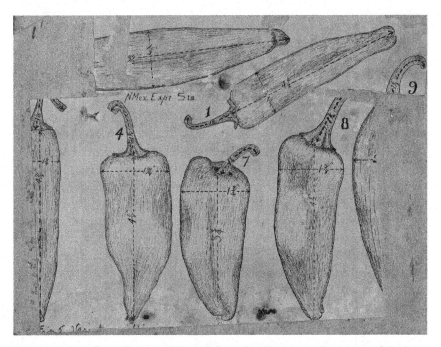

Figure 6.2. Drawings of various chile pods from the New Mexico Experimental Station, New Mexico College of Agriculture and Mechanical Arts, Mesilla Park, New Mexico, 1913–1914. Drawn by J. W. Rigney. Courtesy New Mexico State University Library, Archives and Special Collections.

emerged as the most desirable for industry purposes. It possessed the smooth-
ness, fleshiness, and sloping shoulders that processors desired. It was also less
pungent than landrace chile and, as a side effect of selecting only healthy plants
in the trials, was more resistant to chile wilt.[12]

García approached the chile with a faith that it could be continually perfected
through modern science and the progress of civilization. "Naturally, after the
Spaniards came across and found that this vegetable [the chile pepper] was being
eaten by natives . . . no doubt because of their higher civilization, they developed
more palatable dishes. I believe that the present [chile] recipes . . . have been
improved upon by the Spanish conquistadores," he began a historical account of
the chile in 1934. "Naturally, with highly developed civilizations and home economics developments, the old native methods of preparing these [chile and fri-
jol] dishes have been materially improved upon." Such improvements included
enhancing the enchilada with an "egg that is fried and placed on top of the tortillas after you have put the cheese and the onions on them. It has been stated that
the idea of using an egg with the enchilada originated with the [largely Anglo]
miners in and around Pinos Altos and Silver City, New Mexico, back in the early
80's." For García, technological change drives this teleology of improvement
upon the foodways of the native crop. Chile grinders were a "material improvement," he emphasized, over grinding by hand; and careful, methodical breeding
outperformed the ways of early "New Mexico tribes [who] naturally, had no idea
about plant breeding and plant improvement."[13]

Borderlands

A vision of a more inclusive borderlands shaped García's project of modernizing the chile. He believed in a unified Hispanidad that stretched across the
U.S.-Mexico border. Many intellectuals and elites in northern New Mexico in
the early twentieth century deemphasized historic ties to Mexico, choosing
instead to highlight their whiteness through their Spanish roots and perpetuat-
ing what John Nieto-Phillips has called the "White Legend."[14] Hispanic elites of
southern New Mexico and elsewhere in the U.S.-Mexico borderlands, though at
times employing a similar strategy of claiming whiteness, more often promoted
a "pan-Hispanic" ideology that emphasized Mexican rather than Spanish symbolism and a binational ethnic solidarity among Mexicans and Mexican Americans on both sides of the border. La Alianza Hispano-Americana, a mutual aid
society founded in late nineteenth-century Tucson, helped develop and spread
this ideology.[15]

García paid dues to La Alianza for much of his career and, though hardly
outspoken about his Mexican heritage, embraced the organization's binational
message and his Mexican roots. Alfredo Levy, general attorney of La Alianza in
Mexico City, described García in 1930 as a "Mexican" who represented "a pride

for our race." In 1943, a federal education inspector in Ciudad Juarez told García that he was "a great friend of the Mexicans because he was born in Mexico [and] is of our race."[16] García freely acknowledged his Mexican roots, and kept a copy of the national anthems of both Mexico and the United States in his desk. While some La Alianza members at times claimed whiteness, García did not. He instead claimed a pan-Hispanic Nuevomexicano identity and proudly declared that the blood of "the native New Mexican runs through my veins."[17] Perhaps the most explicit indication that García did not claim whiteness comes from a letter from Bonney Youngblood, a U.S. Department of Agriculture (USDA) Experiment Station official and longtime friend. He wrote to García in 1944: "I recall you are part Yaqui and part Spanish. . . . Perhaps you know that the people of Mexico are much prouder nowadays at least of their Indian than of their Spanish origin, and from the way you have talked with me in the past, I imagine you are of the same opinion. Am I correct?"[18] García's reply, unfortunately, is lost to the historical record.

La Alianza formed in part as a response to pervasive racial discrimination throughout the borderlands. As the country witnessed a rising tide of nativist sentiment during the first decades of the twentieth century, racial tensions in places like Las Cruces only increased. The Ku Klux Klan, while not nearly as prevalent in New Mexico as it was in neighboring Colorado and Texas, nonetheless had a brief but active presence in southern New Mexico in the 1920s that centered in Las Cruces.[19] García likely gravitated to La Alianza in part because of discrimination he felt as the only Mexican American faculty member at the college. One particularly explicit example of direct racism toward García came when he applied for a horticulturalist position at the San Juan, Puerto Rico, experiment station. According to a colleague who supplied a "recommendation letter" for the job, "[García] is a thoroughly honest and conscientious worker and is quite industrious but being a Mexican he shows rather less initiative than would be expected of a white man of equal mental ability."[20]

Racial bias even tinged some of García's closest relationships with white colleagues. His friendship with USDA Experiment Administrator Bonney Youngblood, for example, speaks both to García's ability to bridge cultural borders and the subtle limitations of those efforts. After various visits from Youngblood to New Mexico, the two men developed a close relationship that lasted García's lifetime. In a particularly inspired letter from Youngblood that opened with "Muy Distinguido Don Fabian Mio" and closed with "your hand is kissed by an humble Texan who prides himself in being your friend," Youngblood expressed clear admiration, respect, and affection for García:

Having bedded down at night on the deserts in the days of your youth with your ovejas hombres and mujeres (secretos) with no canopy above you but the stars in the heavens; no music to lull you to sleep but the wail of coyotes or the bleats of hungry borregos y borregas; and with nothing between you and the mujeres secretos y senoritas to signify mutual protection and continence, you have imbibed the beauties of the desert landscape. Living in the midst of natural loveliness and grandeur, you have acquired a depth of thought and aspiration which New Mexican society could ill do without.[21]

García, even in such poetic praise from a close friend, can nonetheless not quite escape Youngblood's tendency to *guisar* the chile breeder's story with racialized sexual stereotypes and clichés of the Wild West. Years later, requesting from García a biographical sketch for a USDA publication, Youngblood perhaps revealed his own desires when describing those of the editors: "They want your story to be as pungent . . . as your peppers themselves."[22]

García envisioned not only an inclusive borderlands but also a more scientific and industrial one. He believed that New Mexicans—Hispanic, native, and otherwise—should embrace science, and that nonnatives and non-Hispanics in New Mexico and throughout the nation should welcome Hispanic culture. In a 1928 speech to the Mesilla School, García relates this attitude in a story about "a friend of mine who was connected with the Department of Agriculture [and] has accepted a very responsible position from the United Fruit Company." García explained that the friend had recently asked if he could "recommend a young man, preferrably [*sic*] a Latin American, who was properly trained in agriculture and could give instruction in Spanish." If not, his friend asked if he could recommend a "North American who could speak Spanish." Regrettably, García explained, he could not recommend anyone to his friend, and a "wonderful opportunity was lost."[23] More than simply asking Hispanic students to modernize, García expressed a vision for a modern United States that accepted and embraced its Hispanic population and neighbors.

García's work in Mexico also reflected his broader vision for the borderlands. Throughout his career, García frequently visited Mexico, informally advised Mexican farmers, occasionally met with high-level Mexican officials throughout the country, and even served as a guest lecturer in Mexico in 1930 for a course on agricultural research and education sponsored by the Department of Agriculture.[24] His particular influence on Mexican agriculture was apparent as early as 1906. In that year, the newly founded Juarez Experiment Station's inaugural report listed various fruit trees that Experiment Stations in Arizona, Texas, New Mexico, the Juarez Station, and "catalogs" had recommended. While the report used the abbreviations "Ariz.," "Tex.," and "E." for Arizona, Texas, and Juarez, respectively, the abbreviation for New Mexico was simply "G.," which "represents that this variety has been recommended by el Sr. D. Fabián García, expert arboriculturist and member of the New Mexico Agricultural Experiment Station."[25] By 1910, García's work in Mexico had extended to high levels of development. In that year, García visited with the Mexican minister of foreign relations (and former governor of Chihuahua), Enrique Creel, in Mexico, "in search of further information in the development of his work." The Mexican Revolution seems to have halted momentum on such "development," though eleven years later the governor of Chihuahua requested García join him on a trip to view "the same farms that will be irrigated by the Conchas, so that [the farmers] will be better able to appreciate your instructions."[26]

García also had a hand in Mexican agriculture through his ongoing relationships with former students either farming or working on agricultural policies in Mexico. For example, Arnulfo Landaverde, a former NMSU student who had recently accepted a post in the Mexican Department of Agriculture, wrote to thank García for sending him copies of the college catalog and to ask García whether he would look over the statement he was to read to the Department of Agriculture regarding Rambouillet sheep. He expressed his "high affection and gratitude for the different ways in which [the college] deigned to help me during my stay in this State [California] and outside it, deeds that are already well known by the leadership of agriculture [Direccion de Agricultura] of my country."[27]

García's influence more often came through casual advice to Mexican farmers. Reynaldo Talavera, a former student of García's living in Chihuahua, Mexico, wrote to García seeking copies of university bulletins on the "tomatoe, potatoe, onions and especially beets for feeding cows or what we call here 'remolacha forrajera.'" In García's reply, in which he stated that he would "be glad to discuss all the problems that you have on your mind on the growing of onions, tomatoes, chile, beets and potatoes," he also mentioned that "the last time I saw you was on the trip to Chihuahua to discuss the building of the highway between El Paso and Chihuahua."[28] Here, García reveals not only his influence over farmers in Chihuahua but also hints at larger connections such as a highway project that would significantly open up agricultural markets throughout the borderlands.

Mexican government officials and farmers were not the only ones to approach García about Mexican agriculture. In 1920, William S. Myers, who had telegraphed him nine years earlier as a representative of Texas-based Mexican Land & Colonization Co., wrote to him, in light of the Mexican Revolution, that "recent changes in Mexico suggest the possibility of our opening an office in that country." Specifically, Myers inquired whether he, or someone García could recommend, would be willing and able to "[carry on] experiments and demonstrations, and generally [be] diplomatic and able to conduct a Propaganda Office" in Mexico. Myers sought an agricultural expert to report on "the big money crops of Mexico, and [give] us some intelligent idea as to whether the growing of these crops is going to expand and whether it would be free from political interference in the future. In other words, is Agriculture going to progress and develop in Mexico, or not?"[29] García served as a mediator, both formally and informally, between U.S. agriculture and Mexican agriculture on several levels: he informed

Mexican officials and educators, farmers on both sides of the border, and perhaps even U.S. investors.

THE NUMBER 9

García's chile-breeding work represents yet another level of mediation. The number 9 had genetic roots throughout the borderlands. García wrote in his *Chile Culture*, "The common strain of Mexican chile that has been grown in this section for a number of years . . . is being replaced in the Mesilla Valley by other better varieties that have been introduced in late years." He used those varieties—the *negro* and *colorado* chiles, along with twelve strains of the *pasilla* chile (then quite popular in Chihuahua)—to develop the number 9. His Chihuahuan *chile pasilla* seeds were brought to him by Carlos Romero, an agricultural student from Chihuahua who later returned to farm in Chihuahua. The *chile negro* seeds he used were from an undisclosed location in Mexico, brought to him by New Mexican farmer Francisco Rivera. The *chile colorado* seeds came from California, secured by local businessman Theodore Rouault, though they also may have had recent New Mexican origins.[30] Emilio Ortega, who founded a cannery in Los Angeles also in 1896 and is responsible for the term "Anaheim pepper," apparently visited New Mexico sometime in 1890 and brought back seeds. As the travel log of these chiles suggests, the number 9 drew its genetic base from throughout the U.S. Southwest and Mexican North.[31]

The strains used for the experiments were themselves shaped over many generations by farmers and gardeners throughout the Southwest, working under a variety of environmental conditions and agricultural systems. These years of labor are embedded, so to speak, in the genes of the chile. The number 9, derived from these experiments, was thus a consolidation of geographical areas across the borderlands. Considering this consolidation of past and distant labor in the genome helps illustrate how the land-grant school facilitated a regionwide interchange of knowledge and material resources.

Professional and university breeders, García included, commonly sourced seeds locally, regionally, and globally to breed modern industrial varieties.[32] As simultaneously a strictly regional and a transnational crop, the number 9 chile differed from most university breeding projects in its reliance on local connections on both sides of the international border. Common intermediaries such as seed catalogs, professional plant hunters, or the USDA seed introduction program were simply not useful. This was a local crop that needed a local border crosser to successfully transform it into a more industry friendly, nationally digestible crop.

It needed, too, an intermediary to encourage changes in both farmers and consumers. García understood the new variety would be a valuable resource only if farmers collaborated in the process by taking on a more diligent and systematic approach to seed selection. "There are always some plants in the field which tend to revert back," García wrote in his bulletin on the pepper in 1921, "consequently, it is very necessary to select seed in the field."[33] This ongoing process required a transformation within the farmers themselves. "As a matter of fact," he wrote in his 1908 *Chile Culture*, "our New Mexico chile growers do not pay any attention to the selection of the seed, and as a result of this we are producing a very variable product."[34] Indeed, throughout his tenure García appealed to farmers to share his strong faith in science. In a lecture based off an 1898 U.S. government publication on hybrids, García repeated the authors' claim that "scientific investigations have shown clearly that the possibilities in the improvement of our useful plants are almost unlimited," but added in his own words that farmers and gardeners frequently miss the opportunity for such improvements because "selection is not made very systematically, perhaps on account of a lack of knowledge on the subject on the part of the operator."[35] The modern, scientifically derived chile, García believed, came part and parcel with more modernized and scientific farmers.

García joined other Experiment Station scientists and extension specialists in various trips throughout the state to spread the gospel of science. His audience received him with both enthusiasm and, occasionally, disdain. In 1923, Bonney Youngblood and García traveled up the Rio Grande together, stopping at various pueblos. One pueblo, however, tried to "run [them] off the reservation."[36] Years later he wrote Youngblood, "I wish I could repeat [that] trip that you and I made," and recalled how "we got into the Indian dance and feared for our scalps."[37] In a letter to García eleven years later relating to a possible project in Navajo country, Youngblood remarks, "I'll not ask you for a letter of introduction to the Navajos, since I already know from experience what at least one group of Pueblo Indians think of you!"[38] A year later, Taos pueblo elders objected to a county extension garden project on the grounds that "anything that had been recommended by the Government had usually been an expensive habit, and that they had found themselves poorer after trying out these things than they had originally." Despite the complaints, the elders were eventually persuaded, and García sent up seeds from Las Cruces.[39] Whether García sent up his newly released number 9 or not, it is clear that García, as with the extension agents throughout the state, experienced a mixed reception depending on the audience and the context.

García's vision for the chile pepper required not only a transformation among those who grew it but also those who ate it. Though he bred primarily for traits that would allow for more efficient canning, García also selected for mildness—presumably to appeal to Anglo consumers throughout the country—and understood that non-Hispanic consumers in the Southwest and beyond needed to develop a taste for the pungent fruit if the industry were to take off. While a less pungent chile would certainly help the pepper's marketability, so too would a change of taste among consumers. "Some of our New Mexico people are becoming quite interested in the use of some of these native products [tortillas, frijoles, and chile]," he wrote to Bonney Youngblood in 1934, "and I only wish it were possible for a national educational campaign to be started to get people to eat these products more than they are doing."[40] In the context of prevalent anti-immigration sentiment—often expressed through food and diet campaigns—in the United States during García's trials and the first decades of the number 9's introduction, García's wish for a "national education program" reflects the subtle challenge of normative U.S. tastes inherent to his work with the chile.

The number 9 never became a fully dominant variety among New Mexican chile growers. While it became quite popular in the southern and central parts of the state, many farmers in the north, where landrace varieties proved hardier, did not grow the variety. In 1924, García reported that production had recently increased 300 percent in Santa Fe County, but growers there were planting landrace varieties, not the number 9, because it was too hot (this, by the way, indicates that while García may have bred for mildness, the final result missed the mark). Farther south, it gained wide popularity but never entirely replaced other varieties. A Las Cruces grower remarked in 1921 that while the number 9 performed well in the field, "we find that the small native chile sells the best. . . . We wish the No. 9 was of the smaller size, as the native people prefer the small hot chile to the mild large variety."[41] Later, in 1934, García wrote that the number 9 was widely used in New Mexico, but because it ripened late, was especially "an excellent variety for the warmer sections."

Despite its limitations, many New Mexicans throughout the state embraced the project of improving the chile pepper. Fabiola Cabeza de Baca, the famed champion of northern New Mexico foodways, exemplifies this cultural acceptance. In an undated speech (likely from the 1940s), she explains that "the chile grown, even 50 years ago, in the northern counties, was a small pepper and very hot. Horticulturalists, from our College of Agriculture, conducted experiments in crossing the early varieties with less pungent, better size and quality chile, which resulted in the improvement of the product."[42] Her approval of the scientifically "improved," and more easily canned, number 9 chile points to an acceptance of new technologies we see in other facets of her work, such as her Spanish-language bulletins that advocate home canning.[43] In this sense, such an openness toward the reworked culturally iconic crop confirms how Cabeza de Baca, in the words of historian Virginia Scharff, "worked to venerate and preserve a more mixed and dynamic New Mexico heritage [and] reworked the world in which she moved, with an eye on both the past and the future."[44]

FUNDAMENTAL SHIFTS IN THE IDEA OF THE CHILE

The creation and popularity of the number 9 chile help illuminate how the greater borderlands shaped this "more mixed and dynamic New Mexico heritage." Cabeza de Baca and Fabián García, who knew each other well and developed a deep mutual respect after traveling on a farm demonstration train together throughout northern New Mexico in 1930, wrote extensive, often affectionate, letters to each other until García's death. "There isn't a person in this country who I admire more . . . than you," Cabeza de Baca wrote him in 1943. She continued, "I believe that every *hispano* should feel honored that we have one of our own blood who was able to lift himself to such an elevated position."[45] Cabeza de Baca certainly drew lines to emphasize the distinctness of Nuevomexicano culture in her writing: she insisted that "one must use New Mexican products" to get a "genuine" New Mexico taste and used cookbooks to distinguish "New Mexican" from both "Mexican" and "American" foodways.[46] Yet her relationship to García and her support of the number 9 suggest she understood such lines to be more blurred than strictly defined. More broadly, her relationship with García and the number 9 offers an important window into how influences from southern New Mexico and the larger borderlands region informed the intellectual, agricultural, and cultural identity of northern New Mexico.

The number 9 represents an important chapter in the history of chile pepper industry in New Mexico and New Mexico's relationship to modernity and nationhood. The number 9 served as one of the genetic strains for the Sandia variety, which was developed in the 1950s and remains an important variety for the New Mexican chile industry. Its significance, however, stretches far beyond its genetic legacy; the development of the number 9 represented a fundamental shift in the idea of the chile. No longer bred primarily for local and seasonal consumption, the scientific chile crossed geopolitical, seasonal, and cultural borders. García's work, as Carmella Padilla states in her 1997 *Chile Chronicles*, "laid the groundwork for turning a regional food into a national food [and] above all . . . made chile into a science."[47] Such change reverberated well beyond the agricultural fields of New Mexico. Bred for a more modern and inclusive region and country, this physically and culturally reworked chile forged new paths of agricultural and cultural exchange both within and beyond the borderlands.

NOTES

1. For examples of scholarship on race, modernity, and New Mexico statehood, see Charles Montgomery, *Spanish Redemption: Heritage, Power, and Loss on New Mexico's Upper Rio Grande* (Berkeley: University of California Press, 2002); John Nieto-Phillips, *The Language of Blood: The Making of Spanish-American Identity in New Mexico, 1880s–1930s* (Albuquerque: University of New Mexico Press, 2008); Robert Larson, *New Mexico's Quest for Statehood* (Albuquerque: University of New Mexico Press, 2013); and David Holtby, *Forty-Seventh Star: New Mexico's Struggle for Statehood* (Norman: University of Oklahoma Press, 2012).

2. "Biographical File," Box 1, Folder 1, and "Correspondence, 1940–1948," Box 5, Folder 3, UA 011, Fabián García Papers, Records of the College of Agriculture and Home Economics, Hobson-Huntsinger University Archives, New Mexico State University, Las Cruces [hereafter cited as FGP]. For biographical sketches of Fabián García, see Kent Paterson, *The Hot Empire of Chile* (Tempe, AZ: Bilingual Press/Editorial Bilingüe, 2000), 15–26; Carmella Padilla, *Chile Chronicles: Tales of a New Mexico Harvest* (Santa Fe: Museum of New Mexico Press, 1997), 6–7; and Rick Hendricks, "Fabián García, Biographical Sketch," http://newmexicohistory .org/people/fabian-garcia-biographical-sketch.

3. Fabián García, *Improved Variety No. 9 of Native Chile*, Bulletin 124, New Mexico College of Agriculture and Mechanic Arts, Agricultural Experiment Station [hereafter cited as NMCAMA, AES] (Las Cruces, NM: Rio Grande Republic, 1921), pp. 3, 4, 16; and Fabián García, *Chile Culture*, Bulletin 67, NMCAMA, AES (Albuquerque, NM: Albuquerque Morning Journal, 1908), 12.

4. William Helmsley Emory, *Notes of a Military Reconnaisance from Fort Leavenworth, in Missouri, to San Diego, in California, including parts of the Arkansas, Del Norte, and Gila Rivers*, (New York: H. Long and Brother, 1848), 51.

5. Fabiola Cabeza de Baca Gilbert, *The Good Life* (1949; repr., Santa Fe: Museum of New Mexico Press, 2005) 45; and Fabiola Cabeza de Baca Gilbert, "Chile," Box 1, Folder 15, p. 1, Fabiola Cabeza de Baca Gilbert Papers, Center for Southwest Research, University Libraries, University of New Mexico [hereafter cited as FCBGP]. Also, "Las Cruces: Manners and Customs of the Native Population as Described by Jimmy McCarthy in the Denver Tribune," *Rio Grande Republican*, July 26, 1884, p. 4.

6. "New Mexico: End of the Chili Line," *Time*, September 15, 1941; "Embudo Rock Pile Monument to Old Chile Line," *Albuquerque (NM) Journal*, September 1, 1941, p. 8; and Fabián García, "Report on Horticulture," 1924, Box 5, Folder 4, FGP. Hugh G. Calkins, "Handling of a Cash Crop (Chili) in the Tewa Basin," USDA Soil Conservation Service Southwest Region Bulletin 46, Conservation Economics Series no. 19 (July 1937), describes chile in northern New Mexico in the 1930s as a critical cash substitute in the region's economy, making it "the important commercial crop in the area . . . [and] the principal means by which flour, beans, lard, sugar, coffee, and clothing become available to the Spanish-American agriculturalist" (p. 4).

7. *Report of the Governor of New Mexico to the Secretary of the Interior* (Washington, DC: Government Printing Office, 1903), 314–317; Fabián García, "Horticulture," 1908, and "Fruits and Vegetables in the Mesilla Valley," April 14, 1910, Box 5, Folder 4, FGP.

8. García, *Chile Culture*, 4. He employs the old agricultural use of the term "culture" here, which refers to the conditions and practices required for successful cultivation.

9. *Report of the Governor of New Mexico to the Secretary of the Interior*, 42.

10. Fabián García to Bonney Youngblood, January 10, 1934, p. 2, Bonney Youngblood Papers, Herbert Hoover Presidential Library, West Branch, IA [hereafter cited as BYP, HL].

11. The advent of widespread refrigeration and freezing in the 1950s helped make year-round green chile even more ubiquitous. The question of traditional or modern along the lines of red and green chile remains relevant today. Most landrace chile in New Mexico continues to be grown in small acreages primarily to be dried and eaten as red chile; most green chile derives from meatier varieties developed by NMSU for industrial growing and processing.

12. García, *Improved Variety No. 9 of Native Chile*. Of the fourteen strains of chile that García used, twelve were of the *pasilla* variety, one was *colorado*, and one was *negro*.

13. García to Youngblood, January 10, 1934, pp. 1–3, BYP, HL.

14. Nieto-Phillips, *Language of Blood*.

15. On La Alianza in New Mexico and its regional variations, see Olivia Arrieta, "La Alianza Hispano-americana, 1894–1965: An Analysis of Collective Action and Cultural Adaptation," in *Nuevomexicano Cultural Legacy: Forms, Agencies, and Discourse*, ed. Francisco A. Lomelí, Víctor A. Sorell, and Genaro M. Padilla, Paso Por Aqui Series (Albuquerque: University of

New Mexico Press, 2002). On La Alianza more broadly, see Geraldo Cadava, *Standing on Common Ground: The Making of a Sunbelt Borderland* (Cambridge, MA: Harvard University Press, 2013); Eric V. Meeks, *Border Citizens: The Making of Indians, Mexicans, and Anglos in Arizona* (Austin: University of Texas Press, 2007); and Manuel G. Gonzales, "Carlos I. Velasco," *Journal of Arizona History* 25 (Autumn 1984): 265. Charles Montgomery argues that Hispano claims to whiteness in northern New Mexico differed from similar claims elsewhere in the U.S.-Mexico borderlands primarily due to class. While the White Legend extended to *paisanos* of all classes in northern New Mexico, elsewhere only wealthy Mexicans and Mexican Americans (while still embracing a *Mexicanidad*) tended to make this claim. See Montgomery, *Spanish Redemption*, 15–17.

16. Letter from Alfredo Levy, Apoderado Gereral en la Republica Mexicana de la Alianza Hispano Americana, to Jose Gonzales, presidente de la Logia #22 (AHA in Las Cruces), Mexico City, July 26, 1930. The original reads: "Efectivamente, hombres de la talla del hermano Fabián García, son un orgullo para nuestra raza y representan lo que el mexicano puede hacer cuando la voluntad y la cultura se unen en ellos." Also, Prof. R. Ramon Espinosa Villanueva to García, Ciudad Juarez, Chih., June 27, 1943, FGP. The original, in part, reads: "El Dr. García es un gran amigo de los mexicanos porque nació en Mexico, de raza nuestra, que al oir español se emociona como un niño."

17. For claims of whiteness among members of La Alianza, see Meeks, *Border Citizens*, 97, 115. For quote, see Fabián García, undated speech (pre-1912), Box 6, Folder 1, p. 4, FGP. García showed skepticism for the term "Spanish American," at one point referring to the "Mexicans and the so-called Spanish Americans" of New Mexico. See García to Youngblood, January 10, 1934, p. 1, BYP, HL.

18. Youngblood to García, Washington, DC, September 26, 1944, FGP. Also, García to A. J. Cook, March 7, 1913, Box 4, Folder 5, FGP.

19. David Correia, *Properties of Violence: Law and Land Grant Struggle in Northern New Mexico* (Athens: University of Georgia Press, 2013), 80.

20. John D. Tinsley to Frank Gardner, September 9, 1901, Box 4, Folder 5, FGP.

21. Youngblood to García, December 13, 1935, Box 2, Folder 1, FGP.

22. Youngblood to García, September 26, 1944, Box 5, Folder 3, FGP.

23. Fabián García, "The Value of an Education," May 24, 1928, Box 6, Folder 1, FGP.

24. "Member of A&M Staff since Graduation 52 Years Ago, Fabián García Is Retired," *Las Cruces (NM) Sun-News*, April 22, 1945.

25. "Variedades de Arboles Frutales propios para la parte norte de la mesa central," Buletin numero 22, Estación Agricola Experimental de Ciudad Juarez, Chihuahua, 1906, p. 9.

26. Governor to García, December 3, 1921, Chihuahua, Chih., Box 5, Folder 1, FGP.

27. Arnulfo Landaverde to Agricultural Experiment Station, December 24, 1925, San Francisco, Box 5, Folder 1, FGP.

28. Reynaldo Talavera to García, December 11, 1944, Chihuahua, Chih., Box 5, Folder 3, FGP; and García to Talavera, November 25, 1944, Mesilla Park, NM, Box 5, Folder 3, FGP.

29. "Mexican Land and Colonization Co. telegram," November 14, 1911, Box 1, Folder 4, FGP; William Myers to García, June 8, 1920, Box 5, Folder 1, FGP.

30. García, *Chile Culture*, 29–30.

31. For more on Ortega, see www.ortega.com/history; *Sunset*, vol. 6, Passenger Dept., Southern Pacific Co., 1901; "Fruit Interest," *Corona (CA) Currier*, December 16, 1899; and "Hundreds of People See Pure Food Display and Get Samples," *Oxnard (CA) Currier*, April 22, 1910, p. 7.

32. García bred onions, for example, with seeds mostly supplied through seed companies such as W. A. Burpee in Philadelphia and Barteldes Seed Company in Lawrence, Kansas. The latter once provided him a particularly early maturing strain of Grano from Valencia, Spain. For examples of major university breeding projects involving foreign germplasm from the USDA introduction program, see Noel Kingsbury, *Hybrid: The History and Science of Plant Breeding* (Chicago: University of Chicago Press, 2009), 148.

33. Fabián García, "Improved Variety Number 9 of Native Chile," Bulletin no. 124, New Mexico College of Agriculture and Mechanic Arts, Agricultural Experiment Station (Las Cruces, NM: Rio Grande Republic, 1921), 16.

34. García, *Chile Culture*, 19.

35. García drew heavily from Walter T. Swingle and Herbert J. Webber, "Hybrids and Their Utilization in Plant Breeding," in *Yearbook of United States Department of Agriculture, 1897* (Washington, DC: Government Printing Office, 1898), 383–420. At times, García lifts entire passages from this early resource on the science of hybridization. See Fabián García, "Variation and the Improvement of Agricultural Plants," undated lecture, Box 5, Folder 4, FGP.

36. Youngblood to García, April 27, 1934, BYP, HL.

37. García to Youngblood, September 28, 1945, Box 2, Folder 2, FGP.

38. Youngblood to García, April 9, 1934, BYP, HL.

39. "Club Work at the Taos Pueblo in Taos County for Year 1924," Box 5, Folder 4, FGP.

40. García to Youngblood, January 10, 1934, p. 4, BYP, HL. See also Danise Coon, Eric Votava, and Paul W. Bosland, "The Chile Cultivars of New Mexico State University Released from 1913 to 2008," Research Report 763, New Mexico State University, Agricultural Experiment Station, Las Cruces. Youngblood alludes to García's work toward making the chile more appealing to non-Hispanic tastes when he states that García has "added vigor and *palatability* to the life-giving mais, chile, frijoles, and uvas" (emphasis mine), in Youngblood to García, December 13, 1935, FGP.

41. Percy W. Barker, Mesilla Park, NM, in García, *Improved Variety No. 9 of Native Chile*.

42. Fabiola Cabeza de Baca Gilbert, "Chile," Box 1, Folder 15, FCBGP.

43. See Fabiola Cabeza de Baca Gilbert and Veda A. Strong, *Boletín de Conservar*, Extension Circular 135 (Las Cruces: New Mexico State University, 1935).

44. Virginia Scharff, *Twenty Thousand Roads: Women, Movement, and the West* (Berkeley: University of California Press, 2002), 118. See also Tey Diana Rebolledo, "Narrative Strategies of Resistance in Hispana Writing," *Journal of Narrative Technique* 20 (Spring 1990): 142.

45. Cabeza de Baca to García, May 9, 1943, Box 2, Folder 2, FGP. In another example of their affectionate correspondence, García sent Cabeza de Baca lyrics to a song he wrote about their travels on the demonstration train in 1930. García to Cabeza de Baca, May 1, 1930, Box 5, Folder 4, FGP. "Las recuerdos del tren agricola me gustan mucho," she responded in Fabiola Cabeza de Baca to García, May 27, 1930, Box 2, Folder 1, FGP. A second letter attached from her adds: "Thanks a lot for the poem. It is very sweet and it brings back dear memories of you. I had not written because I wanted to try and write you an answer in poetry. No creo que jamas olvide aquello.–Fabiola."

46. Cabeza de Baca Gilbert, *Good Life*, 45.

47. Padilla, *Chile Chronicles*, 7.

CHAPTER 7

Constructing Borderless Foods

THE QUARTERMASTER CORPS AND
WORLD WAR II ARMY SUBSISTENCE

Kellen Backer

For two months after David Schreiner left the United States for the Pacific, his Marine troop sat idly at rudimentary bases in the Pacific. Schreiner was a collegiate football star at the University of Wisconsin–Madison and had expected more active combat when he enlisted to fight in World War II. He was frustrated, writing that "as yet we have not done one thing for the good old U.S.A."[1] With no battles to fight, Schreiner's letters detail his leisure activities and the food he ate. Remarkably, halfway across the world, he found familiar foods. He wrote fondly about the meals he ate in the Pacific, which, at times, consisted of "fresh meat—dehydrated potatoes—canned vegetables—bread, plenty of butter, fruit juice or coffee, and <u>excellent</u> pastries."[2] And yet while the foods were familiar, they were also different. He lamented the general lack of fresh eggs and milk—noting that dehydrated products were not nearly as tasty as the fresh ones he was used to. Schreiner could also purchase beers he knew well, such as Pabst and Schlitz, yet for some reason they were "not as good as back home."[3] Many other soldiers also found themselves enjoying the military rations, such as a soldier who remembered always having "good meals" and "plenty" of food.[4] Even William Akers, who worked as a cook and restaurateur before joining the army at the age of forty, praised the military rations: "the food is American and compares quite favorably with what we had at home."[5] How did soldiers stationed around the world manage to find themselves eating foods that were at once familiar yet also, somehow, different?

For the United States, fighting World War II created a massive logistical problem. How could supplies be moved throughout the world to fight a war? To solve this problem for food—known in the military as subsistence—the Quartermaster Corps, the army branch responsible for distributing supplies, focused on creating standardized, heavily processed products—perfecting existing techniques and creating new methods for preserving and shipping foods. Once delivered, soldiers would eat standardized rations in the field and standardized meals on bases. To ensure uniformity, the army developed "Master Menus" that detailed what foods would be used in specific meals; cookbooks and circulated recipes described how to prepare dishes. At the same time, researchers sought to reproduce what they considered to be a typical American diet. Schreiner's experiences highlight the paradox of American military subsistence, which attempted to replicate dishes using processed foods that had new tastes and textures. Moreover, replicating meals in diverse environments—using products shipped from around the world—made it much more difficult to standardize rations.

The army's subsistence plan had the potential to erase national, geographic, and cultural food borders. Most notably, this plan for provisioning troops meant moving foods across national and geographic borders. Under the Quartermaster Corps' subsistence strategy, soldiers stationed in places as diverse as England, the Philippines, and Texas would be eating the same meals. However, the Quartermaster Corps' rationing plan also meant that American cultural food borders—the discursive boundaries that marked different regional and ethnic food traditions—could disappear. The researchers responsible for creating the new rations served during World War II sought to feed all troops a typical diet, but given the diversity of cuisine throughout the country, no foods could meet all soldiers' ideas about taste. Army rations had the potential, then, to erase regional food barriers and create an imagined national cuisine.[6]

As this volume shows, people often attempt to re-create foods across borders. Mark Padoongpatt, for example, describes the challenges that Thais faced in finding ingredients to create certain foods, which forced them to at times rely on smuggled products (chapter 5). Similarly, Teresa Mares and her colleagues show the importance of finding the right chiles and how diffuse distribution networks bring ingredients to rural Vermont (chapter 10). Unlike the immigrant communities described by Padoongpatt and by Mares and her colleagues, the Quartermaster Corps could easily move goods across borders. The army had well-established supply lines, with entire industries working to supply products. Furthermore, the hierarchical structure of the military meant that planners could dictate what happened on the ground across the globe.

And yet even when it is possible to bring foods across borders, cuisines often change as this happens. In this volume, for example, José Antonio Vázquez-Medina describes the ways that Mexican cuisines changed in the United States as migrant cooks created new dishes. In World War II, the Quartermaster Corps reshaped many aspects of the American food system, but it was not able to standardize foods around the world—borders still mattered.

Warfare is an important site for understanding the possibilities and limits of reshaping food systems. The anthropologist Sidney Mintz argues, for example, that "war is probably the single most powerful instrument of dietary change in human experience. In time of war, both civilians and soldiers are regimented. . . . Food resources are mobilized, along with other sorts of resources."[7] As soldiers fight wars, "they must eat together. Armies travel on their stomachs; generals—and now economists and nutritionists—decide what to put in them."[8] World War II mobilization certainly restructured the American food system. Standardizing foods and moving them seamlessly across national and geographic borders required new production facilities and new logistical systems.

As American rations moved throughout the world during World War II, however, food borders still shaped what troops ate. Geographic constraints mattered. While canned, frozen, and dehydrated foods could conceivably be shipped around the world, moving goods across oceans proved difficult. Climate also interfered with plans, as heat, humidity, and cold could spoil rations. In addition, soldiers did not always want the same foods in different climates. While the army believed it could appease many appetites—and change others' taste preferences—troops grew tired of an unvaried diet and found ways to create new meals or procure novel foods. Moreover, the army always relied on local goods when available. So, in terms of supplying soldiers with subsistence, the army's plan was a success. But national, cultural, and geographic food borders also shaped what soldiers ate during the war.

Creating Uniformity

The Office of War Information's wartime film *Food for Fighters* opens with new recruits complaining about military foods. The film's narrator then cuts in, announcing that "since the last war nutrition has become a science and our Army Quartermaster Corps uses that science in planning meals."[9] *Foods for Fighters* is a propaganda film that aims to convince Americans of the quality of military food, yet it does capture several aspects of World War II subsistence strategy.

First, the film highlights how the Quartermaster Corps utilized the most recent technological advances and transformed food to meet military requirements. Consider bread, for example, which could become moldy or stale as it was transported. The Quartermaster Corps sought to solve this problem by creating canned breads. Fresh vegetables were likely to rot; instead, they could be canned. Tin, though, was in short supply, so research extended to other methods of preservation, like dehydration or freezing. All of this processing, however, did tend to change the texture and flavor of foods, so other research sought to find the right combination of ingredients to improve the tastes of these new processed foods.[10]

Food for Fighters also focused on the novelty of World War II subsistence: the Quartermaster Corps' focus on researching food was new, as was its focus on standardizing the meals served to soldiers. In earlier wars and leading up to

World War II, the U.S. Army's subsistence strategies had left ample room for improvisation. Cooks were expected to take various ingredients and create meals for soldiers, but recipes were not standardized. Moreover, distribution chains and limited food preservation technology meant the army relied on local foods. World War I, however, highlighted the haphazard nature of the U.S. Army's food supply. After World War I, the army created a new approach to feeding soldiers. Most directly, the Quartermaster Corps created a new school to train officers. The Quartermaster Corps Subsistence School in Chicago operated from 1920 to 1936 and trained officers in how to purchase, inspect, store, distribute, and cook different foods. The school's staff also developed textbooks for teaching and training. From 1920 to 1936 the school released fifty-two monographs, including *The Army Cook* and *The Army Baker*, which became the standard guides for food preparation in the army. The school closed in 1936, but the army turned the space into the Subsistence Research Laboratory and ramped up its work. Starting in July 1936, the lab partnered with experts in academia and industry to create new rations, new standards, and new techniques, and embarked on a number of other research projects to improve military subsistence.[11]

The development of a pemmican, a highly caloric paste of pounded dehydrated meat, offers insight into the workings of the Subsistence Research Laboratory and the networks of expertise upon which it relied. Pemmican, as a word and as a food, originally came from Native American cultures, particularly the Cree. The lab sought to build on Native American pemmicans and, in 1939, began to create an emergency ration that could better sustain soldiers than any existing ration. As this work proceeded, Robert S. Harris, a professor at MIT specializing in nutritional biochemistry, and Herbert King, a second lieutenant in the Quartermaster Corps, developed two potential formulas for pemmican. To improve on his proposed product, King spoke with representatives from Armour and Company about using "beef muscle and beef liver powder" in the pemmican.[12] Later in the process, another food manufacturer helped create formulas for making different pemmicans. To test the nutritional content of the concentrated ration, the Quartermaster Corps sent samples to L. A. Maynard of the Laboratory of Animal Nutrition at Cornell University, to Merck & Company, and to other academic and industry labs. Ancel Keys, a University of Minnesota scientist, studied how people faired while exerting themselves on a diet of only pemmican. These are just a few of the many experts who helped on this project, and, more generally, on every major Quartermaster subsistence research project.[13]

Based on the Subsistence Research Laboratory's research, the Quartermaster Corps worked to standardize soldiers' diets. To standardize foods, researchers created specifications that detailed every aspect of food production. As was the case with the pemmican research, the Corps relied on outside expertise in industry and academia to help craft these standards. Once the Corps procured products, it distributed cookbooks and menus to make sure that meals were prepared the same way around the world. Again, the Subsistence Research Laboratory worked with experts, in this case largely home economists, to create these recipes and menus. The lab also worked to create new rations for soldiers to eat when they were in the field. What all of this meant is that soldiers in any part of the world were, for the most part, eating the same meals.[14]

As a starting point for standardizing foods, the army created specifications for the products it purchased. During the war, companies worked to meet army standards, as the military was the largest wartime purchaser. Moreover, companies that sold goods to the military could often get favorable treatment from regulators, which provided a large incentive for companies to meet detailed specifications. To create a specification, the Subsistence Research Laboratory would conduct research, writing to manufacturers about what kinds of products were being used. After conducting extensive testing, which often relied on help from academic and commercial research labs, the Quartermaster Corps would craft a specification.[15]

Consider, for example, the specification for dry salami, which attempts to standardize a notoriously variable product. Butchers and companies often use different ingredients and techniques to create unique sausages. For the army, however, such variation presented a problem. Minor variations might end up leading to products that spoiled in different conditions. In order to be able to ship and store provisions, the army needed products made in very standardized, specific ways. The 1941 specification for dry salami began by referencing other applicable federal requirements. Though salami itself had no applicable federal specifications, complex products like field rations referenced dozens of different federal specifications for each of its component parts. The salami specification also required that salami be manufactured in a factory that had been inspected by the Department of Agriculture and that companies follow the provisions of the Food, Drug, and Cosmetic Act of 1938 to help ensure products were manufactured in sanitary ways.[16]

Specifications also mandated "Specific Requirements" for each product that described in detail how the product should be manufactured. For dry salami, the mixture of meats needed to be "beef, 50 to 60 percent, and regular pork trimmings, 50 to 40 percent."[17] Beyond this, the beef had to consist of "beef chucks . . . free from sinews, ligaments, and blood clots," and the sausage could "not contain cereal, vegetable starch or vegetable flour."[18] The filling needed to be "stuffed in sewed beef middles approximately 3½ inches in diameter . . . [and] be uniformly smoked in dry smoke from hardwood, or hardwood sawdust," after which the sausages needed to be "dried for a minimum of 35 days."[19] Finally, the rules noted that "delivered product shall be shrunk not less than 30 percent from green weight, and shall be firm, dry, and in prime condition when delivered."[20] All of these details helped to ensure that the army could procure nearly identical products from different manufacturers.

In addition to specifications, grading was another way to standardize foods. Specifications set a minimum standard for foods the army purchased, but these foods still needed to be graded to determine the price the army would pay for them. An inspection manual described the two most important purposes of grading: to protect the health of the soldiers by preventing "spoiled, damaged, or contaminated food" from being served and to make sure the army "gets what it pays for."[21] Despite all of the efforts to standardize foods, the manual did note the difficulty of grading subsistence, as "no two heads of cabbage are identical."[22] With price controls in place during the war, companies could only hope to make more money by having higher grades of food, which meant they worked to meet grading standards. Because of a shortage of qualified graders, most food grades focused on measurable qualities instead of subjective criteria like taste. Grade A tomatoes, for example, were those that "possess a normal tomato flavor; and are of such quality with respect to wholeness as to score not less than 90 points when scored in accordance with the scoring system outlined herein."[23] The scoring system focused on canned tomatoes' weight, color, and freedom from blemishes. According to this system, even the finest quality tomatoes with a rich flavor would have gotten the same grade as relatively tasteless tomatoes that were the right shade of red and free from blemishes.

Beyond creating specifications and grades, the army produced cookbooks and menus both to standardize foods and to improve the subsistence soldiers ate at mess halls. *The Army Cook*, one of the army's technical manuals, had first been published in 1935, and other army cookbooks dated back to the nineteenth century. During World War II, however, the army worked to implement meal plans based on the cookbooks much more directly, creating Master Menus that outlined complete meals for a garrison. By using updated cookbooks and Master Menus, the Quartermaster Corps aimed to ensure uniform cooking procedures in bases across the globe.[24]

The Master Menu for March 1, 1943, provides a representative example of the Quartermaster Corps' meal planning. Troops would start the day with a breakfast composed of apples, dry cereal, fresh milk, cinnamon French toast, toast, butter, syrup, and coffee. For lunch—called dinner in the menus—soldiers would have soup, boiled corn beef, boiled potatoes, boiled cabbage, shredded carrots with raisins, bread, and butterscotch pudding. For last meal of the day—called supper—soldiers would have baked beans with bacon, spinach, pickled beets, cornbread, butter, fruit gelatin, and cocoa. This Master Menu was dated, but it came packaged with other menus for March, which together were supposed to provide adequate nutrition. Each day specified how much of each ingredient to use to feed 100 soldiers. The packet included a few recipes; for most of the dishes, cooks relied on recipes from other army publications, such as *The Army Cook*.[25]

The sudden expansion of the army during World War II meant that there would need to be mass training of many cooks who had no experience, which the army sought to solve by providing more useful recipes. For example, when the army set out to revise *The Army Cook* in early 1942, Colonel Paul Logan described some of the problems with previous versions: "We did not give much heed to recipes at one time. We felt that every cook knows what to do about cooking."[26] Indeed, when one home economist working on the cookbook pointed out that an error in a previous recipe for roast pork would not bring it to a temperature that would kill trichinosis, an army officer replied that the new cookbook would correct the mistake. But the officer assured the home economist that even with the old recipe, "meat is so generally overcooked in the army that there is no danger of trichinosis."[27] The new cookbook, together with the army's Master Menus, tried to make cooks actually follow recipes to the letter.

Cookbooks and menus helped determine what soldiers ate at bases, but often soldiers depended instead on the army's field rations. Rations provided meals that could be carried and prepared by individual soldiers in the field. C Rations were meant to approximate an actual meal that soldiers could eat for several consecutive days. The D and K rations were emergency foods that soldiers could easily carry and provided subsistence for a short period of time. All of the major rations served during World War II were developed after the First World War.[28]

From the foods the army bought to the meals it served to soldiers, the army strove for uniformity. Quartermaster Corps research had created a food system in which standardized foods could be distributed across the globe, potentially erasing geographic and national food borders. But researchers also needed to decide what kinds of foods to include in rations, and in deciding what kinds of foods to serve, researchers sought to reform soldiers' diets.

CREATING AMERICAN FOOD

In deciding what to include in rations and recipes, the Quartermaster Corps sought to replicate a typical American diet, which would help make foods more acceptable to all soldiers. However, creating foods that all soldiers thought were appetizing was difficult. Would soldiers accustomed to specific ethnic and regional cuisines like these army foods? Furthermore, could army subsistence distributed around the world—including products many soldiers had never tasted, such as frozen or dehydrated foods—be made to conform to existing ideas of taste? To solve these problems, the Quartermaster Corps worked to create foods that were "palatable in accordance with the eating habits of the troops, so that it may be generally acceptable."[29]

The Quartermaster Corps, however, did not undertake systematic research about eating habits and so relied on researchers' intuitions on what soldiers might enjoy. It is possible that records have not survived, but in the letters and research reports that are preserved, there is not a great deal of attention paid to what individual soldiers thought of the foods. The lab would get occasional letters—almost always from officers—that detailed their thoughts on food. Some research would also reference interviews with soldiers, such as a report from the Double "O" Sausage Company, which "interviewed a number of the Personnel at the various Camps" to figure out what soldiers thought of sausages.[30] In general, however, the lab appeared to have no explicit mechanism for receiving input from soldiers about subsistence.

One way to see the kind of feedback the Quartermaster Corps received comes from the detailed reports the secretary of war commissioned about army life. Several of these studies surveyed soldiers about the foods they were eating during World War II. While the studies seem to paint a positive picture of army subsistence, the questionnaires that formed the bases of these studies avoided directly asking soldiers if they liked the food. In 1942, for example, a report found that 80 percent of soldiers believed the army bought "good food"; 90 percent responded that messes served food "fresh and hot"; and 72 percent said the food was "well prepared." A 1944 study focused more on whether soldiers got enough to eat. This survey only asked about food quality in a question about whether military food was "unfit to eat." Fifteen percent of soldiers responded that they did think the food was unpalatable. The kinds of questions on this survey shows that the army was not centrally focused on getting feedback from soldiers about the taste of foods. Indeed, at the close of the war the Quartermaster Corps realized that far more detailed research was needed on soldiers' food preferences and started a new research program. During World War II, however, the lab allowed researchers' intuitions to serve as a guide to what soldiers thought was acceptable.[31]

For companies, developing foods in accordance with what researchers believed soldiers wanted was important. In 1941, a company inquired about selling its products—canned tamales—to the Subsistence Research Laboratory, a common practice for companies that hoped to have food items become a part of rations. A Quartermaster Corps officer, without offering to taste or analyze the tamales, explained the army did not purchase tamales.[32] Generally, when the Subsistence Research Laboratory received samples from companies, it went about testing them for taste, nutrition, and ease of storage, but canned tamales appeared to be too foreign to investigate further. Keeping tamales from the army served to erase cultural food boundaries inside the United States, by serving soldiers a diet that denied a place for regional and ethnic dishes.

In contrast to tamales, researchers' thinking about coffee shows how their ideas about foods and taste could trump research. One Quartermaster Corps officer noted the importance of conducting research to make coffee available in army rations, as "coffee is important in the life of most American soldiers."[33]

As coffee was added to rations, however, research suggested that not all troops enjoyed coffee, and nearly 55 percent of soldiers actually believed it should be removed. The Quartermaster Corps researchers, however, ignored these surveys. One officer argued that if coffee were removed, "I am sure we would have more [soldiers] . . . asking for it."[34] Here, the arguments about including coffee rested on assumptions about what troops would like in terms of taste and diet. Researchers believed coffee was important to Americans and did not let actual feedback from soldiers dissuade them. Similarly, researchers believed that tamales did not fit into the American diet and rejected canned tamales based on intuition, not research.

Researchers' own conceptions about food shaped the diet of millions of soldiers, which had the potential to change food cultures and erase regional and ethnic diets. At a conference to revise *The Army Cook*, Colonel Paul Logan specifically outlined the goal of teaching soldiers proper eating habits: "There is no attempt in the Army to cater to sectional appetites. After a while, the soldier gets the Army appetite."[35] Rather than appease soldiers who might want "hogs and hominy" or some other ethnic or regional food, the army would teach soldiers to eat what researchers considered a proper diet. Logan further argued that soldiers were "going to go home with an Army appetite . . . [that] will spread itself into the nutrition of the American home."[36]

In her history of dietary reform in modern America, Charlotte Biltekoff writes that reformers "see eating habits as a link between individual bodies and the social body, so dietary advice is a way for them to pursue social aims, not just better the health of individuals."[37] In a similar way, the military did not just focus on feeding the army during the war. Logan's comments highlight how military planners sought to reform diets—and sought to do so by creating a national cuisine and erasing food cultures that might value dishes like hogs and hominy.

Getting a sense of what defined American food to Quartermaster Corps researchers requires going back to the early twentieth century, an era in which the growth of immigrant cuisines helped to create a national cuisine defined against the new food cultures. As Helen Zoe Veit argues in her history of these changes, American food came to be based on a New England diet and emphasized plain, simple dishes. Eschewing the complex ingredients, rich sauces, and mixed stews of immigrants, American cuisine emphasized lightly spiced dishes with identifiable ingredients. Veit points out that national cuisine was flexible and often incorporated—and transformed—immigrant foods. At the same time, as Veit argues, food reformers "throughout the early twentieth century aggressively sought to Americanize immigrants' diets by convincing them to eat blander, simpler, and less saucy food." Such ideas about dietary reform and American food continued and would powerfully influence Quartermaster Corps research.[38]

Quartermaster Corps researchers were also heavily influenced by new scientific ideas about food. Starting in the late nineteenth century with the work of Ellen Richards, Wilbur Atwater, and others, conceptions of food began to change. The discovery of new nutrients allowed many scientists to reduce food to nutrients—what Gyorgy Scrinis terms nutritionism. The historian Laura Shapiro sums up one effect of this kind of thinking in the early twentieth century by arguing: "this was the era that made American cooking American, transforming a nation of honest appetites into an obedient market for instant mashed potatoes."[39]

Home economists played an important role in the spread of nutritionism, and would also aid the Quartermaster Corps throughout the war. Home economics straddled a tenuous position, as it was a female-dominated field in a male-dominated academic world. To gain respectability, home economists sought to emphasize the scientific aspects of their work, which included a focus on foods as nutrients. Moreover, the discipline had—from its inception until World War II—helped to promote processed foods. At times, promoting processed foods was inadvertent, such as when home economists worked to make cooking more standardized, which promoted uniform ingredients. Additionally, the discipline's emphasis on the importance of nutrients served food processors as a marketing tool. Finally, many home economists worked for the food industry, where they developed products and new ways of marketing food.[40]

Beyond just aiding the food industry, home economists promoted dietary reform that included broader social goals. For example, Charlotte Biltekoff shows how World War II campaigns to promote nutrition on the home front, which were often led by home economists, did more than teach citizens about nutrition. While campaigns sought to teach citizens how diet could aid the war effort—thus building patriotism as well—the language used helped to promote middle-class values and reinforce gender norms. Dietary reformers in this era—and throughout history—have always mixed ideas about health and nutrition with social and cultural projects.[41]

It is no surprise, then, that Quartermaster Corps officers sought to reform soldiers' diets. Researchers ostensibly worked to improve dietary nutrition. At the same time, however, researchers pursued social goals, such as erasing certain food cultures and replacing them with a national cuisine. Though Quartermaster Corps officers drew on earlier ideas about American food, the researchers were not always consistent in their ideas.

In World War II, the boundaries of acceptable army food were fluid and based more on researchers' intuitive understandings of a national cuisine.[42] The recipes in The Army Cook provide an example of this fluidity. While many of the recipes in the technical manual might fit with traditional conceptions of American food, such as meatloaf, the technical manual contains some recipes that complicate the picture of what researchers would endorse. The 1942 manual includes a recipe for chop suey, though the recipe and its ingredients—bacon, onions, beef, celery, stock, chili powder, tomatoes, turnips, and corn—do not sound like most chop suey recipes. The Corps added the dish to the cookbook before the war because "messes and families have been including a Chinese meal in their weekly menu."[43] Before World War II, messes had freedom to create their own recipes, which helped guide the Subsistence Research Laboratory. During the war, this freedom disappeared, and researchers' own intuitions played an even greater role in shaping the inclusion of different foods. Other recipes in the 1942 cookbook, such as chili con carne and stew el rancho, both referenced—and also transformed—American Latino food cultures. The 1942 version of the manual even included a recipe for tamales, though tamales never seemed to appear on the Master Menus for the war and the Quartermaster Corps was not interested in investing any resources in developing tamales for mobile rations.[44]

THE LIMITS OF STANDARDIZATION

In creating a subsistence strategy for World War II, the Quartermaster Corps attempted to ship standardized foods across national and geographic borders, but this project was not always a success. Quartermaster Corps depot reports, for example, show how borders remained important. At the Newfoundland depot, the Quartermaster Corps found that there were local provisions that could be purchased, such as fresh meat and fresh milk, which the Corps used to feed troops. In Greenland, however, there were no local foods to be purchased, and the depot had to be supplied entirely by a larger depot in Boston. At the Iceland depot, the Quartermaster Corps purchased mutton and fish locally. India had an abundance of agricultural products for sale, and a 1943 report suggested that India could supply 75 percent of all meat and 50 percent of local produce for the depot. The report noted that bases in India "have and use a standard menu," but by procuring so many goods locally, there was certainly some deviation from other regions.[45] In each case, the local food environment shaped the kinds of foods available. Moreover, local climates also helped to shape the kinds of foods distributed. In cold locales, cans could freeze. Frozen foods could be stored for longer times more easily at certain times of the year. So while the Quartermaster Corps might dream of creating food distribution networks that enabled all soldiers to eat similar products, national borders and geography—and particularly climate—served as impediments that helped to keep soldiers eating different products.

The Master Menus also allowed for variations based on local provisions and climate. Many menus noted the importance of geography, such as one from December 1941 that included the note: "for use in December in the latitude of Washington, D.C."[46] Officers had some freedom to modify Master Menus to use local foods, but these modifications needed to follow standardized recipes. A June 1942 menu noted that when substituting foods, planners should ask themselves, "Is it acceptable in relation to other foods on the menu?" and "Is it nutritionally equivalent to the food originally planned or if not, are proper adjustments made?"[47] Master Menus could be modified, but only in specific ways that preserved nutrition and made acceptable substitutions that ensured the food fit within researchers' ideas about food. So while there could be variations based on climate and available products, the subsistence strategy still centered on providing soldiers with standardized, nutritious meals.

For field rations, the army similarly realized that not all soldiers would like the same rations in the same places (Figure 7.1). During the war, the army developed

Figure 7.1. Soldier eating a field ration, 1942. Library of Congress, Prints & Photographs Division, FSA/OWI Collection, LC-USF344–007888-ZB.

mountain rations and jungle rations to suit different climates. One difference in these rations was the packaging; jungle rations, for example, underwent extra rust proofing to deal with the high humidity. There were also differences in the particular food included: mountain rations included dehydrated cheese and a canned butter spread, while jungle rations included peanuts and precooked cereal. The rations had many items in common, but the differences stemmed from practical concerns and from feedback about what items soldiers preferred in warm or cold climates.[48]

While the Quartermaster Corps acknowledged some geographical differences and relied on some local foods, which in turn shaped what soldiers ate, soldiers also appropriated army foods for their own uses. Returning to David Schreiner's letters reveals some of the ways that soldiers modified or avoided army meals. Upon leaving the United States, Schreiner traveled on a Dutch ship, which meant he ate "three excellent Dutch meals" every day while at sea.[49] On a Pacific island, Schreiner described a hunting trip he took with a group of locals, writing: "we slept in a native village, ate their food, and really enjoyed their company."[50] Later in the war, while in the Philippines, Schreiner advanced to trading military food to Filipinos for fruits and other fresh local foods. One time, Schreiner and some friends smuggled steaks outside the kitchens and fried the steaks in butter. Schreiner also described going hunting or fishing for alternatives to military foods. For example, in May 1945 Schreiner and a group of Marines "caught fish by throwing grenades in deep holes."[51] The group then "had a fresh egg and some fresh fish . . . they were sure good."[52] Surprisingly, they did this on Okinawa while the American military was still struggling to defeat an entrenched Japanese army.[53]

As the war went on, many soldiers found themselves growing tired of the monotony of military rations. Even a soldier who initially described military food as "exceptional," finding himself completely "surprised how tasty the food is," later described getting tired of rations: "An even more significant step in the march of civilization was the arrival of some fresh meat, butter, and eggs. In this war the government has done very well in providing edible canned rations, but after several months of repetition they are not too appetizing."[54] One soldier could never again eat chili con carne after surviving on emergency rations of chili for too long. He summed up the combat rations by suggesting that "you could survive on it. You can't live on it, but you can survive on it."[55]

Soldiers seemed to long, in particular, for familiar foods. One former University of Wisconsin student wrote to a kitchen manager for whom he had worked about how he missed the food at the Ann Emery residence hall: "Have thought a lot of those Ann Emery days—and the food. The latter particularly after several weeks of C rations—man those are terrible—man I'd give a fortune for some of Clara's spaghetti."[56] Throughout the end of 1944 and the start of 1945, David Schreiner increasingly wrote about missing his mother's cooking: "How I miss fresh vegetables, your own canned blue plums mother, 3 qts. of milk every day, a couple of eggs for breakfast and many other things I didn't appreciate when I was home. We're all that way—never really appreciate something until you lose it."[57] In one letter home, Schreiner asked his parents to send him some food, including cheese, "canned sardines, anchovies . . . [and] piggled [sic] pigs feet."[58]

As soldiers tired of army rations, they looked to local foods in the foreign locales that might provide different flavors. Rather than eating army foods that were meant to erase borders, these soldiers ate local foods, grounded in particular places. Though food was generally much more plentiful in the Pacific theater than in the European theater, troops throughout the world found alternatives to military food in local cuisines. Sometimes servicemen merely supplemented rations by foraging for fruits and vegetables or trading for meat and dairy products. Discovering local foods and cooking outside of military camps provided troops with memorable meals. When a group of Marines at Iwo Jima discovered a Japanese cache of food and sake, they cooked "the best meal we had."[59] At other times, servicemen tried entirely new cuisines, such as a soldier in Vietnam who "got to like some of their food . . . [such as] this fish sauce, nuoc cham. When they fix [it] up right with hot peppers and lemon juice and so forth, it is pretty tasty."[60] Higher-ranking officers also got the occasional invitation to a more formal meal, such as a colonel who had a dinner at a British castle that included "Scotch . . . famous old Bordeaux wine . . . [and] a famous port."[61]

Looking at soldiers' accounts of the war reveals that not all soldiers readily accepted the standardized army subsistence. Soldiers found foods abroad; they received care packages from home; and they reappropriated military rations for their own uses. Moreover, not all soldiers readily accepted researchers' cultural ideas about food. Rather than being acculturated to enjoy rations, the wartime experience of eating monotonous rations inspired some soldiers to never want these foods again. Some soldiers certainly enjoyed the foods they ate; indeed, experts in the food processing industry believed that soldiers would become accustomed to the tastes of processed foods during the war. The size and diversity of the U.S. military, however, make drawing large conclusions about how standardized rations affected individual food beliefs more complicated.[62]

While assessing changes to food culture may be difficult, food production certainly shifted to meet the Quartermaster Corps' requirements. Companies worked to meet standards, so they could sell products to the armed forces. Because the Quartermaster Corps focused on supplying typically American foods, this benefited companies unequally. LaChoy, which canned Chinese foods, found that in 1942 it would no longer be able to procure tin to can Chinese products. So, for the duration of World War II, LaChoy focused on canning fruits and vegetables. Coca-Cola, in contrast, sought to link itself with the nation. The army clearly did not need Coca-Cola to help fight the war, and the Office of Price Administration could have limited the company's access to sugar. Fortunately for Coca-Cola, many officers believed Coca-Cola was important to national identity and to the war effort. A historian of the company describes letters requesting Coca-Cola from various branches of the armed forces, including from high-ranking officers, as both numerous and "almost pathetically urgent."[63] Coca-Cola was sold at commissaries, and an army order encouraged setting up bottling plants close to the front lines so that all soldiers could purchase the beverage. When selling to the army or navy, Coca-Cola was exempt from sugar rationing. For Coca-Cola, the war helped to create a transnational distribution network that would bring this essentially American food to the world.[64]

The army's strategy in World War II did help to create large-scale distribution networks and processing techniques that could move processed foods around the world. Deborah Cowen has shown how modern corporate logistical systems have their roots in military conflicts. After World War II, a war in which Cowen describes how logistics took "center stage," logistical systems, such as innovations in packing and shipping, spread and became a part of the modern corporation and global capitalism.[65] For American foods, World War II created a standardized food system, centered around processed foods, and an imagined national food culture. The era after World War II is remembered for the homogenized processed foods that came into homes, erasing older food cultures. The increasing globalization of food during the second half of the twentieth century has roots in the Quartermaster Corps' subsistence plan.[66]

Examining the U.S. Army's subsistence strategy during World War II reveals the reality and the artificiality of food borders. As the Quartermaster Corps worked to standardize foods and get all soldiers around the world eating the same meals, it threatened to erase the borders between food systems. In various locales, however, these borders did not disappear. Local foods remained, which provided an alternative to standardized military meals. Food processing technologies allowed foods to be shipped all over the world, but climate could interfere with some technologies and required adjustments in creating meals. Researchers sought to change the American diet, but many soldiers rejected the army diet and found ways to appropriate rations and meals to their own uses. As the Quartermaster Corps' experience in World War II reveals, creating a borderless food system is a nearly impossible task.

NOTES

1. See David Schreiner to parents, March 20, 1944, in David Schreiner Letters, Wisconsin Historical Society Archives, Madison. Henceforth this collection will be referenced as David Schreiner Letters.

2. David Schreiner to parents, February 14, 1944, David Schreiner Letters.

3. David Schreiner to parents, February 23, 1944, David Schreiner Letters.

4. For other soldiers' quotes, see Shaun Illingworth and Tim Fonseca, "Interview with David Wood, for the Rutgers Oral History Archives," October 24, 2002, Rutgers Oral History Archives.

5. Richard K. Long, *A Cook's Tour of World War II* (Ann Arbor, MI: Sabre Press, 1990), 40.

6. By imagined national cuisine, I reference the artificiality of national borders and the role of conceptions in creating nations. For more on how nations are imagined, see Benedict Anderson, *Imagined Communities: Reflections on the Origin and Spread of Nationalism*, rev. ed. (1983; repr., New York: Verso, 2003). For numerous examples of how nationalism can shape food cultures, see Warren James Belasco and Philip Scranton, eds., *Food Nations: Selling Taste in Consumer Societies* (New York: Routledge, 2002).

7. Sidney Wilfred Mintz, *Tasting Food, Tasting Freedom: Excursions into Eating, Culture, and the Past* (Boston: Beacon Press, 1996), 25. For more on the history of food and war, see *Food, Culture, and Society* 10 (Summer 2007), which focuses on this theme.

8. Mintz, *Tasting Food, Tasting Freedom*, 25.

9. See *Food for Fighters* (Washington, DC: Office of War Information, [1943]), black and white MPEG2, http://archive.org/details/FoodforF1943.

10. For canned bread, see "Report of Official Travel" by Walter B. Freihofer, February 9, 1945, and February 20, 1945, in Inspections 1945, General Correspondence "Subject File" 1936–1945, OQG. For a full discussion of this research, see Kellen Backer, "World War II and the Triumph of Industrialized Food" (Ph.D. diss., University of Wisconsin–Madison, 2012).

11. See Backer, "World War II and the Triumph of Industrialized Food"; Walter Porges, *The Subsistence Research Laboratory* (Chicago: Chicago Quartermaster Depot, 1943); Erna Risch, *Quartermaster Support of the Army: A History of the Corps, 1775–1939* (Washington, DC: Center for Military History, 1989); Erna Risch, *The Quartermaster Corps: Organization, Supply and Services* (Washington, DC: Center of Military History, 1995); and Harold W. Thatcher, *The Development of Special Rations for the Army* (Washington, DC: Office of the Quartermaster General, 1944).

12. Quote from Herbert B. King to Rohland A. Isker, February 27, 1941, in Pemmican 1939–Feb. 1941, Combat Rations, World War II and Korea, Box 106, Quartermaster Food and Container Institute, Chicago, Office of the Quartermaster General, Record Group 92, National Archives and Records Administration, College Park, MD. Henceforth this record group and archive will be referenced as OQG.

13. For a description of the two formulas, see Rohland A. Isker to Paul P. Logan, February 21, 1941. For Cerevin's help creating a formula, see Paul P. Logan to Chas. H. James, February 17, 1941. For Ancel Keys's work, see "Proposed Program on Diet and Fatigue," February 26, 1941. All of these documents, and many more related to the various experts who helped on the project, are in Pemmican 1939–Feb. 1941, Combat Rations, World War II and Korea, Box 106, Quartermaster Food and Container Institute, Chicago, OQG. For more on the history of pemmicans, see Edward N. Wentworth, "Dried Meat: Early Man's Travel Ration," *Agricultural History* 30 (January 1956): 2–10.

14. The U.S. Army has a long history of working toward standardization. See David Hounshell, *From the American System to Mass Production, 1800–1932* (Baltimore: Johns Hopkins University Press, 1984); and Merritt Roe Smith, *Harpers Ferry Armory and the New Technology: The Challenge of Change* (Ithaca, NY: Cornell University Press, 1977).

15. For more on the role of specifications in subsistence procurement, see Inspection Handbook, Subsistence, QMC 25–1 November 1944, pp. 10–12, in QMC Manual 23–5 through QMC Manual M608–3, Record Set of Publications: 1944–61, OQG. For a look at a controversy on creating a specification, which led to arguments about the purpose of the specifications, see "Proposed Revision of Tentative Candy Specifications," in 400.1141 (Candy, Hard) MIL-C-3034, General Correspondence Relating to Research and Development, 1928–1954, OQG.

16. For more on the Food, Drug, and Cosmetic Act of 1938, see Charles O. Jackson, *Food and Drug Legislation in the New Deal* (Princeton, NJ: Princeton University Press, 1970). See specification PP-S-96 in 400.1141 Sausage, Salami PP-S #96 1943, General Correspondence Relating to Research and Development, 1928–1954, OQG. The entry General Correspondence Relating to Research and Development, 1928–1954, contains hundreds of boxes related to the development of army specifications.

17. Specification PP-S-96 in 400.1141 Sausage, Salami PP-S #96 1943, General Correspondence Relating to Research and Development, 1928–1954, OQG.

18. Ibid.

19. Ibid.

20. Ibid.

21. Inspection Handbook, Subsistence, QMC 25–1 November 1944, p. 2.

22. Ibid.

23. See "New U.S. Grade Standards for Tomatoes Now in Effect," *Canner*, June 6, 1942, 11–12.

24. For a detailed bibliography of army cookbooks going back to the nineteenth century, see Steven C. Karoly, "US Army Cookbooks and Food Service Manuals," http://www.seabeecook .com/books/milfs_biblio/us_army_books.htm. For a comparison of different versions of *The Army Cook*, see *The Army Cook, TM 10–405* (Washington, DC: Government Printing Office, 1946); *The Army Cook, TM 10–405* (Washington, DC: Government Printing Office, 1942); *The Army Cook, TM 10–405* (Washington, DC: Government Printing Office, 1941); and *The Army Cook, TM 2100–152* (Washington, DC: Government Printing Office, 1935).

25. See Master Menu March 1943 in Menu Planning Branch: Master Menus, 1941–1954, OQG.

26. "Address by Colonel Paul P. Logan, Given at the Conference on the Army Cook," January 14, 1942, in 461 Army Cook, General Correspondence "Subject File" 1936–1945, OQG.

27. C. F. Kearney to Marion C. Pfund, February 15, 1942, in 461 Army Cook, General Correspondence "Subject File" 1936–1945, OQG.

28. For a more detailed look at the development of rations, see Backer, "World War II and the Triumph of Industrialized Food."

29. James C. Longino, "Rations in Review," *Quartermaster Review* (May–June 1946), http://www.qmmuseum.lee.army.mil/WWII/rations_in_review.htm.

30. Quotes from Emil Oppenheimer to Colonel Paul P. Logan, February 3, 1942, in 400.1141 Sausage, Salami PP-S #96 1943, General Correspondence Relating to Research and Development, 1928–1954, OQG.

31. See "What Enlisted Men Think About Their Food, Clothing, and Laundry," Report 29, September 18, 1942, in Field Surveys on Troop Attitudes; "Survey of Quartermaster Operations," November 1944, in Attitude Reports of Overseas Personnel; and "Survey of CBI Quartermaster Operations," January 1945. All of these reports are in Manpower Personnel and Reserve, Research Division, Assistant Secretary of Defense, Secretary of Defense, RG 330, NARA, College Park, MD. For later research program, see Gertrude Dacken, ed., *Food Acceptance Research Conference* (Chicago: Office of the Quartermaster General, [1946]).

32. For information on the tamales, see W. S. Taylor to Quartermaster General, November 5, 1941, and Rohland A. Isker to W. S. Taylor, November 24, 1941, both in Rations "C"-1941, Combat Rations, World War II and Korea, Box 61, Quartermaster Food and Container Institute, Chicago, OQG.

33. Ward B. Cleaves, "Food Service Program," *Quartermaster Review* (July–August 1945), http://www.qmmuseum.lee.army.mil/WWII/food_service_program.htm.

34. Rohland Isker to Lt. Colonel Paul Logan, April 24, 1942, in Rations "C" 1942, World War II and Korea, Box 61, Quartermaster Food and Container Institute, Chicago, OQG.

35. "Address by Colonel Paul P. Logan, Given at the Conference on the Army Cook."

36. Ibid.

37. Charlotte Biltekoff, *Eating Right in America: The Cultural Politics of Food and Health* (Durham, NC: Duke University Press, 2013) Kindle Edition, locations 377–378.

38. Helen Zoe Veit, *Modern Food, Moral Food: Self-Control, Science, and the Rise of Modern American Eating in the Early Twentieth Century* (Chapel Hill, NC: University of North Carolina Press, 2013), Kindle Edition, p. 132.

39. Laura Shapiro, *Perfection Salad: Women and Cooking at the Turn of the Century* (New York: Modern Library, 2001), 4. For nutritionism, see Gyorgy Scrinis, *Nutritionism: The Science and Politics of Dietary Advice* (New York: Columbia University Press, 2015).

40. For more on the history of home economics, see Megan J. Elias, *Stir It Up: Home Economics in American Culture* (Philadelphia: University of Pennsylvania Press, 2008); Harvey Levenstein, *Revolution at the Table: The Transformation of the American Diet* (Berkeley: University of California Press, 2003); Janice Williams Rutherford, *Selling Mrs. Consumer: Christine Frederick and the Rise of Household Efficiency* (Athens: University of Georgia Press, 2003); Amy Sue Bix, "Equipped for Life: Gendered Technical Training and Consumerism in Home-Economics, 1920–1980," *Technology and Culture* 43 (October 2002): 728–754; Sarah Stage and Virginia Bramble Vincenti, eds., *Rethinking Home Economics: Women and the History of a Profession* (Ithaca, NY: Cornell University Press, 1997); and Biltekoff, *Eating Right in America*.

41. Biltekoff, *Eating Right in America*. For more on these themes, see Amy Bentley, *Eating for Victory: Food Rationing and the Politics of Domesticity* (Urbana: University of Illinois Press, 1998).

42. At the end of World War II, the Quartermaster Corps did undertake more systematic food research. See, for example, Dacken, *Food Acceptance Research Conference*.

43. Major W. R. McReynolds, "Food Facts," *Quartermaster Review* (September–October 1937): 43.

44. See *The Army Cook, TM 10–405* (Washington, DC: Government Printing Office, 1942), 91, 112, 113, 116.

45. See Paul Logan, "Report of Circumstances Surrounding Subsistence Activities in the Port of Boston," January 1943; and Paul Logan, "Report of Circumstances Surrounding Subsistence Activities in the Port of Charleston," January 1943, both in 430 Overseas 1943, General Correspondence "Subject File" 1936–1945, OQG.

46. Master Menu December 1941, p. 1, in Menu Planning Branch: Master Menus, 1941–1954, OQG. For the Master Menus of World War II, see this same entry.

47. Master Menu June 1942, p. 1. Both menus are in Menu Planning Branch: Master Menus, 1941–1954, OQG.

48. For a detailed account of the development of these rations, see Thatcher, *Development of Special Rations for the Army*.

49. David Schreiner to parents, February 7, 1944, David Schreiner Letters.

50. David Schreiner to parents, March 28, 1944, David Schreiner Letters.

51. David Schreiner to parents, May 1, 1945, David Schreiner Letters.

52. Ibid.

53. See also David Schreiner to parents, August 29, 1944; David Schreiner to parents, March 24, 1945; David Schreiner to parents, December 28, 1944; and David Schreiner to parents, January 3, 1944. All letters in David Schreiner Letters.

54. R. M. Andressen to Lillian Fried, February 28, 1942; and Mac [R. M.] Andressen to Lillian Fried, June 22, 1945, both in Lillian Fried Correspondence, 1941–1946, Wisconsin Historical Society Archives, Madison.

55. G. Kurt Piehler and Carmen Godwin, "An Interview with P. Richard Wexler, for the Rutgers Oral History Archives of World War II," November 18, 1997, Rutgers Oral History Archives.

56. Stuart Koch to Lillian Fried, December 19, 1943 in Lillian Fried Correspondence, 1941–1946, Wisconsin Historical Society Archives, Madison.

57. David Schreiner to parents, September 4, 1944, David Schreiner Letters.

58. David Schreiner to parents, January 16, 1945. See also David Schreiner to Betty, Hal, and Judy, June 20, 1944; David Schreiner to parents, August 16, 1944; David Schreiner to parents August 8, 1944; David Schreiner to parents, August 20, 1944. All letters in David Schreiner Letters.

59. Sandra Stewart Holyoak and Shaun Illingworth, "Interview with Irving Baker, Rutgers Oral History Archives," May 26, 2000, Rutgers Oral History Archives.

60. Shaun Illingworth, David D'Onofrio, and Jared Kosch, "Interview with Howard Kirkpatrick Alberts, Rutgers Oral History Archives," May 16, 2003, Rutgers Oral History Archives.

61. James H. Polk, *World War II Letters and Notes of Colonel James H. Polk, 1944–1945* (Oakland, CA: Red Anvil Press, 2005), 55. For more descriptions of finding local foods, see ibid., 45; and Shaun Illingworth and Michael Ojeda, "Interview with Edward Bautz, for the Rutgers Oral History Archives of World War II," October 15, 1999, Rutgers Oral History Archives.

62. For food processors' optimism, see William Christopherson, "Refrigeration Makes Possible Attractive Menu at Great Lakes Naval Station," *Ice and Refrigeration*, August 1943, 87; "The Candid Canner," *Canner*, January 24, 1942, 7; and "The Candid Canner," *Canner*, July 17, 1943, 11.

63. Mark Pendergrast, *For God, Country, and Coca-Cola* (New York: Scribner, 1993), 200.

64. For order allowing Coca-Cola to be sold, see Circular No. 51, Vol. 19, Circulars 1944, Reference Collection of DRB Series; Non-Record Materials, Adjutant General's Office, RG 407, National Archives at College Park, College Park, MD. For the story of LaChoy, see "LaChoy Moves from Detroit to Archbold, O. [Ohio], Will Resume Production in August," *Canner*, June 27, 1942, 16.

65. Deborah Cowen, *The Deadly Life of Logistics: Mapping Violence in Global Trade* (Minneapolis: University of Minnesota Press, 2014), Kindle Edition, location 671

66. For the history of the postwar period, see Harvey Levenstein, *Paradox of Plenty: A Social History of Modern America* (Berkeley: University of California Press, 2003); and Laura Shapiro, *Something from the Oven: Reinventing Dinner in 1950's America* (New York: Viking, 2004). For an account emphasizing the diversity of food choices in the postwar period, see Donna R. Gabaccia, *We Are What We Eat: Ethnic Food and the Making of Americans* (Cambridge, MA: Harvard University Press, 1998).

CHAPTER 8

Bittersweet

FOOD, GENDER, AND THE STATE IN THE U.S. AND CANADIAN WESTS DURING WORLD WAR I

Mary Murphy

In March 1918, the Canada Food Board announced that the yearly cost of feeding six useless dogs would be enough to feed one Belgian war orphan. The board recommended that Canadians replace dogs with sheep, which would make "just as good" pets and, more important, provide wool and meat. A dog, at best, might furnish hide enough to make one pair of gloves.[1]

The Food Board's recommendation, absurd as it seems now, was part of the massive campaign conducted on both sides of the U.S.-Canadian border to increase production and curtail domestic consumption of certain foods in order to export more wheat, meat, fat, and sugar for the Allied war effort. The World War I home front campaign involved both federal governments in the intimate daily act of eating, and the acquisition, transportation, and consumption of food gave new meaning to the U.S.-Canadian border. Especially in the North American West, where on both sides of the line states and provinces were young institutions, wartime regulations inscribed more clearly what had been a fairly invisible national border. War brought more consciousness of the role and power of the state and highlighted the differences between Canada and the United States. Governments had certainly investigated and regulated the private aspects of citizens' lives prior to World War I, but the creation of large-scale bureaucracies on both sides of the border that dictated what people should and, in some cases, could eat was an unexpected intrusion into millions of households. The massive propaganda campaigns that linked food to patriotism caused Americans and Canadians to look across the border, not only to monitor their nearby neighbors, but to judge the quality of each citizenry's patriotism and loyalty. Food became a pathway that helped to reshape Americans' and Canadians' attitudes to their respective states and to each other.

140

On one level war is about the making and unmaking of states, the redrafting of borders, and derivatively about the making and unmaking of citizens. The United States and Canada were allies in World War I; their border was not in question. However, the task of waging war and the agendas of both countries drew new attention to the meaning of the border and the meaning of citizenship for residents of both countries.

This was particularly true for women. The states and provinces of the prairie and Rocky Mountain West were among the first in both nations to enfranchise women. Women's heightened awareness of the rights and responsibilities of citizenship found expression in the food campaigns of both countries. Feeding people was traditional women's work, and both the United States and Canada targeted women in their food crusades. Regardless of her race, her marital status, her occupation, or whether she lived in the city or the country, a woman could support or hinder the war effort simply through the ways in which she procured, cooked, and served food. During the course of the war, the meaning of women's work and women's understanding of the connections between domesticity and politics would undergo significant change. As many of the essays in this collection illustrate, the seemingly mundane tasks involved with feeding people have deeply embedded social and political meanings. U.S. and Canadian women would be called upon to turn their daily chores into weapons of war, but there were unintended consequences to that enlistment. Women, asked to think about food in political ways, learned to think about political power in new ways. Access to certain rights of citizenship was a sweet victory, but in the context of war, bitterness tinged women's responsibilities to their respective nations.

"Food Will Win the War":
A Permeable Border and New Institutions

The United States and Great Britain groped their way to a border between the United States and Canada. After the American Revolution, the 1783 Treaty of Paris established the border between the new United States and Canada. Once the United States began acquiring western territories, boundaries needed extension, and in 1818 negotiations set the border at the 49th parallel beginning at the Lake of the Woods and running to the crest of the Rocky Mountains; the two countries agreed on "joint occupation" of the land to the Pacific. In 1846, the line was extended along the 49th parallel to the Pacific, dipping around the southern tip of Vancouver Island. Actually mapping that border took many years. The North American Boundary Commission began surveying the border west of the Rockies in 1858; surveying and marking the section from the Rockies to the Great Lakes only took place between 1872 and 1874. In 1908, the International Boundary Commission was established to demarcate the border more precisely; it repaired and replaced border monuments that had fallen into disrepair and created an unobstructed corridor along the 8,891-kilometer (5,525-mile) border. That now entails keeping clear a 6-meter (20-foot) swath regardless of terrain.[2]

After the 9/11 attacks, the United States pushed for a "thickening" of the U.S.-Canadian border. The term refers to the new layers of security on both sides of the line: requiring U.S. and Canadian travelers to have passports, using a variety of surveillance equipment, carrying out multiple inspections of cargo, and deploying more border agents. It is this "thickening" that has created the climate of fear for dairy workers discussed by other authors in this volume (chapters 10 and 11). Nevertheless, the northern border is still loosely patrolled compared to the U.S.-Mexican border. About 18,600 agents patrol the southern border, 2,200 the northern. But in 2001 only 340 agents had been stationed along the entire U.S.-Canadian line.[3]

For much of the nineteenth and twentieth centuries, the U.S.-Canadian border was remarkably porous. Until the late nineteenth century, collecting duties on trade goods was the primary purpose of the men who worked the border. That shifted in the late nineteenth century when controlling Asian immigration and the movements of indigenous peoples added layers of surveillance and policing.[4] In the prairies and Rocky Mountains on the Canadian side of the line, the North West Mounted Police patrolled the border, concerned mostly with trespassing Native peoples, liquor, and livestock. In the United States, immigration agents worked the line, and army outposts provided troops for containing Native peoples, but there was no official border patrol until 1924.[5]

Montana and Saskatchewan share one of the most sparsely populated stretches of that border—270 miles of prairie. At the outbreak of World War I this region had only recently undergone a transition in which dry land grain farming invaded ranch country.[6] Even by the standards of the empty plains, this was remote country. There were no north–south rail lines connecting the counties, no improved thruway. People crossed the border on foot, horseback, and Model T along a web of dirt section line and county roads, sometimes going through official entry points, often not. Border posts, which often consisted of one lonely cabin, were far-flung and sometimes inauspiciously located. The first customs office at Willow Creek, Saskatchewan, across from Willow Creek, Montana, squatted in a gully out of sight of the road it supposedly monitored (Map 4).[7] At the outbreak of World War I, people and goods continued to crisscross the line, as one historian commented, "as if it were no more substantial than a threshold."[8] Thus, it is a good laboratory for examining how the war produced a more restricted space.

Both Montana and Saskatchewan were relatively new political entities: Montana had become a state in 1889, Saskatchewan a province in 1905. With homestead booms on both sides of the border starting around 1908–1909, the land brimmed full of strangers, many of them immigrants, facing the challenge of residing in a new country at war with their homelands. One German immigrant

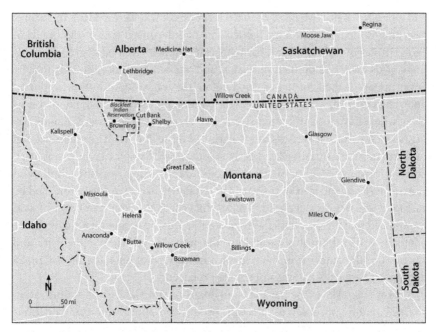

Map 4. Montana and southern Canada showing the Blackfeet Reservation (see chapter 9) and the road network and border crossings as they existed soon after World War I. While the network thickened after the war, most roads remained unpaved and were unguarded where they crossed the border. No north–south train lines crossed the border at the outset of World War I. Willow Creek is in western Saskatchewan, immediately north of the U.S. border. Cartography by Syracuse University Cartographic Laboratory & Map Shop.

to Montana had sons in both the German and American armies.[9] People continually negotiated questions of citizenship and loyalty. In some cases political rights expanded: Montana women won suffrage in 1914; Saskatchewan women in 1916. In other instances, they shrunk: Canada's Wartime Elections Act took away the vote "from immigrants from enemy countries who had been naturalized since 1902."[10] New wartime agencies emerged, and extant institutions took on widened duties. For example, both Montana's and Saskatchewan's universities housed extension services that became deeply engaged in food production and conservation.

From the war's beginning, food had been a critical issue, but in 1917 it took on new urgency. When Britain declared war against the German Empire on August 4, 1914, Canada went to war. By the time the United States joined the Allies in April 1917, Canadians had been fighting and dying, saving and scrimping, for nearly three years. While public support for the war remained strong, the passage of conscription in 1917 fractured Canadian society. Returning soldiers, bearing physical and psychological wounds, peopled the country's farms and cities. No matter where one looked, the costs of war were evident. In Europe, sweeping campaigns and fixed battlefronts had destroyed tens of thousands of square miles of rich cropland. Farms became trench-riven battlegrounds. Millions of farmers had donned uniforms, and women had not been able to fully compensate for their lost labor. Even before the war, western Europe imported enormous quantities of grain: in 1912 the continent purchased 600 million bushels of wheat from foreign sources; Great Britain alone bought nearly 240 million bushels.[11] Wartime blockades sharply curtailed those imports. The intensification of German submarine attacks in early 1917 decimated shipments of grain, meat, and sugar from the United States, the West Indies, Canada, Argentina, India, and Australia. In several parts of the world crop failures had been rife in 1916, and by 1917 food reserves were depleted.[12] In December 1917, the French minister of food announced that civilian stocks were down to a three-day supply of flour.[13] Thus, when the Food Administration adopted the motto "Food Will Win the War!" and stated that "the outcome of the war must be decided in the kitchens of Canada and the United States," it was not simple propaganda.[14]

On the federal level, the Canada Food Board and the U.S. Food Administration shared common purposes: to direct the production, conservation, and distribution of food in the interests of the Allied nations. They also deployed similar tactics and propaganda. Canada borrowed and adapted—with permission—much of the printed and graphic materials the Food Administration generated.[15] But there were some significant differences. When the Canadian government instituted the new Office of Food Controller in 1917 with W. J. Hanna, an Ontario politician, at its head, it signaled that the already long war was not near an end.[16] In contrast, the United States created its Food Administration in the heady days of America's enthusiasm for joining the war, and President Woodrow Wilson appointed as director Herbert Hoover, widely recognized as a hero for leading the Commission for the Relief of Belgium. With flashy propaganda, a famous leader, and momentum as the premier agency mobilizing home front support, the Food Administration enjoyed a popularity that never touched the Office of Food Controller.

In the United States, food work under the guidelines of the Food Administration was completely voluntary. That is, no formal rationing was invoked; no price regulation; no specific laws passed that governed production or consumption. This is not to say that coercion did not exist, but it occurred through heavy-handed peer pressure and "voluntary" regulation. In Canada, a somewhat hybrid structure emerged. The federal government issued licenses that regulated the distribution of commodities in what it termed "their bulk state," but no rationing was imposed on families or individuals. The Food Board's 1918 report summed up the situation with this example: "the sale of sugar in bulk to dealers without certificates was prohibited by order, conservation by families was secured by loyal voluntarism."[17]

Both countries created structures that reached from each nation's capital to, they hoped, the remotest countryside. In Canada, each province had a provincial committee and somewhat ad hoc local committees. George H. Brown, former lieutenant governor of the province, chaired Saskatchewan's Provincial Food Committee, but much of the work devolved to W. J. Rutherford, dean of agriculture at the University of Saskatchewan. By June 1918, eighty-eight committees worked in locales ranging from cities to villages and rural communities. Publicizing food conservation by distributing food service pledge cards and federally produced pamphlets was their primary task.[18] In the United States, each state had a paid supervisor, and, in theory, each county had a volunteer administrator, although in practice not all did. Montana's supervisor was Alfred Atkinson, professor of agronomy at Montana State College in Bozeman. State and county administrators monitored compliance with Food Administration directives. All of the supervisors and administrators were men; their target audience was primarily women. Hoover and Hanna consulted with each other. Hanna visited Hoover in Washington, D.C., and the Food Administration established a Canadian Relations Division, under the charge of William F. Fisher, to coordinate efforts in both countries.[19] Together the two agencies commanded a three-pronged food campaign. The first sought to increase production, the second to preserve foodstuffs, and the third to conserve food by reducing domestic consumption. At first, gender lines on the food front seemed clear: men were in charge of boosting production; women would manage conservation. Labor shortages would complicate that scenario, as would the politicization of conservation.

"Farm to Win 'Over There'": Production

Farmers and ranchers did tackle the food campaign's first charge, to increase food production. Canada labeled the effort the Greater Production Campaign. On both sides of the border, government encouragement, seed loans, easy credit to purchase equipment, and a guaranteed price of roughly $2.20 a bushel for wheat—more than double the prewar price—resulted in record acreage. In 1913, Montana farmers sowed 1.3 million acres of wheat; by 1918 that number had almost tripled to almost 3.5 million acres. In Saskatchewan, wheat acreage doubled between 1914 and 1919. Montana livestock production also skyrocketed. In 1913, Montana ranges hosted 845,000 head of cattle; by 1918 that number had increased to almost 1.5 million. Saskatchewan concentrated on wheat, and while livestock numbers increased modestly, in retrospect, historians gauge the war as turning the province's farmers away from mixed farming and setting them on "the treadmill of cereal monoculture."[20]

Alfred Atkinson viewed women as auxiliary to the task of increasing production. Described by a colleague as a man who "might be wrong, but . . . was never in doubt," in 1914 Atkinson delivered an address entitled "Agriculture for

Women," and pronounced that "if Mr. Jones was a farmer, Mrs. Jones was a nec-essary adjunct, not to farming but to Mr. Jones."[21] An Extension Service bulletin from June 1918, assessing the labor needs for the upcoming harvest, echoed the deep-seated belief that Euro-American women should not engage in fieldwork. The author, E. L. Currier, speculated on just who *would* work the harvest. He suggested that if the usual transient harvest crews were not plentiful enough, help might be gained from the U.S. Boys Working Reserve, a cadre of high school boys training for agricultural labor, or perhaps retired farmers who, "with a little hardening up," could manage the physical demands. Currier admitted that women had "often been mentioned" for farm work. He reluctantly conceded that, while "most of us do not like the idea of asking women to do work of this character," women would be seen in the fields that summer more frequently than ever before. This prospect disturbed his sensibilities, and of all possible options, he favored the proposal that urban men, performing jobs women could easily do, should turn their work over to women and return to the farm. After all, he declared, "public opinion should be such as to force every man in the state to do a man's job."[22]

Neither were Canadian leaders enthusiastic about seeing women in the fields. They, too, encouraged women, girls, and boys to take town jobs for a few months to free up men to work in the fields either at seeding or harvest times. Soldiers of the Soil, the Canadian counterpart to the U.S. Boys Working Reserve, trained over 20,000 boys between the ages of fifteen and nineteen to toil on Canadian farms during the war.[23] Thomas Molloy, labor commissioner of the Saskatch-ewan Department of Agriculture, encouraged women who wanted to help with farm work not to take field jobs, but to provide domestic help to farm wives. He speculated that urban women would like to "engage in the more spectacu-lar work of driving teams or running tractors," but argued that they were really needed in kitchens.[24] Saskatchewan's Department of Agriculture proposed form-ing a women's section of the Farm Labour Committee to appeal to their sisters to forgo more lucrative war industry jobs and take up domestic work on farms during the harvest season, stating "the extra work of the farmer's wife should be shared by the women of the urban communities."[25] It is unclear whether the appeal garnered any success, and just as it was south of the border, by September 1918 Saskatchewan women "were out stooking sheaves."[26]

Beginning in 1890, Canadian railroads had offered special "harvest excursion" rates to workers from eastern Canada and the United States to travel to the prai-rie provinces to reap the harvest.[27] During the war those border crossings became contentious. In both 1917 and 1918, representatives from the Canadian and U.S. governments met to come to an agreement on helping the labor problem in each country. In 1918, they agreed that neither country would try and recruit skilled labor without the approval of the other.[28] Far more volatile was the issue of farm labor. Farmers in both countries resented the rise in wages that the shortage of farm labor precipitated. Agricultural wages on the prairies doubled over the course of the war, and farmers petitioned provincial governments to regulate workers' pay. In 1916, the Balcarres, Saskatchewan, Grain Growers Co-operative Association not only implored the government to set a standard wage, but to require farm laborers to share their new largesse by donating $5.00 a month to the Red Cross or Patriotic Fund.[29] The U.S. and Canadian governments did agree to share farm labor when possible. A jointly prepared advertisement appealed to American workers, stating that while the United States wanted land at home to be "developed first of course . . . it also wants to help Canada." While few workers crossed from the United States to Canada during the war, presumably because wages were even higher in the United States, the American press portrayed Canada as trying to poach desperately needed American farm labor.[30]

Both governments urged everyone—man, woman, and child—to grow food, and as Fred S. Cooley, head of the Montana's Extension Service, noted, "the whole country bent nobly to the task . . . lawns, railroad rights of way, public commons, and vacant lots became alive with people tending gardens and potato patches."[31] Canada, too, launched a widespread vacant lot campaign. With mottoes like "every potato a bullet," cities such as Regina and Saskatoon turned what had been modest prewar hobby and city beautification projects into patriotic service.[32] Charles Lathrop Pack, president of the volunteer-based National War Garden Relief Commission, urged "the patriots of America" to turn vacant lots, or as he called them, "'slacker lands,' as useless as the human loafer," into community gardens (Figure 8.1).[33] Philander Claxton, U.S. commissioner of education, sent a letter to every school in the country, asking boys and girls to conquer the "No Man's Land" of empty lots: "Your trenches are the garden furrows; your ammunition are garden seeds . . . ; your weapons are the spade and hoe."[34]

Women's groups glanced askance. The Industrial and Social Conditions Committee of the Montana Federation of Women's Clubs did not object to the militarization of gardening, but they feared patriotism would veer into child labor. The committee warned against pulling children from school to work on farms. "School gardens for small boys and girls are a wise use of child labor outside of school hours," they wrote, "or as a course in agriculture in the school curriculum, but the ordinary farm in new Montana is no place for young boys or girls." Clubwomen urged the state to keep schools open and enforce the compulsory education law.[35] In Canada, Ethel Hurlblatt, the warden of McGill's Royal Victoria College, expressed a similar sentiment. While she fully supported female students' Red Cross work, she argued that their first duty to the state was to complete their education. She anticipated that Canada would need their "power of thought" with the loss of so many educated young men.[36]

Figure 8.1. Mina Van Winkle, head of the Lecture Bureau of the U.S. Food Administration, explains Victory gardening and food processing to support the war effort, ca. 1917. Library of Congress Prints & Photographs Division, Washington, LC-DIG-ds-09719.

"The Kitchen Is the Key to Victory": Preservation and Conservation

While the majority of women in Canada and the United States supported the war, there were some outspoken opponents and many who had grave reservations. As part of the British Empire, Canada did not have a choice about entering the war, but in the United States, debates had been fierce, and Congress did not unanimously declare war on Germany. On April 5, 1917, Jeannette Rankin of Missoula, Montana, the first woman elected to the U.S. Congress, stood on the floor of the U.S. House of Representatives and famously said, "I want to stand by my country, but I cannot vote for war." Rankin's election came in part because Montana women had won suffrage in 1914 with heavy support from homestead counties. Her wartime choices reflected those of many women. After voting her conscience, Rankin upheld the majority decision and worked to support the war effort, often through the maternalist politics of the time. She gave public speeches to raise money for the Red Cross and Liberty Loan campaigns; she entertained Montana soldiers when they came through Washington, D.C.; she called attention to the poor conditions in military camps; and she responded to women's complaints about the politics of food. Indeed, Rankin's first speech in Congress was not about universal woman suffrage, the cause she had advocated for so many years, but about food. In May 1917, she offered an amendment to a bill that, in addition to instituting measures to increase food production and conservation, also provided for a survey of the food supply. Her successful amendment proposed that when practicable, women would be hired for the survey work. She argued that "food conservation as a national problem is the natural outgrowth of woman's fundamental work."[37]

Conservation became highly politicized on many levels. Government officials negotiated border crossings of food; women negotiated purchasing, cooking, and serving those foods. From small towns along the U.S. side of the border, men and women wrote to food administrators complaining that "there seems to be no food restrictions, whatever, in Canada." One reported, "there is a lot of people going across the line and getting all the flour they need without any restrictions at all."[38] Farmers and ranchers who lived close to the line were accustomed to shopping wherever it was most convenient, regardless of which side of the border a store was located. Distance, not wartime edicts, governed their commercial habits. In the past merchants sold goods without regard to the nationality of purchasers. The war caused new hardships for all concerned. The food administrator for Sheridan County, which abutted Saskatchewan, sympathized. He reported that it was difficult for American merchants to turn down customers from across the line with whom they had been dealing for years because they did not have U.S. sugar certificates. Equally it was "distressing" for Canadian farmers, "living four or five miles from these Montana stores having to turn the other way and drive sometimes 25 or 40 miles."[39] The fact that Canadian and U.S. rules were not always in concert increasingly led to confusion, inconvenience, and resentment. One correspondent reported that a German relative visiting from North Dakota, "near the Canada line," told him there was "much ill feeling and frequent quarrels between the Yankees and Canadians along the line" because of the lax control of Canadian wheat and flour.[40] The writer thought it was all German propaganda and wanted some "authentic information" so he could set people straight. Various food administrators from states along the border feared rumors that Canadians "are not cooperating toward the winning of the war to the same extent we are" would cause a "serious lack of cooperation on the part of the American people."[41]

Henry Thomson, who had succeeded W. J. Hanna as chairman of the Canada Food Board, lost patience with American innuendoes. The Food Board worked with the commissioner of Customs to check leaks of sugar and flour and disciplined border town merchants who violated food rules, seizing goods, suspending licenses, and occasionally closing businesses.[42] But Thomson also wrote to William Fisher, head of Canadian Relations at the Food Administration, asking to have the border states' food administrators "give us a few facts, and name the points where these odd shipments of flour and sugar are coming across," rather than trying to "exaggerate trivial matters into things of huge importance."[43]

Part of the confusion over what was happening in Canada stemmed from the fact that Canadians *were* using more wheat than Americans, simply because they did not have access to the substitutes Americans did. Fisher explained to Edwin Ladd, North Dakota's food administrator, that Canada did not grow much corn, which was one of the major substitutes used in the United States, nor was the United States exporting any corn to Canada. Canadians had implemented many conservation measures, but inevitably they would be more dependent upon wheat than Americans. Because using substitutes was such a key part of the American conservation effort, from the American side, it simply looked like Canadians were not doing their bit.[44]

What ordinary Americans did not see was that Canadians had to bargain for foods they had once easily imported. Major commodities like sugar and coffee, which had often been imported through the United States, were now the object of constantly shifting negotiations.[45] Seeking to reserve food to send overseas, the United States also embargoed certain items. Sometimes low level dickering worked things out. On one occasion, Thomson and Fisher were able to broker a deal whereby Canada dispensed some flour in exchange for the release of seventeen freight cars of Passover food from the Manischewitz Company in Cincinnati, none of which was available in Canada.[46] Of concern to prairie dwellers was a U.S. embargo on California dried prunes and peaches. Dried fruits were a staple in northern territories where soft fruits could not grow. Again, diplomatic negotiations enabled western Canadian merchants to import the fruits under special permits.[47]

Propaganda enjoined cooks to replace wheat flour with barley, rye, corn, and potato flour. In one of its more unusual measures, the Food Administration advocated the use of whale meat as an "economical and excellent" substitute for more traditional meats. It even provided recipes for whale pot roast and, should there be leftovers, for curried whale. Canada shipped more than a thousand tons of frozen whale meat to Boston in 1918, although it did not catch on in either American or Canadian markets.[48] The Food Board encouraged Canadians to eat beaver. Claiming that beaver meat was "relished by woodsmen and trappers," the Food Board recommended the "best way to treat beaver meat is to salt it as has been done with pork."[49] It is unclear if members of the staff who encouraged this practice saw any symbolism in urging Canadians to cook the country's totem animal, one that appeared on the seal of the Food Board itself. While the challenges of acquiring whale meat and preparing beaver may have seemed daunting, women regularly tackled new war recipes that frequently bore erratic and sometimes inedible results.

The pervasive propaganda frequently succeeded in convincing civilians that they were crucial to the historic effort of the war, and it led them to their own innovations. While the government and national women's magazines published cookbooks, pamphlets, and bulletins with wartime recipes, local women's groups also came up with their own creations. Members of the Regina Boat Club Girls' Auxiliary compiled a *Food Conservation Cook Book* with chapters on War Menus and Warming Over "Left Overs."[50] The Hot Springs, Montana, Red Cross Society published a wartime cookbook, stating in its preface that its purpose was not "for the recipes and money derived from the sale of the book only," but that the Society wished it to "serve as a memento of these stirring history-making times, when we showed the world and each other that we could be true, red-blooded Americans in every sense of the word." "We can help win this war by eating," they wrote.[51] But of course one had to eat according to conservation guidelines. Their book included all kinds of recipes using leftover meat, beans, and potatoes, and included such dishes as "Woodrow Wilson's Okey Hash," "General Pershing Salad," "Hoover Corn and Graham Gems," and "General Joffre Pudding." Wilson's hash consisted of chopped meat and barley groats; General Pershing's salad was a concoction of gelatin, cheese, whipped cream, salt, and pepper. The author suggested serving it with cream dressing, and then amended that during the war, French dressing might be more appropriate. It was taxing for cooks to figure out how to make bread, rolls, piecrusts, cakes, and other baked goods with greatly reduced portions of wheat flour and sugar. In the cookbook *War-Winning Recipes*, written by the Young Ladies Sodality of Missoula's St. Francis Xavier Church, one recipe for "Conservation Oatmeal Cookies" was wheatless, eggless, and sugarless—but required three cups of corn syrup.[52]

During World War I, neither Canada nor the United States imposed civilian food rationing. Compliance with conservation directives from the Food Board and the Food Administration—for example, the famous wheatless and meatless meals, and then days—was voluntary. But enormous amounts of propaganda and peer pressure often made acquiescence seem compulsory. The similarity of propaganda on both sides of the border masked some real differences in food supply and government policy. It made it easier for people looking across the line to disparage the dutifulness of Canadians or Americans and their commitment to the war effort. The border, which had been a virtually imperceptible line people crossed to get work, to shop, to visit family and friends, to partake in holiday picnics, now became a line of judgment.

"Are YOU Breaking the Law?": Enforcement

Colorful posters, experimental recipes, and pantry shelves gleaming with packed canning jars represented the constructive side of the food war. But there was a darker side as well. Not all merchants did abide by food directives. Voluntarism could veer into persecution when neighbors turned to spying and tattling on each other for perceived violations of the food rules. And both administrations' commitment to voluntarism also meant there were few meaningful attempts to curb inflation, price gouging, and fraud.

Traveling salesmen, neighbors, business rivals, and self-appointed watchdogs reported to both the Food Administration and the Food Board alleged food rule infractions, as well as all kinds of ways in which they thought people misused food.[53] A traveler wrote to Herbert Hoover about a café in Lewistown, Montana, complaining: "Yesterday I was charged 25 cts for a cup of very weak coffee and 3 small doughnuts[,] the hole being the largest part of said doughnuts." What really irked him was that he discovered locals were charged only 15 cents for the same bad coffee and runty doughnuts.[54] Accusations of food hoarding or failing to use substitutes were common. In Assiniboia, Saskatchewan, authorities charged George Wilder, a soldier home on harvest leave, with hoarding flour. Until he joined the army, Wilder lived on a farm with his seventy-year-old father and had bought a quantity of flour over the allotment in place at that time for the elder Wilder's use while George was away. The local magistrate consulted with the Justice Department and the Food Board, but while waiting for their response, "took the matter into [his] own hands" and dismissed the case, since George Wilder had been recalled to duty. The Food Board subsequently decided that Wilder had not in fact been in violation of its orders.[55] Guilty or not, the label of hoarder could be devastating. Alice Hutchens served her first threshing crew dinner during World War I. She recalled saving all her sugar and coffee for weeks so that she could put on the kind of meal her mother had in prewar years. The men sat down to a long table of "good food, steaming hot and ready." They ate with gusto, but also said within Alice's hearing: "This tastes like real coffee—and so much pie! There must be *hoarders* at this house." The slur was vivid fifty years later: "My heart was broken entirely! There were two words that were anathema in World War I. One was *hoarder*. The other was *slacker*. After all the weeks we had done without! Hoarder!"[56]

Since the Food Administration's rules were technically voluntary, there was a convoluted process to punish violators. Food Administration staff in Bozeman investigated charges, and if they seemed credible, the accused was given a hearing and a decision rendered. If the accused was found to have "failed to properly observe the regulations," he or she was then "allowed" to make a specified donation to the Red Cross, or sometimes forbidden from purchasing sugar, or compelled to return flour.[57]

In January 1918, Atkinson had appealed to Montana women's clubs to form three-person "Food Rule Enforcement" committees to discourage violation of food rules "by word, letter or telephone, or, if necessary, by public remonstrance." These "food police," he said, should be women of "the highest patriotism," certainly no "slackers," who would "pledge themselves to openly take issue with any man or woman whom they find disobeying food rules." Grace Vance Erickson, president of District 1 of the Federation of Women's Clubs and future first lady of Montana, advised Atkinson that he would be unlikely to find women willing to join such committees. Alternatively, she proposed sending "capable strong women" out into the community in an educational campaign, which would, she posited, "do about the same work, without creating the antagonism of the 'food police.'"[58] Cognizant of the dangers of excessive patriotism, James McGregor, western representative of the Food Controller, sought diplomatic men to lead the provincial committees. He wanted them to diffuse the ire of citizens who wrote daily proposing conservation measures that were unnecessarily draconian.[59]

In Canada, enforcement of the Food Board's orders did become a police matter. In April 1918, the Food Board created an enforcement section to investigate and penalize violations of any of the Food Board's orders (Figure 8.2). The Board called upon local and provincial police, who responded with varying degrees of enthusiasm. Without naming any names, the Board noted that in some provinces, "little or no assistance was rendered, due partly to the small numbers on their forces and due partly to lack of sympathy." Perhaps in response to what people read about practices across the border, the Food Board clarified that it had no authority to compel contributions to the Red Cross or Patriotic Funds.[60] But it did take other measures. Those found guilty of selling flour without substitutes or of hoarding had goods confiscated or were ordered to cease business for a certain number of days.[61] Beginning in June 1918, the *Canadian Food Bulletin* publicized lists of "typical cases" that had come to the attention of the enforcement section. It printed individuals' names, the offenses for which they had been found guilty, and the penalties imposed. Everyone up and down the chain of food service was held accountable. Regulations for public eating places governed the amount of bread and butter, the kinds of meats, and the hours during which meals could be served. Not only proprietors and managers, but waiters, cooks, and stewards were held "personally responsible" for compliance.[62] As a result, a waiter in a Saskatoon café was fined $100 and costs with the option of thirty days in jail for serving hamburger during prohibited hours, and another café owner in the city was fined $100 for serving more than two ounces of white bread to a customer at one time. Three caterers in Regina paid a penalty of $100 apiece for selling pork tenderloin on a porkless day. Considering how convoluted the food orders were—Canada passed a total of seventy different food orders between 1917 and the end of the war—the number of punitive actions in the country was not large:[63]

Fines	142
Imprisonments	4
Suspensions	133
Confiscations	17
Forced Sales	8

Judging by the lists in the *Food Bulletin*, Saskatchewan was one of those provinces short-staffed or unsympathetic to enforcement of food orders.[64]

Figure 8.2. "Are You Breaking the Law?" Note the silhouette of a policeman in this Canada Food Board Poster. Library of Congress, Prints & Photographs Division, WWI Posters, LC-USZC4–12666.

In the United States, county food administrators formed the front line of enforcement, and some relished the role. In Prairie County, Administrator Day LeSuer instructed boardinghouse keeper Mrs. R. L. Casselman that she could not place a sugar bowl on the table or pass one to her boarders. If a boarder wanted sugar in his or her coffee or tea, Casselman could put one teaspoon in each cup, but only in the kitchen before it was served.[65] Elmer Johnson, the administrator for Ravalli County, reviewed grocery store records to assess how much sugar people bought and sent them admonitory letters if he thought they had purchased too much. Perhaps the most zealous of the state's food administrators was Jerome G. Locke of Livingston, president of the Park County Loyalty League. Locke was rabid in his opposition to socialists, Wobblies, and anyone he judged to be pro-German. In spring of 1918, a Mrs. Margaret Carlson came to his attention. He alleged that she was known to be "violently disloyal," to have "indulged in seditious utterances," and to have perjured herself in obtaining a draft exemption for one of her sons. He claimed to have spent days in his car watching her, hoping to get sufficient evidence to prove she was, on top of everything else, "a food hoarder." Locke wanted to make her an example, arguing that if "we can get one conviction . . . our troubles will be lessened." Indeed, he told Atkinson that if he could not get a conviction on food hoarding in Park County, he would ask to be replaced as food administrator, so he could "take a job as leader of the Vigilantee Committee."[66]

Some people used the cloak of patriotism and the existence of new government agencies to revive long-standing grievances, to cast aspersions on neighbors of German background, as well as to express well-meaning concerns and fears. Their agendas were tangled and assuredly not always clear even to themselves. One letter from a woman in Wolf Point illustrates the many axes upon which women's cares in particular turned. In September 1918, Mrs. E. Purdy wrote to Atkinson to complain that her neighbor, Ed Bolder, was letting his cattle destroy the corn crop of a young homesteader serving in the war. The young man's mother had planted the field for her son, but she was working in town, and despite chasing off the cattle many times, she could not protect the crop. In her absence, Purdy asserted, the neighbor, a "low-degraded German," let his cattle break the homesteader's fence and eat and trample his crops. She also accused Bolder of breaking into the boy's shack to steal a pair of pliers and accused his wife of stealing eggs from the hen house. Purdy noted that the cattle in question had been eating other neighbors' alfalfa, and that Bolder's hogs had been bothering her for two years. Moreover, she described Bolder as prosperous; he owned his own farm, which had "all kinds of grain[,] cattle & horses," yet he had purchased only $50 in war thrift stamps, while others with much less signed up for $100. Purdy hoped Bolder would be drafted and "put to war where he belongs."[67]

It is hard to know which of the many grievances that Purdy enumerated bothered her most. Farmers on both sides of the border complained that cattle damaged their crops. This old grievance, based on open range laws that required farmers to fence crops but did not require fences to enclose animals, was given new life in the war. Farmers wanted the Food Administration to prosecute live-stock owners on the grounds they were threatening wartime food production. The fact that Bolder was prospering in a time when many homesteaders were struggling; that he was allegedly thieving from a soldier; that he was cheap and unpatriotic and German, all rolled into quite an indictment. But the accusation Purdy saved for her final volley was that Bolder was imposing on this young homesteader's mother: deprived of her only son, she was not even able to protect his crop.

Women, despite their best efforts to remain patriotic, grew increasingly frustrated with the economics of trying to support the war and take care of their families in the face of what they perceived as ill-conceived policies. Besieged by "three hundred old women" who could not get the sugar they needed for canning because of the convoluted way the agency distributed sugar certificates, George Bolster, food administrator in Sheridan County, sounded a bit desperate when he beseeched Atkinson for help.[68] Farmers' wives in Canada complained that posting a food pledge card in the window was a deterrent to getting hired hands. Laborers refused to eat substitutes, demanded excessive amounts of sugar for their tea, and insisted on meat and potatoes.[69] Mrs. W. J. Pennington of Cut Bank testified to the difficulties of heeding the food rules. She documented her attempts to use substitutes, but noted that as soon as the government said "Eat fish," the price of fish skyrocketed. Butter substitutes cost as much as butter. She was eager to do what she could for the war, but "the miserable profiteering" concerned her, and she hoped that "all the crooked things [would] soon be straightened out for all."[70]

In cities across the region, women decided to attack "the miserable profiteering" and high cost of living through housewives' leagues, consumer councils, and efforts to create or reinvigorate city markets. At the beginning of the war, Mrs. Newhall, president of the Calgary Consumers' League, visited Regina to describe women's impressive efforts to cut the cost of living by revivifying Calgary's city market. To dramatize their efforts, they bought a railcar load of vegetables from British Columbia and then sold the produce themselves in the market. The women sent 250 letters to women's institutes and farmers' unions to urge producers to bring their meat, eggs, and produce directly to the market, and from a paltry four stalls, they soon had a waiting list of fifty potential vendors.[71] As the food crisis intensified, the Butte Housewives' League bypassed middlemen by arranging for farmers to ship carloads of produce to Butte, and then sold the goods directly to consumers at the railroad freight house. Two delegates from every woman's club in the city comprised a Women's Council that investigated the food distribution system. Women monitored wholesalers who apparently tried to dump edible food in attempts to decrease supply and drive up prices.[72]

Many women proclaimed that they would not support food conservation until Prohibition had been put into effect, since, as one farm wife put it, "as long as the breweries are allowed to buy up the grain and use it up for poisin, what little we save won't amount to much."[73] The government's "continual prodding" of housewives to save small portions, while "it deals with gluttonous and traitorous speculators in a soft and piffling manner," angered other women. Why should they be overworked—planting, growing, harvesting, canning, conserving—"while Mr. Exploiter exists uncontrolled and reaps that which we have sown."[74] It raised the hackles of Eva Little of Plains, Montana, to read in the newspaper advice from an English lord on what Americans should eat and how they should economize. From food she moved to the wartime concentration of political power, "How can we call our allies democratic when they have kings, queens, lords, dukes, etc.? Have we not also got to be careful or we will have a greater autocracy in this country . . . are we not giving our President more power than even he [the Kaiser] has?"[75]

Producing, cooking, and serving food had always been traditional women's work. During the war those domestic tasks took on added political significance. In order to gain women's cooperation, Herbert Hoover and others told women that what once was considered necessary but insignificant work now had global consequences. It is not surprising that women, bombarded with new messages about the political importance of their daily chores, could expand that thinking to other political and social issues. Women used their domestic tasks as a springboard to critique the economics of food distribution, the priorities of conservation, and the very nature of democracy. As Una Herrick, dean of women at Montana State College, reflected, the country had sent women into unprecedented public spaces to work for the war. It was naive to think they would be unchanged. "Women," she wrote, "went into war in a hobble skirt but came out less hampered in mind and body."[76] Abigail DeLury, director of women's work at the University of Saskatchewan, in her 1919 report to the Homemakers' Clubs, looked back at the experience of the war and the influenza epidemic and mused, "because of these experiences we shall be able to bring more kindness, more sympathy, more tolerance, better judgment, more intelligent and independent thinking to the great tasks that are before us."[77]

Indeed, western women, while willing to make sacrifices for the war, were not willing to make those sacrifices unconditionally. In 1917, the Montana Federation of Women's Clubs, which lent its considerable organizational skills to the war effort, outlined what women expected in return for their cooperation. The Federation argued that if mothers of the country freely gave their sons, then those "boys" should be housed in "morally clean camps"; that if there really was a serious food shortage, then national prohibition should be enacted as a war measure to save grain; and that if the future of the nation and of world peace depended on the next generation, boys and girls must be kept in school.[78] Women did not absolve government policies that ignored consideration of regional differences, that seemed arbitrary, unfair, and sometimes corrupt. Her wartime experiences caused at least one Canadian woman to profoundly change her attitude toward the state. Mrs. Addams supported the war when her son was sent to the front, but even before she received word that he had been killed and his body tossed "in a lonely swamp," she had begun to reassess the impact of the war on Canadian life: "gradually through the months, when always more of the people's food supply and constantly more men were taken by the government for its military purposes, when I saw the state institutions for defectives closed, the schools abridged or dismissed, women and children put to work in factories under hours and conditions which had been legally prohibited years before . . . the State itself gradually became for me an alien and hostile thing."[79]

Canada and the United States asked housewives, mothers, servants, and students, women of all sorts, to do their duty to their respective nations during World War I. For some this meant figuring out just what their relationship to the state was. In part they looked to their neighbors across the border to measure the meaning and scope of duty and citizenship. Jeannette Rankin had argued that dealing with food was natural for women, but she also insisted that women's relationship with food was political and global. Presaging contemporary food activists, she stated in 1917, "Women as housewives should consider the food problem in the carload lot and in the market and in transit and in storage and in the Board of Trade and in the national market as well as in the small portions used on the family table."[80] Whether women's wartime experiences had a lasting effect on the ways in which they thought about food is hard to determine. Una Herrick attributed increased postwar enrollment in home economics to the fact that "the world," including women, "was becoming food conscious."[81] It is clear that the call to participate in the food war opened unanticipated modes of political thinking and action for Canadian and American women. Through gardening, canning, shopping, and cooking they came to new understandings of what they owed their respective nations and what their nations owed them in return.

World War I made the plains and prairie dwellers in the North American West more cognizant of a border that required them more than ever before to be Canadian or American. The borderlands between Montana and Saskatchewan remained remote and loosely policed compared to parts farther east and west. Nonetheless, crossing the border to find work or to buy food became more complicated and more bureaucratized. By their very nature borders imply surveillance—someone monitors who and what crosses borders—or else they are meaningless. World War I accelerated the surveillance that both countries would further institutionalize in coming decades. In the context of the war, seemingly innocuous items like sugar and flour became instruments of policing and judgment. As neighbors looked across the border to places where they had picnicked, stores they had patronized, cafés in which they lunched, the once nearly invisible line between them became ever more tangible.

NOTES

1. *Canadian Food Bulletin*, no. 13 (March 28, 1918): 17.
2. Peter Sullivan, David Bernhardt, and Brian Ballantyne, "The Canada-United States Boundary: The Next Century," http://www.internationalboundarycommission.org/docs/ibc -2009-01-eng.pdf; Elizabeth Jameson and Sheila McManus, eds., *One Step over the Line: Toward a History of Women in the North American Wests* (Edmonton: University of Alberta Press, 2008).
3. "The United States–Canadian Border Undefended No More," *Economist* (November 8, 2014), http://www.economist.com/news/americas/21631103-violence-ottawa-has-thickened -once-seamless-border-souring-mood-both.
4. See discussions of these issues in Kornel S. Chang, *Pacific Connections: The Making of the U.S.-Canadian Borderlands* (Berkeley: University of California Press, 2012); Bruno Ramirez, *Crossing the 49th Parallel: Migration from Canada to the United States, 1900–1930* (Ithaca, NY: Cornell University Press, 2001); and Sheila McManus, "Unsettled Pasts, Unsettling Borders: Women, Wests, Nations," in Jameson and McManus, *One Step over the Line*, 29–54.
5. Ramirez, *Crossing the 49th Parallel*, 56.
6. On the borderlands economy, see Andrew R. Graybill, *Policing the Great Plains: Rangers, Mounties, and the North American Frontier, 1875–1910* (Lincoln: University of Nebraska Press, 2007).
7. Dave McIntosh, *The Collectors: A History of Canadian Customs and Excise* (Toronto: NC Press, 1984), 377.
8. Beth LaDow, *The Medicine Line: Life and Death on a North American Borderland* (New York: Routledge, 2001), 98.
9. Alice S. Hutchens, *The Gift of Little Things* (Caldwell, ID: Caxton Printers, 1968), 67.
10. Bill Waiser, *Saskatchewan: A New History* (Calgary: Fifth House, 2005), 222.
11. Avner Offer, *The First World War: An Agrarian Interpretation* (Oxford: Clarendon Press, 1989), 86.
12. William Clinton Mullendore, *History of the United States Food Administration 1917–1919* (Stanford, CA: Stanford University Press, 1941), 47; Maxcy Robson Dickson, *The Food Front in World War I* (Washington, DC: American Council on Public Affairs, 1944), 11–12.
13. Canada Food Board [hereafter cited as CFB], *Report of the Canada Food Board* (Ottawa, 1918), 2.
14. *Canadian Food Bulletin*, no. 5 (December 1, 1917): 13.
15. T. B. Macaulay to William F. Fisher, December 22, 1917, Record Group 4 [hereafter cited as RG4], Records of the United States Food Administration, Canadian Relations Division, General Records, 11/1917–01/1919, National Archives Identifier 1865634, box 940, file "General Correspondence, Nov. 1917–Jan. 1919," National Archives and Records Administration, Kansas City [hereafter cited as NARA-KC].
16. R. E. Gosnell, "Food Control," in *Canada in the Great World War*, vol. 3 (Toronto: United Publishers of Canada, 1919), discusses the impetus for food control in Canada and the United States.
17. CFB, *Report*, 4–5.
18. For the structure of the Food Administration, see Mullendore, *History of the United States Food Administration*; for the Food Board, see CFB, *Report*; and James M. Pitsula, *For All We Have and Are: Regina and the Experience of the Great War* (Winnipeg: University of Manitoba Press, 2008), 209.
19. Robert Cuff, "Organizing for War: Canada and the United States during World War I," *Historical Papers/Communications historiques* 4.1 (1969): 144.

20. For Montana statistics, see Department of Agriculture, Labor and Industry, *Montana Resources and Opportunities*, vol. 1, no. 1 (Helena, MT: Department of Agriculture, Labor and Industry, Division of Publicity, June 1926), 59, 96. On Saskatchewan, see John H. Archer, *Saskatchewan: A History* (Saskatoon: Western Producer Prairie Books, 1980), ch. 10; and Pitsula, *For All We Have and Are*, 195.

21. Robert Rydell, Jeffrey Safford, and Pierce Mullen, *In the People's Interest: A Centennial History of Montana State University* (Bozeman: Montana State University Foundation, 1992), 34; Una B. Herrick, "Twenty Years at Montana State College" (typescript, ca. 1931, Renne Library, Montana State University), 42–44.

22. E. L. Currier, *A Farm Survey of Montana* (Bozeman: Montana Extension Service in Agriculture and Home Economics, no. 25, June 1918), 9–10.

23. CFB, *Report*, 25.

24. *Canadian Food Bulletin*, no. 14 (April 13, 1918): 8.

25. *Public Service Monthly* [Regina] 6, no. 12 (July 1918): 207.

26. Pitsula, *For All We Have and Are*, 201.

27. John Herd Thompson, "Bringing in the Sheaves: The Harvest Excursionists, 1890–1929," *Canadian Historical Review* 59.4 (1978): 470.

28. "Memorandum regarding conference held in the Dept. of Labor . . . ," January 1918, Joseph Wesley Flavelle fonds, Imperial Munitions Board Correspondence, file 122, Library and Archives Canada [hereafter cited as LAC].

29. John Herd Thompson, *The Harvests of War: The Prairie West, 1914–1918* (Toronto: McClelland and Stewart, 1978), 62; Thompson, "Bringing in the Sheaves," 484; "Petition of Balcarres Grain Growers Co-operative Association," February 21, 1916, Department of Agriculture Records, General Correspondence, RG 17 I-1, vol. 1253, file 247408, LAC.

30. "Memorandum regarding conference held in the Dept. of Labor . . . ," January 1918. Statistics are sketchy, but according to John Herd Thompson, only 1,181 Americans were harvest excursionists in 1917 and 1918, compared to 5,000 in 1911. Thompson, "Bringing in the Sheaves," 472. On the U.S. press, see "Re the alleged effort of the Canadian Government to bring farm labour from the United States," February 11, 1918, RG 17, vol. 1298, file 259222, LAC.

31. F. S. Cooley, *A History of the Montana Extension Service* (Bozeman: Montana Extension Service, 1933), 22.

32. Pitsula, *For All We Have and Are*, 205–207.

33. Charles Lathrop Pack, *The War Garden Victorious* (Philadelphia: J. B. Lippincott, 1919), 10.

34. "Five Million Boys and Girls Wanted for the United States School Garden Army," *Touchstone* 3.3 (June 1918): 204.

35. *Montana Federation of Women's Clubs, 1916–1917* [Annual Report], 40–41. Montana had instituted compulsory education in 1883.

36. Linda J. Quiney, "'Bravely and Loyally They Answered the Call': St. John Ambulance, the Red Cross, and the Patriotic Service of Canadian Women during the Great War," *History of Intellectual Culture* 5.1 (2005): 6–7.

37. James J. Lopach and Jean A. Luckowski, *Jeannette Rankin: A Political Woman* (Boulder: University Press of Colorado, 2005), 148–152; "Votes $14,770,000 for Food Survey," *New York Times*, May 29, 1917.

38. John G. Clark to George A. Prescott, March 28, 1918; John Munro to E. F. Ladd, March 30, 1918, RG4, Canadian Relations, box 940, file "Canadian Food Conservation Complaints." [hereafter cited as "Canadian Food Complaints"], National Archives and Records Administration, Denver [hereafter cited as NARA-Denver].

39. Sheridan County Food Administrator to Louis Wessel, September 27, 1918, RG 4, Mont., box 31, file "Sheridan County (1) 127H-A33," NARA-Denver.

40. L. E. Hendricks to Herbert Hoover, March 9, 1918, "Canadian Food Complaints."

41. F. J. Lingham to William Fisher, May 6, 1918, "Canadian Food Complaints."

42. CFB, *Report*, 60–61; CFB to Charles A. Dunning [hereafter cited as CAD], September 6, 1918, Charles A. Dunning fonds, Document 41908, Saskatchewan Archives Board [hereafter cited as SAB].

43. Henry D. Thomson to William Fisher, May 7, 1918, "Canadian Food Complaints."

44. William Fisher to Edwin F. Ladd, April 8, 1918, "Canadian Food Complaints."

45. The *Canadian Grocer* gave extensive coverage to the issue of commodity supply during the war.

46. Henry D. Thomson to William Fisher, February 20, 1918, RG4, Canadian Relations, box 940, file "General Correspondence, Nov. 1917–Jan. 1919."

47. S. C. Burton to CFB, July 29, 1918, Dunning fonds, doc. 41869–73; CFB to CAD, August 7, 1918, Dunning fonds, doc. 41888.

48. *Canadian Food Bulletin*, no. 19 (October 1918): 19.

49. *Canadian Food Bulletin*, no. 13 (March 28, 1918): 14.

50. R.B.C. [Regina Boat Club] Girls' Auxiliary of the Salisbury Chapter, I.O.D.E. comp., *Food Conservation Cook Book* (March 1918).

51. Hot Springs Red Cross Society, *Red Cross Cook Book* (Missoula: Missoulian Pub[?], 1918[?]), 9, 13.

52. Young Ladies Sodality, *War-Winning Recipes* (Missoula, MT: St. Francis Xavier Church, 1918), 12.

53. There are hundreds of these complaints in the Food Administration records. Unfortunately, the records of the Canada Food Board were not preserved, so no comparable trove of letters exists, although one tantalizing document states that the agency's "average daily incoming and outgoing mail is round 4000." Henry Thomson to A. L. F. Jarvis, April 20, 1918, RG 17, vol. 1301, file 260317, LAC.

54. P. C. Franklin to Herbert Hoover, July 13, 1918, RG4, box 8, folder "Base H Div R, Subdiv D-F (127A-A1)," NARA-Denver.

55. All correspondence re this case is in RG 13, Dept. of Justice, vol. 228, file 2232, LAC.

56. Hutchens, *Gift of Little Things*, 128.

57. Press release from U.S. Food Administration, September 14, 1918, RG4, Mont., box 5, file "Base E Div D All (127A-A1)," NARA-Denver.

58. Alfred Atkinson to Montana Women's Clubs, January 30, 1918; and Mrs. J. E. Erickson to Atkinson, March 25, 1918, MC 286, Grace Vance Erickson Papers, box 3, folder 1, Montana Historical Society.

59. James D. McGregor to CAD, February 28, 1918, Dunning fonds, doc. 41704–708.

60. CFB, *Report*, 57–59.

61. For examples, see telegrams from CFB to CAD, August 21 and 22, 1918, Dunning fonds, doc. 41899–90.

62. CFB Educational Division, press release, March 27, 1918, Dunning fonds, doc. 41724–29.

63. The Board considered this a very reasonable number of rules, citing the fact that the British Ministry of Food had issued 130 orders in the first three months of 1918. CFB, *Report*, 19. For statistics on enforcement, see CFB, *Report*, 61.

64. *Canadian Food Bulletin*, see issues from June 1918 through November 1918.

65. Day LeSuer to Mrs. R. L. Casselman, July 8, 1918, RG4, Mont., box 30, file "Prairie County (1) 127H-A28," NARA-Denver.

66. Jerome G. Locke to Atkinson, March 22, 1918, RG4, box 6, file "Base E Div R (127A-A1)"; Park County Loyalty League to B. K. Wheeler, April 16, 1918, RG4, box 3, file "Base A Div R, Subdiv, all (127A-A1)," NARA-Denver.

67. Mrs. E. Purdy to Atkinson, September 21, 1918, RG4, Mont., box 31, file "Richland County (2) 127H-A30," NARA-Denver. There are many similar letters in the Food Administration files.

68. Geo. E. Bolster to Atkinson, July 30, 1918, RG4, Mont., box 32, file "Sheridan County (4) 127H-A33" NARA-Denver.

69. Barbara E. Kelcey and Angela E. Davis, eds., *A Great Movement Underway: Women and The Grain Growers' Guide, 1908–1928* (Winnipeg: Manitoba Record Society, 1997), 168–171.

70. Mrs. W. J. Pennington to Atkinson, July 20, 1918, RG4, Mont., box 32, file "Teton County (5) 127H-A37," NARA-Denver.

71. Undated newsclippings, ca. 1914, in Minutes, 1909–1915, R-136, Regina Council of Women fonds, SAB.

72. Mary Murphy, *Mining Cultures: Men, Women, and Leisure in Butte, 1914–41* (Urbana: University of Illinois Press, 1997), 27–28.

73. Birdie Runnalls to Jeannette Rankin, August 24, 1917, MC147, Jeannette Rankin Papers, box 7, folder 1, Montana Historical Society.

74. Mrs. J. E. Erickson et al. to Rankin, July 12, 1917, Erickson Papers, box 3, folder 1. See Pitsula, *For All We Have and Are*, 211, for similar comments from Regina women.

75. Eva C. Little to Rankin, June 26, 1917, Rankin Papers, box 2, folder 5.

76. Herrick, "Twenty Years at Montana State College," 68, 75.

77. Abigail DeLury, "Ninth Annual Report, Saskatchewan Homemaker's Clubs," June 1919, p. 1, Saskatchewan Homemakers' Clubs and Saskatchewan Women's Institute fonds, RG11 s.4.A, Directors' Reports, 1917–1971, University of Saskatchewan University Archives and Special Collections.

78. *Montana Federation of Women's Clubs*, [Annual Report], 51.

79. Linda Rasmussen et al., comps., *A Harvest Yet to Reap: A History of Prairie Women* (Toronto: Women's Press, 1976), 116.

80. "Votes $14,770,000," *New York Times*, May 29, 1917.

81. Herrick, "Twenty Years at Montana State College," 69.

CHAPTER 9

The Place That Feeds You

ALLOTMENT AND THE STRUGGLE FOR
BLACKFEET FOOD SOVEREIGNTY

Michael Wise

During the vast expansion of industrial capitalism that reconfigured the American West after the Civil War, the U.S. Office of Indian Affairs (OIA) sought to transform the Blackfeet and other indigenous peoples of the northern plains from bison hunters into cattle herders. The initiative supported the agency's broader goal of assimilating American Indians into the nation's economic and cultural fabric, not necessarily as free and equal citizens, but as laborers and colonial subjects in the globalizing world of industrial meat production. For the next fifty years, the OIA worked to enforce this transformation on the Blackfeet Reservation of northern Montana by imposing new political borders that constrained the Blackfeet to ever smaller parcels of land and foreclosed their historical means of tribal subsistence.

The process began with the criminalization of off-reservation hunting in the 1870s, an adjustment to Blackfeet livelihood that killed over a third of the reservation's inhabitants through mass starvation and left survivors dependent upon federal beef rations.[1] It continued through the 1880s and 1890s with sporadic OIA efforts to establish the reservation as an income-producing cattle ranch that exported beef to meatpackers in Chicago and other eastern markets. Despite the construction of two OIA slaughterhouses designed to control local meat production and prevent the subsistence killing of agency cattle by the reservation's starving residents, this exportation scheme was largely a failure.[2] By 1900, the OIA's agents had settled on leasing large tracts of reservation land to non-Native cattle growers as the most convenient means of extracting a colonial income from the reservation, a high patch of grass on North America's rocky backbone (see Map 4 in chapter 8). A handful of Blackfeet families tried to assemble their own private cattle herds, but the majority remained poor and destitute, largely alienated from a land that had fed and sustained them just a generation earlier.

On the heels of these colonial tragedies came allotment—the forced privatization of American Indian tribal lands authorized by the Dawes Act of 1887—and a revolutionary process of rebordering the interior of Indian country that the OIA instituted on the Blackfeet Reservation beginning in 1907. The overarching goal of the Dawes Act was to further force the incorporation of Native people as subjects in the world of colonial capitalism by dissolving their historical ties to land as a communal resource.[3] The bill's author, Senator Henry Dawes of Massachusetts, described American Indians as "idle tramps" who occupied valuable western lands without using them productively to generate a market income.[4] Converting their tribal lands into small, individually owned parcels of private property would force Indians to use their land efficiently and within the boundaries of market constraints, or else sell their labor for wages. The so-called surplus tribal lands left over from the allotment process could be retitled by the state and then sold to non-Native purchasers. In short, by the time the OIA ended allotment in 1934, a massive 90 million acres of reservation land had passed into non-Native ownership, an amount approaching two-thirds of the total acreage held by tribes in 1887.[5]

Allotment also constituted another weapon in the OIA's long-term mission of colonizing the Blackfeet through their stomachs. Rebordering reservation lands from tribal ownership into the ownership of individual Indians allowed the OIA to further transform Blackfeet food provisioning from its egalitarian, socially oriented roots in cooperative bison hunting to an individual, market-oriented trade in livestock capitalism—a livelihood based on beef, labor, and dollars. By carving communally owned reservations into individually owned 160-acre allotments, privatization, in the end, not only diminished the possible scale of Native agricultural production but also profoundly reshaped food sovereignty from a community endeavor to an individual subsistence problem.[6]

But this transformation was never complete, since the Blackfeet used allotment to suit their own tribal ends and cooperative needs even as they became an outpost for beef production in the far West. Under the leadership of a young Blackfeet activist named Robert Hamilton, they successfully resisted the most onerous part of allotment—the surplus land sales—and succeeded in increasing the size of their 320-acre allotments by 80 acres by 1919. Perhaps even more notable, many Blackfeet used their individual allotments to reinvigorate past cooperative food provisioning obligations. A dramatic example was the 1921 establishment of the Piegan Farming and Livestock Association (PFLA), a collection of twenty-nine Blackfeet-led farming districts across the reservation, organized around the cooperative use of individual land allotments for the common goal of reservation food security. By 1923, the Blackfeet were raising enough chickens, pigs, and cattle, and were growing enough wheat, potatoes, and other vegetables through the PFLA, to satisfy their own annual needs as well as some market demand off the reservation. During a decade when regional industrial agriculture on both sides of the U.S.-Canadian border—in Montana, Alberta, and Saskatchewan—faced economic crises of unprecedented magnitude, the Blackfeet had organized an alternative agricultural community that sustained its members through an emphasis on the local production, distribution, and consumption of mixed food crops.[7]

This agricultural cooperative was a new development in Blackfeet cultural and environmental history, but it also reflected older understandings of sustenance that had long been an essential component of Blackfeet conceptions of home and territory. The Blackfoot word for territory, *auasini*, translates into English as a combination of food and place, something like "the place that feeds you."[8] The word expressed broader Blackfoot knowledge of human-nonhuman kinship and relational selfhood—an acknowledgment that one does not autonomously feed oneself, but necessarily relies on a wider set of social and environmental relationships to acquire sustenance. A community's economic value did not simply materialize through the sum total of the individuated, productive labor of its discrete members, but it coursed instead through holistic systems that connected human and nonhuman beings with the lands they inhabited. This understanding, what anthropologist Enrique Salmón has called "kincentricity," and what Blackfoot scholar Betty Bastien has described as "kinship alliances," drew on Blackfoot understandings of social selfhood that were unlike the production-focused individualism residing at the core of OIA assimilation policies.[9] Living in a world shaped by these kinship alliances diluted the colonial power of privatization and facilitated the flow of food across the newly erected borders of the allotment-era Blackfeet Reservation.

In spite of political criticisms from within the tribe and beyond the reservation that depicted the PFLA, alternately, as both "old-fashioned" and "Bolshevistic," the project earned praise for establishing a level of food security unheard of in Blackfeet country since the 1860s. Indeed, thanks to the PFLA's success in incubating Blackfeet notions of place within the exigencies of allotment and federal assimilation policy, by 1924 its Blackfeet members claimed that they had become "the most progressive tribe of Indians in the United States."[10]

This chapter explores how the Blackfeet confronted the bordering of their tribal lands under allotment and charted their own modern path toward food sovereignty. The first half traces the roots of the PFLA in the anticattle, antiland sale activism of Robert Hamilton in the 1910s. The second half tells the story of the agricultural cooperative itself. The legacy of allotment is not just a "Native issue," but a lesson for thinking more broadly about modern historical relationships between community food sovereignty and private landownership. Our own neoliberal society often repeats the farcical ideological assertions of allotment—that private property extends individual freedom and that privatization provides limits to the extension of state power. The experience of the Blackfeet with allotment reflected the opposite outcome. Efforts to "liberalize" Native landownership resulted in the deeper exploitation of indigenous land and labor. Nevertheless, the Blackfeet succeeded in bridging some, if not all, of the borders inscribed by allotment. With the development of the PFLA, the Blackfeet developed a new mode of livelihood that constructed an alternative set of environmental and social relationships atop the reservation's individuated grid of private property. These new relationships hinged on the Blackfeet's reinterpretation of some older ontological understandings of human-nonhuman kinship, such as animist practices of medicine power, recast to fit within the exigencies of twentieth-century industrial agriculture. Rather than accept the fruits of modern agriculture as the sole productive force of human actors, PFLA members understood agriculture production as a broader endeavor that spanned the boundary between human and nonhuman. By reconnecting their individuated allotments under the cooperative system of the PFLA, members worked to reintegrate their concepts of human-nonhuman kinship into reservation agriculture, helping expand the potential for Blackfeet food sovereignty within and across the borders of their colonized community.

Blackfeet food activism from the past century shows how the present-day struggles for food sovereignty have roots reaching far beyond our own neoliberal moment. The Blackfeet's historical struggles show that even the dissolution of the political borders wrought by capitalism and private property may not be sufficient, or even necessary, to create a more just and equitable future. The colonial changes that revolutionized indigenous food economies over a century ago cannot be undone simply by reforming free trade agreements or slackening immigration laws. In addition to these questions about political borders, the problems posed by food's ontological borders should also set a major agenda for scholars of food colonialism, as well as for food sovereignty activists. Considering food, along with its production and distribution, as a more-than-human endeavor might allow us to take seriously a more radical idea that food sovereignty can liberate our places and our nonhuman kin in addition to ourselves.

ALLOTMENT AND THE POLITICS OF BEEF

Beef production and land allotment made for strange bedfellows on the Blackfeet Reservation.[11] Left completely unallotted until 1907, a full twenty years after the passage of the Dawes Act mandated privatization, the reservation had become a unique grazing landscape on the northern plains precisely because of its stubborn history of communal ownership. As surrounding homesteaders carved up the Montana plains and plowed under its cattle trails, many Native and non-Native ranchers viewed the reservation as a final refuge for open-range stock raising. OIA personnel were well aware of this fact. Clarence Churchill, who served as reservation's head agent during the allotment process, explained, "stockmen who are acquainted with all the grazing sections of the State, admit that there is no better grazing in any part of Montana than the Blackfeet Reservation."[12] In managing the reservation's preallotment grasslands, the OIA was tasked with balancing the grazing needs of a tribal herd along with the needs of private herds owned by a few prosperous Blackfeet, and, after 1904, the private herds of non-Native ranchers who had leased significant portions of the reservation's acreage. This was a challenging job that the OIA was ill-suited to undertake. Within a few years Blackfeet resistance to the allotment process made it more difficult.

By 1912, a loose coalition of Blackfeet cattlemen and off-reservation, non-Native lessees had stocked the reservation with over 20,000 head of cattle. Oscar Lipps, the OIA's livestock supervisor, suggested the reservation's grasslands could sustain an additional 80,000 animals, declaring that "the country needs the beef, and the Indians would like to produce more of it." He suggested a postallotment cattle plan endorsed by Churchill's replacement, Arthur McFatridge, and a coalition of Native cattlemen. The plan called for the expansion of a common tribal herd, from which cattle would be issued to individual Blackfeet who demonstrated that they could take proper care of the animals. This plan would work in a similar way to the Dawes competency commissions that were awarding land titles to Indians elsewhere. If landholders demonstrated enough "competency," federal agents removed their lands from OIA trust provisions.[13] Under this plan, cattle belonged to individual Blackfeet under a trust arrangement. In order to actually sell or otherwise dispose of their animals on the market, individual Blackfeet needed to demonstrate their competency as stockmen. Demonstrating competency, in this case, required the Blackfeet to sell their cattle on the market, rather than kill their issued cattle for food.[14]

Lipps also recommended another controversial solution to the problem that the reservation's allotment posed to the agency's cattle leasing program. On the reservation's unallotted lands, which the OIA planned to put up for sale under the terms of the Allotment Act, Lipps suggested the retention of a least "a few townships of land" that would be set aside for open-range grazing leases to fund the agency budget. Despite its ongoing allotment, McFatridge and Lipps set about maintaining the Blackfeet Reservation as an open range, a clear expression of the OIA's continued intention of incorporating Blackfeet land into the North American beef industry. McFatridge was backed by Blackfeet cattlemen who defended the pending sale of the surplus unallotted lands as a means of purchasing additional cattle for issue to tribal members.

Leading the opposition to this cattle-focused vision of reservation land use and to the sale of surplus unallotted lands was Robert Hamilton, a young Blackfeet whose skills as an organizer eventually seated him at the head of the Blackfeet's reorganized Tribal Business Council (BTBC). From this position

Hamilton developed access to influential members of the U.S. Congress who went to battle against the interests of the reservation's cattlemen and the OIA.

Hamilton aspired to achieve Blackfeet economic independence by managing their land base for the direct benefit of the entire tribe, rather than for the OIA and its wealthy stock-owning allies in Browning, the reservation's largest town. The OIA first recognized Hamilton as an anathema to its control over Blackfeet labor in 1906, when he organized a strike of workers on the Two Medicine irrigation project. The workers struck in October, a critical moment to complete excavations before the ground froze. Their demands were simple: an increase in wages from the Bureau of Reclamation. Within two days, and without violence, Hamilton and his supporters succeeded in negotiating a raise that brought their wages to parity with white workers. An infuriated agent Churchill arrested Hamilton and threatened to remove him from the reservation, but was denied this authority by his superiors. Explaining the incident to the commissioner of Indian Affairs, Churchill wrote: "The Indians have worked well and have done good work. They have been told so, and a few of them were led to believe that their labor and that of their teams, was equal to that of the white men with larger horses."[15] In fact, the workers struck not because of the agent's praise for their contribution to the Two Medicine project—which would establish an irrigated valley that the OIA would later attempt to sell as unallotted land—but because they were being paid below subsistence-level wages that brought them away from their homes and families. The strike's success brought Hamilton to the center of popular politics on the reservation.

The focus of Hamilton's career as a tribal organizer for the next decade would be his opposition to allotment's proposed sale of the Blackfeet Reservation's unallotted lands. By an act of Congress on March 1, 1907, the Blackfeet Reservation was ordered to be allotted, each enrolled member of the tribe receiving 320 acres. This plan left over 800,000 unallotted acres on the reservation, roughly half of its total area, most of which would be returned to federal domain and sold to settlers under the terms of the original Dawes Act of 1887. Not surprisingly, the reservation's allotment was popular throughout the rest of northern Montana, as the region's cattlemen eyed the possibility of purchasing—possibly for pennies on the dollar—its unallotted grasslands.

Hamilton and his supporters sought to stop this surplus land sale, which threatened to eliminate over half the Blackfeet's remaining tribal lands. They eventually achieved this goal, not by resisting allotment in its entirety, but by organizing the tribe against only its surplus land sale provisions. At one council meeting in 1909, Hamilton collected the statements of dozens of tribal leaders who accepted the allotting process but objected to the sale of unallotted land.[16] After twelve years of fighting that stalled any general land sales, Hamilton and his supporters accomplished this goal in 1919, when Congress passed a bill exempting the Blackfeet from selling any surplus lands. The bill also allotted each enrolled member an additional 80 acres.

Hamilton and his supporters developed relationships with legislators and bureaucrats in Washington, D.C., who were willing to hear and act on his stories of agency corruption and the shortcomings of the OIA's cattle strategy. Hamilton's first trip to D.C. was reluctantly sponsored by the OIA, and resulted in an internally administered inspection of the agency that, not surprisingly, concluded that the agency was well run and that its administration worked toward the benefit of all Blackfeet. Although his visit was held under the tutelage of the commissioner of Indian Affairs, Hamilton also met separately with U.S. senator Harry Lane of Oregon. In Washington, Hamilton convinced Lane to lead a separate inspection of the reservation and its management. This inspection drew a much different conclusion—that the majority of Blackfeet lived in a state of destitution, ruled over by an agent and a clique of stock growers more interested in the private acquisition of government-issued cattle than in improving the reservation's broader economic conditions.[17]

McFatridge sought to discredit Hamilton and his supporters by characterizing them as lazy Indians with little personal initiative who survived off agency largesse. In a letter exposing his breathtaking colonial hubris, the day after McFatridge explained to the commissioner of Indian Affairs why he ended the distribution of annuity goods—guaranteed by treaty—to the "able-bodied," he requested authority to spend $1,250 from the same Blackfeet annuity fund to buy himself a new Buick. Upon Hamilton's return to the reservation, McFatridge fumed that "[Hamilton] had not worked one single day." Despite the damning evidence from the Lane inspection, McFatridge continued to rule with an iron fist. He answered reports of destitution with a familiar refrain that Indians, like Hamilton, simply would not work. "There are a number of Indians on the reservation," he explained, "that are able to earn a living who have refused to perform labor for rations for themselves and their families, and I have refused to issue rations to such people." "Those who do not have enough to live on," he continued, "can blame themselves."[18]

The next year, Hamilton tried to organize a second trip to Washington, which brought him into a series of direct clashes with McFatridge. Over the winter, Hamilton had organized a meeting of the BTBC without notifying McFatridge. The council voted to send Hamilton back to D.C. along with two other representatives, Wolf Plume and Young Man Chief, who would help finance the trip. After discovering the plan, McFatridge was enraged, telling his superiors that Hamilton was "simply an agitator and has caused more trouble in this tribe of Indians than any other person." McFatridge ordered the tribal police after the trio and had them arrested at the Browning railroad station. After their release, they tried a second time, riding off the reservation to pick up the Great Northern

Railroad at Cut Bank. McFatridge gave chase and once again arrested them. But the OIA could no longer overlook the agent's constant overreaches of authority, and McFatridge was fired later that month. He fled to Alberta with $1,200 of tribal funds, cash raised from the annual grazing tax.[19]

McFatridge's sudden departure left the agency administration in disarray. From 1916 until 1920, seven different OIA employees managed the agency. During these years, the center of power on the reservation shifted from the OIA to Hamilton and the BTBC, his grassroots governing body that stalled the sale of unallotted lands and pressured Congress to overturn the provision altogether. Hamilton and his supporters sought to use allotment to their advantage to secure a victory against the reservation's Native and non-Native cattlemen.

Emerging centers of radical power in Montana politics took notice, including the Non-Partisan League. In 1918, the tribe selected its former allotment agent, Louis S. Irvin, to serve as their tribal attorney.[20] Irvin was married to a Blackfeet woman and quickly sided with Hamilton's faction against the OIA's plans to sell oil leases on the reservation to non-Native speculators. In 1920, Irvin served as Burton K. Wheeler's running mate in Montana's gubernatorial election.[21] Although "Bolshevik Burt" and Irvin's run on the Non-Partisan League ticket was an electoral disaster, the campaign catapulted Wheeler into the U.S. Senate as a Montana Democrat two years later, during the height of the northern plains' regional economic depression. By the 1930s, Wheeler was chair of the Senate Committee on Indian Affairs, and the primary sponsor of the Indian Reorganization Act, which the Blackfeet were one of the first tribes to sign.

Although unsuccessful in reversing OIA policies regarding the stock industry, the reservation's anticattle faction took the lead in the Blackfeet's effective resistance to the Allotment Act's provision for surplus land sales. These debates revealed conflicting visions of how the reservation's land and resources would be best utilized, but also tensions over understandings of labor, selfhood, and food sovereignty that underlay the OIA's assimilation project and its reception by enrolled Blackfeet.

The Piegan Farming and Livestock Association

Far from signaling the disappearance of Blackfeet understandings of land and livelihood, allotment opened a door for an interwar renaissance of Blackfeet food sovereignty. Through the development of the PFLA, the Blackfeet accommodated allotment to Blackfeet notions of *auasini*. Even a colonial institution like allotment could be reworked by the Blackfeet to fit within their broader communal kinship traditions. As the radical positions of Robert Hamilton and his supporters indicated, many Blackfeet saw in their individual allotments opportunities to reconnect their individual labor back to a broader communal tradition of value creation, one that spanned colonial conceptions of discrete individual selfhood. Through the PFLA, Blackfeet sought to use their individual allotments to develop a cooperative subsistence economy on the reservation. By the mid-1920s, many Blackfeet had utilized their allotments to develop an effective organization that blended subsistence and market agriculture in a way that resonated with Blackfeet understandings of place, sustenance, and selfhood.

Several generations of American Indian historians have now studied the PFLA, approaching it mainly as a bureaucratic anomaly of early twentieth-century Blackfeet history. John Ewers, Paul Rosier, and Tom Wessel, working from mostly OIA sources, have ascribed the PFLA's successful emergence primarily to the good-hearted efforts of Fred Campbell, the reservation's superintendent throughout most of the 1920s.[22] They are right to point out that Campbell's earnest administration represented a radical departure from the corrupt and inefficient tenure of previous Blackfeet agents. But the PFLA, borne from Campbell's ambitious "Five-Year Industrial Program," succeeded in spite of the OIA's economic motivations for the reservation. It succeeded because it offered the Blackfeet opportunities to refashion their indigenous understandings of production and relational selfhood into a viable and modern social alternative to the forms of commodity agriculture that had bankrupted the northern plains over the previous decade.

The PFLA emerged during the fall of 1921 as a reservation-wide Blackfeet organization committed to reaching the subsistence goals of Campbell's Five-Year Industrial Plan (FYIP). Adopted in March 1921, the FYIP aggressively focused agency energies around the task of expanding subsistence agriculture on the reservation, with the main objective of achieving Blackfeet agricultural self-sufficiency by 1926. Although the plan did place its faith in a kind of mixed agriculture sure to conjure images of white yeoman farmers, the program's emphasis on communal self-sufficiency nevertheless signaled a radical departure from the OIA's traditional emphasis on assimilation and livestock capitalism. Paired with the Blackfeet-organized PFLA, the FYIP-PFLA achieved widespread popularity with the Blackfeet. It also generated economic results that were, perhaps, unprecedented and unrepeated anywhere else in Indian country. For his part, Campbell became the OIA's brightest star, and by 1923 he spent most of his time away from Browning, touring other reservations throughout the United States and Canada, giving lectures, and trying to convince other agency administrators to adopt his program, a task in which he was mostly unsuccessful. In 1928, he was "fired" by Hamilton's BTBC, in some ways a victim of his program's own success, the BTBC claiming his administration was no longer needed. Reinstated by the commissioner of Indian Affairs—the BTBC's legal authority to fire agency personnel was questionable—Campbell's tenure boiled down to a controversy over Blackfeet sovereignty and OIA administration that led directly to the desks of Senator Wheeler and, eventually, John Collier, the authors of the Indian Reorganization Act six years later.[23]

The FYIP set fairly modest goals in its first year. Sending out a wide call for participation, Campbell offered all enrolled Blackfeet the necessary fencing materials to enclose a 40-acre field on their allotment. Each family that built fences also received one milk cow, twenty sheep, and twelve chickens. Using agency funds, Campbell also built a flour mill in the Heart Butte district, optimistically awaiting the reservation's first major harvests of grain. More significant, Campbell visited every household on the reservation that summer, along with an interpreter, the agency's doctor, farmer, and livestock supervisor. He explained the program personally, encouraged Blackfeet participation, wrote reports, and photographed the reservation's population outside of Browning where previous agents had seldom ventured.

Because of the way it engaged Blackfeet understandings of relational selfhood, this personal attention during the summer of 1921 may have been one of the keys to the FYIP-PFLA's success. The Blackfeet concept of "medicine power" had been invoked earlier by OIA assimilationists to explain Blackfeet reluctance to pursue agriculture. According to this understanding of power, individuals needed to borrow or beg abilities with which they were not originally endowed. Rather than personal initiative amounting to the basis for individual success—one of the base truisms of Anglo-American autonomous selfhood—Blackfeet selfhood, *mokaksin*, constituted an assemblage of personal capabilities gathered from other human and nonhuman persons. In the pre-reservation era, Blackfeet commonly forged these relationships through dreams and ritual fasts. Sometimes the powers derived could be embodied within collections of objects—medicine bundles—and then exchanged with others. The animal world was the original source of ability and knowledge. Animals held powers in their pure forms; humans drew on a panoply of watered-down powers granted them by their nonhuman patrons.[24]

Although the ritual practices associated with medicine power, particularly those misunderstood as "self-torture," had been severely curtailed by OIA administrators from the 1880s onward, reservation Blackfeet continued to organize their confidences around the concept. In 1923, for instance, the Blackfeet adopted Tom Gibbons, Jack Dempsey's challenger in the title fight for heavyweight boxing held that summer in Shelby, Montana, just east of Browning on the Great Northern rail corridor. They granted Gibbons the name Pony-kick-in-hands to describe his unique boxing abilities, surely derived from his kinship with horses. Despite losing to Dempsey in fifteen rounds, Pony-kick-in-hands remained a folk hero on the reservation and a testament to the modernization of medicine power in Blackfeet popular thought by the 1920s. Campbell's house-by-house canvas of the reservation thus fell within an established Blackfeet framework of medicine power, ritual, and relational selfhood that undoubtedly encouraged the success of Blackfeet agriculture. Through these personal interactions, Campbell transferred agricultural abilities that his medicine powers represented, this embodied knowledge increasing the share of relational selfhood accessible by PFLA members.

The third year of Campbell's program rolled out the FYIP's most revolutionary goal: "Elimination of the necessity for the Indian to leave his home in search of employment and to help him work out a plan whereby he may spend a three hundred sixty-five day working year on his own allotment." Unlike three decades of OIA programs that sought to subordinate and incorporate Blackfeet labor into Montana's livestock industry, the FYIP emphasized the goal of eschewing Blackfeet wage labor altogether. More than anything else, this goal of the FYIP provided a complementary element to Blackfeet understandings of food and place. The land and its interrelationships could provide livelihood for those who dwelt upon it.

It would be a mistake to characterize the FYIP and the PFLA as being entirely subsistence-based. An auxiliary goal of the organization was to "work out a system of marketing whereby the Indian can place upon the open market any surplus farm or live stock products." The PFLA was not a retreat from the market economy, but a program to establish Blackfeet means of production that could accommodate the reservation's subsistence requirements and also accumulate capital. Accordingly, the program sought to have 75 percent of allotments producing at least 10 acres of wheat by year four, enough to feed the reservation. By year five, they hoped to have 70 percent of the reservation's allotments producing an agricultural surplus for sale—either in grain, vegetable crops, livestock, or hay, which was probably the most common surplus commodity. This food surplus would have been sold off the reservation, crossing the OIA's political borders on its way to markets in Montana and elsewhere.[25]

During the first summer, the Blackfeet developed twenty-nine PFLA chapters to administer the project, each chapter loosely organized around existing kinship relationships (Figure 9.1). About fifteen different families, most of which were interrelated through marriage, comprised each chapter. This familial geography was the legacy of a previous relocation effort. In 1902, agent James Monteath relocated a substantial number of full-blood families to Heart Butte and other southern districts in anticipation of irrigation projects that were never completed.[26] When the reservation was allotted between 1907 and 1912, most of these neighbors were allotted together, "so that a chapter membership [of the PFLA]," wrote a reporter for the *Indian Leader* in 1923, "in many instances comprises a large family group."[27] Organized around existing family units, PFLA chapters existed similar to band units, drawing on pre-reservation Blackfeet social structure.

One major way that PFLA chapters formed a cooperative organization was through group purchases and shared equipment. All twenty-nine chapters shared the same flour mill, constructed in 1921. They also shared two grain threshers that traveled across the reservation during harvest season. But most chapters bought other machinery for use by their own chapter members, including hay

White Grass Chapter

Figure 9.1. Piegan Farming and Livestock Association, White Grass Chapter, ca. 1924. Photographer unknown; photograph courtesy of William Farr.

binders and rakes, and other machines. The *Indian Leader* also reported on this phenomenon: "This farming machinery is turned over to the president of the chapter and he is held responsible for its housing and safe-keeping and the various chapters all over the reservation are building community machinery sheds for this purpose." The cooperative use of machinery helped PFLA members avoid the large debts faced by regional farmers forced to purchase equipment on their own.

The PFLA's cooperative mission also extended beyond the bounds of financing machinery purchases. One of the PFLA's strongest admirers, General H. L. Scott, inspected the reservation for the Indian office in 1925. Scott lauded the program through the story of George Wren, an older chapter member who suffered from blindness and was unable to plant crops in 1924. "The other members of his chapter, noting his condition," wrote Scott, "got together and put in his crop in addition to their own, a circumstance which would not have happened had there not been a chapter organized."[28] Belonging to the PFLA chapter expressed a series of kinship obligations that extended to providing labor beyond the boundaries of one's individual allotment.

Even after the first year, the PFLA's results impressed commentators. The old-time Indian office inspector Oscar Lipps visited the reservation in the fall of 1921. He reported on one Blackfeet man, purportedly named "After Buffalo": "The old man and wife and two grandsons live together," Lipps remarked. "They raised nothing last year except a few potatoes. This year they raised 40 bushels of wheat, 30 bushels of oats, 50 sacks of potatoes, some rutabagas, beets, carrots, peas, corn, etc. They put up hay, sold 20 tons and have one stack left."[29] With hay selling for around $12 a ton, After Buffalo and his family not only grew enough food to sustain themselves for an entire year, but generated a cash income of over $200— a fortune by early twentieth-century reservation standards. Satisfied with the program's results, Lipps ended his report: "Thus stands the record of the efforts of these old buffalo-eaters and hunter-sportsmen in their first attempt at subsistence farming." Even a veteran representative of the OIA grudgingly admitted the PFLA's success. In the fall of the 1921, the Blackfeet harvested and milled 1,100 bushels of grain. The following year they milled 15,000 bushels, enough to feed the entire reservation.[30]

The PFLA was not without controversy. An older generation of assimilationists denounced the program from the start as an unrealistic experiment in agriculture that was "doomed to failure," as James Willard Schultz put it. Schultz, a white settler on the reservation in the late 1800s and the popular author of *My Life as an Indian*, a book that described his marriage to a Blackfeet woman and their life in Browning, published a scathing editorial on the PFLA from his retirement home in Southern California in 1921. On the reservation, Schultz had been an advocate of the cattle regime that had bankrupted the Blackfeet during the 1910s. He published the editorial under the title "The Starving Blackfeet," drawing upon a long-standing tradition of similar charges against the OIA that reflected a Progressive Era white philanthropic mission to lessen the suffering of American Indians. This time, however, the charges of starving Blackfeet were unfounded. Schultz represented the Blackfeet as "starving" under the PFLA to help justify a return to previous administration tactics that focused on procuring livestock for the reservation's previously well-off stock growers. Schultz did not advocate the growth of Blackfeet communal self-sufficiency, but instead worked as an apologist for the failed policies of individuation and assimilation that the PFLA overturned. He ended his editorial with one last admonishment for the project: "There remains but one hope for the Montana Blackfeet, and that is, to obtain from the government a portion of the value of the vast territory arbitrarily taken from them by presidential executive orders."[31] Although Schultz was right to request compensation for lands stolen from the Blackfeet during the nineteenth century, his opposition to the PFLA revealed his shortsightedness in retreating toward the prospect of "trading land for food," the old tactic that he believed would spare the Blackfeet from colonial annihilation, but that could not ensure their long-term prosperity.

Other critics decried the project as Bolshevist and Communistic. These charges mostly came from men like Schultz who continued to cling to the promise of an individuated cattle economy. Supporters of plans to sell oil and mining leases on the reservation also resorted to harnessing the Red Scare to support their political mission. In a report written in 1924, General Scott responded to these criticisms, arguing that "the program is in no way communistic, it works for individual effort in a cooperative way." He added that the PFLA was on the leading edge of other cooperative associations forming throughout the United States and Canada in response to the challenges of industrial agriculture: "The white farmers are forming cooperative societies all over the country for mutual support and benefit as many other industries are organized."[32] Scott realized that the PFLA was situated within a broader Progressive movement, not toward radical Communism, but toward a cooperative social democracy based on understandings of social selfhood.

In this sense, the PFLA drew on Blackfeet traditions of relational selfhood to inform its cooperative endeavors, but it would be a mistake to characterize the program as traditional. The PFLA was significant because it provided a means to blend Blackfeet knowledge of the world with nontraditional forms of food and market production. Its goal was not the assimilation and incorporation of the Blackfeet into the American body politic as colonial subjects, but to establish Blackfeet communal self-sufficiency by partnering modern agricultural procedures with an organization that drew on Blackfeet understandings of selfhood, labor, and the origins of value.

Across the high and remote northwestern plains, the 1920s brought massive disruptions to the world of industrial agriculture that American and Canadian immigrants had tried to build over the previous generation. Postwar price depressions in wheat and barley bankrupted the region's commercial farmers, and a decade of aggressive bumper crops had reduced entire fields to "a solid mat of Russian thistle," as Wallace Stegner remembered the fate of his own childhood homestead near the Milk River. Along with thousands of other settlers, Stegner's family fled the landscape they had desiccated; by the end of the decade, few remained.[33]

These combined misfortunes of climate, commerce, and industrial agriculture ravaged the Blackfeet as well, but unlike their non-Native neighbors, the Blackfeet could not simply pick up and move their capital to greener pastures. Incorporated into the free market of twentieth-century agriculture under the legal conditions of the Allotment Act, they were forced to stay and negotiate the flurry of privatization in an era of broader economic crisis. Managing economic catastrophes that originated outside the boundaries of the Blackfeet Reservation required that the Blackfeet attend to the internal borders that reconfigured their reservation under allotment. No longer able to forge a subsistence from their tribal lands, PFLA members in the 1920s united their individual landholdings under an agricultural cooperative. Intratribal debates over OIA grazing leases and reservation cattle trespass had led many Blackfeet to resist the agency over the previous decade. One of the leaders that emerged from these debates was Robert Hamilton, whose tireless campaign against the surplus land sale provision succeeded with its repeal in 1919. Hamilton's focus on land as the basis for Blackfeet economic independence drew on a wellspring of Blackfeet notions of *auasini* that informed the PFLA during the 1920s. As the capitalist dissociations of industrial agriculture collapsed around the postwar northern plains, the PFLA offered the Blackfeet an alternative means to reconfigure their world.

With the PFLA, the Blackfeet were not simply "reviving tradition" but also articulating a new vision of cooperative, community food sovereignty that negotiated their newly inscribed borders of private property. Since the 1870s, the OIA had worked to divest the Blackfeet of their tribal obligations and assimilate them as individuated selves through institutions. But drawing on their own indigenous knowledge of kinship and selfhood, and on the lessons learned from their experience with industrial agriculture, the Blackfeet were in a suitable position to address the challenges that drove so many of their non-Native neighbors from the land.

The Blackfeet's struggle for food sovereignty represented, at its core, a battle over ontological boundaries as well as political borders. While the tribe ultimately had little power to oppose the federal government's allotment and division of reservation lands, they did succeed in accommodating the new political landscape to a cooperative form of agricultural production that reflected communal practices rooted in the Blackfeet's precolonial past. Relative to the private cattle industry that had dominated the reservation economy in the twenty years prior to allotment, which had focused on the exportation of meat to markets off the reservation, the PFLA's cooperative vision instead comprised both the production of food for subsistence and for market sale. Moreover, this vision necessarily drew from older conceptions of *auasini* and *mokaksin* that emphasized the continuity of human and nonhuman beings as kindred food producers, each involved in a holistic process of feeding on and from a particular place. In such a world, food sovereignty represented more than just the transcendence of political boundaries, but also the reconsideration of the ontological borders of modern capitalism that sought to abstract, separate, and devalue nonhuman inputs to community livelihood. With the PFLA, the Blackfeet had sought to fashion this alternative route to food sovereignty, and, for a time at least, they succeeded in their struggle.

NOTES

1. There are only a few records related to these mass starvations on the Blackfeet Reservation, and the incidents have not been closely studied by historians. The most lethal starvation occurred in the winter of 1883–1884, when 600 Blackfeet perished out of a total population of about 1,300. See James Welch, preface to *The Reservation Blackfeet: A Photographic History of Cultural Survival*, by William Farr (Seattle: University of Washington Press, 1984), 8; and Inspector Benedict, "Inspection of Blackfeet Agency," July 26, 1883 (3443), in United States Bureau of Indian Affairs (BIA), *Reports of the Inspection of the Field*

Jurisdictions of the Office of Indian Affairs, 1873–1900 (Washington, DC: National Archives Microfilm Publications), M1070, Reel 2.

2. For a detailed history of the criminalization of Blackfeet hunting and meat-making, see Michael Wise, "Colonial Beef and the Blackfeet Reservation Slaughterhouse, 1879–1895," *Radical History Review* 110 (Spring 2011): 59–82.

3. Despite the role of land allotment in accelerating Native poverty and dispossession, many of the Allotment Act's nineteenth-century architects considered themselves humanitarian reformers and advocates of American Indian people. See Frederick Hoxie, *A Final Promise: The Campaign to Assimilate the Indians* (Lincoln: University of Nebraska Press, 1986); C. Joseph Genetin-Pilawa, *Crooked Paths to Allotment: The Fight Over Federal Indian Policy After the Civil War* (Chapel Hill: University of North Carolina Press, 2012).

4. See Henry Dawes, "300,000 Tramps: The Red Men Increasing and Not Passing Away," *New York Herald*, December 30, 1885. For a deeper discussion of this discourse of work in the history of assimilation reform, see Daniel Usner, *Indian Work: Language and Livelihood in American History* (Cambridge, MA: Harvard University Press, 2009).

5. See Peter Iverson, *When Indians Became Cowboys: Native Peoples and Cattle Ranching in the American West* (Norman: University of Oklahoma Press, 1994), for a classic discussion of this transformation in the twentieth century. For detailed histories of the complex processes and legacies of the allotment era, see David Chang, *The Color of the Land: Race, Nation, and the Politics of Land Ownership in Oklahoma, 1832–1929* (Chapel Hill: University of North Carolina Press, 2010); David Chang, "Enclosures of Land and Sovereignty: The Allotment of American Indian Lands," *Radical History Review* 109 (Winter 2011): 108–119; Emily Greenwald, *Reconfiguring the Reservation: The Nez Perces, Jicarilla Apaches, and the Dawes Act* (Lincoln: University of Nebraska Press, 2002); Melissa Meyer, *The White Earth Tragedy: Ethnicity and Dispossession at a Minnesota Anishinaabe Reservation, 1889–1920* (Lincoln: University of Nebraska Press, 1999); and Kristin Ruppel, *Unearthing Indian Land: Living with the Legacies of Allotment* (Tucson: University of Arizona Press, 2008).

6. For a description of these historical Blackfoot methods of cooperative hunting, see Russell Lawrence Barsh and Chantelle Marlor, "Driving Bison and Blackfoot Science," *Human Ecology* 31 (December 2003): 571–593; David Nugent, "Property Relations, Production Relations, and Inequality: Anthropology, Political Economy, and the Blackfeet," *American Ethnologist* 20.2 (May 1993): 336–362; and Clark Wissler and Alice Beck Kehoe, *Amskapi Pikuni: The Blackfeet People* (Albany: State University of New York Press, 2012).

7. For a discussion of these interwar economic crises on the northern plains, see Rod Bantjes, *Improved Earth: Prairie Space as Modern Artefact, 1869–1944* (Toronto: University of Toronto Press, 2005); Mark Fiege, "The Weedy West: Mobile Nature, Boundaries, and Common Space in the Montana Landscape," *Western Historical Quarterly* (Spring 2005): 22–47; and Deborah Fitzgerald, *Every Farm a Factory: The Industrial Ideal in American Agriculture* (New Haven, CT: Yale University Press, 2003).

8. I do not speak Blackfoot. For my reconstructions of Blackfoot words and concepts, including *auasini*, I have relied mainly on two sources: Betty Bastien, *Blackfoot Ways of Knowing: The Worldview of the Siksikaitsitapi* (Calgary: University of Calgary Press, 2004), 197–198; and C. C. Uhlenbeck, *An English-Blackfoot Vocabulary Based on Material from the Southern Peigans* (Amsterdam: Koninklijke Akademie van Wetenschappen te Amsterdam, 1930), 54.

9. See Bastien, *Blackfoot Ways of Knowing*; and Enrique Salmón, *Eating the Landscape: American Indian Stories of Food, Identity, and Resilience* (Tucson: University of Arizona Press, 2012), 21.

10. "Minutes of Meeting: Resolutions Committee," March 30, 1925, Record Group 75, CCF-1, File 27506-1923-BF-100, National Archives and Records Administration (NARA), published in Paul Rosier, *Rebirth of the Blackfeet Nation, 1912–1954* (Lincoln: University of Nebraska Press, 2001), 36.

11. Blackfeet politics grew increasingly complicated as the early twentieth century pro-gressed, and although my historical analysis here distinguishes procattle and anticattle fac-tions on the reservation, the contemporary divisions between these groups were not always entirely clear. Political alliances moved and shifted rapidly, and were shaped by family and class identities in addition to the perspectives on cattle and allotment discussed in this essay.

12. Agent Churchill to the Commissioner of Indian Affairs (CIA), September 15, 1909, in *Thomas R. Wessel Indian Claims Commission Research Papers, 1855–1979*, Collection 2059 (*TW-ICC*), Box 2, Folder 4, Montana State University (MSU) Special Collections, Bozeman.

13. One original element of allotment in Oklahoma that was later transferred to the pro-cess's implementation elsewhere with the Curtis Act of 1906 was that allotment titles were held in trust by the OIA for a varying number of years, or until Native allottees appeared before a local commission of magistrates who could validate their "competency" to assume full fee title. Owning an allotment with this trust encumbrance made it impossible for allot-tees to lease or sell their lands until they acquired full title. In the meantime, the only income they could generate from their allotment came from agricultural uses. On the former Creek Reservation in Oklahoma, for instance, Indians who could not support themselves on their small allotments without the capital to purchase necessary farming equipment sold their lands to non-Native buyers. As the historian David Chang has demonstrated, in such cases the local competency commissions seemed more than happy to assist the non-Native buyers by freeing up Native titles. See Chang, *Color of the Land*.

14. Oscar Lipps, Supervisor, "Report on the Education, Industrial, Economic, and Home Conditions, Blackfeet Reservation, Montana," October 20, 1913, in *TW-ICC*, Box 4, Folder 1, 5.

15. Dare to CIA, October 4, 1906, in *TW-ICC*, Box 2, Folder 1.

16. Churchill to CIA, July 12, 1909, in *TW-ICC*, Box 2, Folder 4. Blackfeet opponents of allotment did not necessarily view privatization itself as a means of dispossession, only the sale of surplus lands. See Churchill, "Transcript of Tribal Council Meeting at Blackfeet Agency," April 24, 1909, in *TW-ICC*, Box 2, Folder 4: "The Indians are very anxious to have the allotting completed so that they can make permanent improvements and establish suit-able homes. They have been looking forward to the time when allotments would be made them for about ten years. While there have been several instances of personal differences arising from disputes over selections for allotment, there have been no general complaints nor individual opposition to allotment." In the future, I plan to further analyze Blackfeet debates over allotment in comparison the earlier allotment of the "closed reservations" of the Blackfoot, Blood, and Piegan Reserves in Alberta. See Hana Samek, *The Blackfoot Con-federacy, 1880–1920: A Comparative Study of Canadian and U.S. Indian Policy* (Albuquerque: University of New Mexico Press, 1987).

17. See Rosier, *Rebirth of the Blackfeet Nation*.

18. See McFatridge to CIA, April 17, 1914, in *TW-ICC*, Box 4, Folder 2; McFatridge to CIA, January 31, 1914, in *TW-ICC*, Box 4, Folder 2; and McFatridge to CIA, April 16, 1914, in *TW-ICC*, Box 4, Folder 2.

19. See McFatridge to CIA, January 19, 1914, in *TW-ICC*, Box 4, Folder 2; McFatridge to CIA, January 29, 1914, in *TW-ICC*, Box 4, Folder 2; McFatridge to CIA, January 31, 1914, in *TW-ICC*, Box 4, Folder 2; and Robert Hamilton to A. R. Serven, January 31, 1914, in *TW-ICC*, Box 4, Folder 2.

20. Rosier, *Rebirth of the Blackfeet Nation*, 43.

21. See Burton K. Wheeler, *Yankee from the West*, with Paul F. Healy (New York: Double-day, 1962), 177.

22. See John C. Ewers, *The Blackfeet: Raiders on the Northwestern Plains* (Norman: Univer-sity of Oklahoma Press, 1958); Rosier, *Rebirth of the Blackfeet Nation*; and Thomas R. Wessel, "Agriculture on the Reservations: The Case of the Blackfeet, 1885–1935," *Journal of the West* 17 (October 1979): 18–23.

23. For a narration of this story, see Rosier, *Rebirth of the Blackfeet Nation*.

24. For a good description of these Blackfeet concepts, see Clayton C. Denman, "Cultural Change among the Blackfeet Indians of Montana" (Ph.D. diss., University of California, Berkeley, 1968).

25. See Fred Campbell, "Five-Year Industrial Program from April 1, 1921 to April 1, 1926," in *TW-ICC*, Box 9, Folder 1.

26. See Wessel, "Agriculture on the Reservations," for background on the Monteath relocation.

27. "The Five-Year Program on the Blackfeet Indian Reservation," *Indian Leader* 26 (1923): 3.

28. "Extract of the Report of General H. L. Scott, dated October 10, 1925," in *TW-ICC*, Box 8, Folder 6.

29. Oscar Lipps, "Subsistence Farming on the Blackfeet Reservation; Memorandum for Mr. Cooley," in *TW-ICC*, Box 8, Folder 5.

30. "Five-Year Program," 3.

31. James Willard Schultz, "The Starving Blackfeet Indians" (Los Angeles: National Association to Help the Indian, 1921).

32. "Extract of the Report of General H. L. Scott."

33. Wallace Stegner, *Wolf Willow* (1952; repr., New York: Penguin Press, 2000), 282–283.

CHAPTER 10

Eating Far from Home

LATINO/A WORKERS AND FOOD
SOVEREIGNTY IN RURAL VERMONT

Teresa M. Mares, Naomi Wolcott-MacCausland, and Jessie Mazar

By the tenth grocery store visit with a friend and colleague, the first author of this chapter was exhausted and increasingly annoyed about the prominence of canned chili and crispy taco shells in the "Hispanic" aisle of these retail outlets. Having been to at least four big box stores, two food co-ops, a dollar store, and several smaller ethnic markets owned by refugee families resettled in the Burlington area, she was exasperated by the inability to find the necessary ingredients to make tamales with Alma, the wife of a dairy farmworker, for an upcoming *Dia de los Muertos* festival at the Vermont Folklife Center.

This should not have been a surprise; finding *real tortillas* and *real salsa picante* along the northern border had been a source of frustration before. Yet this time, with the challenge of feeding more than 100 people, the lived reality of searching out the components of such a beloved and culturally meaningful dish drove home the significance of our collaborative research on the foodways of Latino/a migrants in the state of Vermont. Along with this frustration came the insight, theoretical turned experiential, that having the resources necessary to search out these ingredients (specifically a driver's license and a fairly serviceable car) was a mark of privilege linked to the benefits of U.S. citizenship and flexibility of time and labor. For the estimated 1,200–1,500 Latino/a farmworkers living in the state of Vermont, this kind of culinary expedition would be impossible, particularly in the cold winter months when temperatures of ten below zero and three-foot snowdrifts are not uncommon.

We arrived at Alma's apartment the day after the shopping mission with some semblance of the list that she had sent via text message while planning the menu for the event.[1] Upon setting down the items, the bag of *masa* was met with a disapproving frown and a proclamation that the dried *chiles* that had been procured "*no son los correctos!*"[2] Assuring us that we would make do with the assortment of desirable and less-than-desirable ingredients, Alma quickly unearthed her own stash of the correct *chiles*, and we started the ten-hour process of making several dozen chicken tamales with red *and* green salsa, using a half-functioning stovetop and a blender that threatened to catch on fire. As we were completing the process of assembling the tamales and carefully placing them into large steamer pots, the doorbell rang, and Alma returned with a large box postmarked in Queens, New York. With great excitement, and under the watchful eye of her young daughter, she showed us the dried herbs, candies, packaged foods, and other small gifts that had been sent by her sister who was enjoying greater access to a network of *tiendas* in a culturally diverse urban environment. Contained within this package was Alma's strategy of procuring the right ingredients to prepare dishes that cross national borders and connect migrant households in the United States with cultural meanings, traditions, and foodways back home.

Throughout our ethnographic and applied work in Vermont, individuals like Alma have revealed the diverse food procurement strategies common in migrant households, ranging from ordering items through the mail to receiving deliveries from mobile market enterprises that bring food, phone cards, and Hello Kitty piñatas from as far away as New Jersey. These complex negotiations of geographic and linguistic borders and barriers, markets (both formal and informal), and social networks reveal that, for migrant farmworkers, food access often entails much more than a simple trip to the grocery store. This chapter illuminates some of these complexities by connecting vignettes about the household food practices of Latino/a migrant workers with an analysis of the broader historical, economic, and cultural forces that have shaped Vermont's dairy industry and its changing labor force. Drawing upon insights gained from our collaborative work on a kitchen garden project and applied ethnographic research, this chapter examines how living and working alongside the U.S.-Canada border influences the foodways sustaining Vermont's Latino/a dairy workers and their choices over the foods they consume. Through this examination, we argue in this chapter that isolation, fear of border enforcement, and anxieties around leaving the home combine to create marginal spaces through which migrant workers reformulate ideas of good food and where the layered and often contested meanings of food sovereignty are revealed.

Our long-term objective is to illuminate and challenge the links between food sovereignty and structural vulnerabilities in nontraditional destinations of migration and among farmworkers employed in year-round production—a group that often falls outside the purview of most food security, antihunger, and food justice efforts. In doing so, we interrogate the consequences of living and working alongside *la otra frontera*—a space where many of the same processes of surveillance, dehumanization, and social marginalization return to shape the lives of workers who have already endured the violence endemic to the southern borderlands and within their countries of origin. A key difference between our work and the majority of the scholarship on farmworker food access is that Vermont, as a "new destination of migration," presents a geographic and social context very different from regions with longer histories of Latino/a migration. These different contexts necessarily entail variations in the scale and scope of resource provisioning, social networks, and food access, only exacerbated by federal border proximity. With workers dispersed across wide expanses of the rural landscape, the processes of accessing, preparing, and sharing food present both distinct challenges and spaces where human ingenuity and agency are revealed in everyday practices of food sovereignty. Yet, for workers who are living and working within these northern borderlands, the difficulties associated with accessing basic needs and maintaining the cultural meanings connected to food conspire to leave workers never truly satiated, even while ensuring the food security of consumers and continued profits for the farm owners who manage to stay afloat.

ETHNOGRAPHIC AND THEORETICAL CONTEXT

Often characterized as a "new" or "nontraditional" destination for Latino/a migration, the state of Vermont has seen a steady increase in the number of migrant farmworkers from Mexico and other Latin American countries since the late 1990s. Despite the newness of this trend, the Latino/a population in the state grew twenty-four times faster than the overall population between 2000 and 2010.[3] Currently, there are approximately 1,200–1,500 Latino/a migrant dairy workers in Vermont, and the vast majority—roughly 90 percent—of these workers are likely undocumented. While the majority of migrant workers in Vermont's dairies are men, a steady number of women are now living, and sometimes working, on these farms. However, as Claudia Radel and colleagues underscore, farm owners often view the presence of women on dairies as problematic. This is due to the substandard housing that many workers are provided, the fact women are often viewed as incapable of operating heavy machinery, and the notion held by some farmers that if women become pregnant, this could call greater attention to the presence of undocumented workers as they seek pre- and postnatal health care services.[4]

As one of the whitest states in the nation, these demographic changes have not gone entirely unnoticed, and the presence of these workers reveals the hidden dynamics behind Vermont's iconic working landscape. Latino/a migrants working in the state's dairy industry face a perplexing conundrum in their daily lives, as they are simultaneously invisible in the milking barns where they work and hypervisible when they enter public spaces outside of the home or workplace. These workers experience a great deal of fear, isolation, and anxiety connected to their status in Vermont as "invisible workers" laboring in what geographer Susannah McCandless has characterized as a "carceral countryside."[5] These anxieties tend to intensify the closer one is living and working to the northern border, as the concentration of active U.S. Border Patrol agents increases with closer proximity. The majority of the state, including 90 percent of the state's residents, falls within the 100-mile expanse where Immigration, Customs, and Enforcement (ICE) officers have the authority to stop and search travelers without reasonable suspicion or a warrant. However, the "primary operating domain" of Border Patrol is said to be 25 miles within the Vermont-Canada border, meaning that the majority of routine enforcement takes place within a much smaller region of the state (see Map 1 in chapter 1). This domain encompasses three of the four border counties (Grand Isle, Franklin, and Orleans) that are home to a significant number of the state's dairy farms employing Latino/a workers.[6]

In neighboring New York State, the experiences of Latino/a migrant workers living in rural areas have been examined from multiple disciplinary angles. These studies illuminate the difficult realities that Latino/a migrants face in a state where the federal border has become increasingly "Mexicanized" since 2001, whereby the number of border agents has increased and policing has become more militaristic amid concerns of terrorism and lax surveillance.[7] Vermont shares many of the same rural dynamics as New York, yet has a particular history of rural inclusion and exclusion distinct from other northern border states. For workers in the border region, the international border manifests itself into everyday decisions about the risks of leaving the farm and encountering Border Patrol versus exercising one's autonomy and right to mobility. For most, the risks of detention and deportation do not outweigh the benefits of continued employment, resulting in dependency on others for accessing food and medications, inequitable access to health care, and generalized anxiety and other mental health concerns.[8] While there are a number of individuals who provide services to these workers on the farm, namely delivering food and other goods or transportation for hire, many of the individuals take advantage of these dynamics and charge a premium for goods and services, only exacerbating the vulnerabilities and inequalities that farmworkers experience.

To fully understand Vermont's contemporary border dynamics, it is essential to situate them within the historical and strategic production of the state's rural countryside. As Clare Hinrichs has highlighted, the production of Vermont's countryside has been mired in a set of exclusionary politics and cultural boundaries based on race/ethnicity, social class, and national origin. The promotion of the state as a "distinctive rural place" steeped in Yankee values of hard work, modesty, and wholesomeness has been carefully geared toward select groups of outsiders, particularly those with economic capital they might infuse into the rural economy.[9] These outsiders have primarily included white northerners from the broader region who might visit the state to establish a second home or small business, to ski or otherwise recreate in the wilderness, or to consume the state's specialty agricultural products (namely maple and dairy). Decidedly absent from this welcome embrace have been groups "of foreign stock," including in-migrating French Canadians coming south across the border from Quebec in search of greater economic opportunity. While the state's Quebecois influence is now celebrated, perhaps because of the dependence upon tourist revenue from visiting Canadians, a newfound uneasiness about "foreign" newcomers has come to rest squarely upon the backs of Latino/a workers who have crossed the U.S.-Mexico border to work in the state's dairies.

The dairy industry is the cornerstone to Vermont's agrarian image, and the state's agricultural economy depends more on dairy production than any other state in the nation.[10] As in most agricultural sectors across the nation, milk production in Vermont has grown increasingly industrialized since the 1950s, resulting in both the consolidation of thousands of small family farms into a much smaller number of large farms with larger herds and an intensification of milking throughout the year, rather than relying upon seasonal production. The technologies and labor practices associated with milking have also shifted to become more uniform, mechanized, and less amenable to small-scale family farming. With these changes and challenges, Vermont has lost as many as 80 percent of its dairy farms, seeing a decrease from 11,000 dairies in the 1940s to fewer than 1,000 in 2011.[11] As of 2014, informal counts estimate that the number of dairies has fallen below 900. Across the U.S. dairy industry, hiring Latino/a workers has become more commonplace alongside the mounting technological and financial challenges of farming. In Vermont, Latino/a migrant workers have enabled the state's dairy industry to produce more milk than ever before, even while the total number of farms has dwindled. As of 2005, as many as two-thirds of Vermont's dairies employed migrant laborers, with a sizable percentage of the state's milk being produced by these workers.[12]

What distinguishes labor in the dairy industry from other food sectors is that, unlike other agricultural production, dairy production takes place year-round, rather than following seasonal schedules of planting and harvesting. Because of these labor patterns, migrant dairy workers are excluded from federal seasonal work programs, such as the H-2A visa program that brings apple pruners and harvesters from Jamaica into the state for approximately five months each year. This differential access to documented work in the U.S. food industry is reflective of the broader and deeper contradictions and inequalities that plague the food chain. Organizations like the Food Chain Workers Alliance, Restaurant Opportunities Centers (ROC) United, and the Coalition of Immokalee Workers (CIW) have documented and challenged these contradictions, drawing attention to the fact that food-related jobs, from production through disposal, are often filled by workers of color with limited access to the benefits and protections associated with U.S. citizenship. More recently in Vermont, the farmworker-led organization Migrant Justice has developed a "Milk with Dignity" campaign to pressure large companies like Ben and Jerry's to agree to a worker-driven social

responsibility program, taking inspiration from the innovative organizing strategies of the CIW.

The growing dependence on exploiting immigrant communities of color
to produce a food long associated with "white social dominance" reveals yet
another cruel contradiction within industrial dairy production. In examining
the promotion of milk as a cure for bodily and social illness in the early 1900s,
Melanie DuPuis notes, "milk became not only one of the reasons for Northern
European white racial superiority but also a way to pass that superiority onto
other races and ethnicities."[13] While today's industrial dairies share little in common with the "cow and milkmaid" pastoral representations circulating during
earlier times, the values of purity and wholesomeness that are still invoked to sell
milk products belie the racialized labor systems that leave workers vulnerable
to abuse and the political and economic conditions that make small-scale dairy
farming next to impossible.

The racialized labor patterns embedded within Vermont's dairy sector
and the assumed undocumented status of Latino/a workers in the industry put
them at risk for compounding structural vulnerabilities and inadequate and
irregular access to many basic needs. Structural vulnerability is both a process
through which the "vulnerability of an individual is produced by his or her location in a hierarchical social order and its diverse networks of power relationships and effects" and an analytical stance that examines ". . . the forces that
constrain decision-making, frame choices, and limit life options."[14] The concept
of structural vulnerability has become instrumental within the field of medical
anthropology, including within studies of health disparities confronting migrant
workers. Scholars in this field have offered important insights into the lives of
farmworkers during and after the process of migration, focusing mostly upon
the well-being and health of those employed in seasonal agricultural production
in states with a long history of Latino/a migration. Together, these studies highlight the structural vulnerabilities that leave Latino/a migrant workers at risk for
health complications and decreased life chances.[15]

Despite the growing consciousness around these inequalities, the intersection
of food sovereignty and structural vulnerability within farmworker populations
has not been examined in much depth, even though it has proven to be a fruitful
line of theoretical inquiry in studies of food access within nonfarmworker communities and families.[16] Yet amid concerns around social isolation, hazardous
working conditions, and barriers to accessing health care, it is clear that disparities in access to food, especially food that is healthy and culturally familiar, is of
paramount concern for farmworkers. Studies in more traditional destinations of
migration have repeatedly documented the disproportionate rate of food insecurity among farmworkers.[17] These studies have found that farmworkers experience food insecurity rates between three and six times the national average,
which currently hovers around 14 percent, with rates even higher among families

with children. Yet, as we argue below, the concept of food security itself presents a limited vantage point to understand the broad range of choices and principles of taste (see Meredith Abarca's chapter in this volume) that shape the everyday foodways of migrant farmworkers, necessitating a deeper engagement with the concept of food sovereignty.

Throughout their journeys, migrant farmworkers transgress, reside within, and are constrained by political and cultural borders. As a conceptual category tied to multidimensional and continuously shifting geographic and social spaces, the borderlands have long been a compelling theme of scholarship across the humanities and social sciences. Theorizing the borderlands has extended out from studies of migration and settlement between Mexico and the United States to enable examinations of difference, inequality, and the desire for proximity to new experiences and lifeways in many spaces around the globe.[18] Gloria Anzaldúa, whose work has become canonical within border studies, describes the borderlands as those spaces that are "physically present wherever two or more cultures edge each other, where people of different races occupy the same territory, where under, lower, middle and upper classes touch, where the space between two individuals shrinks with intimacy."[19] This view emphasizes that the borderlands are markers of difference and of closeness, of deterritorialization and reterritorialization, and of sovereignty of the nation-state and of individual bodies. In this vein, it is essential that border scholars examine both movement across and maintenance of borders, and the dialectical relationships between geopolitical spaces, social practices, and cultural identity. The relationships between people and the food that sustains them presents a compelling entry point into these examinations.

Cultivating Food Sovereignty in the Borderlands of Vermont

If we, as eaters, reflect for a moment about our motivations for leaving the home as we move through our daily lives, grocery shopping, meeting friends and colleagues for lunch or dinner, and running by the convenience store for a quick gallon of milk for tomorrow's breakfast are surely central to our daily tasks. These realities are entirely different for migrant workers in Vermont who face significant geographic, cultural, and linguistic barriers in accessing food and other basic needs. Since late 2011, the three authors of this piece have collaborated on an applied kitchen gardening project that works to increase food sovereignty among Latino/a migrant workers. The Huertas project (*huerta* is Spanish for kitchen garden), which supports migrant farmworkers in planting home gardens, is connected to University of Vermont (UVM) Extension's Bridges to Health Program. In the summer of 2015, we worked with farmworkers on forty-four farms, many of whom had gardened for the past several years, in addition to a few first-time gardeners. These gardens range in size from a few square feet to hundreds of square feet of growing space, providing varying amounts of food for farmworker families and those with whom they share extra produce. Farmworkers who have participated in the project have been primarily identified through ongoing outreach coordinated by Bridges to Health and have expressed interest in growing some of their own food. There are no minimum standards for program participation, and Huertas serves a diverse group of households, ranging from groups of men sharing cramped living quarters to nuclear families with young children.

What is unique about Huertas is that the majority of gardens are located on land owned by dairy farmers, given that most Latino/a farmworkers are living on the farms where they work. Unlike most community gardening initiatives, the community aspect of Huertas is fostered by the social relationships between volunteers and members of migrant worker households, rather than the social ties facilitated by the shared use of space. Many of the volunteers involved with the project are university students, though supportive neighbors living in rural Vermont have also been involved in the project. The majority of farmworkers with whom Huertas collaborates are geographically isolated, and most do not have access to personal transportation, much less public transportation, while living thousands of miles away from family and friends. Moreover, as discussed earlier, those living near the federal border face significant risks in entering and utilizing public spaces, making traditional community gardening approaches next to impossible. By connecting farmworkers with volunteers, materials, and the permission from the dairy owners to plant these gardens within this set of constraints, Huertas aims to address the disparities in access to nutritious food while simultaneously bridging the barriers of social isolation that are sustained and reproduced in this type of working landscape.

The Huertas project began in 2010 as an informal program to distribute seeds and plants to farmworkers and increase their access to more localized and culturally appropriate sources of food. Over the last few seasons, in our effort to learn about and prioritize the cultural preferences of the dairy workers with whom we work, our project team and student interns have begun dialogues early in the season to gain a better understanding of the preferred selection of vegetables and herbs for each participating farm. These vegetables have ranged from the everyday staples easily found in U.S. grocery stores like lettuce, tomatoes, carrots, and onions to culturally familiar herbs like *cilantro, epazote, hierba buena,* and several varieties of *chiles* (including *poblano, miracielo, jalapeño, habanero,* and *serrano*) used in preparing various Mexican dishes (Figure 10.1). Based on the preliminary list, we have received the generous support of local greenhouses and farmers who have provided supplies, seeds, and transplants for the gardens. Several of the gardeners have also planted their own seeds that they saved themselves or brought from home. Volunteers from the broader community are matched with gardeners to do two outreach visits: plot planning and

Figure 10.1. A farmworker garden showing intercropping of beans, maize, and squash. Photo by Jessie Mazar.

preparation in the late spring as well as a planting day in the early summer. However, several of these partnerships have extended past these visits, resulting in regular visits and shared meals between farmworkers and project volunteers.

Although the population of farmworkers in Vermont is relatively small and the number of farmers is also on a continual decline, it is difficult and perhaps also counterproductive to generalize the relationships between farmworkers and farm owners within the dairy industry or the cultural and livelihood backgrounds that farmworkers bring with them into the state. While cases of worker abuse are well documented and there are significant concerns of exploitation, many workers with whom we have collaborated have expressed their appreciation for their employer and the opportunity to work, and some are regularly welcomed into their employers' families for celebrations and meals. Yet the power dynamics between farmers and farmworkers are necessarily borne out of imbalances of power and privilege, though it must be acknowledged that farmers themselves are also caught in a cycle where their productive work is continually devalued by the market economy and where pressures from corporate consolidation and failed agricultural policies are ever-present. Still, on the farms where Huertas is active, all of the farm owners are supportive of the project, though this support ranges from a simple granting of permission to utilize a small plot of land to helping to prepare the soil and add compost enriched by manure generated by the herd. Within the group of participating farmworkers, some have extensive agricultural experience in their home countries and reflect upon their families' farms with a sense of fondness and nostalgia, while others were already disconnected from an agrarian tradition long before they arrived in Vermont.

As Huertas has expanded over the last few years, we have become increasingly guided by and committed to a food sovereignty framework. Within food-related projects and the many food movements in which they are embedded, multiple discourses guide activist and advocacy efforts, including local food, community food security, food justice, and food sovereignty.[20] The promise of a food sovereignty framework stems from its bottom-up perspective that demands a deeper conversation of rights, control, and choice. Perhaps most important, food sovereignty moves beyond a focus on food security to advocate for a deeper connection to food that challenges a narrow consumer-commodity relationship. Developed most intensively by the international peasant movement *La Via Campesina*, food sovereignty has been primarily conceptualized as an all-encompassing movement with the end goal of rebuilding locally controlled food systems, rather than a set of everyday practices and choices that individuals and families make over the food that sustains them. In our work, we have become convinced that food sovereignty can and should operate at both levels, and that the household (or garden) is a crucial space where food sovereignty might emerge.

In examining how food sovereignty plays out within the home and on the plate, theoretical concepts like "principles of taste" and "culinary subjectivities," as described by Meredith Abarca in this volume, prove to be helpful in understanding the material realities that shape and are shaped by the foodways of Latino/a farmworkers. For Alma, whose story opened this chapter, the *right chiles* and the *right masa* are key to reproducing tastes from home, revealing a depth of culinary subjectivity that illustrates a keen sense of agency and autonomy over the food that sustains her and her family. However, the lengths she must go to secure these foods reveal the challenges present in everyday practices of attaining food sovereignty in a place beset by structural vulnerability. In the narratives below, the practices of food sovereignty demonstrated by Huertas participants are placed into conversation with the structural vulnerabilities that shape their lives.

NARRATING THE SELF THROUGH THE GARDEN

A central component of building a community-engaged research project connected to Huertas has been to share the stories of the gardeners with whom we work not only in academic literature but also with local audiences in Vermont who are often unaware of the particular challenges facing the workers who are producing the dairy products for which the region is known. What follows is an attempt to share the narratives of some of the farmworkers with whom we have collaborated and what we have learned about their relationships with their gardening spaces, the experience of migration, and the food that sustains them.

These vignettes reveal that, even while these gardens are significant in rebuilding some sense of place and fostering practices of food sovereignty, our efforts are necessarily limited by constraints of a short growing season, demanding work schedules, and the deeper structural vulnerabilities these workers face.

Since early 2012, we have regularly visited with farmworkers, planning and preparing garden beds, witnessing the births of calves, deciding the best place to plant tomatoes, and hauling away hundreds of pounds of squash that had transformed overnight from *calabicitas* to what we have jokingly termed *"calabazones."* During the harvest seasons over the past few years, we have set aside several full days to visit gardeners during the height of the gardens' productivity to gain a better understanding of what has worked well and what we might consider doing differently the following year. These visits have also provided important ethnographic insights, allowing us to refine our long-term research interests and objectives. In anticipation of a series of visits in 2012, Wolcott-MacCausland warned Mares and Mazar, half-jokingly, that we would need to make sure the car was empty to carry all of the produce that would be given to us as we made our rounds. This turned out to be fair warning, as we soon found ourselves the lucky recipients of pounds and pounds of extra veggies, most of them coming from the garden of Tomás.

Tomás, born in 1950, had been working on and off in the United States since he was twenty-four years old. Raised in the state of Guerrero, he is the father of eight children, six of whom live and work in various states north of the border. Until arriving on a Vermont dairy farm in 2002, he traveled back and forth frequently between jobs working on large farms that grew tobacco, lettuce, cabbage, cauliflower, and beets while in the United States and tending to his *maiz y frijoles* (corn and beans) while at home in Mexico. With increased border security following 9/11, Tomás and millions of other migrant workers have found themselves less able to visit Mexico for fear that they would not be able to return to work in the United States. While he reminisced frequently about caring for his land in Mexico, until connecting to the Huertas project, he had never grown food for his own sustenance in the United States. After decades of working in U.S. agriculture, Tomás permanently returned to Mexico in January 2015 after his employer sold the remaining herd and retired. His return to Mexico occurred just months after he appeared in immigration court and had been granted deferred deportation proceedings until late 2015.

In the fall of 2012, as Mares and Mazar entered the small two-bedroom mobile home that he shared with two other men, Tomás quickly pushed into our hands three gallon-sized bags of frozen wild black raspberries that he had picked from the surrounding hills in anticipation of our visit. After scooting us through the trailer and out the back door, bags in hand, we were stunned to see the vibrant intercropped garden that spanned almost the full length of the home. We were even more taken aback when we learned that the space in which we were standing was just one of four gardens that he tended around the property, all the while working more than sixty to seventy hours per week milking cows. Over the next hour, we followed him around the garden as he proceeded to fill bags and bags of tomatoes, ground cherries, herbs, winter squash, corn, and zucchini that he insisted we take home. This produce, which he regularly calls "gifts from the earth," was shared with the two men with whom he lived, health outreach volunteers from UVM Extension, and the wife of the farm owner for whom he worked (in fact, she was quite jealous of his garden). He was even known to package up produce to send to his children in various states in the eastern and southeastern United States.

At a more recent visit, we asked Tomás why he had not grown a garden previously given his extensive agricultural experience and enthusiasm for growing. He replied that until he was approached by Huertas, he never even thought planting a garden was a possibility. Despite having a tremendous wealth of agricultural knowledge and experience and a deep love of growing food, he was unable to access the seeds and other necessary materials needed for his garden, a connection that was successfully established through participating in the project. After this brief discussion, he quickly returned to the tour of his garden, pointing out the sunflowers and *flor de viuda* (widow flowers) he had planted around the perimeter of the space and the dry beans he had received from his family in Mexico. Over the course of our many visits, Tomás regularly requested that we take pictures of him in his garden so that he could share them with his children and so that he could bring them with him back to Mexico. In these instances, the sense of pride and sovereignty that is cultivated through these gardens becomes clear, as is the desire to share the bounty of the food produced in these spaces. Before he returned home to Mexico, he made sure to let our team know that he was looking forward to growing his own food again on a greater scale on the land he had been accumulating in his home state of Guerrero.

As our visits with Tomás grew more regular throughout 2013 and 2014, and more focused on socializing than gardening, he began to prepare elaborate meals in anticipation of having guests. These meals nearly always centered upon homemade tortillas that he prepared with Maseca purchased from the mobile vendors, and were accompanied by a rotating assortment of vegetables, chicken *mole*, *posole*, *atole*, beans, salsas, rice, and candied squash that suited his own principles of taste. When asked if he cooked these kinds of dishes in Mexico, he gave a sly laugh and stated, "No, in Mexico, I was the king! I did not need to cook or clean, nothing!" Commenting on the "*machista*" ways of men in Mexico, he acknowledged his gender privilege during this conversation but also hypothesized that when he returned home for good, he most certainly would not continue to cook if he could find a woman who would do so. However, as his stay in the United States stretched longer than he had originally planned, he sought out the expertise of women, particularly when he was working in seasonal crop production where women were more commonly employed. These women shared with him their cooking knowledge and skills, which he began to employ in his own kitchen. While tortillas were an everyday staple in his Vermont home, as he repeatedly reminded us, cooking more elaborate meals was really only worth the time and effort if it brought visitors to his home. In this way, Tomás engages his culinary subjectivity and practices of food sovereignty to rebuild a sense of commensality that was often absent while he worked in the United States.

During Huertas site visits, what has been particularly striking are the daily lives of women, especially mothers with very young children, who are living at these dairies. Unlike Tomás, who would likely give up his cooking duties if he could find someone else to cook for him, for Juana, preparing meals that resemble those from home is what she loves most about her garden. As a newer gardener, Juana's success growing food for the first time in 2012 was impressive, especially given that the farm owner periodically cut off the water supply to her family's home during the hottest period of the summer to redirect it to the cows in the barn. At this farm, Juana lived with her two small boys, her husband, and a few other men in a small manufactured home, though she has since moved to a new farm and now lives only with her immediate family. For Juana, cultivating her own food has given her an opportunity to get outside and re-create some of the meals she misses from home, and also to develop new skills in food production that she had only witnessed while living in Chiapas, Mexico. Although she has jokingly complained about the fact that her husband and children do not have enough appreciation for vegetables, she has continued to find new ways of sneaking them into the meals she prepares. Over the past few years we have regularly visited and shared meals with Juana, and during this time, her garden has increased exponentially in size and productivity.

Unlike many of the gardeners with whom we have worked, Juana had little experience growing her own food before becoming involved in Huertas, despite having been raised in an agricultural community. However, she has thrown herself into the project with both feet, growing flowers and vegetables that she regularly shares with other volunteers who come to her home and with our project collaborators whenever she gets a chance. Whether it is fresh salsa or a bouquet of recently picked flowers, Juana has developed a firm sense of pride in her ability to create something from the ground where she resides. Even with this personal growth, her autonomy and sense of pride are rooted to land that she does not own, a connection that remains tenuous and seemingly impermanent. Nevertheless, Juana has grown increasingly active in local farmworker activism efforts and has recently taught a cooking class focusing on tamales at a local food cooperative, in addition to starting to work a few hours at a nearby dairy. Despite the fact that these events require her to leave the home—which is a risky venture given where she lives—Juana's relationships to the local community are deepening despite all odds.

Another woman, Lourdes, lives with her young daughter and husband, along with several other workers, at a farm very close to the border. The Huertas project has given her and her daughter an outlet for creativity, experiencing the outdoors, and cultivating fresh food with deep cultural resonance. She reflected upon these experiences during a 2014 visit with Wolcott-MacCausland:

> I used to only leave the apartment to go to the milking parlor to help my husband sometimes. I never went outside. I didn't see the sun. Three years ago I started to have a garden. I didn't know anything about having a garden here. Jessie [Mazar] and Teresa [Mares] came to talk to me about it. They explained how to prepare the soil and asked about the plants I wanted. The boss gave us a place to plant in an area in between the barns and farm machinery. Immigration always passes by on the roads next to the farm so it was difficult to find a place that was not visible from the road.

Because of this continual fear of immigration enforcement, Lourdes explained that prior to having a garden, there were periods where she would not leave her apartment for as long as two months at a time because there simply was not anywhere enjoyable to go. This apartment, tucked behind a makeshift farm office, has a small kitchen and sleeping quarters for the workers, and little else.

As Lourdes recalled, in deciding upon the location of the garden we had to take extra care that it was out of sight from the small state highway that loops around the barn and their housing unit. To get to the raised beds, Lourdes and her daughter put on their rubber boots and muck their way through the milking parlor and then the cow barn, wading through inches of animal waste to arrive at a sunny area tucked between two sections of a free stall barn and bunker silos that store the majority of the cow feed. Despite these obstacles, Lourdes has repeatedly expressed that the garden has given her and her daughter a reason to get outside, often as much as three or four times a day, and reconnect with dishes like *chile rellenos* that she prepares with the produce that she is growing with her own hands (Figure 10.2). As important, she has expressed her appreciation for the project for the ways it has allowed her to meet more people and form lasting friendships.

During the summer months, the produce from her garden provides a significant percentage of the fresh vegetables her family consumes, and throughout the winter, she has added dried herbs from the garden to flavor her dishes and has saved seeds to replant the herbs the following year. For her, this is a meaningful addition to her household's food supply and a practice in food sovereignty, though there are seasonal limitations. She explains:

> The rest of the year, the manager on the farm buys us the vegetables we ask for once a week. We make a list and request what we need. It's difficult to know how much I need each week, and there are times that we eat all the vegetables I

Figure 10.2. A gardener harvesting *poblano* peppers to prepare *chiles rellenos*. Photo by Jessie Mazar.

ask for in a few days and then we don't have any for the rest of the week. Other times, we have too much, and they rot before we can use them. With the garden, I harvest what I need daily without the vegetables going bad or not having enough for the meal. Since I started harvesting this year I haven't purchased any vegetables. Every day I harvest what I want that day. I covered my garden a few weeks ago to protect it from the frost and am still able to harvest.

Lourdes's garden continues to be one of the most productive we have seen, an abundant space where she grows corn, tomatoes, several varieties of *chiles*, tomatillo, lettuce, radishes, summer squash, carrots, watermelon, cucumbers, onions, and garlic, in addition to many different herbs (cilantro, oregano, mint, chamomile, *epazote*, dill, thyme, *papalo*, and *cepiche*). While the variety and quality of vegetables are of clear benefit, Lourdes's ability to choose which vegetables she wants to pick and eat, and avoid waste, is perhaps even more significant in terms of everyday practices of food sovereignty. Unlike all of the other women involved with Huertas, Lourdes has no interest in planting flowers, preferring to dedicate this precious space to food production only.

Over the last two years she and her husband have made special efforts to construct raised bed borders and extend the overall footprint of the garden, in addition to adding a large umbrella to provide shade for relaxation. This has transformed the garden from a space of producing only vegetables to one of broader impact: "One benefit of the garden is the distraction. If I didn't have the garden, I'd be inside all day in the kitchen watching TV. I don't get bored in the kitchen but it's different being outside. Now I go outside and listen to the birds sing. I feel more free, like I'm in the fields in my village. The memories of what it was like there come back. Another benefit is to breathe fresh air and have fresh vegetable and herbs and no more rotten cilantro!" In these connections, we can observe the desire to create a sense of belonging and tranquility, even amid the challenging conditions and fear in which she lives. She has repeatedly told us that when the time comes for her to return to her home state of Guerrero, Mexico, she would like to take the skills she has learned through gardening in Vermont and grow vegetables for sale on land that she owns.

As Lourdes's young daughter has grown increasingly talkative and precocious, Lourdes has made an effort to expand her social networks as much as possible, recognizing the importance of her interacting with other children. At times, this has involved Lourdes sending her to Easter egg hunts and birthday parties for the children of other farmers in the area with the farm owner's wife, an opportunity that her daughter has because she was born in the United States and is not subject to the same fear of immigration enforcement that confronts Lourdes. The sad fact is that Lourdes does not feel safe going to these parties herself, though she will sometimes make exceptions and endure the risk for the parties of children of other Mexican mothers. These kinds of contradictions are fueled by a misguided and unjust set of immigration and agricultural policies that leave migrant farmworker households in a state of structural vulnerability where even the most mundane events—like an Easter egg hunt—become a point of disconnection between mother and child.

The final vignette is brief and brings us back to the individual whose story opened this chapter. During the long process of assembling tamales in 2013, we asked Alma whether she had any interest in starting a garden. She hesitantly explained that she had tried small container gardens before, but that she was fearful that the family who lived below her, all U.S. citizens, would destroy any effort she might make toward expanding her gardening space. She described how this family had a long history of stealing and breaking any items that she and her children left outside and repeatedly threatened to call Border Patrol on them if they made any complaints. Despite her love of cooking, and the elaborate steps she regularly takes to access food that is familiar and meaningful, the risks of starting a garden did not outweigh the benefits. Fortunately, Alma has since moved to a new home with her family, and her overall living situation has become more comfortable. She has recently started a garden at her new home and also hopes to support the project through providing outreach to other workers in the area, many of whom purchase food from the informal catering business that she runs out of her home. Alma's story reminds us that while Huertas has enabled participating farmworkers to expand their everyday practices of food sovereignty, the overall impact of the program is small in relationship to the needs, and hundreds of farmworkers still stand to benefit not only from the familiar food that the project aims to provide but also from the social connectedness that is perhaps even more needed.

Moving toward Sovereignty in a Vulnerable Place

Over the past few summers, as the gardens were bursting with produce, we have planned several fiestas to bring many of these gardeners together and to celebrate and share the literal fruits of our labor. Over a large gas-fired stove at the Wolcott-MacCausland family farm, the individuals and families described in these vignettes have come together to share homemade tortillas, prepare and can fresh salsas and black raspberry jam, and use up some of the baseball-bat-size *calabacita* in zucchini cakes. We have done this all with the goal of building a sense of commensality and community that is often missing from the daily lives of these workers. In a small way, these events have challenged the isolation that is produced by and reproduces Vermont's rural working landscape. In these fiestas and in the gardens themselves, we see the glimmers of sovereignty and autonomy over the sources and diversity of foods these individuals are consuming. Yet, in planning these events, we must remain constantly aware that for farmworkers, leaving one's home and entering the public sphere, for a reason as simple as cel-ebrating a birthday or sharing one's tomatillos, puts them at risk for surveillance and potential detention by Border Patrol. These individuals take these risks, fully aware of the consequences, because of their deep desire for social connection.

In this snapshot of a man in his beloved gardens where he tends to "the gifts of the earth," the rejection of planting flowers in favor of vegetables, or the firm commitment to provide healthy foods for one's husband and children, we can observe how these individuals claim a sense of agency and a connec-tion to meaningful meals in a borderland region that is far from welcoming. We also can observe how these individual efforts, and the broader objectives of the Huertas project, call into question the complicated dynamics of how food sovereignty efforts play out on the ground and the challenges of working toward greater autonomy over one's food access in an environment that is beset by so few choices. As we continually develop the Huertas project, questions of food access are of central concern, but it is not a straightforward connection to mere calories or nutrients that we are aiming to enable. Rather, in working alongside individuals like Juana, Tomás, and Lourdes, we seek to expand the choices and decisions that socially marginalized individuals have over how to source their food and what kinds of foods are available close to home. While the *chile* or corn plants they cultivate are just one small contribution to the household's food supply, as these stories demonstrate, the meaning of these plants goes deeper than their nutritional value to more fundamental issues of self-sufficiency and sustaining ties to cultural identity.

In previous work, Mares has written about the ways that kitchen gardens can serve as a source of sustenance and the maintenance of cultural identities, especially in the midst of migration and settlement.[21] This is something that we have seen very clearly through our work with Huertas. Our project team is also aware that no matter how many gardens we plant, or how successful they may be, they are just one small part of addressing basic needs year-round, and it is imperative to underscore that these gardens are only productive for a few months out of the year. While most of the gardeners make an effort to freeze, dry, and otherwise preserve foods for the winter months, all remain dependent on others to do the majority of their shopping for them, often the manager or owner of the farm who rarely speaks Spanish. In this way, their ability to choose and have regular access to food in these northern borderlands—particularly fresh foods with cultural significance—remains compromised, and their practices of food sovereignty remain constrained. While many of the Huertas participants have indicated that they have consistent access to food, they do not often have total control over what they are eating or when the food arrives. We have observed that gardens are one part of a broader patchwork of responses that have sprouted up because of unpredictable and inconsistent food access and that in this northern climate, year-round access to healthy, sustaining, and culturally relevant food is of utmost importance.

As a border state, many of the same fears, anxieties, and dangers that are connected to the southern border are reproduced in Vermont, with significant consequences for the food sovereignty, health access, and overall well-being of migrant workers sustaining the state's dairy industry. While the number of migrant workers in these northern borderlands is much smaller than at the U.S.-Mexico border, significant experiences of structural vulnerability have been expressed by the workers involved with Huertas, a vulnerability that both is produced by and serves to reproduce the ongoing fear and anxieties of living and working in a landscape where one is so visibly out of place. While the cultural and political contexts in these northern states are very different from those in California, Texas, and other areas with large numbers of migrant farmworkers, the political possibilities of Vermont's political progressiveness remain limited by a failed set of agricultural and immigration policies at the national level. More broadly speaking, we must recognize that our agricultural system is built upon a systematic and often violent denial of sovereignty to workers across the food chain, both in the United States and in their countries of origin. Until we as a nation are ready to come to terms with the needs of those who feed us, and do all that we can to ensure that they can feed themselves in a way that they deem appropriate and nourishing, the mealtimes of individuals like Tomás, Juana, and Lourdes will continue to be incomplete.[22]

NOTES

1. Throughout this chapter, "we" and "us" refer to two or more of the authors of this chapter.
2. "aren't the right ones!"
3. Daniel Baker and David Chappelle, "Health Status Needs of Latino Dairy Workers in Vermont," *Journal of Agromedicine* 17.3 (2012): 277–287
4. Claudia Radel, Birgit Schmook, and Susannah McCandless, "Environment, Transnational Labor, and Gender: Case Studies from Southern Yucatán, Mexico, and Vermont, USA," *Population and Environment* 32.2/3 (2010): 177–197.
5. Susannah McCandless, "Mapping the Carceral Countryside: Affect, Mobility and Gender in the Lived Spaces of Vermont Latino Farmers" (paper presented at the Annual Meeting of the Association of American Geographers, Las Vegas, March 26, 2009).
6. American Civil Liberties Union of Vermont, "Surveillance on the Northern Border" (2013), http://acluvt.org/surveillance/northern_border_report.pdf.
7. Peter Andreas, "The Mexicanization of the US-Canada Border: Asymmetric Interdependence in a Changing Security Context," *International Journal* 60.2 (2005): 449–462; Carlos Ulises Decena and Margaret Gray, "Introduction: The Border Next Door: New York *Migraciones*," *Social Text* 24.3 (2006): 1–12; Thomas R. Maloney and David Grusenmeyer, "Survey of Hispanic Dairy Workers in New York State," *Research Bulletin* 05–02 (2005), Cornell University Department of Applied Economics and Management; Melanie Nicholson, "Without Their Children: Rethinking Motherhood Among Transnational Migrant Women," *Social Text* 24.3 (2006): 13–33; Pilar A. Parra and Max J. Pfeffer, "New Immigrants in Rural Communities: The Challenge of Integration," *Social Text* 24.3 (2006): 81–98; see also the chapter by Kathleen Sexsmith in this volume.
8. Naomi Wolcott-MacCausland, "Health Access Negotiations among Latino Dairy Workers in Vermont" (M.S. thesis, University of Vermont, 2014).
9. C. Clare Hinrichs, "Consuming Images: Making and Marketing Vermont as a Distinctive Rural Place," in *Creating the Countryside: The Politics of Rural and Environmental Discourse*, ed. E. Melanie DuPuis and Peter Vandergeest (Philadelphia: Temple University Press, 1996), 259–278.
10. Bob Parsons, "Vermont's Dairy Sector: Is There a Sustainable Future for the 800 lb Gorilla?," University of Vermont Opportunities for Agriculture Working Paper Series 1.4 (2010), http://www.uvm.edu/crs/reports/working_papers/WorkingPapaerParsons-web.pdf; Radel et al., "Environment, Transnational Labor, and Gender."
11. Ross Sneyd, "Total Number of Dairy Farms Falls Below 1000," Vermont Public Radio, July 8, 2011, http://www.vpr.net/news_detail/91330/total-number-dairy-farms-in-vt-falls-bellow-1000/.
12. Radel et al., "Environment, Transnational Labor, and Gender"; Parsons, "Vermont's Dairy Sector"; Baker and Chappelle, "Health Status Needs."
13. E. Melanie DuPuis, *Nature's Perfect Food: How Milk Became America's Drink* (New York: New York University Press, 2002), 118.
14. James Quesada, Laurie K. Hart, and Philippe Bourgois, "Structural Vulnerability and Health: Latino Migrant Laborers in the United States," *Medical Anthropology* 20.4 (2011): 339–362.
15. Teresa Figueroa Sanchez, "California Strawberries: Mexican Immigrant Women Sharecroppers, Labor, and Discipline," *Anthropology of Work Review* 34.1 (2013): 15–26; Seth Holmes, "Structural Vulnerability and Hierarchies of Ethnicity and Citizenship on the Farm," *Medical Anthropology* 30.4 (2011): 425–449; Seth Holmes, *Fresh Fruit, Broken Bodies: Migrant Farmworkers in the United States* (Berkeley: University of California Press, 2013); Joan Vincente Palerm, "Immigrant and Migrant Farmworkers in the Santa Maria Valley," in *Transnational Latina/o Communities: Politics, Processes, and Cultures*, ed. C. Velez-Ibenez and A. Sampiao (Lanham, MD: Rowman and Littlefield, 2002); Quesada et al., "Structural Vulnerability and Health."

16. Megan Carney, *The Unending Hunger: Tracing Women and Food Insecurity Across Borders* (Berkeley: University of California Press, 2015).

17. The literature is large: Kirsten Borre, Luke Ertle, and Mariaelisa Graff, "Working to Eat: Vulnerability, Food Insecurity, and Obesity among Migrant and Seasonal Farmworker Families," *American Journal of Industrial Medicine* 53.4 (2010): 443–446; Sandy Brown and Christy Getz, "Farmworker Food Insecurity and the Production of Hunger in California," in *Cultivating Food Justice: Race, Class, and Sustainability*, ed. A. Alkon and J. Agyman (Cambridge, MA: MIT Press, 2011), 121–146; Katherine Cason, Sergio Nieto-Montenegro, and America Chavez-Martinez, "Food Choices, Food Sufficiency Practices, and Nutrition Education Needs of Hispanic Migrant Workers in Pennsylvania," *Topics in Clinical Nutrition* 21.2 (2006): 145–158; Jumanah Essa, "Nutrition, Health and Food Security Practices, Concerns and Perceived Behaviors of Latino Farm/Industrial Workers in Virginia" (M.S. thesis, Virginia Polytechnic Institute and State University, 2001); Jill F. Kilanowski and Laura C. Moore, "Food Security and Dietary Intake in Midwest Migrant Farmworker Children," *Journal of Pediatric Nursing* 25.5 (2010): 360–366; Lisa Kresge and Chelsea Eastman, "Increasing Food Security among Agricultural Workers in California's Salinas Valley," California Institute of Rural Studies (2010), http://cirsinc.org/index.php/publications/current-publications/category/3-rural-health.html; Laura-Anne Minkoff-Zern, "Knowing 'Good Food': Immigrant Knowledge and the Racial Politics of Farmworker Food Insecurity," *Antipode* 46 (2012): 1190–1204; Katherine Moos, *Documenting Vulnerability: Food Insecurity among Indigenous Migrants in California's Central Valley* (Washington, DC: Congressional Hunber Center, 2008); Sara A. Quandt, Thomas A. Arcury, Julie Early, Janeth Tapia, and Jessie D. Davis, "Household Food Security among Migrant and Seasonal Latino Farmworkers in North Carolina," *Public Health Reports* 119.6 (2004): 568–576; Yoshie Sano, Steven Garasky, Kimberly Greder, Christine C. Cook, and Dawn E. Browder, "Understanding Food Insecurity among Latino Immigrant Families in Rural America," *Journal of Family and Economic Issues* 32.1 (2011): 111–123; Don Villarejo, David Lighthall, Daniel Williams, Ann Souter, Richard Mines, Bonnie Bade, Steve Samuels, and Stephen A. McCurdy, *Suffering in Silence: A Report on the Health of California's Agricultural Workers* (Davis: California Institute for Rural Studies, 2000); Margaret M. Weigel, Rodrigo X. Armijos, Yolanda Posada Hall, and Rubi Orozco, "The Household Food Insecurity and Health Outcomes of U.S.-Mexico Border Migrant and Seasonal Farmworkers," *Journal of Immigrant and Minority Health* 9.3 (2007): 157–169; Cathy Wirth, Ron Strochlic, and Christy Getz, *Hunger in the Fields: Food Insecurity among Farmworkers in Fresno County* (Davis: California Institute for Rural Health, 2007).

18. Robert R. Alvarez, "The Mexico-US Border: The Making of an Anthropology of the Borderlands," *Annual Review of Anthropology* 24 (1995): 447–470; Geraldine Pratt, "Geographies of Identity and Difference: Making Boundaries," in *Human Geography Today*, ed. D. Massey, J. Allen, and Philip Sarre (Cambridge: Polity Press, 1999), 151–167.

19. Gloria Anzaldúa, *Borderland/La Frontera: The New Mestiza* (San Francisco: Aunt Lute Book Company, 1987), preface.

20. Teresa Mares and Alison Hope Alkon, "Mapping the Food Movement: Addressing Inequality and Neoliberalism," *Environment and Society: Advances in Research* 2 (2011): 68–86.

21. Teresa Mares and Devon Peña, "Environmental and Food Justice: Toward Local, Slow, and Deep Food Systems," in *Cultivating Food Justice: Race, Class, and Sustainability*, ed. A. Alkon and J. Agyman (Cambridge, MA: MIT Press 2011), 197–219.

22. The authors gratefully acknowledge the farmworkers in Vermont who have shared their stories, their time, their freshly picked produce, and many delicious meals. Funding for this study on farmworker food access has been provided by the University of Vermont's Graduate College REACH Award, College of Arts and Sciences Joan Smith Award, and the Center for Research on Vermont's Frank Bryan Award. Sections of the chapter are drawn from the following conference paper: Teresa Mares, Naomi Wolcott-MacCausland, and Jessie Mazar, "Cultivating Food Sovereignty Where There Are Few Choices" (Food Sovereignty: A Critical Dialogue, Yale University, 2013).

CHAPTER 11

Milking Networks for All They're Worth

PRECARIOUS MIGRANT LIFE AND THE PROCESS OF CONSENT ON NEW YORK DAIRIES

Kathleen Sexsmith

In April 2014, I pulled up to a small, worn-out trailer on Applewood Dairy Farm,[1] just a few miles from the Canadian border in the northernmost stretches of upstate New York. I waited in the shadows of the farm's enormous 1,200 cattle stables for a Guatemalan farmworker named Felipe, pondering the trailer's strategic invisibility from the road. I was about to turn back, dejected, when a young man appeared at the door, still beguiled by his early morning dreams. He appeared so tired that I nearly asked him how he had managed to walk across the trailer in his sleep. As our interview that day eventually revealed, a full night's rest was a luxury for Felipe: he works eighty hours per week, alternating between eight hours on-duty and eight hours off, six days in a row. (Three of his colleagues maintained this "eight-on, eight-off" schedule seven days in a row to maximize their earnings.) Felipe says he used to work ninety hours per week, often requiring sixteen-hour shifts, but "you finish [your shift] without any desire to eat and you feel uncomfortable. You are completely exhausted and have no strength. It's something ugly." With no more than four or five consecutive hours for rest at any given time, the daily work routine on this industrial dairy was literally milking his body dry, leaving only enough energy to drift like a *sonámbulo* (sleepwalker) between the milking parlor and the trailer after his shifts. I wondered, what did Felipe make of his working conditions? Did he think this situation was fair? And how did everyday life come to be this way for undocumented farmworkers on Applewood Dairy Farm and for others like them on dairies throughout the northern borderlands of upstate New York?

Answering these questions requires close attention to the ways that the international border is inhabited in everyday life by both farmworkers and their employers. The border looms as a constant threat, creating an exacerbated sense of "immigrant deportability in everyday life," which shapes the terms of exchange between milking parlor labor power and basic social support.[2] Take, for example, Felipe's twenty-year-old nephew, Norberto, whom I interviewed at the same farm a few weeks later. Norberto had left Guatemala one month after his fourteenth birthday with a straightforward motivation: "I saw that my father [who was working at Applewood] had money, and I decided that I would go, too." Norberto explained that he was earning 350 Guatemalan Quetzales (about $50 at the time) per week working in the construction industry when he left home; thus, the $600 per week he was soon earning at Applewood (in cold, hard cash) felt like a windfall in comparison. In exchange for his economic gain, however, he lives under conditions of social enclosure: Norberto said he had not set foot beyond the perimeter of the Applewood farm property for two full years. One worker interviewed for this study had not left the farm he worked on, except to receive emergency medical care, for ten years.

Norberto says that "when I started to build a house [in my home country via the remittances I was sending], I stopped going out because I had a responsibility now." What Norberto meant was that Border Patrol agents regularly circle the farm property, sometimes parking their cars on the road within the line of sight from the milking parlor where he usually works. Since the farm is located within 25 miles of an international border, Border Patrol agents have broad powers within this space to stop, search, and investigate those they suspect of committing immigration crimes. Since leaving the farm to shop entails the risk of being detained (and possibly deported), Norberto and his coworkers are instead kept alive by their employers, who bring them groceries and other basic necessities. These expenses are deducted from their weekly pay. Under this system, farmers maintain their access to a constant supply of labor, on which the supply of fresh milk—the farm's main cash flow—depends.

This chapter analyzes how migrants negotiate their consent to precarious conditions of life and work in the agro-industrial landscape of northern upstate New York. Farmers in the state's $14 billion, rapidly consolidating dairy production and processing industry struggle with the ethics of maintaining a migrant labor force, which many believe necessary to keep their farm businesses afloat. Meanwhile, and unbeknownst to their employers, migrant farmworkers create clandestine markets for lucrative dairy farm jobs, as they struggle to dig themselves out of the pit of debt incurred in migrating to the United States. Thus, farmers and farmworkers negotiate, stretch, and redefine the ethical codes around hired labor relations to justify the ethic of unceasing work that industrial dairy farming requires. In this extractive yet assentive labor system, which I refer to as a "borderlands moral economy," the operation of power is diffuse and obscured within shadowy, transnational circuits.[3] As such, farmworkers are both subjected to and participants in the reproduction of the structural and symbolic violence of the modern global food system.[4] This systematic precarity of farmworker life is the human cost of cheap milk in the contemporary United States.

The Making of a Modern New York Dairy Industry

Our state government is working closer together with the private sector than ever before, rolling back bureaucratic red tape and addressing the burdens that are facing job creators. With New York State officially being crowned the Yogurt Capital of America, it is clear that our approach to growing the economy and creating an entrepreneurial government is paying off.

—New York governor Andrew Cuomo

"Time Is Money"

The dairy industry is the focal point of New York governor Andrew Cuomo's earnest efforts to grow and modernize the agricultural economies of rural upstate New York. Dairy production and processing is seen as a promising vector through which Cuomo's self-described "entrepreneurial government" can attract corporate investment and create local jobs. This is because, with milk sales of $3.48 billion in 2014, dairy farming is New York's leading agricultural sector and boasts the highest community economic multiplier of all major industries in the state: for each new job created in dairy processing, 4.72 jobs are created in other industries.[5] Hence, a series of regulatory reforms and new investments to help expand dairy processing capacity have been made under Cuomo's governorship. Incentives to the dairy manufacturing industry helped to double the production of yogurt between 2005 and 2011,[6] and to make New York the nation's largest producer of yogurt, cream cheese, sour cream, and cottage cheese.[7] Cuomo's stated plans to remake upstate New York's pastoral landscape into the "Silicon Valley of Yogurt" have been a resounding success.

Yet this vision of dairy processing industry expansion and innovation depends entirely on significant increases in the milk supply—by some estimates, a 15 percent increase over five years.[8] Hence, technical solutions and regulatory reforms designed to boost milk production at the farm level have been heavily promoted. For one, to encourage farmers to increase their milking herd size, the state government announced plans in 2012 to lift costly environmental regulations for smaller farms, and to invest hundreds of thousands of dollars in a "Dairy Acceleration Program" that "provides business assistance to farmers looking to expand their operations."[9] Boosting milk output has also entailed the introduction over several decades of new technologies that have dramatically boosted the production capacity of individual cows. High protein cattle feed, production-boosting hormone injections, and automated milking equipment have generated a scale and efficiency of production that would hardly be recognizable to dairy farmers just a few generations before.[10] Perhaps most important for labor demand, many, particularly large-scale farmers, have moved from two to three milkings per cow each day, to maximize output and reduce the risk of cows falling ill. These farms are estimated to be larger, more productive, and more efficient than those farms where cows are milked only twice per day. As a result of these and other production-enhancing solutions, the average New York dairy cow now produces 22,330 pounds of milk per year, a 29 percent increase in per cow productivity over 2000 levels alone.[11]

Dairy farmers, however, benefit unevenly from these reforms; as the *New York Times* pointed out, "even dairy farming has a 1 percent."[12] The economic impacts of neoliberal policies in the national and global agricultural sectors, in combination with the consolidation pressures of an agro-industrial vision of dairying, have contributed to the evisceration of many of the state's smaller dairies. State-wide, the total number of dairy farms dropped by 30 percent between 2000 and 2010, with just over 5,000 dairy farms remaining today; meanwhile, the average number of milking cows per farm grew by 26 percent.[13] New York dairy farmers have been hard-hit by diminished federal price supports and the opening of U.S. dairy markets to foreign competition since the 1980s. Moreover, as the prices of feedstuffs like corn and soybeans have risen, the average cost of production for New York farmers is rising to its highest levels ever (in 2014, $20 per hundredweight—just over 11 gallons—of milk produced). Hence, producers have become more sensitive to fluctuations in supply and demand precisely as milk prices (their income) have become more volatile. For example, while the milk price soared to $25.52 per hundredweight in 2014—a significant increase over its previous five-year average of $18.81—by spring of 2015 it had fallen below the cost of production for many New York farmers.[14] Given the unpredictability of their economic position, farmers typically strive to maximize output during peak price periods to generate savings that help them to weather the low points.

Dairy farm owners are clearly subject to the structural violence of the neoliberal global food system. The effects are manifest not only in terms of shrinking margins but also as the emotional devastation wreaked by the rising risk of losing a livelihood that has been in their families for six generations or more.[15] For these farmers on a personal level, and for the rural upstate economy, dairy farms feel too big to fail. For example, Applewood Dairy Farm has been in Thomas's family since the late nineteenth century (when the first fluid milk sales were recorded). Agnes says that when she and her husband came into the partnership in the early 1980s, they were milking only sixty cows. She says that, "as our family grew, we realized that a sixty-cow farm was not going to be able to put our children through school and college that we wanted to provide. So it meant growing." Providing for their children's futures meant expanding the dairy herd and constructing a new housing facility for their cattle. Today, they are one of only 103 New York dairy farms (less than 2 percent of dairy farms in the state) to have a milk cow herd over 1,000 cows.[16] Farm expansion, however, cannot be achieved without incurring significant debt. The debt-to-asset ratio of a farm of their size is approximately 0.36 (or $3,592 per cow); as this debt rises, so does the urgency of generating the "white gold" needed to pay it off. Seen in this light, finding the manual labor to milk cows three times a day—and hence to keep the farm's main source of income flowing—is a matter of both economic survival and cultural reproduction.[17]

Agnes explained that, by around year 2000, the reengineering of their production system had dramatically reshaped the labor requirements and occupational structure of the farm. Specifically, a labor hierarchy emerged, as tasks became more specialized. She said that, "as we got bigger, we needed more higher-trained employees here to work . . . in driving trucks, being able to use computers, knowing animal health issues more. . . . You can't hire anyone off the street to do that." In other words, they required a workforce differentiated between "high-skilled" tasks in fields and "low-skilled" jobs in milking parlors. At the same time, their expansion had transformed the milking parlor and milk production process, by adopting a production line with thirty-two automated milking units (sixteen on each side of the narrow parlor). As Cornell University extension materials carefully explain, the parlor "throughput" (number of times a new group of cows enters the parlor for milking) should be four to five times per hour, for efficiency's sake. "Time is money," as the publication declares.[18] In order to maximize income per cow, they milk their herd three times per day and keep the parlor in operation around-the-clock. The restructuring of their milking system around a modernist theory of agro-industrialization had assumed the availability of an unlimited supply of labor. Yet finding milking labor on Applewood for these long hours and arduous tasks turned out to be a complicated, even furtive task.

Industrial Production, Invisible Labor: A Dialectical Relationship

Given the industrial milking system's requirement for long, overnight shift-work, there are significant advantages to having a labor force that resides as close to the milking parlor as possible—ideally, on the farm itself. Agnes and Thomas were feeling these demands as their production structure changed, and they became exasperated with a local workforce they saw as "unreliable." They said: "We called it 'weekend-it is.' They'll work Monday through Friday afternoon, when their paycheck is handed over you don't see them again until Monday . . . [but] cows cannot be turned off. You have to milk cows no matter if somebody calls in on a Friday night. . . . We had worked all day long and then we'd have to go to the barn at 8 p.m. and work all night long, and then we'd go to bed and sleep for four hours and get up and do the same thing again." In 2002, they sought a solution to their sense of being tethered to the farm. Thomas explained: "I knew [a nearby] farmer that had one or two. And I went over to visit with him and talk to him about it. . . . We got some shortly after." The "some" Thomas was referring to? His undocumented Guatemalan employees. He and Agnes described a covert trip to the nearest city, when they "drove down in the middle of night to pick them up in a dark parking lot and bring them up here." Ever since, undocumented workers, primarily from the same Guatemalan hometown as Felipe and Norberto, have provided what Agnes and Thomas say is high-quality, "reliable" labor for their milking parlor. They are provided their housing on the farm free of charge, conveniently located within a few minutes' walk of the milking parlors, and obscured from street view. They are reliable, of course, because their exacerbated deportability means they have nowhere else to go.

The farmworker population in the dairy industry is heavily undocumented. Due to the year-round nature of work in this industry, dairy farm employers are barred from the national H-2A agricultural guestworker visa program. Therefore, dairy farmers believe that hiring undocumented migrants is their only alternative to the economically unfeasible, "unreliable" local labor force. As Thomas and Agnes provided this justification for their current labor situation, I felt both empathy and unease. When they explained that they had had no choice but to work all day and night when their irresponsible local employees failed to show up to work, I had instinctively offered in response, "But you can't sustain that." They agreed: "We were wearing ourselves out." Yet, as I continued to reflect, it became clear that the alternative they had settled on meant trading in their labor force's right to a good night's sleep in order to protect their own, even if their employees said the "eight hours on, eight off" schedule worked well for them. Moreover, Thomas acknowledges that if they hadn't begun to hire immigrant employees, "we certainly wouldn't have expanded as far as we have." The benefit of this workforce, he further explained, was their "reliability. . . . First of all, they're on the farm. And their work ethic is different from the labor force that we were dealing with. They wanna work, they wanna get a paycheck, they wanna send that money home." This discourse of mutual financial gain through "hard work" serves as a rationale for the fact that industrial production consumes a significant share of workers' social reproduction time, or perhaps it can even be said, delays it until they return home.

This exchange of social reproduction time for profit is made possible by the disciplinary "deportation regime" that impedes them from leaving the confines of the dairy.[19] As mentioned above, Applewood is located within 25 miles of an international border, a special jurisdiction where Border Patrol agents may stop and search vehicles when they have "reasonable suspicion" that an immigration crime has been committed, and may enter private property, other than dwellings, without a warrant (see Map 1 in chapter 1).[20] In addition to their expanded powers, Border Patrol agents have significantly expanded their presence along the northern border region. In New York, the number of Border Patrol agents has risen tenfold (from 39 to 400) since 2002 alone, an even higher increase than the 558 percent growth in agents across the U.S. northern border more widely.[21] This increase forms part of a national trend that has seen the U.S. immigration enforcement apparatus expand rapidly, reaching a total budget of $18 billion dollars in fiscal year 2012—more than the sum of spending on all federal criminal law enforcement agencies combined.[22] One study found that the "flooding" of the northern border region with agents has coincided with a decrease in the number of actual deportations, suggesting "there is not enough work for them to do." As a result, these agents make work for themselves—for example, by providing interpretation services at the scenes of accidents, which enables them to identify undocumented immigrants.[23] Workers are effectively terrorized by the penetration of Border Patrol agents and the border itself into all spheres of their lives.

In the area near Applewood Dairy, Border Patrol agents felt omnipresent. I even found myself parking my car behind the farm stables to hide my plates from view, out of the fear that my repeated presence on area farms would raise suspicion. The constant presence of Border Patrol agents was much more exasperating for local farmers. So much so, Agnes said, that they tried, somewhat successfully, to take matters into their own hands:

> What was happening was Border Patrol was coming onto the farms say like at 2 in the morning, they might drive up to the front of our milking parlor. . . . And they would sit outside the door, blow their horn, and one of the guys would come out, and once they're out they're off the premise, they would get them. So a couple other farms organized this meeting with Border Patrol and our government representation was there, to say, you know, this is the issue we're facing. We're only trying to milk cows, what can we do to help resolve this? Can you understand what we're doing? . . . Since that meeting, I think there was some understanding of maybe backing off a little bit. Because that type of presence stopped. They didn't do that 2 a.m. call anymore.

Although, as they said, Border Patrol agents seemed to have silently "backed off" from harassing migrants at work, their patrol cars are still often seen parked on public roadways adjacent to farm properties. Norberto says that the regular presence of a Border Patrol cruiser so close to the Applewood farm feels so menacing to him that "sometimes I just raise up my hands [in a gesture of giving himself up]." He told me that he hadn't left the farm in months. The risk of encountering a Border Patrol agent creates extraordinary apprehension among workers, in some cases even too much fear to cross the road in front of the farm. They are also fearful of Border Patrol agents who engage in direct racial profiling on roadways and in the community. As Agnes explained it, "This is northern New York, we're not really an integrated community up here. We're primarily a white sect community, okay? So these guys stood out like sore thumbs." Agnes and Thomas, like other farm employers I interviewed, said that "we don't tell them they can't leave the farm, just that they shouldn't." In this sense, the fear of deportation creates an imagined border around the farm perimeter itself, one that workers dare not cross so long as they want to avoid deportation. Thus, whereas the consolidation of capitalism in agriculture has historically necessitated dispossessing peasants from their land (see the chapter by Laura-Anne Minkoff-Zern in this volume), it is the dispossession of hired workers from their most basic rights that pushes rural modernization in upstate New York along its path.

Thomas and Agnes's ethical quagmire is replicated across the traditional Northeast and Midwest dairy belt, where undocumented workers have been incorporated onto large and increasingly also onto small dairies.[24] Thousands of undocumented immigrants are employed in the dairy-farming sector of upstate New York alone: by 2009 estimates, there are 2,600 immigrant workers on New York dairies, representing 24 percent of the sector's hired labor force.[25] Farmers in this study explained that they sought out migrant workers from nearby apple fields, or through labor contractors, when dairy farm industrialization took off in earnest in the early 1990s. So long as they tread carefully, farmers are relatively protected from prosecution for employing undocumented immigrants. That is, under federal legislation passed in 1996, it is only a crime to hire undocumented immigrants if there is traceable proof of the employer's knowledge of their illegal status.[26] Relatively few dairy farmer employers of undocumented migrants in upstate New York have faced any legal repercussions. Indeed, some farmers work hard to maintain this public secret—for example, by providing workers with sequestered housing and limiting their (more visible) outdoors work. The invisibility of workers is essential to keep industrial milking parlors in operation around the clock.

The Process of Consent
Employer Paternalism

The ontological insecurity generated by immigrants' partial belonging to U.S. society has been aptly termed "deportability in everyday life" by migration studies scholars.[27] Yet inquietude also cuts deep among farmers, as they stitch together new moral codes for labor treatment in the interstices of the formal and clandestine labor markets. Under the gaze of the state, borderlands farmers experience liminality in a moral sense, that is, they suspend old value systems in order to make way for alternatives adapted to the imperatives of hiring undocumented workers whose presence they must technically deny. That is to say, a paternalistic social system has emerged in this borderlands moral economy, in which farmers provide hours of work upon arrival, basic supplies, and a sense of protection from immigration enforcement on the farm itself, in return for farmworkers' labor and consent to the terms and process of milking parlor work.

Loyalty is an essential condition for paternalism. Agnes and Thomas cultivated gratitude among their Guatemalan employees from the time they first arrived by offering them part-time work. Given the twenty-four-hour milking schedule, hours of work are a financially abundant resource on industrial dairies, and can be dispensed like gifts to those seeking to cover their personal expenses while looking for full-time employment. For example, with no full-time openings on the farm at the time of his arrival, Felipe was offered short shifts feeding calves, cleaning stables, or occasionally covering for others in the parlor. By telling Felipe that the extra hours were "just for your food," Agnes helped to diminish his sense of financial insecurity. Though meager, his checks were translated into a new social idiom of generosity and care.

Workers often construct ideas about the fairness of their treatment not on the basis of the number of hours they are assigned or the timing of their shifts, but rather through the degree to which employers are willing to "help" them meet their social reproduction needs. As Felipe explained it, "Sometimes the bosses aren't good people. They look at you, you don't do it well, and they throw you to the street in the same moment. There are things you have to take into account before changing your job. Maybe because of looking for a better job, you encounter something even worse." Employers who offer "help" are seen as protectors because they bring workers what they need from stores, where they are too afraid to set foot. Thomas and Agnes described the elaborate system of provisioning for their workers that they have put into place: weekly grocery shopping services, free housing, utilities, cable TV, and occasional gifts of pizza dinners on holidays. They say, "You know we understand that they're here, they're away from home, and because of our location they're not able to go out for entertainment. They're not able to go to the store and buy their own needs. So we try to ease that lifestyle the best we can by providing some other perks for them." The workers at Applewood confirmed this system: "[The bosses] say they will bring us whatever we need . . . there is no need for us to go out and put ourselves into risk." In this way, the intensity of border patrolling creates a "moral alibi" for farmers, that is, a justification for workers to stay on the farm, where they can evade unwanted attention from immigration law enforcement while staying constantly available for milking parlor work.[28]

Finally, the on-farm enclosure and paternalism of this system include providing for the transnational social reproduction of families. By staying on the farm, they reduce their local consumption to almost zero, other than their food and clothing, and are able to send extremely high proportions of their salaries as remittances to Guatemala. Many of my interviewees said they sent 70 percent to 80 percent of their earnings to their family members and personal savings accounts at home. By not paying rent, workers say, they can maximize the amount of money invested in their families and their futures. Felipe said that a significant reason for not following up on job networks in other parts of the United States was that, "even though you make more there, you spend more. . . . My cousin says that he hardly sends any money to Guatemala because he has nothing left [after paying rent and utilities]." Staying on the dairy farm allows workers to fulfill obligations to their wives, children, parents, and siblings. By enabling this transnational social reproduction, farm owners are further revered as patrons with vast economic reach.

Importantly, farmers negotiate the dimensions of their paternalism by comparing their own "helpfulness" toward their workers to that of their farmer peers. Agnes and Thomas said that they know of some "bad farms . . . where the workers aren't treated very well. . . . They're made to pay for their housing . . . or they're just not treated well by the boss." They referenced one neighbor with a reputation so bad that "he wouldn't hesitate to physically strike [his immigrant employees]." When that farmer had asked them if they knew of any migrants seeking work, they simply told him they could not find anybody, without actually having tried to look. Through constant dialogue with and comparison to their peers, farmers are defining the moral contours of employee care and control.

These paternalistic practices differ from the forms of patronage classically analyzed by agrarian studies scholars. That is, moral economists have suggested that when patrons attempt to extract themselves from their traditional obligations to the rural poor, the latter engage in resistance, and the constant threat of revolt keeps the patronage system intact.[29] Yet these models cannot predict paternalistic behavior in this borderlands context because of unequal citizenship status between farmers and workers. That is, in the moral economy framework, workers must enter public space to stage their ultimate resistance, but undocumented migrant farmworkers are effectively excluded by immigration enforcement activity from any such act. Instead, they engage in more clandestine acts of resistance, through illicit exchanges of jobs that demonstrate counterhegemonic intentions but may actually exacerbate the structural conditions of their powerlessness.

"Securing" Precarious Work

If, as I have suggested, workers on northern New York borderlands dairies are living a life of social enclosure on the farm under paternalism, how do they participate in shaping the terms of consent? After all, workers are not bound to the farm by physical force; they make daily cost-benefit analyses about whether to leave the farm property for another workplace, or for a fuller social life in Guatemala. Understanding how people rationalize and justify their difficult daily decisions in this irresolute borderlands condition of permanent "deportability" requires close interpretation of their discourse, which I undertake in this section.[30] I attend to how people define and express concepts of justice and injustice, often in coded ways—a phenomenological method that James Scott refers to as "listening carefully."[31] During interviews with farmworkers, I inquired about how they arrived to the farm, the process of adjusting to a life without the freedom of mobility, their perceptions of their schedule and pay, and their motivations for staying put at Applewood. Surprisingly, I found that workers often saw their dairy farm jobs as a privilege compared to other forms of agricultural or even urban employment, because the work was *seguro* (safe) and the job itself ensured by a *garantía* (guaranty). Yet these exhausting, low-wage jobs, performed under the intense scrutiny of Border Patrol agents, are by most standards a highly insecure way of life and work. Why, then, did migrant farmworkers justify these seemingly precarious jobs as "secure"?

I propose that the answer to this question can be gained by taking into account the "spatial imaginaries"—or "cognitive frameworks, collective and individual, constituted through the lived experiences, perceptions, and conceptions of space itself"—formed during migration journeys and the many border crossings they entail.[32] That is, spatial forces of confinement and clandestinity contribute to the process of subject formation as migrant workers travel toward and through the U.S. borderlands. Joselito says that when traveling north across Mexico after leaving Guatemala, he spent days locked in a trailer with other immigrants to avoid detection by Mexican police. As he described the experience, "It was very hot. There were some holes for ventilation above, but not very much air got in because there is a lot of people in there. There are people above and below. There was only room for standing in there." In an effort to avoid these dangers, border-crossers go into hiding in covert spaces where they can prevent the detection of their illegalized bodies by authorities.[33]

The self-invisibilization learned en route is constantly adapted when facing the dangers of the later stages of border crossing. In the Mexico-U.S. borderlands, migrants become accustomed to making tactical movements by night. For days on end in the United States' southern borderlands, border-crossers must carefully hide from the militaristic U.S. Border Patrol apparatus of drones, helicopters, migration agents, and infrared cameras. Felipe says: "We slept where we could find trees, because the helicopters couldn't see us there. The helicopter was there circulating at night and by day. So we had to find a way to hide. . . . We waited in the sand, or in the stones and hid there." These Border Patrol agents compete for sovereignty of the borderlands space with gang members who take rape victims and dead bodies as trophies representing their territorial control. Felipe said how in 2012 he walked for ten days in the desert to cross from Sonora, Mexico, to Arizona, and had his water and food supplies stolen from him under attack by *narcotraficantes* (drug traffickers). He said they "controlled the entrance to the desert" and forced migrants to purchase drugs from them to "maintain their energy" before allowing them to pass. The state-sanctioned violence and criminal extortion these migrants encounter on their journeys shape a spatial imaginary of the borderlands as a protracted "state of exception,"[34] one in which a sense of lawlessness is created by the severity of the border protection apparatus itself.

The border crossing is a physically and emotionally disciplining experience, and surviving it contributes to narratives of a shared migrant identity characterized by individual strength and the sheer will of survival. As Felipe put it, he was given courage by the fear of abandonment and death. He would tell himself, "Not here, nobody will stay behind here. Just follow and don't get separated from the group. . . . Nobody is coming to get us from here." Self-discipline is cultivated alongside a sense of unity and shared trajectory; E. P. Thompson might say that, in the desert, undocumented immigrants are "made" as a liminal working class.[35] This collective self-discipline is transported to the opposite border of the United States, in the northernmost stretches of upstate New York, where migrants once again find themselves dodging Border Patrol agents in the shelter of dairy farms to circumvent deportation. Yet the risks of the borderlands extend beyond the physical; the economic and ethical ties in migrant networks are adapted to these imperatives, too.

In order to arrive to Applewood on his first trip to the United States, Felipe had borrowed 50,000 Guatemalan Quetzales (over $6,000) from a moneylender in his hometown, leaving the title to the home where his wife and mother lived as collateral. This loan covered his journey all the way to New York City, where he had to borrow an additional $1,000 to pay for his ride to northern New York. According to the norms of money lending in his hometown, Felipe was to be responsible for repaying the loan, plus accumulated interest, from the moment he arrived in the United States—regardless of whether he had found work. If he were to fail in his mission to get to the dairy farm, his debt would be literally unrepayable, considering that his only other option in Guatemala was to earn 75 Quetzales (less than $10) per day in construction. In this worst-case scenario, he would lose his family's home.

Similarly, eighteen-year-old farmworker Joselito left Guatemala at sixteen years old in an attempt to make it to Applewood, where his older brother Norberto and their father worked at the time. He borrowed 57,000 Quetzales (over $7,000) from his father to make the journey. When I asked if he wasn't afraid of crossing the border through the desert, he said: "Of the journey, no I wasn't worried. What worried me was my debt. That I wouldn't make it . . . [at that point I already owed] 20,000 Quetzales which is like $3,000." What Joselito means is that the journey is typically paid in installments to various smugglers along the way, who ask for payment for the travel segment they provided upon its successful completion. To this amount, migrants must add the money needed to pay off corrupt Mexican officials who detect them traveling through their territory without visa authorization. Felipe said that "if you tell a police officer that you have no money, the response will be: 'If you don't have any [money], you stay here. You don't pass.'" Under the crushing financial risk that newly arrived immigrants have incurred, paid hours of work are in high demand. Hence, the "security" of dairy farm work comes from the regularity of paid hours: round-the-clock schedules of milking parlors like Applewood's promise workers the paid hours they covet to pay off their loans from the moment they step on the farm. Felipe, for example, described his job as highly "secure" because of the sheer quantity and reliability of hours, even though he was unsure if he earned the legal minimum wage and said he did not believe there was any possibility of a promotion or raise. The sense of job "security" is a product, therefore, of the industrial structure of modernized dairying, and ironically helps to fashion worker consent to a production system that denies their physiological need for adequate rest.

Like any other commodity, however, dairy farm jobs come at a price. Both of the times he arrived to his new workplace after crossing the border, Felipe was asked by the departing Guatemalan worker he replaced to pay $1,000 for a ninety-hour per week job. He said:

> It's a chain that goes back to the first person who was here [on this farm]. I don't know if that person was charged for his job or not, but the person who came after him had to pay for the job. So, the [next person] has to pay him. So it becomes a chain. To not lose the money you have invested in that job, you tell the next person who will stay there working, "I need you to return my money to me because I paid so much for this." The person who goes has their money returned to them, and the other one stays working. It's like a guarantee, nothing more, that the job is for sure.

Felipe expressed no moral troubles with this system. He implied that it was completely justified because the person was not simply "changing jobs" to make a profit, but rather would be returning to Guatemala, and was therefore completely in his or her right to recuperate his or her "investment." A "job-changer" would, on the other hand, be seen as taking advantage of newly arrived workers to turn a profit. Joselito described how he was asked to pay $1,000 for his eighty-hour per week job when a Guatemalan worker left for home. The worker who asked him to pay? His own father. Other farmworkers I interviewed confirmed that $1,000 was the going rate for a full-time posting, but that a *garantía* of work could range between about $500 and $1,500. One Guatemalan informant on a farm nearby told me he had paid $1,500 for his job; while he felt that this price was unjust, he said he had no choice in the matter. Often, newly arrived workers are only told about these charges once they arrive to the farm. With nowhere else to stay, they cannot refuse to pay.

Migration theorists have begun to pay more attention to the role of such risks in the reformulation of moral norms around money and debt in migrant communities. David Stoll shows that a vicious cycle of "debt-migration" degrades social relations in Guatemalan sending towns; my research shows that this pattern is replayed among those who seek to offset the risk of their journeys when they land in the United States.[36] In these upstate New York cases, migrants who

have been in the United States for longer, have already paid off their migration
loans, and have greater financial freedom become implicated in holding deeply
indebted migrants captive in these labor markets. In this way, those workers who
are economically better off participate in producing the financial precarious-
ness of their newly arrived coworkers. The Mexico-U.S. border crossing therefore
has the effect of laying new ethical rules for helping and lending money to others,
justified by the exceptional acts and costs of the migration journey itself.

Importantly, this is a labor system with counterhegemonic intentions, in the
sense that it has formed autonomously, in defiance of the farmers' paternalistic
social system. That is, workers explained that farm employers are deliberately
kept in the dark about these clandestine job markets because "they wouldn't like
it." Indeed, one farm employer told me he had discovered one worker charging
a "finder's fee" for jobs on his farm, and promptly fired him, believing he had
stamped out the problem for good. I later discovered through my interviews
with the employees that the practice had continued, maintained in a more diffuse way by multiple participants who had since learned the trick of the trade.
It is through the crowding of farmworkers in secluded housing and their ability to conduct such "business" in Spanish, or even in a Guatemalan indigenous
language, that these underground economies continue to thrive right under the
eyes and ears of employers. Hence, these independent, clandestine labor markets
are created as a way to undermine the social control of paternalism. Yet by further indebting them and bonding them to the farm to pay off those debts, these
counterhegemonic intentions reinforce farmworker consent to a precarious life
on borderlands farms.

Remaking the Moral Landscape

As Wendy Wolford reminds us, spatial relations are constitutive of social relations.[37] As such, spatial relations in the borderlands produce distinct social
spaces, where danger and state surveillance compel inhabitants to develop new
moral frameworks to grapple with risk. Undocumented immigrants inhabit
borders in their everyday lives in clandestine spaces, where their labor is readily
bought and sold, but their access to social membership continues to be denied.[38]
To adapt to these conditions of exclusion, immigrants internalize interstitial
ways of being and belonging; as I have shown, the stretching of moral economic
norms is central to this process. Workers must find ways to accommodate their
socially constructed "illegality," in what Giorgio Agamben would consider camp-
like conditions of near total social enclosure in remote northern New York.[39]
Hence, they create a parallel economic system, through which jobs are "secured"
in expensive, sometimes predatory underground markets, and their own powerlessness is temporarily reproduced.

Employers, meanwhile, compensate for the extreme risks of the debt incurred in expanding their operations by taking on another risk: that of an undocumented and precarious labor force. This risk is, in turn, mitigated by a strategy of provisioning for workers' basic needs, and by the silence that language barriers and social distancing create around the clandestine activities taking place on their farms. Taken together, uneasy terms of consent are fashioned by farmers and their employees, in a system that creates and reproduces systematically precarious conditions of work and life. This is a truly modern, moral economy, one in which a dialectical relationship between industrialization and labor invisibilization creates uneasy new ethical rules for production and social reproduction, under conditions of social enclosure on the farm.

As the physical landscape of New York dairying communities has been fundamentally altered by the modernist vision of an upstate "Silicon Valley," so too have social relations and cultural norms. The production of this peculiar, modern dairy sector has therefore entailed remaking the landscape in both material and moral terms, under conditions created by a unique, intensely surveilled border enforcement regime. If uncovered and acted upon, these migration and labor conditions can challenge the powerful myth of the incorruptible morality of the countryside.[40] Ultimately, dairy consumers also participate in the diffuse system of power that shapes these hidden labor relations, as do members of the public whose political actions contribute to the formation of immigration and border surveillance policies. Yet there is hope that exposing the labor impurities behind this national emblem of wholesomeness will motivate popular and political action toward systemic change.

NOTES

1. Names of farms, towns, and people have been changed.

2. Nicholas de Genova, "Migrant 'Illegality' and Deportability in Everyday Life," *Annual Review of Anthropology* 31 (2002): 419–447.

3. Gerardo Francisco Sandoval, "Shadow Transnationalism: Cross-Border Networks and Planning Challenges of Transnational Unauthorized Immigrant Communities," *Journal of Planning Education and Research* 33.2 (2013): 176–193.

4. Seth Holmes, *Fresh Fruit, Broken Bodies: Migrant Farmworkers in the United States* (Berkeley: University of California Press, 2013).

5. "Ag Facts," New York State Department of Agriculture and Markets, http://www .agriculture.ny.gov/agfacts.html; "New York Milk Cash Receipts Increase 22 Percent in 2014," United States Department of Agriculture National Agricultural Statistics Service, http:// www.nass.usda.gov/Statistics_by_State/New_York/Latest_Releases/Latest_Releases/NY %202014%20Milk%20PDI%20News%20Release.pdf; "Governor Cuomo Hosts First New York State Yogurt Summit," August 15, 2012, New York State Governor Andrew M. Cuomo News, https://www.governor.ny.gov/press/08152012-nys-yogurt-summit; Pathstone Corporation and Cornell Farmworker Program, "The Yogurt Boom, Job Creation, and the Role of Dairy Farmers in the Finger Lakes Regional Economy," *Office for New Americans*, http://www .newamericans.ny.gov/pdf/yogurtBoomBrochure19.pdf.

6. Cited in Pathstone Corporation and Cornell Farmworker Program, "Yogurt Boom."

7. "Governor Cuomo Thanks New York's Hard Working Dairy Industry and Celebrates June as Dairy Month in New York State," June 3, 2014, New York State Governor Andrew Cuomo News, https://www.governor.ny.gov/news/governor-cuomo-thanks-new-yorks -hard-working-dairy-industry-and-celebrates-june-dairy-month-new.

8. Mary Jo Dudley, "The Importance of Farm Labor in the NYS Yogurt Boom," *Research and Policy Brief Series*, Community and Regional Development Institute, Department of Development Sociology, Cornell University, October 2014, https://cardi.cals.cornell.edu/ sites/cardi.cals.cornell.edu/files/shared/documents/ResearchPolicyBriefs/Policy-Brief -October-2014.pdf.

9. "Governor Cuomo Announces New York State Is Now Top Yogurt Producer in the Nation, Delivers on Key Promises Made at Yogurt Summit to Help Dairy Farmers," April 18, 2013, New York State Governor Andrew Cuomo News, https://www.governor.ny.gov/news/ governor-cuomo-announces-new-york-state-now-top-yogurt-producer-nation-delivers -key-promises.

10. For a detailed and insightful discussion of the transformation of New York dairy farm-ing over time, see Melanie DuPuis, *Nature's Perfect Food: How Milk Became America's Drink* (New York: New York University Press, 2002).

11. Calculated by the author from National Agricultural Statistics Services data. Official statistics on the historical change in the number of farms milking cows three times per day are not available, but an approximation is possible by comparing findings from the (nonrepresentatively sampled) Cornell University annual Dairy Farm Business Summary reports. It was reported that in the year 2000, 25 percent of 293 dairy farms participating in the survey milked their dairy herd three times per day. The 2011 report states that 50 percent of participating farms milked cows three times per day. On average, these farms were larger by fifty-two cows and produced more milk (33 percent more per cow, and 52 percent more per worker) than farms that milked only twice per day. Their operating costs were also lower, by $0.07 per hundredweight of milk. Data from Wayne Knoblauch, Linda D. Putnam, Jason Karszes, Richard Overton, and Cathryn Dymond, *Business Summary New York State, 2011*, Dairy Farm Management (Charles H. Dyson School of Applied Economics and Manage-ment, College of Agriculture and Life Sciences, Cornell University, 2012); and Wayne Knob-lauch, Linda D. Putnam, and Jason Karszes, *Business Summary New York State, 2000*, Dairy Farm Management (Charles H. Dyson School of Applied Economics and Management, Col-lege of Agriculture and Life Sciences, Cornell University, 2001).

12. Mattias Adolfsson, "Even Dairy Farming Has a 1 Percent," *New York Times*, March 6, 2012, http://www.nytimes.com/2012/03/11/magazine/dairy-farming-economy-adam-davidson .html.

13. Calculated by the author from National Agricultural Statistics Service data.

14. Ronald Knutson, Robert Romain, David Anderson, and James Richardson, "Farm-Level Consequences of Canadian and U.S. Dairy Policies," *American Journal of Agricul-tural Economics* 79.5 (1997): 1563–1572; Chris Laughton, "Northeast Dairy Farm Sum-mary, 2014," Farm Credit East, https://www.farmcrediteast.com/~/media/Files/Knowledge %20Exchange/Dairy%20Farm%20Summary/FCE_NEDFS_2014_FINAL.ashx, 7; "Low Milk Prices, Glutted Market Put Strain on Dairy Farmers," *New York Times*, May 3, 2015, http:// www.nytimes.com/aponline/2015/05/03/us/ap-us-dairy-farmers-milk-prices.html?_r=0.

15. This point is also made with respect to the West Coast berry industry in Holmes, *Fresh Fruit, Broken Bodies*.

16. Data on size of New York dairy farms obtained from the USDA 2012 Census of Agricul-ture for New York, http://www.agcensus.usda.gov/Publications/2012/Full_Report/Volume _1,_Chapter_1_State_Level/New_York/st36_1_017_019.pdf.

17. Debt statistics for dairy farms with 900 cattle or more. This data was gathered in 2012 from 112 farms of 300 cows or more in New York. Jason Karszes, Wayne Knoblauch, and Cathryn Dymond, *New York Large Herd Farms, 300 Cows or Larger, 2013*, Dairy Farm

Business Summary (Charles H. Dyson School of Applied Economics and Management, College of Agriculture and Life Sciences, Cornell University, 2014), 38. See also Wayne A. Knoblauch, George J. Conneman, and Cathryn Dymond, "Ch. 7: Dairy Farm Management," Published Proceedings of the Cornell University Charles H. Dyson School of Applied Economics and Management 2014 Agribusiness Economic Outlook Conference, http://dyson .cornell.edu/outreach/outlook/2015/Chap7FrmMgt_2015.pdf, 7–2.

18. Hal F. Schulte III, "Parlor Efficiency," Cornell University College of Veterinary Medicine, Quality Milk Production Services, https://ahdc.vet.cornell.edu/Sects/QMPS/ FarmServices/parlorefficiency.cfm.

19. Nicholas De Genova, "The Deportation Regime: Sovereignty, Space, and the Freedom of Movement," in *The Deportation Regime: Sovereignty, Space, and the Freedom of Movement*, ed. Nicholas De Genova and Nathalie Peutz (Durham, NC: Duke University Press, 2010). See also the chapter by Teresa Mares and her colleagues in this volume.

20. "Customs and Border Protection's (CBP's) 100-Mile Rule" American Civil Liberties Union, http://legalactioncenter.org/sites/default/files/CBP%2010,0%20Mile%20Rule.pdf.

21. New York Civil Liberties Union, *Justice Derailed: What Raids on NY Trains and Buses Reveal About Border Patrol Interior Enforcement Practices* (New York: New York Civil Liberties Union, 2011); Lisa Graybill, *Border Patrol Agents along the Northern Border: Unwise Policy, Illegal Practice* (Washington, DC: Immigration Policy Center of the American Immigration Council, 2012), 5.

22. Doris Meissner, Donald Kerwin, Muzaffar Chishti and Claire Bergeron, *Immigration Enforcement in the United States: The Rise of a Formidable Machinery* (Washington, DC: Migration Policy Institute, 2013).

23. Graybill, *Border Patrol Agents*.

24. For a comprehensive overview of the role of undocumented immigrant workers in the U.S. dairy industry, see D. Susanto, C. P. Rosson, D. P. Anderson and F. J. Adcock, "Immigration Policy, Foreign Agricultural Labor, and Exit Intentions in the United States Dairy Industry," *Journal of Dairy Science* 93 (2010): 1774–1781.

25. Thomas Maloney and Nelson Bills, *Survey of New York Dairy Farm Employers 2009* (Charles H. Dyson School of Applied Economics and Management, Cornell University, 2011). It is also worth noting that this survey was farmer-reported, thus the number of immigrant workers on New York dairy farms may be higher. Nationally, it is estimated that 41 percent of dairy farmworkers in the United States are undocumented immigrants (Susanto et al., "Immigration Policy").

26. Juliet Stumpf, "The Crimmigration Crisis: Immigrants, Crime, and Sovereign Power," in *Governing Iimmigration through Crime: A Reader*, ed. Julie A. Dowling and Jonathan Xavier Inda (Stanford, CA: Stanford University Press, 2013).

27. de Genova, "Migrant 'Illegality.'"

28. Roxanne Lynn Doty, "Bare Life: Border-Crossing Deaths and Spaces of Moral Alibi," *Environment and Planning D: Society and Space* 29.4 (2011): 599–612.

29. James Scott, *The Moral Economy of the Peasant: Rebellion and Subsistence in Southeast Asia* (New Haven, CT: Yale University Press, 1976); E. P. Thompson, *The Making of the English Working Class* (New York: Pantheon, 1966).

30. de Genova, "Migrant 'Illegality.'"

31. James Scott, *Weapons of the Weak: Everyday Forms of Peasant Resistance* (New Haven, CT: Yale University Press, 1985), 42.

32. Wendy Wolford, "This Land Is Ours Now: Spatial Imaginaries and the Struggle for Land in Brazil," *Annals of the Association of American Geographers* 94.2 (2004): 409–424.

33. Susan Bibler Coutin, "Being en Route," *American Anthropologist* 107.2 (2005): 195–206.

34. Giorgio Agamben, *State of Exception* (Chicago: University of Chicago Press, 2005).

35. Thompson, *Making of the English Working Class*.

36. David Stoll, *El Norte or Bust: How Migration Fever and Micro-Credit Produced a Financial Crash in a Latin American Town* (London: Rowman and Littlefield, 2013).

37. Wolford, "This Land Is Ours Now."

38. Bibler Coutin, "Being en Route"; Leo Chavez, *Shadowed Lives: Undocumented Immigrants in American Society* (Fort Worth, TX: Harcourt Brace Jovanovich College Publishers, 1992); Menjívar, "Liminal Legality."

39. Giorgio Agamben, *Homo Sacer: Sovereign Power and Bare Life* (Stanford, CA: Stanford University Press, 1998).

40. Raymond Williams, *Country and the City* (Oxford: Oxford University Press, 1973).

CHAPTER 12

Crossing Borders, Overcoming Boundaries

LATINO IMMIGRANT FARMERS AND A NEW SENSE OF HOME IN THE UNITED STATES

Laura-Anne Minkoff-Zern

Corn and soybean fields blanket the Northern Neck of Virginia's picturesque agrarian landscape. Situated between the Potomac and the Rappahannock Rivers, the Northern Neck is one of three peninsulas (or "necks") that jut out into the Chesapeake Bay. One can drive many miles bordered by monocropped scenery, only occasionally spotting farmhouses and machinery between the fields. But if you have the pleasure to slow down and look more closely, you might start to notice that some of the farms do not look like the others. Nestled among the seemingly never-ending uniform acres of commodity crops are farms with diversely planted rows containing hundreds of varieties of fruits and vegetables. These farms are primarily owned by Latino farmers, who often arrive in the United States with experience from farming their own land in Latin America and use this experience, as well as what they have learned as migrant workers in the United States, to start their own family-operated farms (Figure 12.1).[1] I explore this new category of farmers in the United States, as they not only cross geographical boundaries as immigrants but also cross class and cultural boundaries as they transition from subsistence farmers in Mexico, to workers on industrial farms in the United States, to family-based small-scale farm owners in the United States.

This chapter tells the story of people moving across borders and the practices and land-based identities that travel with them. There are approximately thirty Latino immigrant families farming in the Northern Neck, almost all part of an extended family from Jalisco, Mexico. Although most of the area is cultivated by corn, wheat, and soybean growers, immigrant farmers represent half

Figure 12.1. An immigrant farmer's field in the Northern Neck of Virginia. Photo by the author.

to two-thirds of the fruit and vegetable farmers in the northern peninsula, or "Neck," according to estimates by farmers themselves and local U.S. Department of Agriculture (USDA) and extension staff. As part of a national study of Latino farmers, I interviewed half the Latino farmers in this area, meeting with them at their farms, homes, and markets where they sell. I also conducted interviews with staff members of programs that advocate for and work with low-resource and "socially disadvantaged" farmers, at the county, state, and national levels.[2]

Most of the farmers interviewed for this chapter expressed a desire to farm in a way that allowed them independence to make decisions on their farms and helped them develop a sense of place or home in the United States. Rather than seeing farming as merely a way to make money, farming allows them the opportunity to live off the land as they had in Mexico. They articulated an aspiration to maintain this scale and farming style, to remain living on or near the land they cultivate, in the style they prefer, and in personal control of their markets. As many explained, their farm in the United States is part of trying to recreate a "*recuerdo*," or memory, of their former lifestyle in Mexico. It is also a new opportunity to find a way to belong and feel permanence in a country where they have been migrating as seasonal laborers for decades. Returning to farming reinforces their land-based identity, connecting them to their previous lives, while also allowing them a new chance to establish autonomy in the global agricultural system.

Latino farmers' ability to reclaim land and succeed as farmers in the United States is constantly being defined and redefined in relation to their positioning to others. In this chapter, I employ these complex notions of home, identity, and place to understand how and why immigrant farmworkers are farming in the United States, despite particular challenges based in their racial and ethnic social positioning. I argue that the rationale and motivation of immigrant farmers in the United States can only be understood through the lens of identity described above, as their challenges as well as their motivations are unique to their racialized and ethnic positioning. I show the ways these farmers are re-creating a new sense of home through cultivation and consumptive practices, ultimately arguing that these connections to an agrarian identity keep them farming, despite challenges.

AGRARIAN TRANSITIONS

In the Northern Neck, an assemblage of extended families have found a place to root themselves, a place where brothers, sisters, and cousins are re-creating a community that reminds them of the life they left in Mexico. All of them settled in the Neck after spending years—and for some, even decades—migrating with fruit harvests up and down the East Coast and midwestern United States. Although no one could identify exactly what year, one farmer interviewed claimed to be the first to settle down in the area and rent land for himself, about twenty years ago. Other family members followed after him, finding the moderate climate and low rents suitable to establishing a new home in the United States. While transitioning to renting and then eventually owning land, many worked in the local berry and tree scrub industries, eventually saving enough money to start their own farm businesses.

The Neck plays a significant role in U.S. political and agrarian history. Birthplace of three U.S. presidents, including George Washington, it was the home to wealthy large-scale plantation owners during the colonial period.[3] Tobacco, cultivated by slave labor, was the key crop grown in the area during colonial settlement, but the crop declined by the time of the Civil War, as the region was not deemed worthy of defense. Mixed vegetables and grains became the staple crops in the Neck, with fisheries providing the bulk of the agricultural employment in the region over the last centuries. Agricultural prosperity boomed in the early twentieth century. Unfortunately, the area has become increasingly impoverished over the past 100 years due to its geographic isolation, losing its food processing plants and sawmills. Historically connected to urban areas by its ample waterways, railways came late to the region, as its steamboats were owned by the railroad company, which did not see the need to lay rail tracks.

Although it is still a productive agricultural area, specializing in winter wheat, farmers have struggled to compete in global markets. Not seeing farming as a viable economic option, the young population is migrating to urban centers with more stable employment as previous generations of farmers are retiring and selling off their farmland.[4]

The Northern Neck is representative of a pattern of out-migration throughout the rural South. As white agrarian communities struggle to retain their youth, new immigrant populations are ascending both culturally and economically.[5] This migration of white youth is an opportunity for immigrant farmers to enter the agricultural market. This agrarian transition is occurring on a national scale. While the majority of U.S. farm ownership remains white, Latino immigrants from Mexico and Central America are rising in the ranks of farm ownership and operation. The number of farms whose principal operators were of "Spanish, Hispanic, or Latino origin" in the United States has grown from 50,592 in 2002 to 55,570 in 2007 to 67,000 in 2012.[6] In the most recent count, 64,439 were primary farm business owners as well. Although not all of these operators are farm business owners, this increase represents more Latinos in leadership roles on farms.

As many scholars have noted, re-creating food and agricultural practices from their home countries often enables Latino immigrants in the United States to maintain particular land- and food-based identities and cultural traditions as they cross spatial and political boundaries.[7] Yet as Doreen Massey points out, although capital and the relatively recent process of globalization force people to forge a new sense of home geographically, for many, especially those from the colonized world, "home" has never been constant.[8] Dislocation and reorganization of a sense of home, in terms of social relations and one's identity in relation to home, are never fixed. Similarly, Stuart Hall contends that the cultural identity of diasporic peoples must always be understood as hybrid, through the process of transformation and change, rather than stuck in an essentialized notion of home.[9] The immigrant farmers in this study are reclaiming agricultural practices as a way of creating a new sense of home—one building on past experiences of landedness, but entrenched in new relations with state power, borders, and citizenship.

Meredith Abarca (chapter 2) introduces the notion of "culinary subjectivities," whereby people's food choices and related practices are conceived of as an "active process by which people create, maintain, and constantly renegotiate their own sense of cultural, social, and historical self." These processes and food-related identities, she argues, are not bound by place and time. Similarly, Teresa Mares and her colleagues (chapter 10) and Tanachi Mark Pandoongpatt (chapter 5) tell stories of immigrants using foodways to reclaim a sense of place and self when immersed in a new country and culture, where much of their former livelihood has been lost. In this chapter, I build on and engage with these complex notions of migration, food, borders, and identity, analyzing the difference that social, political, and cultural borders make for redeveloping a land-based home.

The specific forms of farming in this study are representative of this desire for re-creating a home place, where farmers are able to define their own livelihoods and spaces. Specific practices include growing biodiverse fruit and vegetable crops on a small scale (3 to 80 acres, with most between 10 and 20), direct sales at farmers' markets, and maintaining family-based labor. They sell almost all their produce at farmers' markets at relatively low costs. Although they use little or no synthetic inputs, none are certified organic, so they do not get the organic premium. Except for family labor, none of these practices are necessarily the most cost effective way to cultivate, yet it is what they know and the way they want to maintain their farms. In contrast to many white farmers who grow using these practices, they do not self-identify as part of an alternative farming or local food movement. Rather, they see farming as a way of life, a way to utilize the knowledge they have to run their own business and feed their family, and a way to reconstruct a sense of home that they lost through migration.

Immigrant farm businesses in the United States also function to help farmers reclaim land and agricultural production across geopolitical borders. Some farmers in this study dream of returning to their birth country, while others are more accepting of their new lives and communities in the United States as permanent. A few said they would eventually retire in Mexico, once their children had been educated. Regardless of whether they plan to stay, like most immigrants in the United States, they still sent home remittances to their original hometowns. While living in the United States, some have actually established new farms in Mexico, which they have family maintaining for them, whereas others help family members buy or sustain landownership there. Irrespective of their desire to return to their home country, all the farmers I interviewed expressed a longing to re-create a sense of home in the United States for their immediate future.

Yet they struggle with this transition. Gaining access to land, resources, and markets is a struggle for immigrant farmers, especially in the context of a largely white rural landscape. Below, I describe the complex set of conditions they face as immigrants and farmers of color in the United States.

Obstacles to Agricultural Success for Latino Farmers

On a national scale, non-white immigrant farmers have fewer financial resources and less access to land and capital than their white counterparts. Even when farmers of color succeed in climbing the "agricultural ladder," their social positioning means that they do so with limited resources and with varying level of success.[10] In this section I discuss the challenges faced by Latino and other farmers of color in gaining access to land and capital in the United States historically.

I then follow with the stories of farmers in this study, as they struggle to access USDA funding and support.

Although the vast majority of agricultural land ownership in Virginia is held by white farmers today, the state has one of the longest histories of black land ownership in the country, dating back to colonial times. Yet even in places, like Virginia, that have strong histories of non-white land ownership, farmers of color are squeezed out by differential opportunities by the state, ranging from overtly racist treatment at USDA offices at the local and federal levels, to problems with literacy, legal counsel, and general knowledge of available opportunities that help non-white farmers maintain their land and markets.[11]

As immigrants, and particularly as immigrants of color, participants' experience of U.S. citizenship varies. Although most farmers interviewed had documents to legally live and work in the United States, their ease and opportunity in accessing land and support to farm were significantly affected by their racialized identity. The United States has a long history of constituting citizenship (and related rights to land and resources) through whiteness. The earliest colonists utilized social constructions of race to justify the taking of Native lands and exploitation of Native labor in the founding and expansion of the nation. Ever since, non-white slaves and immigrants have composed the majority of the agrarian labor force. Farmers and landowners have historically taken advantage of racialized immigrants' politically vulnerable citizenship status, be it as documented temporary workers, undocumented workers, or even documented workers with relationships in the undocumented worker community, to deny workers human rights and a living wage.[12]

Previous groups of immigrants and farmers of color have been excluded from full citizenship rights in the United States due to state-sanctioned policies, which have been reinforced by everyday experiences of racial exclusion. Non-white immigrant farmers have been explicitly dispossessed of land and resources, in many cases due to their racial and citizenship status.[13] The Alien Land Laws in the early twentieth century excluded Japanese immigrants from holding land and forced practicing farmers off land they were already cultivating.[14] Although they are not immigrants, African American farmers in the United States, like Latino and other immigrant farmers of color, have been displaced from their livelihoods many times over. They were first dispossessed through the processes of capture from their homelands, and more recently as landowners and tenant farmers, mostly in the southern United States. Systematic discrimination by the USDA contributed to black farmers' 93 percent decline from 1940 to 1974.[15] These processes have succeeded in creating agricultural racial formations, the end result being that ownership and operation of U.S. farms remain in primarily white hands.[16]

All but a few farmers interviewed were indeed documented and able to apply for USDA assistance. Yet not being able to read, write, or understand the required forms in English necessary to become established farmers in the United States can prove very challenging. Among immigrant farmers, language skills, literacy, and education levels vary. Most have had very little formal education. Many have completed elementary school, others even high school, and all speak some English, usually enough to get by at a market, but not much more. Most have limited reading, writing, and business skills, and struggle to navigate the bureaucracy of the U.S. agriculture system. Local USDA staff informed me that very few Latino farmers enter their offices, although the "local" (or white) farmers usually come and ask for what they need. "They don't know about the cover crop program, they don't know about the high tunnel program if it doesn't go to their mailbox. Because I don't see them at all, unless I go to their farm. They don't come in here unless they hear about the program from their neighbor, or brother, or sister or something. They just don't walk in here like most of my clients do. They're [white farmers] in here all the time. They're calling all the time, 'Can you help me get funded?' And they [Latino farmers] never do that."

Many immigrant farmers do not have the linguistic or literacy skills to fill out paperwork. Additionally, they find government offices intimidating and oftentimes unwelcoming. Of all the farmers I interviewed, only three had attempted to receive services from the USDA. One farmer in Virginia, who has 60 acres in production, was the only farmer I interviewed who had crop insurance, which he secured through his local USDA Risk Management Agency office in Virginia. It took three trips to the offices to get the proper paperwork filled out. He does not read or write well in English and found the process intimidating and frustrating. It was also time consuming, beyond what he felt he could afford. As the owner-operator of a family-run business, his physical presence was needed on his farm.

Another farmer told me of her experience trying to get access to hoop house funding from a USDA funded project. After not receiving funding on her first try, she started questioning why she didn't receive funding when other farmers around her did.

> I went to the local NRCS office to ask about funds for building a hoop house. They told me in the office that they did not currently have funds, so I couldn't apply. I was telling this to a [white] customer at the market who had worked for the USDA. She told me they should still take my application. The customer contacted the office for me and they then told me to come in and to get an application. In the meantime, I noticed that other [white] neighbors were receiving the funding, while I was turned away. I applied and we eventually got the funding, although we are still waiting for it to go through.

A former federal USDA staff member reaffirmed this kind of racial discrimination at local offices. "Now, some of what happens today, when there is actually overt racism, it's still not as overt. It's more like, 'Oh, your forms aren't complete.'

And they'll hold persons' forms to higher scrutiny than they would a white person's forms."

Farmers also often feel unwelcome in the primarily white farming community. A farmer in Virginia stated that his previous employers were angry when they learned he was starting his own farm. He had managed their farm for twenty-seven years, yet they were not supportive of his transition and started talking badly about him to other farmers. He started selling his own produce at the same market where he had sold on behalf of his white employer for almost thirty years. He only did so after his former employer decided to stop going to the market and focus on wholesale. He found the other vendors were not tolerant of a Mexican farmer selling his own produce at the market. Two white farmers tried to get him ousted from the market, which he believes was motivated by jealousy and racial discrimination. "I have had clients there for twenty-five, thirty years. Regularly, for years, they have bought from me [selling for his former employer]. I bring 200, 300 watermelons in the truck and I sell it all. They [other vendors] brought 70, and they couldn't sell them. It made them mad and they wanted me kicked out. The next year two white women tried to get me expelled because I sold a lot. So the people [his customers] started to help me, so they couldn't run me out."

Other immigrant farmers cited similar stories of discrimination. Some stated market managers, customers, and other white farmers whom they believe were jealous of their sales often accused them of not bringing their own produce to the market. "Even if they [customers] point the finger at the gringos, they come inspect the Hispanics. Even if they're the clients who are complaining, they all come the same. . . . So, if someone complains about a gringo, they come inspect us. And they say that the gringos have everything [in order] and to all of us, they give us a paper to see if we have everything [that we say we have]. But we know it's all lies, but what are we going to do? . . . Yes, especially if it's a gringo [complaining], they only inspect the Hispanics."

Of course, entrepreneurs do not typically cheer on their competition. But at the markets where these farmers sell, there are dozens of farmers selling at a range of prices. Latinos do not stand out as the lowest sellers or particularly different than the other vendors, other than their race and nationality and somewhat larger variety of produce, with some additional Latin American varieties. In the case of immigrant farmers, the negative reactions are rooted in a suspicion of outsiders in a white farm-operator community. A local extension agent affirmed this type of discrimination against "newcomers," entrenched in a general mistrust of a new group of farmers they do not know. "They're good growers, and I think, pretty successful. And I think that can cause other farmers to be jealous. Not necessarily in the area, but across the board at a market. And I think a lot of fingers get pointed. And I think that the things that people say they do. . . . I think the biggest thing a lot of times is that there's mistrust, in terms of if they're actually growing what they saying they're growing, that's probably the biggest" (Figure 12.2).

At the institutional level, immigrants are made to feel their place is working in the fields, not in government offices or farm management positions. Very few USDA forms are available in Spanish, and at the local Virginia offices we visited a translator was not available. A USDA staff member acknowledged that the language barrier, in addition to literacy and general aversion to paperwork, was a large reason for this discrepancy. "Most of our [Latino] producers—we used to have some come in the office. They don't come in anymore. I think it's English. Because we had one that couldn't speak English, and he would always bring his son in here. And then the forms. We have some forms that are in Spanish, but most of our forms aren't . . . where they're used to dealing with more cash than a lot of paperwork. I think they find the paperwork a little overwhelming."

Further, it has been documented that the USDA has historically discriminated against Latino farmers. In 2000, a class action suit was filed against the USDA on behalf of Hispanic farmers and ranchers who were discriminated against from 1981 to 2000 while applying for USDA loans. The USDA admitted to discrimination, and this case is currently being settled via a claims process, where farmers

Figure 12.2. "They're good growers, and I think, pretty successful." An abundance of produce from an immigrant's farm. Photo by the author.

are eligible to receive from $50,000 to $250,000 based on the evidence they submit.[17] National outreach for the claims process was conducted during the summer of 2013, via television and radio ads. Those who believe they are eligible are able to fill out forms online. Although they did not technically need a lawyer to file a claim, USDA employees I spoke with said they recommended legal assistance to properly submit a claim. The process is complicated, they told me, and required a variety of forms and documentation. The USDA, with the assistance of the legal nonprofit the Lawyer Legal Action Group, created a list of lawyers trained to help with the claims. Individuals still had to pay the lawyers out of their own pocket, a cost unreasonable for most small-scale immigrant farmers.

According to my contact with the Office of General Counsel at the USDA, the claims administrator received over 50,000 claims. Around 85 percent of claims filed by Hispanic farmers and ranchers were deemed complete by the claims administrator and sent to the adjudicators for a determination on the merits. A third party has been hired to adjust the claims. As of July 2015, the USDA approved 14.4 percent of the claims, while the rest of were rejected due to lack of "sufficient documentation."[18] Although the claims process will help a small number of people of Latino decent recover profits lost due to discrimination, most are not aware of the process or their right to file as part of the suit. And as the results of the process make clear, even when steps are made to attempt to create fairer opportunities, problems of literacy and language continue to be obstacles.

It is the responsibility of the staff at the USDA local office to reach out to farmers in their region. Yet when I asked the staff at the local office in Virginia about outreach, they told us they had a flier in the office, but no one had applied. This is the same office where they told me Mexican farmers rarely enter. Of the farmers I interviewed, most stated they had never even applied for USDA funds or entered its offices, thereby making the claims process irrelevant in rectifying the type of structural discrimination they face.

Those who experienced discrimination after the year 2000 are not able to submit a claim. At the federal level, the secretary of agriculture in the Obama administration, Tom Vilsak, claimed to be ushering in a "new era" at the USDA. Yet a former staff member at the USDA's Socially Disadvantaged Farmer and Rancher Program expressed that most of the changes to address discrimination are equivalent to offering "coffee and donuts," rather than getting to the root of the problem. She claimed that the USDA outreach to socially disadvantaged farmers, as a result of the discrimination claims, are mostly rhetoric. The program does not provide technical assistance that farmers really need:

> "Here have a cookie and some coffee, honest we'll give you a loan." But then they leave. And actually, "No honest, we won't give you a loan," because nobody actually stopped eating the donut and the coffee and figured out how to get financed, because that would be hard work. . . . "Here's information about

the USDA. Hey, by the way, the USDA doesn't discriminate anymore. And we really hope that when you come to our office you'll meet someone that looks like you and treats you with respect, and if they don't, here's your civil rights." But not, "So let's sit down with your tax return now."

In her opinion, although there is a genuine intention of creating more racially just programs from the top levels of the administration, in effect, the USDA's claims of making institutional change to combat historic discrimination are merely oratory performance. She argues that to improve opportunities for disadvantaged farmers, they need technical assistance with their finances. For immigrants who have experience with working in the field, but do not have a background in business or a family member to teach them, technical skills, such as bookkeeping and business planning, tend to be primary boundaries to starting a functioning business.

In order to convert from worker to farmer, immigrants must successfully navigate entrenched racial, social, and political borders. Despite discrimination and obstacles related to language, literacy, and documentation status, some immigrant farmers are beating the odds, and, in the process, re-creating a new and promising sense of place and home. These multiple forms of displacement underlay their deep commitment to an agrarian profession and livelihood and their quest to carve out a social as well as physical place they can call their own.

CREATING A NEW SENSE OF HOME THROUGH AGRICULTURAL PRACTICE

Although all of the farms I visited were owned and operated by separate and distinct nuclear families, resources and knowledge were commonly shared among the close-knit group. Many of them have been in the region for over twenty years, yet most of the immigrant generation still speaks primarily Spanish, with just enough English ability to navigate markets. They depend on their teenage and adult children to communicate with market managers, equipment salespeople, government representatives, and other neighbors. This language barrier, while it keeps this community somewhat isolated among a largely white and English-speaking regional population, also functions to maintain closeness among Latino immigrant farmers, where they depend on each other before looking to outsiders for assistance.

One young farmer who owns and operates a farm with his parents, who emigrated from Jalisco about twenty years ago, noted that this part of Virginia is unique in having so many farmers of Mexican origin. This makes them feel comfortable and has given them a reason to stay. He explained that for his parents, who both migrated throughout the United States as farmworkers before settling in Virginia, having their own farm in the United States was always their dream.

"My parents always talked about having acres. Having a country home. Having pigs, cows, and chickens, and growing your stuff, and whatever goes bad, give it to them to fatten up." He also told me that farming and living in rural Virginia feels like home. "This is what I know. I go to the cities, and come in through the bridge . . . and I'm just like, 'Oh, I'm home.' I guess it's just the country life. It's very peaceful. I don't know what it is." For this farmer and his family, establishing a stable agrarian life the Northern Neck allows them to realize the lifestyle they wanted for themselves and their children, after many years traveling from place to place.

Another farmer told me that she found life in the United States "very, very ugly. . . . Each person stays in their own house. There is no time. People live by their watch and there is a lot of stress." In contrast, on her farm, "It is a little bit like Mexico. It makes me feel the same. It is not the same exactly, but more free. In the city there is more pressure." She explained that on her farm she had the crop varieties she liked to eat in Mexico, could view her fields from her windows, and spent her days cultivating food for her family, which all made her feel closer to her home and family she left in Jalisco.

When I asked farmers how large they wanted their farm to grow, farmers repeatedly expressed that they didn't want to get too large. Oftentimes those who owned between 10 and 40 acres stated they didn't want to grow any bigger. They were working as hard as they could to make ends meet and did not see scaling up as a goal. Additionally, they were struggling to sell the produce they already grew. Instead of aspiring to develop in size, they desired to find more markets for what they were already growing.

In Virginia, land prices are reasonably affordable, and almost all the farmers had bought land with an established home on the property, or are currently working toward building a home on their land. This is the goal for all the immigrant farmers I interviewed—to live and farm in the same place. It is important to them to raise their children on a homestead and teach them to grow food, as most of them were taught in Mexico. The farms functioned with almost only family labor. Most of the farm business owners were a couple who employed their teenage or grown children and sometimes a sibling or cousin. Oftentimes more family would come and help during a particularly busy part of the harvest season. Many told me they would like to keep it that way—they did not want to take on the task of finding outside labor or manage the complications of hiring strangers.[19]

Maintaining family labor on the farm is a way for immigrants to ensure that their children experience a similar lifestyle as they did growing up in Mexico. Although some of their children have worked as farm laborers to make extra cash, most have grown up on family-owned farms and have been educated in the United States. Not all desire for their children to take over their farm operation, yet many see farming as a good profession for their children, if they are interested. They see teaching their children about farming as a way to pass on their culture and traditions, as well as a skill to fall back on. One farmer's son told us that although his father encourages him to think broadly about his future, he sees farming as a skill he will always have should he need it. "My dad tells me, one day you don't have a job and you want to do something, you already know how to do the farming."

Another farmer agreed, telling us that although she did not expect all her children to farm, she wanted them to be proud of their agricultural background and know that they always have farming skills as a backup plan to make a living. "I tell my kids, 'You don't want to do it [farming]. Stay in school. Stay in school, but just don't forget where you came from. There's always, you always will find a job farming, in case you don't find whatever you want to do. You can always come back. There's nobody that's going to tell you, "Oh, you don't know how to do it." Yes you do. Yes you do.'"

On the farms with teenagers or children in their twenties, most of the children are working on the farm full time, and in many cases they manage promotion and selling at markets. After watching their parents struggle to transition from farmworkers to small business owners, many of the adult-age children of farm owners said that they wanted to help their parents' businesses grow. It might not be their only professional goal, but all the young adults I interviewed want to support their parents' farm in one way or another.

All the farmers are growing diverse crop mixes, similar to the fields they cultivated when subsistence farming in Mexico. They are producing a combination of fruits and vegetables, covering the spectrum of food demanded by farmers' market customers. This includes Latin American specialty herbs like *mora* and *chepilin*, produce varieties preferred by U.S. food aficionados such as heirloom tomatoes and little gem lettuces, as well as crops requested by other immigrant communities, such as Chinese long beans and eggplant varieties.

Their growing techniques include a mix of those learned working in the United States and those from their home country. Although they discussed their farms as a place to remember or a way to return to their lifestyle before emigrating, they have learned new farming techniques to adjust to new climates, markets, and generally different farming conditions in the United States. Technologies like drip irrigation and tractors are welcomed advances, creating less demand of their physical labor and allowing them to produce the quantities needed to compete in U.S. markets.

All of the farmers I spoke with were selling primarily at farmers' markets. Since their farms are small scale and they are cultivating a diversity of crops, they are limited to marketplaces where there is an emphasis on product variety. This restricts them to direct markets such as farmers' markets or to selling specialty crops in small batches to restaurants and small grocery stores. None had started a Community Supported Agriculture (CSA) program yet, although some had discussed it. To sell to larger wholesale distributors, they would have to grow a more consistent amount of fewer products, which none of the farmers were interested in doing. Additionally, growing directly to customers allows them to maintain a certain level of control over production without being beholden to wholesalers or other large buyers. This is a familiar way for them to grow and sell, most similar to their family practices selling in open-air markets in Mexico.

Despite their success at starting and maintaining their farms, all farmers I interviewed expressed challenges to sustaining the scale and form they desired. In a marketplace that demands uniformity and large-scale production, they were struggling to find enough direct markets to sell to. The most lucrative farmers' markets are saturated with mixed crop and vegetable growers and will not take in more vendors with similar products. Although they are surviving at the scale and style of farming they preferred, they all expressed frustration at a lack of outlets to sell their produce. None of the farmers said that they were considering a shift away from growing diverse crops, yet most were finding it difficult to sell all the produce they grew. Markets were the most commonly cited limiting factor to the survival of their farm businesses.

In addition to growing small-scale and diverse crops, all were committed to growing using low amounts of synthetic inputs, often citing integrated pest management techniques. Although none were certified organic, most told me they used little to no nonorganic pesticides, herbicides, or fertilizers. Many of the farmers involved in this study are coming from backgrounds of subsistence farming, where they used minimal off-farm inputs and often saved seeds each year. Their experience growing organically before emigrating provides many immigrant farmers with the knowledge to start as organic farmers by default.

Some expressed that after working in the fields in the United States, they no longer wanted to be exposed to the pesticides and herbicides they had worked with in others' fields. Being that they hire almost strictly family labor, maintaining a healthy atmosphere on the farm is important to them. Their children are on the farm in the summers and after school, and they did not want to see them exposed to harmful chemicals.

Many also said they are interested in becoming certified organic, but do not have the resources to pay or are intimidated by the paperwork involved in the certification process. Some feel that the regulations are too strict. For those that do not own all the land they are growing on, it is difficult to confirm that the land has not been cultivated using synthetic additives in recent years, a requirement for certification. Furthermore, they do not want to invest in improving land where they are unsure of their tenure.

Farming is not an easy way to earn a living, especially when you have not inherited a family farm, have little capital input, and do not have the advantages of being born in the United States and coming from the white majority of farm owners and operators. For Mexican immigrants who are converting from farmworker to farm owner, the explanation for their persistence in the profession must be understood beyond one of simple class mobility. As I argue above, their growing presence in small-scale farming in the United States must be understood as one connected to agrarian culture and identity, as they create a sense of place defined by their own experience.

CROSSING BORDERS, OVERCOMING BOUNDARIES

Despite struggling against deep-rooted racial and ethnic agrarian hierarchies, immigrant farmers are starting their own farms, where they reestablish agricultural livelihoods and foodways. They cultivate not only to sustain themselves financially but also as a way to re-create a new sense of place and home, one that has been complicated by many years of economic and cultural dislocation. After being dispossessed from their homelands by transnational agricultural policies and forced to work as migrant laborers in the global industrial food system, these farmers are in part motivated by a desire to reclaim a land-based identity, stripped from them through processes of migration. Through the practice of then repossessing land and their own labor, they then recross the class border, again claiming the means of production as their own.

For many immigrant farmers, establishing a farm is not only a survival strategy but also a way to create a new life in the United States, one where they are able to draw on their culture and traditions as food producers to create a space of their own. Their nostalgia for home draws on both an idea of the past and a dream for the future. In establishing farms in the United States, workers cross geopolitical, class, and racial borders, as they strive to re-create memories of what an attachment to land and food means to them. Looking forward to establishing a real home, they draw on notions of an idealized one, ultimately creating a hybrid version of the place they remember combined with the realities of a new life.

The growing presence of non-white immigrant farmers and other farmers of color forces us to question whether farming must and will always reaffirm historical race and citizenship relations. As these farmers' stories remind us, agriculture and foodways across America's borders and borderlands are wrought with stories of struggle and suffering, but they are also full of hope and survival.

NOTES

1. I define a farmer foremost as someone who identifies himself or herself as a farmer (*campesino, agricultor,* or *ranchero* in Spanish)—more specifically, one who currently owns his or her farm business, so as to differentiate him or her from a farm laborer, who works for an employer. He or she must also perform at least some of the manual labor on the farm. They do not need to own the land they farm, or the machinery they use. I did not include a sales minimum for inclusion in this study, only that they must be selling at least some of

their crops and self-identify as a farmer. A minority of the farmers I interviewed have other jobs, some in farm work, others in construction, but they all make at least some, if not all, of their income from their own farming business. The National Agricultural Statistics Service defines a farm as any business "from which $1,000 or more of agricultural products were sold or would normally be sold during the year" (U.S. Department of Agriculture [USDA], 2014, "National Agricultural Statistics Service-History of Agricultural Statistics," www.nass .usda.gov/About_NASS/History_of_Ag_Statistics/index.asp).

2. Fieldwork took place June 2013–July 2014. I conducted all research with the assistance of three student research assistants, in Spanish and English. A research assistant or I translated interviews conducted in Spanish to English. Specific locations and names will remain anonymous. I conducted eighteen interviews with farmers and twenty interviews with employees in the nonprofit and government sectors who work with immigrant farmers. This included three regional farmers' market managers and staff at the Latino Farmers and Ranchers Association, the Rural Coalition, Telemon Foundation, Virginia Cooperative Extension, and the USDA. At the USDA, I interviewed staff who work in the office of Advocacy and Outreach and the Socially Disadvantaged Farmers and Ranchers Program in Washington, D.C., and the Natural Resources Conservation Service (NRCS) and Farm Service Agency (FSA) local offices in Virginia. Additionally, I interviewed employees who work at the federal level on the Hispanic and Women Farmers and Ranchers discrimination suit and claims process at the USDA. The national study is ongoing at the time of this publication and includes additional research sites in California, New York, and Washington states.

3. Minor T. Weisiger, "Northern Neck and Proprietary Records," Library of Virginia. Research Notes 23 (2002).

4. Frank Delano, "Area's Proud Past Fades into Troubled Present." *Free Lance Star* 117.274 (2001): A1–A6.

5. J. D. Kasarda and J. H. Johnson. *The Economic Impact of the Hispanic Population on the State of North Carolina* (Chapel Hill, NC: Frank Hawkins Kenan Institute of Private Enterprise, 2006); A. Zandt, "Northern Neck, Virginia. State of the South: Building an Infrastructure of Opportunity for the Next Generation" (Durham, NC: MDC, 2014), http:// stateofthesouth.org/profiles/northern-neck-virginia/.

6. U.S. Department of Agriculture, "Census of Agriculture," 2014, www.agcensus.usda .gov/. These numbers do not tell us how many are first-generation immigrants. This 67,000 number is out of 2,109,303 total principal operators in 2012 (USDA, "Census of Agriculture"). The number of operators who were also owners is not available from before 2012.

7. Meredith E. Abarca, *Voices in the Kitchen: Views of Food and the World from Working-Class Mexican and Mexican American Women* (College Station: Texas A&M University Press, 2006); Teresa Mares, "Tracing Immigrant Identity through the Plate and the Palate," *Latino Studies* 10.3 (2012): 334–354; Teresa Mares and Devon G. Peña, "Urban Agriculture in the Making of Insurgent Spaces in Los Angeles and Seattle," in *Insurgent Public Space: Guerrilla Urbanism and the Remaking of the Contemporary City*, ed. Jeffry Hou (New York: Routledge Press, 2010); Devon Gerardo Peña, *Mexican Americans and the Environment: Tierra y Vida* (Tucson: University of Arizona Press, 2005).

8. Doreen Massey, *Space, Place, and Gender* (Minneapolis: University of Minnesota Press, 1994).

9. Stuart Hall, "Cultural Identity and Diaspora," in *Identity: Community, Culture, Difference*, ed. J. Rutherford (London: Lawrence and Wishart, 1990).

10. Pete Daniel, *Dispossession: Discrimination Against African American Farmers in the Age of Civil Rights* (Raleigh: University of North Carolina Press, 2013); Neil Foley, *The White Scourge: Mexicans, Blacks, and Poor Whites in Texas Cotton Culture* (Berkeley: University of California Press, 1997); Jess Gilbert, Gwen Sharp, and M. Sindy Felin, "The Loss and Persistence of Black-Owned Farmland: A Review of the Research Literature and Its Implications," *Southern Rural Sociology* 18.2 (2002): 1–30.

11. Gilbert et al., "Loss and Persistence of Black-Owned Farmland"; Loren Schweninger. "A Vanishing Breed: Black Farm Owners in the South, 1651–1982," *Agricultural History* 63 (Summer 1989): 41–60.

12. See, among others, Matt Garcia, *A World of Its Own: Race, Labor, and Citrus in the Making of Greater Los Angeles, 1900–1970* (Chapel Hill: University of North Carolina Press, 2001); Don Mitchell, *The Lie of the Land: Migrant Workers and the California Landscape* (Minneapolis: University of Minnesota Press, 1996); Cindy Hahamovitch, *The Fruits of Their Labor: Atlantic East Coast Farmworkers and the Making of Migrant Poverty, 1870–1945* (Chapel Hill: University of North Carolina Press, 1997); Deborah Barndt, *Tangled Routes: Women, Work, and Globalization on the Tomato Trail* (Lanham, MD: Rowman and Littlefield, 2008).

13. Sucheng Chan. *This Bittersweet Soil: The Chinese in California Agriculture, 1860–1910* (Berkeley: University of California Press, 1989); Laura-Anne Minkoff-Zern, Nancy Peluso, Jennifer Sowerwine, and Christy Getz, "Race and Regulation: Asian Immigrants in California Agriculture," in *Cultivating Food Justice: Race, Class and Sustainability*, ed. Alison Alkon and Julian Agyeman (Cambridge, MA: MIT Press, 2011): 65–85; Valerie J. Matsumoto, *Farming the Home Place: A Japanese American Community in California, 1919–1982* (Ithaca, NY: Cornell University Press, 1993); Miriam J. Wells, "Ethnic Groups and Knowledge Systems in Agriculture," *Economic Development and Cultural Change* 39 (1991): 739–771; Miriam J. Wells, *Strawberry Fields: Politics, Class, and Work in California Agriculture* (Ithaca, NY: Cornell University Press, 1996).

14. Matsumoto, *Farming the Home Place*.

15. Daniel, *Dispossession*.

16. Minkoff-Zern et al., "Race and Regulation."

17. Hispanic and Women Farmers and Ranchers Claims and Resolution Process, www .farmerclaims.gov//; Juan Martinez and R. Edmund Gomez, "Identifying Barriers That Prevent Hispanic/Latino Farmers and Ranchers in Washington State from Participating in USDA Programs and Services" (Yakima, WA: Rural Community Development Resources Center for Latino Farmers, 2011).

18. John Zippert, "USDA Approves Only 14% of Completed Claims in the Hispanic and Women Farmers and Ranchers Discrimination Settlement," *Greene County Democrat*, http:// greenecountydemocrat.com/?p=14384.

19. I am not claiming that family labor is inherently a better system or more equitable, only that it is evidence of a particular form of farming. The question of labor is always looming, as most would prefer to not hire outside their families. Yet if they are to survive economically, which may mean getting bigger, they may also have to start to hire some non-family labor. Some farms did have a few nonfamily laborers. In these cases, they were hiring other immigrants from Jalisco, Oaxaca, Chiapas, and other parts of Mexico. Miriam Wells's research in *Strawberry Fields* shows that Mexican farmers in the United States (in comparison to Japanese and Anglo farmers) are more likely to emphasize the importance of family labor as a key to farming success. She credits this difference largely to Mexican farmers' lack of economic resources and the simultaneous wealth of available family labor.

CHAPTER 13

(Re)Producing Ethnic Difference

SOLIDARITY TRADE, INDIGENEITY, AND
COLONIALISM IN THE GLOBAL QUINOA BOOM

Marygold Walsh-Dilley

In August 2013, I sat in a small, cement-floored room in San Juan de Rosario on the southern high plateau (altiplano) in Bolivia. With a warm knit cap and gloves to ward off the chill of the Andean winter night, I was meeting with Don Max and a small group of other senior leaders of the community to present the results of research I had conducted in the village over the previous five years. Our conversation turned to current economic conditions, and the group spoke gleefully about the contemporary quinoa boom. People in the village couldn't believe their luck when the price they received for a 100-pound sack of quinoa went above US$100, but last year it climbed even higher, surpassing 1,000 Bolivianos (about US$145). These prices, and the sustained demand from the United States, Europe, and elsewhere, have significantly altered livelihoods in rural highland Bolivia. Expanding quinoa production has reversed out-migration, transformed production strategies, and improved the standard of living immensely. The economic shift is tangible: the village now buzzes with automobiles on its dusty dirt streets, and in each home I enter I see new evidence of material consumption: stereo systems, refrigerators, microwaves. Local residents are better able to access markets and to pay for new purchases, and as a result are consuming more fruits and vegetables. People tell me that they are better able to support the education of their children, and the money from quinoa production pays for young adults to specialize beyond their high school degree. As an elderly man told me, "The quinoa is saving us."

This marks a significant shift in a relatively short amount of time. Before the 1980s, there was an extremely limited market for quinoa, and the majority of production in San Juan was for subsistence only. At my meeting with the village leaders, Don Max laughed: "And to think, they used to call quinoa a *comida del indio*"—an Indian food. The irony Don Max was pointing to is that up until relatively recently, quinoa was marginalized as a food grown and eaten by high-land indigenous peoples and was considered unfit for consumption by urban mestizos and elites in Bolivia and elsewhere in the Andes.

I recalled Don Max's words recently when walking down the aisle of my local grocery store in upstate New York. I was looking at a packet of Alter Eco quinoa on the shelf. This Organic Royal Black Quinoa is marketed as the "wild, crunchy supergrain of the Andes." The package features a photo of a smiling dark-skinned man in a cap, words in the native languages of Andean Aymara and Quechua peoples, and a short description of how "traditional Quechua and Aymara farmers" cultivate this "ancient variety" near the desolate Uyuni salt flat. Through this narrative, and many others in supermarkets, cookbooks, and else-where across the Global North, quinoa continues to be constructed as an "Indian food." The naming of quinoa as *comida del indio* was once a mark and means of marginalization in Bolivia, reflecting colonial and ongoing mistreatment of native peoples. Now, the linking of quinoa to indigeneity is a central element of a Northern campaign to build North-South solidarity and create ethical markets.

This chapter is about these two parallel constructions of quinoa as an Indian food. I ask: how has it come to be that what was once marginalized and eschewed has become a global superfood? I argue that as quinoa flows north, destined for upscale restaurants and homes in the United States, quinoa's border crossing is closely linked to shifting ideas about indigeneity and how boundaries around ethnic difference are mobilized and reproduced. The discursive treatment of quinoa and the people and places of its production—often created by well-meaning allies seeking to aid Bolivians and improve their welfare—nonetheless relies upon and reproduces racialized boundaries: between consumer and producer, North and South, the unmarked category and its marked Other, indeed the beneficiaries and victims of historic and ongoing colonial encounters. I suggest this problematic reproduction of ethnic difference adds to the ethical dilemma of projects that pursue alternative ("fair" or "solidarity") trade as a strategy for economic development in the South.[1] Thus, this chapter is also about the chal-lenge of how consumers in the North can make ethical consumption choices in solidarity with or that support poor and historically marginalized producers in the South.

CROSSING BORDERS

While quinoa has been cultivated in the Andes for 5,000 years, an international market for the pseudo-grain began to emerge only in the 1980s. Prior to this, qui-noa production was largely undertaken as a subsistence strategy, alongside llama husbandry, potato cropping, and out-migration. There was, quite simply, a very limited regional demand for the crop.

The governments in the region did attempt to promote quinoa as a means to improve nutrition in the highland Andes. These efforts began with a 1948 United Nations–sponsored nutrition conference that suggested that quinoa could "play a major role in feeding the Upland Indians, whose nutrition problems are among the most serious in the Americas."[2] Research in the following decades identified the superlative nutritional and other qualities of quinoa. With a high level of complete protein, quinoa also supplies substantial amounts of iron, calcium, and various vitamins and minerals. Although it is not technically a grain since it is a leafy rather than grassy plant, quinoa can be eaten like rice or ground into flour and is thus a nutritious substitute for wheat and other grains.

In the mid-twentieth century, with support from international agencies, donors, and foreign governments, a small group of researchers and agronomists in the Andes began to investigate and promote quinoa production and consumption.[3] In line with modernization theories of development that were dominant at the time, this work sought to develop improved varieties, identify optimum levels of fertilizer applications and appropriate pesticides, and devise new techniques and technologies for quinoa production and postharvest processing. This was done in an attempt to address the high degree of malnutrition and poverty along the highlands.

But quinoa was already being consumed along the Andean altiplano. Despite the marginalization, neglect, and disruption of indigenous agricultural systems and communities since the Conquest, highland communities continued to produce and eat quinoa, and indeed the varieties and techniques they used were already very well adapted to local ecological and social conditions.[4] John McCamant writes: "Quinoa has endured among them because it co-evolved with their societies and thus fits their needs precisely."[5] The problem, thus, was not that highland communities were not familiar with quinoa or did not have access to adequate varieties, techniques, or inputs, but that there was no market for it because affluent mestizo and urban elites eschewed quinoa and other native foods in favor of European crops like wheat. Efforts by the Bolivian government to promote quinoa did nothing to reverse its marginalization in broader Bolivian society. For example, a law was passed in the mid-1970s requiring that all bread sold by bakeries contain a minimum of 5 percent quinoa flour.[6] While this did create a market demand and led to a doubling of area planted to quinoa in the highlands, these efforts were ultimately undermined as bakers and consumers resisted and the law went unenforced. Quinoa production returned to its former level within just two years. Thus, the emergence of a quinoa market in the Global North precipitated an unprecedented shift from primarily subsistence production to cash cropping.

Two overlapping processes aided the emergent quinoa market. First, the expansion of quinoa was directly linked to the development efforts of foreign missionaries and international organizations. Belgian Catholic missionaries, for instance, promoted the mechanization of quinoa production by providing tractors in the Nor Lipez region of Bolivia, which is today one of the principal production zones for the variety that is most desired on the international market. These tractors enabled producers to clear new land and expand production, and were identified as a key factor in the shift from subsistence to cash-cropping.[7] Technical assistance from the United Nations, the European Union, and the United States' Inter-American Foundation contributed to early industrialization efforts as well, funding the construction of quinoa processing plants.[8] These efforts supported the growing producers associations and cooperatives that became the principal actors in building quinoa production and processing capacity and developing linkages with importers in the North.

Second, in the 1980s consumers in the Global North developed an interest in exotic fruits, vegetables, grains, and other health foods from the South, leading to a non-traditional agricultural export (NTAE) boom. At the same time, "fair" and other alternative trade pathways emerged out of the interest of Northern consumers to make ethical consumption choices to support economic development and ecological sustainability in producing areas. The idea behind fair and other ethical trade organizations was to link and therefore build solidarity between consumers and producers. Quinoa, as a relatively unknown but superlatively nutritious crop grown by rural communities in one of the poorest regions in the hemisphere, was a terrific candidate for solidarity trade networks. The Quinoa Corporation, established in 1983, was the first company to import quinoa into the United States.[9] Like many of the other importers to follow, the Quinoa Corporation was established in part out of a desire to support the development of native peoples in the Andes, and it remains motivated by commitments to ethical and sustainable sourcing.[10] Alternative trade organizations, along with fair trade criteria, significantly influenced the emergent quinoa value chain; they have been the principal importers of quinoa, especially in the early years when Northern consumers were unfamiliar with the Andean crop.

For many of the quinoa importers and distributors in the United States, there was a second motivation beyond building a market for poor and marginalized farmers. For both the Quinoa Corporation and Inca Organics (the longest-standing and principal fair trade company importing quinoa from Ecuador), a principal goal was the "revaluation" of quinoa as a food item within the Andes, not just among North American and European consumers. That is, these and similar companies sought to promote domestic consumption of quinoa, particularly among the Andean poor, and they thought that promoting quinoa in the United States was the best way to do this.[11] Tonya Kerssen writes: "They figured that if quinoa consumption were accepted in the US (symbol of progress and modernity) they might succeed in remaking its image [in Bolivia]."[12] In a

2006 interview, Inca Organics founder Robert Leventry remarked: "We feel very happy that the Ecuadorians are starting to eat the quinoa they had given up on for so long. That's been one of the major things for us, I think."[13]

Thus, quinoa is unlike many NTAEs in that it was dominated from its inception by "solidarity trade" built on values-based relationships between local producer associations and alternative trade organizations rather than being directed by corporate interests.[14] This international trade has benefited Andean quinoa producers in ways that regional or local markets never did, and it is perceived by the oft-marginalized indigenous farmers to be more reliable and fair.[15]

SOLIDARITY TRADE AND THE LINKING OF QUINOA AND INDIGENEITY

Because quinoa was a relatively new and little known food in the North, building quinoa markets required introducing the pseudo-grain to Northern consumers. Various agents have been involved in educating this new public about quinoa, from development organizations and institutions, quinoa importers, fair trade and other alternative trade organizations, health food stores, academics, cookbook authors, restaurateurs, and the alternative as well as, increasingly, mainstream media. Private companies, many of them at least partly motivated by solidarity, fairness, and sustainability, have been particularly important, and how they frame quinoa has served the dual purposes of building a market and upholding ethical commitments to producers. This fits into the broader project of fair trade, which seeks to raise awareness among consumers about producers and production conditions in order to promote social, environmental, and economic justice.[16] Fair trade is seen as a way to shorten the "social distance" between Northern consumers and Southern producers and reduce the inequalities between them.[17] Part of the aim is to contextualize commodities and make visible the producers and histories of imported goods—and thereby to avoid the colonial impulse and decontextualization of commodified border crossings of food so heavily critiqued by bell hooks and others.[18] That is, it seeks to defetishize commodities by revealing the social and ecological conditions under which they are produced.[19] Thus, solidarity trade involves not just the "traffic in things" but also the traffic in information, knowledge, and meanings about things and the people who produce them.[20]

As quinoa is packaged discursively for reflexive but unknowledgeable consumers, ethnicity has emerged as a central, if not always explicit, theme. These discourses show up in many different places, but the materials generated by the importers and distributors are particularly instructive. In these discursive spaces, quinoa is associated with indigeneity in many different ways. Sometimes this is very explicit, directly identifying the producers as indigenous. The website of Inca Organics, for example, emphasizes the ethnicity of its producers in the first sentence of text stating that its product is "grown by over 4,000 indigenous farmers in Ecuador." They also describe the grain itself as indigenous: "Our heir-loom Quinoa is the . . . true traditional blend of indigenous varieties grown by the Incas and their descendants in the high altiplano of Ecuador for centuries."[21]

Often, however, indigeneity is not made explicit, but an image is deployed to reflect race. As noted, Alter Eco's packages of pearl, black, red, and rainbow quinoa all carry the photograph of a smiling man, presumably a quinoa farmer, presumably native. The text alongside this image reads: "13,000 feet up on the arid, desolate Salar De Uyuni salt flat of Bolivia, traditional Quechua and Aymara farmers tend to fields of highly coveted 'quinoa real,' or royal quinoa, an ancient variety grown only in this very spot." Frequently, these discourses are gendered; common tropes frame women as "more Indian,"[22] and discursive treatments of quinoa often highlight images of women in "traditional" dress and other markings of indigeneity. For example, the central image on Inca Organic's homepage is of four barefoot women in long, dark blue wrap-around skirts and bright shawls, with braids down their backs. Andean Naturals, a principal fair trade importer of quinoa, features on its website a photo of a woman with a child on her back, wrapped in a brightly colored woven shawl. This extends to popular media coverage of quinoa as well. For example, a recent set of articles in the *Guardian* showed women dressed in the skirts and bowler hats of the region's Aymara and Quechua women.[23]

Packaging also frequently evokes pre-Conquest groups or civilization as a way to construct quinoa as an Indian food. Most notable are references to the Inca Empire, which at its zenith spread across the Andean region from Ecuador to northern Argentina, and which was extinguished with the Conquest. For instance, Ancient Harvest, one of the principal distributors of quinoa in the United States, has branded one of its varieties of quinoa "Inca Red." The packaging visually makes the link as well, featuring precolonial iconography as its background. Similarly, Alter Eco packages trace quinoa back to its cultivation by the Incas, stating that "[quinoa] was so revered by the Incas that they called it 'chisaya mama' or 'mother grain.'" Seeds of Change, which packages a quinoa and brown rice pilaf that is widely available in supermarkets, notes that "for the people of the Bolivian Altiplano, the tradition of cultivating Quinoa has endured since the time of the Incas." This Inca reference is among the most common themes in North American quinoa packaging.

Cookbooks are another site where this discursive link between quinoa and pre-Conquest civilizations is forged. In *Quinoa the Supergrain: Ancient Food for Today*, the first quinoa cookbook written in English for North American consumers (in 1989), author Rebecca Wood spends four pages outlining the importance of quinoa to the Tiahuanaco civilization (A.D. 100–1200) and the later Inca empire (A.D. 1300–1532), emphasizing the central role of quinoa in their diets and the symbolic connection between quinoa and the legitimacy of the Inca state. She writes, "The golden taquiza [planting stick] . . . was the Inca's symbol of state." The ruler would study the stars and "divine a propitious time to plant quinoa [and] would ceremoniously break the first ground with his golden taquiza. The Sapa Inca (god-king) was held personally responsible for the crop's success and his people's well-being."[24] Most cookbook authors do not devote so much space to rendering precolonial history, but they nearly always link quinoa to the Inca Empire. In Rena Patten's 2011 book *Cooking with Quinoa: The Supergrain*, for example, the very short two-page introduction implicates the Inca: "An ancient plant native to the Andes mountains in South America, quinoa has been around for over five thousand years and is known to have been a staple food of the Incas. They used it to supplement their diet of potatoes and corn. It was commonly referred to as the 'mother grain' or 'gold of the Incas' and was considered sacred."[25]

This tracing of quinoa back to the precolonial Inca is an overarching narrative in the discursive treatment of quinoa in North America that does important symbolic work. It not only frames quinoa as an "Indian food," but it specifies a particular construction of Indian-ness—one that draws on well-known tropes about American Indians in the United States, including prominent themes of authenticity, harmony, purity, simplicity, and sustainability. Purity enters these discourses frequently, with the use of temporal and other language to make the claim that quinoa is not perverted by modern technology or industrial practices—and the discord of modern life. Food packaging and other materials of quinoa importers and distributors use words such as "heritage" and "heirloom" to connect quinoa to a simpler time. Ancient Harvest, a company that specializes in "ancient" grains including quinoa, emphasizes that these crops are "practically unchanged since their origin."[26] Inca Organics notes: "These ancient heirloom grains are not genetically modified or hybrids."[27] They are thus constructed as "authentic" and "traditional." For example, the Inca Organics website hosts a slide show entitled "Mother Grain: Bringing Back the Lost Crop of the Inca" that notes that its quinoa is grown "the old-fashioned way," using "traditional . . . centuries old techniques."[28] Related to this is the notion of harmony that emerges in these discursive materials. For example, Ancient Harvest calls another of its quinoa products its "Harmony Blend," and the website for Inca Organics describes the quinoa harvest as cooperative and harmonious.[29]

These discourses both reflect a nostalgia among Northern consumers for a simpler time, before modern technologies and systems became so complicated, sullied, and profit-driven, and map closely onto common ways that Indian-ness has been constructed in the history of the United States. Indeed, these two elements are intimately linked. "As exemplars of a natural life thought to be pure and unchanging," Philip Deloria writes, "Indians were among the most important symbols used to critique the modern. Indians, it seemed, possessed the community spirit lacking in the city, a spiritual center desired by those troubled by secular science, and the reality so missing in a world of artifice. . . . Indians evoked a nostalgic past more authentic and often more desirable than the anxious present."[30] Thus, these discourses place quinoa temporally, and consumption of quinoa allows consumers to access that space. The discursive linking of quinoa to native culture in this way is a critique of contemporary society and a means to escape its destructive consequences.

This link is drawn out explicitly by Noble Savage Foods, a company that sells prepared meals inspired by the Paleo diet.[31] The company's name was chosen to indicate "an idealized concept of uncivilized man, who symbolizes innate goodness of one not exposed to the corrupting influences of civilization."[32] The website goes on: "We believe that modern civilization/agriculture has corrupted our diet. Grains, sugar, highly processed foods—they all have similar negative effects on our bodies. Our intent is to Uninvent The Meal—take the science out of ingredients and use only whole foods that are found naturally." This company links this desire to avoid "corrupted" and processed industrial foods with a widely used trope about indigenous peoples as the ideal, pure, true, natural—and uncivilized—race. This is precisely the conception of indigeneity that discourses of quinoa draw upon. However, the term "noble savage" and its accompanying ideas have been used for centuries in highly problematic ways to sentimentalize North American Indians and other native peoples to legitimize a colonialist mentality, and indeed to legitimize the elimination of a people.[33] Nonetheless, these tropes continue to hold symbolic currency.

Another reproduction of the idea of indigenous purity is the trope of the "ecological Indian," which constructs Native Americans as ecologists and conservationists who fundamentally interact with the land and natural resources differently than settlers and white Americans did and do.[34] Environmental commitments are central to the fair trade movement, and in 2004 the Fairtrade Labeling Organization (FLO) established fair trade criteria for quinoa involving environmental protection and impact.[35] The "time-honored tradition" of indigenous production practices (as the packaging on truRoots Organic Quinoa notes) and suggestions of non-industrialized production strategies are used to rhetorically support sustainability claims that are frequently made on quinoa packages or which are indicated by the value statements of importers.

These claims are made as a sort of strategic essentialism, valuing indigeneity in order to help contemporary Indians who are poor and to build profitable markets that support development goals. Of course, in this instance, the essentializing is done in discourses unfolding halfway around the world rather than by the essentialized people themselves. Nonetheless, the language of indigeneity is currently ascendant as a way to organize knowledge and make claims at various scales. Claiming indigeneity and performing native culture have become a central tactic of marginalized groups to resist and transgress marginalization and to access resources available on the national and international stage.[36] It is thus an effective strategy for quinoa importers, both to sway consumers to buy their products and as a means to build feelings of "solidarity" on the part of quinoa consumers. And, indeed, contemporary Quechua and Aymara quinoa producers have benefited a great deal from the quinoa boom, though they are not necessarily involved with or even aware of how they are represented in this market.

(Hi)stories of Race in Andean Bolivia

The language of indigeneity is a curious thing in Latin America. Notwithstanding the contemporary uses of "indigeneity" and even "*indio*" in contemporary leftist social movements throughout the globe, hemisphere, and Andean region, such terminology sits uneasy for many of the marginalized rural people who might rightfully lay claim to it. In my own fieldwork in rural Bolivia, I frequently ask people what identity they claim. "We're *campesinos!*" they assert. They express themselves more often in relation to their residence and livelihoods on the land than with the language of racial difference.

This makes sense when placed in the context of colonial and neocolonial racial histories of the region. The native population was named "Indian" by their conquerors, and this ethnic category not only circumscribed their exploitation by the Spanish but later, after political independence from Spain, excluded them from full citizenship as well.[37] Indeed, many "Indians" in Bolivia lived in de facto servitude under the *pongueaje/hacienda* system until as late as the land reform of 1952.[38] For others, and continually to the present, ethnicity and class have been closely aligned, with indigenous communities experiencing disproportionately high and pervasive levels of poverty. The term "Indian" has long served as a marker of both exclusion and presumed inferiority, and "*indio*" remains highly derogatory in Andean Bolivia.

Thus, the historical construction of quinoa as an "Indian food" served to indicate that it was not acceptable for consumption outside of the marginalized indigenous peasantry. Quinoa, along with many other Andean grains, legumes, roots, and tubers, was replaced by wheat-based foods throughout the colonial and republican periods, and the agricultural and trade modernization and liberalization of the twentieth century exacerbated this tendency as rural and urban Bolivia became increasingly delinked.[39] Until quite recently, quinoa was simply considered to be an inferior food item—"a third-rate 'Indian' or 'rural' food,"[40] or even "pig food."[41] As recently as 2006 I was staying with a mestizo host family in Cochabamba City; when I asked if they bought quinoa, they nodded yes, but then pointed to the dog's food bowl to indicate the only appropriate use for quinoa in their household.[42]

This history tells us why it is profoundly uncomfortable to talk about contemporary constructions of quinoa as a "*comida del indio*" with my interlocutors in San Juan de Rosario, where I have been conducting ethnographic field research for nearly fifteen years. Indeed, when I followed Don Max's comment about the irony of quinoa's popularity vis-à-vis its past construction as an Indian food with an observation that quinoa remains linked with indigeneity in contemporary discourses in the United States, I was answered only with a very awkward silence—the type of discomfort that led my interlocutors to close up and effectively end the interview. Even with very well known and trusted friends and informants, my attempts to raise and ask about this issue were uncharacteristically avoided or dismissed. "I don't know anything about this," one said shortly, before changing the topic. This is not surprising to me, since the words "*indio*" and "*indigena*" have been off limits in all my time conducting fieldwork in the region. The closest acceptable word I can use is "*originario*," which captures the idea of "original inhabitant" but avoids entirely the issue of race.[43] For the quinoa producers in the rural Bolivian highlands where I have worked, this linkage between quinoa and indigeneity—regardless of how indigeneity itself is constructed—remains much too pregnant with past marginalization, exclusion, and abuse to be anything but an insult.[44] As Meredith Abarca notes in this volume, food is often a sensory embodiment of memory and identity. Here, the quinoa farmers with whom I work have an active memory of racialized exclusion. Yet the transit of quinoa north reproduces a racialized difference without acknowledging that past discourses of race created the conditions for exclusion and marginalization.

Shifting Boundaries of Ethnic Difference

Even as contemporary discourses about quinoa in the North seek to value indigeneity (in sharp distinction to past constructions of indigeneity in the Andes), these constructions are also deeply problematic. The discursive formation in quinoa packaging is familiar. They closely map on to long-standing tropes about native peoples in North America and tap into deeply held "knowledge" about Indians, ideologies that have become so ingrained that they are unquestioned. These discourses around quinoa often revolve around two interconnected constructions of indigeneity: indigene as ancient relics of the past; and indigene in need of development, backward, and primitive, but only to be saved by a reclamation of this premodern past. Crisscrossing these two constructions are the hidden assumptions of interchangeability of Indians (that is, the idea that all Indians are alike) and the identification of women as more Indian.

The invocation of the Inca and the continual framing of quinoa as ancient place quinoa's origins in premodern space, irrespective of the fact that the Tawantinsuyu (Inca) civilization was a relatively short-lived blip in quinoa's history. This move serves the purpose of the contemporary critique of modernity through food choices. Untainted by modern industry, "simple and pure" quinoa allows consumers to feel as if they can nourish their bodies in a way that might push back against the embodied disciplining wrought by modern capitalist society.

Indeed, by so completely placing quinoa in premodern aboriginal space, these discourses conveniently side-step the messy history of the colonial encounters and ongoing formulations of indigenous inferiority, ignoring how "Indian" as a category and the accompanying subordination of native peoples were enforced by European and then North American dominance. These discourses trace quinoa to precolonial civilizations, but in doing so they avoid the messy truth about why quinoa is so exotic, why it has nearly been lost to time—that it was marginalized, that native agricultural systems were destroyed, that other crops (European or valorized by Europeans) were systematically privileged over quinoa and many other native crops—and that it has only survived because indigenous peoples themselves were similarly marginalized and relied on non-market production systems and native varieties for survival. Thus, there is a fundamental contradiction between the use of indigeneity as a critique/resistance of modernity while simultaneously avoiding the colonial dark side of modernity.[45]

Racial categorization was one of the principal means through which colonial power operated, and remains one of the most general forms of domination today.[46] Race was used in the colonial encounter to rationalize and codify difference between the conquerors and the conquered. This biological interpretation gave the impression that these ideas of difference, and the relations of domination and subordination based upon them, were natural and objective.[47] Such hierarchies were established and operationalized through military and juridical-political practices (enforced through forced labor, for example) but also importantly through discursive means.[48] Discourses that link indigeneity to quinoa, even if they seek to valorize indigenous peoples or show solidarity with them, reproduce colonial categories of race precisely as they seek to critique and resist the disciplines of modernity.

Furthermore, by placing quinoa so firmly in the Andean past, these discourses place indigenous peoples of the Andes themselves in the past tense. For example, note the use of the past tense in the description of Bob's Red Mill Organic Quinoa: "Quinoa (pronounced keen-wa) *was* a staple food for the South American Indians living in the high altitudes of the Andes Mountains. It *was* immensely popular because it *was* one of few crops that could survive in such high altitudes (10,000–20,000 feet above sea level)."[49] This ignores, of course, how subordinated indigenous peasants, who were either completely excluded from regional economies or were enslaved to them, frequently relied upon quinoa and other "*indio*" crops to ensure their basic survival from the colonial encounters through to the emergence of quinoa markets in the 1980s. It also completely erases the communities and people who continue to farm and eat quinoa throughout the region—the very same people who produce the quinoa enjoyed by elite consumers in the North. But it also frames indigeneity within the Myth of the Vanishing Race, the illusion that a natural and wild landscape and population will necessarily vanish as they are taken over by modern forms of interaction between modern people (white North Americans; mestizo Latin Americans). Such myths long served the ideological purpose of forgiving the invaders,[50] but avoiding the colonial encounter in quinoa discourses also allows quinoa's consumers to avoid any complicity as well.

The contemporary lived experience of indigeneity in Latin America is obscured in other subtle ways. For example, the growing numbers of cookbooks on quinoa nearly universally integrate quinoa into Eurocentric cuisine rather than providing recipes for South American or Andean dishes. Rena Patten's *Cooking with Quinoa: The Supergrain* features over ninety recipes that include quinoa as a principal ingredient, including Christmas Fruit Cake, Pear Clafoutis, and Spanish-style Mussels, but not a single recipe inspired by or identified as Andean or South American.[51] Even Rebecca Wood's fascinating book *Quinoa the Supergrain*, which reads in places as a travelogue of the Andes and even uses Spanish words to indicate some categories of recipes, features few recipes inspired by Andean influences. The few exceptions among over 120 recipes for Cold Beef, Quinoa, and Watercress Salad; Scottish Shortbread; and Quinoa Jambalaya are Sopa de Quinoa y Tomate (which the author writes is based on a white rice soup she ate in Cusco) and the Traditional Altiplano Quinoa Chowder. To the credit of Bob's Red Mill, the highlighted recipe for use with its Organic Quinoa is Sopa de Quinoa, a regular midday meal throughout the Andes. (Yet the website describes the recipe as "inspired by a traditional quinoa dish eaten in South and Central America," missing the fact that quinoa is not "traditional" in Central America at all.[52]) The tendency to portray indigenous peoples in the past tense, even if unintentional or well-intentioned, obscures their ongoing lived experience as well as the histories of colonial violence and the ongoing legacies of colonialism that continue to shape contemporary rural communities in the Andes.

Some narratives do emphasize the contemporary experiences of Andean quinoa producers, highlighting the poverty and lack of development of Andean peoples and promoting quinoa as a way out. As noted, importing companies emphasize external valuation of quinoa (especially from North America and Europe) in order to prompt Andean people to consume it. These stories suggest that the poor Indians of the Andes need to return to the past—excavate their own "traditional" culture and practice—as a cure for their inability to successfully confront and respond to modern life. They point to the failure of native communities to value their indigenous "supergrain," sidestepping how colonial practices and institutions systemically devalued both quinoa and the people who grew it, creating the conditions of depravity.

These new constructions of quinoa as Indian thus continue the destructive representation of Indians as primitive, uncivilized, and underdeveloped that were common in the past. Consider, for example, how this trope is reproduced in the packaging of Red Quinoa distributed by Wegmans (Figure 13.1). This package demonstrates many of the tendencies outlined above: the pattern around

Figure 13.1. A box of Wegmans Red Quinoa.
Photograph used with permission of Wegmans
Food Markets, Inc.

the package is vaguely "tribal," the precolonial iconography of a bird (incidentally, an Aztec bird rather than an Inca rendering—recall the "interchangeable
Indian" trope noted above), and even the red package subtly but indubitably
mark the contents as "Indian." Most troubling, however, is the package's label;
the childlike and error-ridden font discursively identifies the "Indians" linked to
quinoa as cognitively underdeveloped, primitive, and backward—all done without any hint of how this representation is not only offensive but also reproduces
damaging North American "knowledge" about native peoples. That this package is a second-generation, nonsolidarity representation of quinoa, after years of
discursive production by fair and other solidarity trade companies, shows precisely how calling on ethnic difference in marketing strategies can quickly lead to
highly problematic ends.

It is often noted in American Indian studies that contemporary American
Indians are frequently portrayed via decrepitude, poverty, and homelessness
(that is, an inability to adequately cope with modern society).[53] While such
forms of dislocation are frequently central to the experience of native peoples,
the overwhelming repetition of stories and metaphors of dereliction "allow us
to imagine only certain kinds of Native history . . . the parts we are prepared to
see by the stories we tell."[54] As Bruce Braun writes, these representations can have
important effects: "they justify political and territorial erasures."[55] Discursive
treatments have material effects; they materialize ways of thinking and help to
create institutions and expectations that illustrate, support, confirm, and naturalize destructive (albeit prevalent) ideas.[56]

CONCLUSION: POWER AND THE PRODUCTION OF ETHNIC DIFFERENCE

When a food like quinoa is commodified and ferried across national borders, a host of contradictions arise. The contemporary quinoa boom relies upon and reproduces racialized boundaries between consumers and producers in order to build market opportunities for a group of farmers long excluded from regional economies. Borders, whether between nations or people, are never natural; they are made through continual citation and need to be acted upon, narrated, and performed for them to remain meaningful.[57] By referencing and giving shape and form to these differences, discourses around quinoa contribute to the accepted knowledge about Andean quinoa producers (in particular) and native peoples (in general). But borders are not just produced through such action; they also continuously do their own work, enhancing social frictions and hierarchies.[58]

Kathleen Sexsmith (chapter 11) and Mary Murphy (chapter 8) help elucidate how the border is a moral as well as physical space, and border crossings frequently involve moral transgressions and reconfigurations. In this case, quinoa's border crossing, prompted by the ethical commitments of its proponents and consumers, produces a moral conundrum requiring an ethical negotiation as well-meaning individuals (including quinoa importers and consumers) seek to both support and exploit, build solidarity with and appropriate, the Andean producers of quinoa. But while these discourses use simplistic and essentialized framings of native peoples to build "solidarity" or to pursue more ethical market systems, they in fact reproduce the very hierarchical logics and systems of power that produce and support global inequality.

Indigeneity can be a powerful category for calling attention to the effects of the colonial encounter and ongoing neocolonial relations of power. Yet who has the power to construct ethnic identities? Because, when it comes down to it, these are constructed categories: "Indian" does not describe an actual essence of peoples, but a set of ideas belonging to North Americans and other Westerners.[59] "*Indio*" remains a highly derogatory term among highland Andean peoples.[60] To call quinoa a "*comida del indio*," or Indian food, remains insulting to them even with the new valuation of indigeneity in the North. But what of the material benefits from strategically mobilizing essentializing ideologies to reach a broader set of consumers? And what alternatives to this strategy are there?

Ideologies that legitimize racial hierarchies and construct indigenous peoples in troubling ways contribute to the creation of economic opportunities for long-marginalized communities in the Andes, a region that has historically had some of the highest rates of poverty in the Western Hemisphere. But, as these ideologies have in the past justified terrible and terrifying acts of genocide, dispossession, and slavery, as well as routine processes of cultural suppression, subordination, and appropriation, the reproduction of such ideologies of difference is disquieting. This ethical dilemma is made worse as the Northern demand for quinoa makes it too expensive for many Bolivians to eat—meaning that the "revaluation" is not necessarily to the nutritional benefit of Bolivians unable to grown their own quinoa.

It's not as if extraction and appropriation are simply a thing of the past, either. One of the bitterest contemporary debates regarding quinoa relates to attempts by researchers at Colorado State University to patent the germplasm of a variety of quinoa developed there.[61] This patent was an affront to Bolivians and others in the region who saw quinoa's genetic diversity as resulting from the efforts of indigenous farmers over millennia. This incident prompted the inclusion of a clause in the 2009 Bolivian constitution marking genetic diversity of native plants as Bolivia's intellectual property. As a result, Bolivia refuses to share its seed stock—the greatest holding of genetic diversity of quinoa in the world—with researchers and farmers in other countries. Control over these seeds is understood in Bolivia as a means to protect food sovereignty and contest ongoing processes of neocolonial appropriation and extraction.[62] But it also directly limits the adaptation of quinoa to other environments, such as Malawi or Pakistan, where the superlative nutritional characteristics and tolerance of poor growing conditions have the potential to improve food security.

Quinoa is a unique commodity because solidarity trade overwhelmingly influences its market today as well as how this market emerged over the past thirty-five years. But in trying to build solidarity and contextualize quinoa for North American consumers, quinoa producers and the places of its production are framed in ways that reproduce ethnic differences and maintain colonial racial hierarchies. Building solidarity around difference reinforces and reproduces ethnic hierarchies and produces the "Other" in ways that fail to place difference in historical context.[63] On one hand, this has undoubtedly helped quinoa producers as they find markets and are remunerated for their crops. But this benefit comes at the cost of reproducing ethnic hierarchies in ways that remain little changed from past colonial constructions, and colonial racial hierarchies continue to justify contemporary constellations of power in Latin America.[64] How can we build solidarity between North and South while also reproducing the very categories and hierarchies that have been so destructive in the past? Building solidarity between white elites and the global poor requires a deep reflection on and reconciliation of colonialism and its ongoing effects.

NOTES

1. See Michael K. Goodman, "Reading Fair Trade: Political Ecological Imaginary and the Moral Economy of Fair Trade Foods," *Political Geography* 23 (2004): 891–915. Goodman points to the exclusivity of fair trade and the reliance on consumer choice for social and environmental change as additional ethical dilemmas. See also Julie Guthman, "Unveiling the Unveiling: Commodity Chains, Commodity Fetishism, and the 'Value' of Voluntary, Ethnical Food Labels," in *Frontiers of Commodity Chain Research*, ed. J. Bair (Palo Alto, CA: Stanford University Press, 2009), 190–207.

2. Quoted in John F. McCamant, "Quinoa's Roundabout Journey to World Use," in *Chilies to Chocolate: Food the Americas Gave the World*, ed. N. Foster and L. S. Cordell (Tucson: University of Arizona Press, 1992), 129.

3. Ibid., 123–141.

4. Ibid.

5. Ibid., 192.

6. Ibid.

7. Marygold Walsh-Dilley, "Negotiating Hybridity in Highland Bolivia: Moral Economy and the Expanding Market for Quinoa," *Journal of Peasant Studies* 40 (2013): 659–682.

8. Zina Cáceres, Aurélie Carimentrand, and John Wilkinson, "Fair Trade and Quinoa from the Southern Bolivian Altiplano," in *Fair Trade: The Challenges of Transforming Globalization*, ed. Laura T. Raynolds, Douglas Murray, and John Wilkinson (New York: Routledge, 2013), 180–199; Kevin Healy, *Llamas, Weavings, and Organic Chocolate: Multicultural Grassroots Development in the Andes and Amazon of Bolivia* (Notre Dame, IN: University of Notre Dame Press, 2001).

9. Pablo Laguna, Aurélie Carmentrand, and Zina Cáceres, "Del Altiplano Sur Boliviariano Hasta el Mercado Global: Coordinación y Estructuras de Governancia de la Cadena de Valor de la Quinoa Orgánica y del Comercio Justo," *Agroalimentaria* 11 (June 2006): 65–76.

10. "Our Commitment," Ancient Harvest, http://ancientharvest.com/about-us/commitment/.

11. Laguna, Carmentrand, and Cáceres, "Del Altiplano Sur," 68; Tanya Kerssen, "Food Sovereignty and the Quinoa Boom in Bolivia" (paper presented at the International Conference on Food Sovereignty: A Critical Dialogue, Yale University, New Haven, CT, 2013), http://www.yale.edu/agrarianstudies/foodsovereignty/pprs/79_Kerssen_2013b.pdf.

12. Kerssen, "Food Sovereignty," 9.

13. Mike Adams, "Interview with Robert Leventry of Inca Organics on Healthy, Versatile Quinoa," *Natural News*—NaturalNews.com., January 1, 2013, http://www.naturalnews.com/016242_quinoa_organic_farming.html#.

14. Kerssen, "Food Sovereignty"; Cáceres, Carimentrand, and Wilkenson, "Fair Trade and Quinoa."

15. Rachel Soper, "Local Is Not Fair: Indigenous Campesino Discourse on Market Trade" (paper presented at the Annual Meetings of the American Sociological Association, San Francisco, 2014).

16. Douglas L. Murray and Laura T. Raynolds, "Globalization and Its Antinomies: Negotiating a Fair Trade Movement" in Raynolds, Murray, and Wilkinson, *Fair Trade*, 4–14.

17. Laura T. Raynolds, "Consumer/Producer Links in Fair Trade Coffee Networks," *Sociologia Ruralis* 42 (2002): 404–424.

18. bell hooks, *Black Looks: Race and Representation* (Boston: South End Press, 1992); I. Cook, "Geographies of Food: Mixing," *Progress in Human Geography* 32 (2008): 821–833; Lisa Heldke, "Let's Cook Thai: Recipes for Colonialism" in *Pilaf, Pozole, and Pad Thai: American Women and Ethnic Food*, ed. Sherrie A. Inness (Amherst: University of Massachusetts Press, 2001), 175–193.

19. Guthman, "Unveiling the Unveiling"; Goodman, "Reading Fair Trade."

20. Peter Jackson, "Commodity Cultures: The Traffic in Things," *Transactions of the Institute of British Geographers* 24 (1999): 95–108; Goodman, "Reading Fair Trade."

21. The Inca Organics website, formerly hosted at http://www.incaorganics.com/quinoa.htm, appears to be no longer available. I last accessed the website on July 9, 2013, when I also copied the text and images into a word document.

22. Marisol de la Cadena, "'Women Are More Indian': Ethnicity and Gender in a Community near Cuzco," in *Ethnicity, Markets, and Migration in the Andes: At the Crossroads of History and Anthropology*, ed. Brook Larson and Olivia Harris (Durham, NC: Duke University Press, 1995), 329–348.

23. See Dan Collyns, "Quinoa Brings Riches to the Andes," *Guardian* online, January 14, 2014, http://www.theguardian.com/world/2013/jan/14/quinoa-andes-bolivia-peru-crop;

Joanna Blythman, "Can Vegans Stomach the Unpalatable Truth about Quinoa?," *Guardian* online, January 16, 2013, http://www.theguardian.com/commentisfree/2013/jan/16/vegans -stomach-unpalatable-truth-quinoa.

24. Rebecca Wood, *Quinoa the Supergrain: Ancient Food for Today* (Tokyo: Japan Publications, 1989), 50.

25. Rena Patten, *Cooking with Quinoa: The Supergrain* (Sydney: New Holland Publishers, 2011).

26. "Ancient Grains," Ancient Harvest, http://ancientharvest.com/ancient-grains/.

27. "Welcome to the Home of Inca Organics!" Inca Organics, http://www.incaorganics .com/index.html.

28. "Mother Grain," Inca Organics, http://www.incaorganics.com/cleaning_&_packaging .htm.

29. Ibid.

30. Philip J. Deloria, *Indians in Unexpected Places* (Lawrence: University Press of Kansas, 2004), 166.

31. While quinoa is technically a seed and not a grain (which the paleo diet avoids), it is often excluded from the diet for other reasons.

32. "Frequently Asked Questions—Why Did You Choose This Name?," Noble Savage, http://noblesavagefoods.com/questions/.

33. Ter Ellingson, *The Myth of the Noble Savage* (Berkeley: University of California Press, 2001).

34. Shepard Krech III, *The Ecological Indian: Myth and History* (New York: W. W. Norton, 1999).

35. Murray and Raynolds, "Globalization and Its Antinomies"; Cáceres, Carimentrand, and Wilkinson, "Fair Trade and Quinoa."

36. Daniel Mato, "Transnational Networking and the Social Production of Representations of Identities by Indigenous Peoples' Organization of Latin America," *International Sociology* 15 (2000): 343–360; John McNeish, "Globalization and the Reinvention of Andean Tradition: The Politics of Community and Ethnicity in Highland Bolivia," *Journal of Peasant Studies* 29 (2002): 228–269; Gayatri Chakravorty Spivak, "Subaltern Studies: Deconstructing Historiography," in *Selected Subaltern Studies*, ed. Ranajit Guha and Gayatri Chakravorty Spivak (Oxford: Oxford University Press, 1988), 3–33.

37. Karen Spalding, *Huarochirí: An Andean Society Under Inca and Spanish Rule* (Palo Alto, CA: Stanford University Press, 1984).

38. Laura Gotkowitz, *A Revolution for Our Rights: Indigenous Struggles for Land and Justice in Bolivia, 1880–1952* (Durham, NC: Duke University Press, 2007).

39. Cáceres, Carimentrand, and Wilkinson, "Fair Trade and Quinoa"; Jon Hellin and Sophie Higman, "Crop Diversity and Livelihood Security in the Andes," *Development in Practice* 15 (2005): 165–174.

40. Teo Ballvé, "Pachamama Goes Organic: Bolivia's Quinoa Farmers," *NACLA Report on the Americas* 40 (2007): 15–18.

41. Adams, "Interview with Robert Leavantry."

42. It was only in 2007 that the international market for quinoa exploded. Between 1983 and 2007, the price for quinoa was stable and relatively high. But the unprecedented spike in price after 2007 marks this as the turning point where quinoa became the international phenomenon that it remains today.

43. "*Originario*" was a term indicating the original inhabitants of a village once it was "reduced" into modern villages under Spanish rule. Thus, "*originario*" traces back to a colonial relationship rather than a claim of precolonial or primordial lineage. "Comunidad Originario" is a technical category indicating the type of governance in effect. These "original communities" are those where village councils hold collective property rights and resources are governed by traditional "uses and customs." This is precisely what in English would be called an indigenous community, but this category does not rely upon race or

ethnicity. See Herbert Klein, *Bolivia: The Evolution of a Multi-Ethnic Society*, 2nd ed. (New York: Oxford University Press, 1992).

44. With the election of Evo Morales as president, along with his and other social movements' rhetorical use of ethnicity and indigeneity, the reception of this word is changing to some degree in urban or political spaces in Bolivia, although, as Albó notes, there is widespread disagreement, and words including "*indio*" and "*indigena*" are still considered disrespectful. Xavier Albó, ". . . y de Mnristas y Kataristas? La Sorprendente y Audaz Alianza Entre Aymaras y Neoliberals en Bolivia," *Boletín de Antropología Americana* 25 (1992): 53–92.

45. Water Mignolo, *The Idea of Latin America* (Malden, MA: Blackwell, 2005); Walter Mignolo, "Delinking: The Rhetoric of Modernity, the Logic of Coloniality and the Grammar of Decoloniality," *Cultural Studies* 21 (2007): 449–514.

46. Aníbal Quijano, "Coloniality of Power, Eurocentrism, and Latin America," *Nepantla: Views from the South* 1 (2000): 533–580; Aníbal Quijano, "Coloniality and Modernity/Rationality," *Cultural Studies* 21 (2007): 168–178; Walter Mignolo, "Coloniality at Large: The Western Hemisphere in the Colonial Horizon of Modernity," *New Centennial Review* 1 (2001): 19–54; Walter Mignolo, "Introduction," *Cultural Studies* 21 (2007): 155–167.

47. Quijano, "Coloniality and Modernity/Rationality"; Deloria, *Indians in Unexpected Places*.

48. Quijano, "Coloniality and Modernity/Rationality"; Edward Said, *Orientalism* (New York: Random House, 1978); Bruce Braun, *The Intemperate Rainforest: Nature, Culture, and Power on Canada's West Coast* (Minneapolis: University of Minnesota Press, 2002), 8.

49. "Organic Quinoa Grain," Bob's Red Mill, http://www.bobsredmill.com/organic-quinoa-grain.html (emphasis added).

50. William Cronon, "Present Haunts of an Unvanished Past," in *Native Seattle: Histories from the Crossing-Over Place*, by Coll Thrush (Seattle: University of Washington Press, 2007), vii–xi.

51. There are two "Mexican" dishes.

52. "Organic Quinoa Grain."

53. For example, Thrush, *Native Seattle*.

54. Ibid., 10.

55. Braun, *Intemperate Rainforest*, 8.

56. Shelly Errington. *The Death of Authentic Primitive Art and Other Tales of Progress* (Berkeley: University of California Press, 1998).

57. Gabriela Valdivia, Wendy Wolford, and Flora Yu, "Border Crossings: New Geographies of Protection and Production in the Galápagos Islands," *Annals of the Association of American Geographers* 104 (2014): 686–701.

58. Ibid.

59. Errington, *Death of Authentic Primitive Art*.

60. See Luis Morató Peña for an impassioned critique of the American tendency to call Andean people Indians. Luis Morató Peña, *Quechua Boliviano Curso Elemental* (Cochabamba: Los Amigos del Libro, 1999).

61. Lisa M. Hamilton, "The Quinoa Quarrel: Who Owns the World's Greatest Superfood?," *Harpers* (May 2014), 35–42.

62. Ibid., 39.

63. See Goodman, "Reading Fair Trade."

64. Latin American postcolonial scholars call this "coloniality of power." See especially Quijano, "Coloniality of Power"; Quijano, "Coloniality and Modernity/Rationality"; Mignolo, "Coloniality at Large"; Mignolo, "Introduction."

Acknowledgments

This book is a moment of convergence that has been in the making for some time. Each of the editors has pursued the twin subjects of food and "borders" for several years. It was with tremendous enthusiasm and mutual respect that we came together for this book, which is more urgent than ever given the state of our nation and its relationship to its neighbors.

Food Across Borders would not have been possible without the generous support of two institutions, one press, and twelve amazing contributors. Arizona State University (ASU) president Michael Crow generously provided support for the creation of Comparative Border Studies at ASU—a project inspired by Jim Scott, K. Sivaramakrishnan, and the Program in Agrarian Studies at Yale University. Matt Garcia leveraged this investment by forging a generative relationship with the premier borderlands research institute in North America, the William P. Clements Center for Southwest Studies at Southern Methodist University (SMU). The Clements Center codirectors, Andrew Graybill and Sherri Smith, recognized the importance of our project immediately, and welcomed (and partially funded) a two-part, yearlong symposia on the subject in 2014–2015. Part one convened in the historic Taos, New Mexico, SMU campus, part two at the swanky midcentury resort hotel The Valley Ho in Scottsdale, Arizona. The contributors, editors, Andrew, and Sherri traveled many miles to engage in review, debate, and discussion of multiple drafts. This is the magic of the Clements Center symposia, which has worked for many scholarly collaborations over the years and now ours. Ruth Ann Elmore of the Clements Center facilitated everything on the Taos end, while Norma Villa and my sharp administrative team in the School of Historical, Philosophical, and Religious Studies at ASU organized the Scottsdale gathering. None of this would have been possible without the abiding support of our editor and friend Leslie Mitchner, the editor-in-chief of Rutgers University Press who championed this project from the moment she heard about it. She joined us in Scottsdale and offered invaluable criticism and guidance throughout the entire publishing process.

We deeply appreciate the additional support for maps and illustrations provided by the Clements Center. Maps were drawn by Syracuse University cartographer Joe Stoll, and Don Mitchell thanks Jamie Winders, Margie Johnson, and the Department of Geography at Syracuse for assuring Joe's great skills were freely available to us. Copyediting was provided by Robert Burchfield. Finally, the labor, skill, and perseverance of those who put food on North American tables inspired the authors in this volume and compel us to confront the challenges that we now face as a nation.

Notes on Contributors

MEREDITH E. ABARCA is Professor of Latina/o Literature and Food Studies; her current work focuses on Afro-Latina/o food narratives. She is the author of *Voices in the Kitchen* and coeditor of *Rethinking Chicana/o Literature through Food* and *Latin@'s Presence in the Food Industry*.

KELLEN BACKER is a Humanities Faculty Fellow at Syracuse University. He studies the ways that science, medicine, and technology have shaped people's understanding of food. His research and writing focus primarily on modern America, though his work has also extended to transnational food networks.

WILLIAM CARLETON is a Ph.D. candidate in the History Department at the University of New Mexico. His research focuses on the intersections of industrial and non-industrial agriculture in the twentieth-century New Mexico borderlands.

E. MELANIE DuPUIS is Professor and Chair of Environmental Studies and Science at Pace University and Professor Emerita, University of California, Santa Cruz. She has a B.A. in Anthropology from Harvard University and a Ph.D. in Development Sociology from Cornell University. She is author of *Dangerous Digestion: The Politics of American Dietary Advice* and *Nature's Perfect Food: How Milk Became America's Drink*; coauthor of *Alternative Food Politics: Knowledge, Practice and Politics*, with David and Mike Goodman; and editor of two edited collections, *Smoke and Mirrors: The Politics and Culture of Air Pollution* and *Creating the Countryside: The Politics of Rural and Environmental Discourse*.

MATT GARCIA is Professor of Latin American, Latino & Caribbean Studies and History at Dartmouth College in Hanover, New Hampshire. He previously taught at Arizona State University; the University of Illinois, Urbana-Champaign; the University of Oregon; and Brown University. He is the author of *A World of Its*

Own: Race, Labor and Citrus in the Making of Greater Los Angeles, 1900–1970 and *From the Jaws of Victory: The Triumph and Tragedy of Cesar Chavez and the Farm Worker Movement.*

TERESA MARES is Assistant Professor of Anthropology at the University of Vermont. Her research focuses on the intersection of food and migration studies.

KATHERINE SARAH MASSOTH is Assistant Professor of History at the University of Louisville. Her research focuses on gender, ethnic identity, and the home in the nineteenth-century U.S.-Mexico borderlands.

JESSIE MAZAR received her M.S. in Food Systems from the University of Vermont in 2016. Her thesis explored food access and food sovereignty issues within Vermont's farmworker community.

LAURA-ANNE MINKOFF-ZERN is Assistant Professor of Food Studies at Syracuse University. Her research focuses on the intersection of food, race, and immigration.

DON MITCHELL is Professor of Cultural Geography at Uppsala University, Sweden, and Distinguished Professor Emeritus at Syracuse University. He is the general editor of *Revolting New York: How 400 Years of Riots, Revolts, Uprisings, and Revolutions Shaped a City* and the author, most recently, of *They Saved the Crops: Labor, Landscape and the Struggle over Industrial Farming in Bracero-Era California.*

MARY MURPHY is Distinguished Professor of History at Montana State University, Bozeman. She teaches and writes about the history of gender in the North American West and is the author of *Hope in Hard Times: New Deal Photographs of Montana, 1936–1942* and *Mining Cultures: Men, Women, and Leisure in Butte, 1914–41,* among other books. She is currently collaborating on a Montana cookbook that will combine essays about food and cooking with recipes drawn from historical cookbooks.

TANACHAI MARK PADOONGPATT is Assistant Professor in the Interdisciplinary Degree Programs at the University of Nevada, Las Vegas. His research examines Asian/Pacific Islander American history, race and ethnicity in the United States, immigration, and urban/suburban cultures.

KATHLEEN SEXSMITH is a Ph.D. candidate in Development Sociology at Cornell University. Her research focuses on labor migration in the global agri-food system.

JOSÉ ANTONIO VÁSQUEZ-MEDINA is a postdoctoral researcher at the Mexican Food Observatory of the Universidad Autonoma Metropolitana. His research focuses on social dynamics and narratives about food preparation among Mexican migrant cooks.

MARYGOLD WALSH-DILLEY is Assistant Professor of Social and Behavioral Sciences in the Honors College at the University of New Mexico. She received her Ph.D. in Development Sociology from Cornell University, and her research focuses on the politics of food and agrarian transformation.

MICHAEL WISE is Assistant Professor of History at the University of North Texas who studies food and the colonial experience in western North America. He is the author of *Producing Predators: Wolves, Work, and Conquest in the Northern Rockies*.

NAOMI WOLCOTT-MACCAUSLAND is Migrant Health Coordinator for Bridges to Health, a program of the University of Vermont Extension. She received her M.S. in Community Development and Applied Economics from the University of Vermont in 2014.

Index

Page references followed by *fig* indicate a photograph or illustrated figure; followed by an *m* indicate a map.

indigenous peoples: global quinoa boom
benefiting Bolivian, 236–237; historical
construction of quinoa as *comida del
indio*, 244–245; misguided efforts of the
OIA to assimilate, 163–164; Myth of the
Vanishing Race framing indigeneity and,
246–247; myth that North Americans
brought civilization and modernity to,
55–57; solidarity trade and linking quinoa
marketing to Bolivian, 19, 237, 240–244,
245, 250. *See also* Blackfeet
Invisible Man (film), 38, 39
Iron Curtain speech (Churchill), 5
Irvin, Louis S., 170

Jacobo's story, 66
Jim Pandol & Company, 18
Johnson, Elmer, 155
Joselito's story, 211, 212–213
José's story, 76
Josué's story, 69–70
Juana's story, 193
Juarez Experiment Station (New Mexico),
112

kaffir limes (citrus hystrix), 85–86, 92
Kaufman, Frederick, 5
Kennedy, Diana, 2
Keys, Ancel, 124
Khrung Kaeng (Shrimp Curry) recipe
[Wilson], 84–85
King, Herbert, 124
kinship. *See* family/kinship
kitchens. *See* Anglo kitchens; restaurant
kitchens
"Kitchens" (Levins Morales), 33–34
Kropp, Phoebe, 53
Ku Klux Klan, 111

La Alianza Hispano-Americana
(nineteenth-century), 110–111, 119n17
Laboratory of Animal Nutrition (Cornell
University), 124
labor relations: challenges to differential
access by dairy industry workers, 185–186;
commercial growers' desire for "cheap
labor," 12; how the border regulates
food industry, 12. *See also* guest worker
programs
land allotment. *See* Blackfeet food sovereignty struggle
Landaverde, Arnulfo, 113
Lane, Harry, 169
Lane, Lydia Spencer, 49, 59
Lane, William Bartlett, 49

Larios (el abuelo), 24, 25*fig*
Larios Cárdenas, Aurora, 24
Latin America: Afro-Latina/os of, 26;
marginalization of natives under
pongueaje/hacienda system of, 244;
Spanish Casta System/Las Castas during
colonial period of, 27; United Brand's
control of agriculture from California
to, 16–17
Latina/os: food sovereignty of rural Vermont workers, 181–198; how migrants
negotiate their consent to precarious
dairy conditions, 201–215; remapping
African culinary influence on New York,
28–29. *See also* Hispanas/os
Latina/os immigrant farmers: creating
sense of home through agricultural
practices, 229–233; differentiating farm
laborer from, 233–234n1; estimated
number in U.S., 220, 222; examining
how food and place shape, 6–7; family
labor primarily used by, 230–231, 232,
235n19; Northern Neck of Virginia location of, 219–220*fig*; obstacles to agricultural success for, 223–229; seeking a
sense of place in U.S., 220–221; selling
at farmers' markets, 226–227*fig*, 231–232;
successfully overcoming boundaries,
233; USDA staff discrimination against,
224–226, 227–229
Laudan, Rachel, 6
LeSuer, Day, 155
Leviathan (Hobbes), 4
Levins Morales, Aurora, 33–34, 39
Levi-Strauss, 5
Levy, Alfredo, 110
Liberty Loan campaign, 148
Linda's story, 68
Lipps, Oscar, 167, 174–175
Little, Eva, 157
locally grown produce: country of origin
labeling (COOL) legislation support-
ing, 19; Latino immigrant farmers selling
their, 226–227*fig*, 231–232; "local food"
as an oxymoron, 19; politics of localism
driving advocates of, 19
Locke, Jerome G., 155
Logan, Paul, 127, 129
"longing for taste," 6–7
Los Angeles Times: "Product of Mexico"
series by, 18; "They Treated Us Like
Slaves" exposé by, 18
Lourdes's story, 194–196
Lummis, Charles Fletcher, 48, 49, 53, 57
Luz's story, 72

modernity (*continued*)
  Americans brought indigenous societies, 55–57; New York state's "Silicon Valley" vision of, 203–205, 215
Mogoffin, Susan Shelby, 47
mokaksin (selfhood) [Blackfeet notion], 172–173, 177
Molloy, Thomas, 146
Montana: "Farm to Win 'Over There'" production outcomes in, 145–147; food conservation enforcement by women's clubs of, 156–158; food conservation support by women's clubs of, 147, 152–153; Non-Partisan League of, 170; U.S.–Canada border shared along Saskatchewan, 142–143*m*; women's suffrage (1914) won in, 141, 148. *See also* Blackfeet Reservation (Montana)
Montaño, Mario, 47
Monteath, James, 173
Montejo, Esteban, 32–33, 39
mulato: acknowledged as African root ("third root") of *mestizaje*, 27, 40; efforts to address inclusion in *mestizaje* identity, 36–38; label identifying people of African and European background, 26–27
Murphy, Carlos, 58
Murphy, Mary, 9, 140
Myers, William S., 113
My Life as an Indian (Schultz), 175
Myth of the Vanishing Race, 246–247

national cuisine: Mexican food has become part of U.S., 44, 52–57; problem of inventing a, 21n12; social and cultural functions of, 6
National Economic and Social Development Plans (NESDP) [Thailand], 88
national identity: the body as metaphor for nation and, 3, 4–9; cultural customs central to acceptance and U.S., 45; Ortiz's transculturation theory on blacks informing, 41n21–22
national threats: American nativism's metaphors on contamination of immigrants, 5; the body metaphor of solidarity and perceived, 5; body metaphors to describe Communism, 5
nations: the body as metaphor for national identity and, 3, 4–9; Hobbes's idea of the body as, 4; how border foodways define and redefine, 2, 20. *See also* citizenship
nativism. *See* American nativism
New Deal agricultural policies, 17
Newhall, Mrs., 156

New Mexican cuisine: Americanized, 58; Anglo appropriation of, 52–59; Anglo's early rejection and distaste for, 45, 46–52; concerns over spicy foods and cleanliness differences, 47–50; concerns over whiteness and negotiations over, 45–54, 57–58; Erna Fergusson's role in importing into Anglo kitchens, 44, 45–46, 53–59; extended families living across borders and the transformation of, 14. *See also* cuisine; Mexican cuisine
New Mexican foodways: Anglos producing and selling spicy foods to Anglos, 51; cookbooks used to define for Anglo women, 45–54, 57–58; embraced by Anglo women, 45; Erna Fergusson's selective appropriation of, 54–59
New Mexico: after U.S.–Mexico War and territorial period (1850–1912), 45; border between "Old" Mexico and, 44–45; chile pepper crop grown in, 106, 108; Hispanas/os population (1848) in, 47; political advantages of Hispanas/os in, 52; "Red or Green?" state question (1996) of, 58, 105; reshaping of New Mexican culture for statehood, 45, 51–52. *See also* Southwest America
New Mexico number 9 chile: genetic roots used in García's work, 2, 114–116; representing a fundamental shift in chile peppers, 117
New Mexico State University (NMSU), 14, 55, 105, 106, 107, 109
New York: CPB's jurisdiction and authority in border zone of, 10, 11*m*, 202, 206–208; risks taken by immigrants traveling to, 10, 208–214; "Silicon Valley" vision of industrial reforms in, 203–205, 215; studies on Latina/os migrant workers living in, 184
New York dairies: "Dairy Acceleration Program" restructuring of, 203–205; economic realities reshaping labor requirements of, 204–205; interviews of migrants working on, 201–203
New York dairy workers: barred from H-2A visas and fear of Border Patrol, 202, 206–208; government reforms and changing labor requirements for, 204–205, 215; how "deportability in everyday life" leads to their invisibility and consent, 208–214; interviews of, 201–203, 212–214; "job-changers" and debt-migration cycle experienced by, 213–214; relationship of industrial production and invisible labor